GAMSAT-Prep

The Gold Standard textbook is a critical component of a multimedia experience including live courses on campus, MP3s, smartphone apps, online videos and interactive programs, *Heaps* of Practice GAMSATs and a lot more.

GAMSAT-Prep.com

The only prep you need.™

Gold Standard Live GAMSAT Courses are held in the following cities:
Sydney • Melbourne • Dublin • London • Brisbane • Perth • Adelaide • Cork

GOLD STANDARD
MULTIMEDIA EDUCATION

* GAMSAT is administered by ACER which does not endorse this study guide.

THE GOLD STANDARD

GAMSAT

Editor and Author

Brett Ferdinand BSc MD-CM

Contributors

Lisa Ferdinand BA MA
Sean Pierre BSc MD
Kristin Finkenzeller BSc MD
Ibrahima Diouf BSc MSc PhD
Charles Haccoun BSc MD-CM
Timothy Ruger BA MA
Jeanne Tan Te

Illustrators

Harvie W. Gallatiera BSc
Daphne McCormack
Nanjing Design
• Ren Yi, Huang Bin
• Sun Chan, Li Xin

RuveneCo

Free Online Access Features*

Additional Section 1 practice questions
Additional corrected Section 2 essays that you can peruse online
Worked Solutions for the GS-1 Exam
Access to relevant, topical teaching videos from our GS Video Library for GS-1

*One year of continuous access for the original owner of this textbook using the enclosed online access card.

Be sure to register at www.GAMSAT-prep.com by clicking on Register in the top right corner of the website. Once you login, click on GAMSAT Textbook Owners in the right column and follow directions. Please Note: benefits are for 1 year from the date of on-line registration, for the original book owner only and are not transferable; unauthorized access and use outside the Terms of Use posted on GAMSAT-prep.com may result in account deletion; if you are not the original owner, you can purchase your virtual access card separately at GAMSAT-prep.com.

Visit The Gold Standard's Education Center at www.gold-standard.com.

Copyright (c) 2017 RuveneCo (Worldwide), 1st Edition

ISBN 978-1-927338-38-4

Address all inquiries, comments, or suggestions to the publisher. For Terms of Use go to: www.GAMSAT-prep.com

The reviews on the back cover represent the opinions of individuals and do not necessarily reflect the opinions of the institutions they represent.

Gold Standard GAMSAT Product Contact Information

Distribution in Australia, NZ, Asia	**Distribution in Europe**	**Distribution in North America**
Woodslane Pty Ltd	Central Books	RuveneCo Publishing
10 Apollo Street Warriewood	99 Wallis Road	334 Cornelia Street # 559
NSW 2102 Australia	LONDON,	Plattsburgh, New York
ABN: 76 003 677 549	E9 5LN, United Kingdom	12901, USA
learn@gamsat-prep.com	orders@centralbooks.com	buy@gamsatbooks.com

RuveneCo Inc. is neither associated nor affiliated with the Australian Council for Educational Research (ACER) who has developed and administers the Graduate Medical School Admissions Test (GAMSAT) nor The University of Sydney. Printed in China.

This is not a typical 1st edition textbook.

The Gold Standard GAMSAT, the first GAMSAT textbook ever, had already gone through 5 editions with significant revisions. In the last edition, hundreds of new pages were added and it grew to just over 3 kilograms (the weight of a healthy baby!). Unfortunately, that met with some student complaints, it had become unwieldy - especially if the aim was to review a small section of the book on campus or at work. Meanwhile, we had plans to revise and expand the book yet again.

And so, with more content, more images and more practice questions, the 1 textbook has become 3. We hope that studying will now be more convenient!

Besides adding more content, we have added more online access. Previous editions had 10 hours of video access over the 1-year online access period. Now, for the first time ever, we have increased access to unlimited viewings of our small number of Section I and Section II videos, and our large number of cross-referenced Section III videos during your 1-year access period. The Section III videos provide helpful background information for many of the science MCQs in the full-length GS-1 practice test at the back of this textbook.

Over 8 years, we have been teaching monthly GAMSAT webinars, science review GAMSAT courses on campuses in Australia, the UK and Ireland, as well as producing over 100 YouTube videos providing step-by-step worked solutions to the official (ACER's) practice materials for the GAMSAT. We have met the full range of GAMSAT students: 'young' and 'old', hoping for a career vs. having built one already, arts vs. science, experts vs. neophytes, etc. In all likelihood, we have heard your voice expressed, to one degree or the other, among the thousands of students that we have taught over the years. Each time, we grew and improved with that voice in mind.

We hope to impart to you our excitement about the awesome beauty of learning, and of sharing the mental manoeuvres of those who are still here, and others throughout history from Aristotle to Pythagoras, and from Freud to Newton.

Your formula for GAMSAT success comes in 3 parts: content review, practice problems, and full-length testing. We will guide you through the process.

Let's begin.

– B.F., MD

The Graduate Medical School Admissions Test (GAMSAT) is a paper-based test (no calculators are allowed) and consists of 2 essay writing tasks and 185 multiple-choice questions. This exam requires approximately 5.5 hours to complete and is comprised of 3 Sections. There is no break between Section I and II. There is a lunch break between Section II and III. The following are the three subtests of the GAMSAT exam:

1. **Section I: Reasoning in Humanities and Social Sciences - 75 questions; 100 min.**

   • Interpretation and understanding of ideas in socio-cultural context. Source materials: written passages, tabular or other visual format.

2. **Section II: Written Communication - 2 essays; 60 min.**

   • Ability to produce and develop ideas in writing. Task A essay: socio-cultural issues, more analytical; Task B more personal and social issues.

3. **Section III: Reasoning in Biological and Physical Sciences - 110 questions, 170 min.**

   • Chemistry (40%), Biology (40%), Physics (20%). First-year undergraduate level in Biology and Chemistry and Year 12/A-Level/Leaving Certificate course in Physics. Chemistry is equally divided into General and Organic.

> The overall GAMSAT score is calculated using the following formula*:
>
> Overall Score = (1 x Section I + 1 x Section II + 2 x Section III) / 4

* Note: the formula applies to all medical schools that require the GAMSAT in Australia, the UK and Ireland except for the University of Melbourne and University of Sydney which currently weigh all 3 sections equally. Please carefully review the admissions information for all of your target programmes.

Common formula for acceptance:

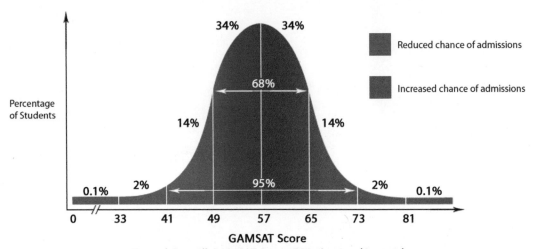

Typical Overall GAMSAT Score Distribution (Approx)

Written Communication

B. Review for Section 2

GOLD STANDARD GAMSAT EXAM

ANSWER KEY AND ANSWER DOCUMENTS

The GAMSAT is challenging, get organised.

gamsat-prep.com/free-GAMSAT-study-schedule

1. How to study:

1. Study the Gold Standard (GS) textbook and videos to learn
2. Do GS Chapter review practice questions
3. Consolidate: create and review your personal summaries (= Gold Notes) daily

2. Once you have completed your studies:

1. Full-length practice test
2. Review mistakes, all solutions
3. Consolidate: review all your Gold Notes and create more
4. Repeat until you get beyond the score you need for your targeted medical/dental school

Recommended GAMSAT Communities:

- All countries (mainly Australia): pagingdr.net
- Mainly UK: thestudentroom.co.uk (Medicine Community Discussion)
- Mainly Ireland: boards.ie

Is there something in the Gold Standard that you did not understand? Don't get frustrated, get on-line: gamsat-prep.com/forum

GAMSAT Scores*

50% not science   50% science

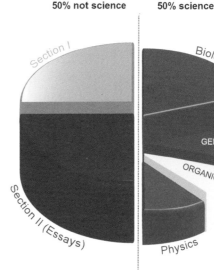
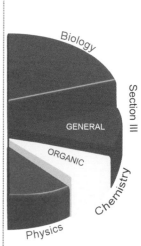

*see exceptions on previous page.

3. Full-length practice tests:

1. ACER practice exams
2. Gold Standard GAMSAT exams
3. Heaps of GAMSAT Practice: 10 full-length exams

4. How much time do you need?

On average, 3-6 hours per day for 3-6 months; depending on life experiences, 2 weeks may be enough and 8 months could be insufficient.

To make the content easier to retain, you can also find aspects of the Gold Standard programme in other formats such as:

THE GOLD STANDARD MULTIMEDIA EDUCATION

Good luck with your studies!

Gold Standard Team

Let's discuss medical school admissions!

Patients and medical professionals often point to three key characteristics of a successful doctor: knowledge, reasoning and interpersonal skills. Clearly, in order to successfully treat illness, knowledge of the condition and treatment options is important. However, reasoning is required to distil all that is possible down to the most likely diagnosis and create an appropriate plan. Despite the preceding, the patient may not want to comply with treatment if interpersonal skills are lacking.

The medical school admissions process has been designed - in part - to address societal concerns. To determine if you are capable of acquiring knowledge at the agreed standard, your GPA is examined. This reflects the sad reality that the majority of undergraduate studies focus more on memory and less so on higher-order thinking skills. But here comes the GAMSAT! The first word in the description of both Section 1 and Section 3 is "Reasoning." Once you start practicing, you will quickly see how memory is downplayed and reasoning is elevated.

The medical school interview - in particular, the MMI (multiple mini-interview) - was born to address the issue of interpersonal skills. Of course, the skills required for the 3 main criteria of medical school admissions overlap to some degree.

In summary, your GPA and GAMSAT score can write the ticket for a medical school interview where success opens the door for admissions. Our aim is to be of help every step of the way.

We begin with a concise examination as to how you can improve your grades at school; even if you have finished your formal studies, you will find some of the advice helpful for your GAMSAT preparation.

Then we take a 'to the point' approach regarding the non-academic aspects of the admissions process: in particular, medical school interviews and, for those who require them, autobiographical materials and letters of reference. Of course, the advice would also be helpful if your aim is dental school or some other professional school.

The next section of the book, 'Understanding the GAMSAT', takes a closer look at the structure of the exam, strategies for all sections, and how to continue to plan your preparation moving forward.

And then what follows is the *sine qua non* of this textbook, where you will even learn to apply *'sine qua non'* in context: Section 1 and Section 2 preparation.

We have prepared hundreds of practice questions with helpful, worked answers in Reasoning in Humanities & Social Sciences (RHSS). We start with simple ideas and then we work up to GAMSAT-level reasoning. Whatever your skill level, you will be able to acclimatize to the challenge while developing and/or expanding your English skills.

And then we present Written Communication (WC) with the dual purpose of further developing your language skills and exploring essay-writing techniques and strategies. You will learn the operating procedure to develop a conservative (safe) essay structure vs. a more risqué, creative structure with its many pros and cons. You will have the opportunity to practice until you develop your own style. You will also be able to read more than 50 essays corrected – in the book and online – from our essay correction service so that you can observe the mental gymnastics involved and note the rewards and penalties.

For both RHSS and WC, we comply with our mantra: *practice, practice, practice*.

And finally, the full-length practice test GS-1 is at the back of this book. It is a 'pull-out' exam so you can make booklets to simulate the real test. If you have no science background, then of course it is strongly recommended that you complete your GAMSAT science preparation prior to sitting GS-1. The exam is followed by answers and the worked solutions are online and accessible using your GS Online Access Card. Aside from the helpful explanations for all 3 GAMSAT sections, many of the worked solutions for the sciences include cross-referenced videos that help with background information.

Truly, The Gold Standard has evolved into a comprehensive, multimedia programme for the premedical student and other students who may need to sit the GAMSAT. Learn well and it will be reflected in your performance.

GAMSAT-Prep.com

MEDICAL SCHOOL ADMISSIONS

PART I

IMPROVING ACADEMIC STANDING

1.1 Lectures

Before you set foot in a classroom you should consider the value of being there. Even if you were taking a course like 'Basket-weaving 101', one way to help you do well in the course is to consider the value of the course to **you**. The course should have an *intrinsic* value (i.e. 'I enjoy weaving baskets'). The course will also have an *extrinsic* value (i.e. 'If I do not get good grades, I will not be accepted...'). Motivation, a positive attitude, and an interest in learning give you an edge before the class even begins.

Unless there is a student 'note-taking club' for your courses, your attendance record and the quality of your notes should both be as excellent as possible. Be sure to choose seating in the classroom which ensures that you will be able to hear the professor adequately and see whatever she may write. Whenever possible, do not sit close to friends!

Instead of chattering before the lecture begins, spend the idle moments quickly reviewing the previous lecture in that subject so you would have an idea of what to expect. Try to take good notes and pay close attention. The preceding may sound like a difficult combination (esp. with professors who speak and write quickly); however, with practice you can learn to do it well.

And finally, do not let the quality of teaching affect your interest in the subject nor your grades! Do not waste your time during or before lectures complaining about how the professor speaks too quickly, does not explain concepts adequately, etc... When the time comes, you can mention such issues on the appropriate evaluation forms! In the meantime, consider this: despite the good or poor quality of teaching, there is always a certain number of students who **still** perform well. You must strive to count yourself among those students.

1.2 Taking Notes

Unless your professor says otherwise, if you take excellent notes and learn them inside out, you will *ace* his course. Your notes should always be up-to-date, complete, and separate from other subjects.

To be safe, you should try to write everything! You can fill in any gaps by comparing your notes with those of your friends. If you do not type then create your own shorthand symbols or use standard ones. The following represents some useful symbols:

|·|	*between*
=	*the same as*
≠	*not the same as*
∴	*therefore*
Δ	*difference, change in*
cf.	*compare*
c̄ or w	*with*
c̄out or w/o	*without*
esp.	*especially*
∵	*because*
i.e.	*that is*
e.g.	*for example*

Many students retype or rewrite their notes at home. Should you decide to rewrite your notes, your time will be used efficiently if you are paying close attention to the information you are rewriting. In fact, a more useful technique is the following: during class, write your notes only on the right side of your binder. Later, rewrite the information from class in a complete but condensed form on the left side of the binder (*this condensed form should include mnemonics which we will discuss later*). If you retype, again, your focus should be to condense your notes (this requires that you continually decide what you already know).

Some students find it valuable to use different colour pens. Juggling pens in class may distract you from the content of the lecture. Different colour pens would be more useful in the context of rewriting (condensing) one's notes.

1.3 The Principles of Studying Efficiently

If you study efficiently, you will have enough time for extracurricular activities, movies, etc. The bottom line is that your time must be used efficiently and effectively.

During the average school day, time can be found during breaks, between classes, and after school to quickly review notes in a library or any other quiet place you can find on campus. Simply by using the available time in your school day, you can keep up to date with recent information.

You should design an individual study schedule to meet your particular needs. However, as a rule, a certain amount of time every evening should be set aside for more in depth studying. Weekends can be set aside for special projects and reviewing notes from the beginning.

On the surface, the idea of regularly reviewing notes from the beginning may sound like an insurmountable task which would take forever! The reality is just the opposite. After all, if you continually study the information, by the time mid-terms approach you would have seen the first lecture so many times that it would take only moments to review it again. On the other hand, had you not been reviewing regularly, it would be like reading that lecture for the first time!

You should study wherever you are <u>comfortable</u> and <u>effective</u> studying (i.e. library, at home, etc.). Should you prefer studying at home, be sure to create an environment which is conducive to studying.

Studying should be an active process to <u>memorize</u> and <u>understand</u> a given set of material. Memorization and comprehension are best achieved by the **elaboration** of course material, **attention, repetition,** and practising **retrieval** of the information. All these principles are borne out in the following techniques.

1.4 Studying from Notes and Texts

Successful studying from either class notes, university textbooks, or Gold Standard GAMSAT textbooks, can be accomplished in three simple steps:

- **Preview the material**: read all the relevant headings, titles, and sub-titles to give you a general idea of what you are about to learn. You should never embark on a trip without knowing where you are going!

- **Read while questioning**: <u>passive studying</u> is when you sit in front of a book and just read. This can lead to boredom, lack of concentration, or even worse - difficulty remembering what you just read! **Active studying** involves reading while actively questioning yourself. For example: how does this fit in with the 'big picture'? How does this relate to what we learned last week? What cues about these words or lists will make it easy for me to memorize them? What type of question would my professor ask me? If I was asked a question on this material, how would I answer? Etc...

- **Recite and consider**: put the notes or text away while you attempt to **recall** the main facts. Once you are able to recite the important information, **consider** how it relates to the entire subject.

<u>N.B.</u> if you ever sit down to study and you are not quite sure with which subject to begin, always start with either the most difficult subject or the subject you like least (usually they are one in the same!).

1.5 Study Aids

The most effective study aids include practice exams, mnemonics and audio MP3s.

Practice exams (*exams from previous semesters*) are often available from the library, upper level students, online or directly from the professor. They can be used like maps which guide you through your semester. They give you a good indication as to what information you should emphasize when you study; what question types and exam format you can expect; and what your level of progress is.

One practice exam should be set aside to do one week before 'the real thing.' You should time yourself and do the exam in an environment free from distractions. This provides an ideal way to uncover unexpected weak points.

Mnemonics are an effective way of memorizing lists of information. Usually a word, phrase, or sentence is constructed to symbolize a greater amount of information (i.e. LEO is A GERC = <u>L</u>ose <u>E</u>lectrons is <u>O</u>xidation is <u>A</u>node, <u>G</u>ain <u>E</u>lectrons is <u>R</u>eduction at <u>C</u>athode). An effective study aid to active studying is the creation of your own mnemonics.

Audio MP3s can be used as effective tools to repeat information and to use your time efficiently. Information from the left side of your notes (*see 1.2 Taking Notes*) including mnemonics, can be dictated and recorded. Often, an entire semester of work can be summarized into one 90 minute recording.

Now you can listen to the recording on your smartphone while waiting in line at the bank, or in a bus or with a car stereo on the way to school, work, etc. You can also listen to recorded information when you go to sleep and listen to another one first thing in the morning. You are probably familiar with the situation of having heard a song early in the morning and then having difficulty, for the rest of the day, getting it out of your mind! Well, imagine if the first thing you heard in the morning was: "Hair is a modified keratinized structure produced by the cylindrical down growth of epithelium..."! Thus MP3s become an effective study aid since they are an extra source of repetition.

Some students like to **record lectures**. Though it may be helpful to fill in missing notes, it is not an efficient way to repeat information.

Some students like to use **study cards** (tangible flashcards and/or smartphone apps) on which they may write either a summary of information they must memorize or relevant questions to consider. Then the cards are used throughout the day to quickly flash information to promote thought on course material.

1.5.1 Falling Behind

Imagine yourself as a marathon runner who has run 25.5 km of a 26 km race. The finishing line is now in view. However, you have fallen behind some of the other runners. The most difficult aspect of the race is still ahead.

In such a scenario some interesting questions can be asked: Is now the time to drop out of the race because 0.5 km suddenly seems like a long distance? Is now the time to reevaluate whether or not you should have competed? Or is now the time to remain faithful to your goals and give 100%?

Imagine one morning in mid-semester you wake up realizing you have fallen behind in your studies. What do you do? Where do you start? Is it too late?

Like a doctor being presented with an urgent matter, you should see the situation as one of life's challenges. Now is the worst time for doubts, rather, it is the time for action. A clear line of action should be formulated such that it could be followed.

For example, one might begin by gathering all pertinent study materials like a complete set of study notes, relevant text(s), sample exams, etc. As a rule, to get back into the thick of things, notes and sample exams take precedence. Studying at this point should take a three pronged approach: i) a regular, consistent review of the information from your notes from the beginning of the section for which you are responsible (i.e. *starting with the first class*); ii) a regular, consistent review of course material as you are learning it from the lectures (*this is the most efficient way to study*); iii) regular testing using questions given in class or those contained in sample exams. Using such questions will clarify the extent of your progress.

It is also of value, as time allows, to engage in extracurricular activities which you find helpful in reducing stress (i.e. sports, piano, creative writing, etc.).

THE MEDICAL SCHOOL INTERVIEW

2.1 Introduction

The application process to most medical schools includes interviews. Only a select number of students from the applicant pool will be given an offer to be interviewed. The medical school interview is, as a rule, something that you *achieve*. In other words, after your school grades and GAMSAT scores (and/or references and autobiographical materials for international schools) have been reviewed, you are offered the ultimate opportunity to put your foot forward: a personalized interview.

Depending on the medical school, you may be interviewed by one, two or several interviewers. You may be the only interviewee or there may be others (i.e., *a group interview*). There may be one or more interviews lasting from 20 minutes to two hours. And, of course, there is the increasingly popular multiple mini-interview (MMI) which includes many short assessments in a timed circuit.

Despite the variations among the technical aspects of the interview, in terms of substance, most medical schools have similar objectives. These objectives can be arbitrarily categorized into three general assessments: (i) your <u>personality traits</u>, (ii) <u>social skills</u>, and (iii) <u>knowledge of medicine</u>.

Personality traits such as maturity, integrity, compassion, sincerity, honesty, originality, curiosity, self-directed learning, intellectual capacity, confidence (*not arrogance!*), and motivation are all components of the ideal applicant. These traits will be exposed by the process of the interview, your mannerisms, and the substance of what you choose to discuss when given an ambiguous question. For instance, bringing up *specific* examples of academic achievement related to school and related to self-directed learning would score well in the categories of intellectual capacity and curiosity, respectively.

Motivation is a personality trait which may make the difference between a high and a low or moderate score in an interview. A student must clearly demonstrate that they have the enthusiasm, desire, energy, and interest to survive (typically) four long years of medical school and beyond! If you are naturally shy or soft-spoken, you will have to give special attention to this category.

Social skills such as leadership, ease of communication, ability to relate to others and work effectively in groups, volunteer work, cultural and social interests, all constitute skills which are often viewed as critical for future physicians. It is not sufficient to say in an interview: "I have good social skills"! You must display such skills via your interaction with the interviewer(s) and by discussing specific examples of situations which clearly demonstrate your social skills.

Knowledge of medicine includes <u>at least</u> a general understanding of what the field of medicine involves, the curriculum you are applying to, and a knowledge of popular medical issues like abortion, euthanasia, AIDS, the national healthcare system, etc. It is striking to see the number of students who apply to medical school each year whose knowledge of medicine is limited to headlines and popular TV shows! It is not logical for someone to dedicate their lives to a profession they know little about.

Doing volunteer work in a hospital is a good start. Alternatively, getting a part-time job in a hospital or having a relative who is a physician can help expose you to the daily goings-on in a hospital setting. An even better strategy to be informed is the following: (i) keep up-to-date with the details of medically-related controversies in the news. You should also be able to develop and support opinions of your own; (ii) skim through a medical journal at least once; (iii) read the medical section of a popular science magazine (i.e. Scientific American, Discover, etc.); (iv) keep abreast of changes in medical school curricula in general and specific to the programs to which you have applied. You can access such information at most university libraries and by writing individual medical schools for information on their programs; (v) do a First-Aid course.

2.2 Preparing for the Interview

If you devote an adequate amount of time for interview preparation, the actual interview will be less tense for you and <u>you</u> will be able to control most of the content of the interview.

Reading from the various sources mentioned in the preceding sections would be helpful. Also, read over your curriculum vitae and/or any autobiographical materials you may have prepared. Note highlights in your life or specific examples that demonstrate the aforementioned personality traits, social skills or your knowledge of medicine. Zero in on qualities or stories which are either important,

memorable, interesting, amusing, informative or "all of the above"! Once in the interview room, you will be given the opportunity to elaborate on the qualities you believe are important about yourself.

Email or call the medical school and ask them about the structure of the interview (i.e., one-on-one, group, MMI, etc.) and ask them if they can tell you who will interview you. Many schools have no qualms volunteering such information. Now you can determine the person's expertise by either asking or looking through staff members of the different faculties or medical specialties at that university or college. A cardiac surgeon, a volunteer from the community, and a medical ethicist all have different areas of expertise and will likely orient their interviews differently. Thus you may want to read from a source which will give you a general understanding of their specialty.

Choose appropriate clothes for the interview. Every year some students dress for a medical school interview as if they were going out to dance! Medicine is still considered a conservative profession, you should dress and groom yourself likewise. First impressions are very important. Your objective is to make it as easy as possible for your

interviewer(s) to imagine you as a physician. Please keep in mind: Although you should explore possible ideas and information that you might present in an interview, you cannot permit your preparation to devolve into preprogrammed responses. No one wants to interview a robot!

Do practice interviews with people you respect but who can also maintain their objectivity. Let them read this entire chapter on medical school interviews. They must understand that you are to be evaluated *only* on the basis of the interview. On that basis alone, one should be able to imagine the ideal candidate as a future physician.

2.3 Strategies for Answering Questions

Always remember that the interviewer controls the *direction* of the interview by his questions; you control the *content* of the interview through your answers. In other words, once given the opportunity, you should speak about the topics that are important to you; conversely, you should avoid volunteering information which renders you uncomfortable. You can enhance the atmosphere in which the answers are delivered by being polite, sincere, tactful, well-organized, outwardly oriented and maintaining eye contact. Motivation, enthusiasm, and a positive attitude must all be evident.

As a rule, there are no right or wrong answers. However, the way in which you justify your opinions, the topics you choose to

discuss, your mannerisms and your composure all play important roles. It is normal to be nervous. It would be to your advantage to channel your nervous energy into a positive quality, like enthusiasm.

Do not spew forth answers! Take your time - it is not a contest to see how fast you can answer. Answering with haste can lead to disastrous consequences as happened to a student I interviewed:

Q: *Have you ever doubted your interest in medicine as a career?*
A: *No!*
Well,...ah...I guess so. Ah ... I guess everyone doubts something at some point or the other...

Retractions like that are a bad signal but it illustrates an important point: there are usually no right or wrong answers in an interview; however, there are right or wrong ways of answering. Through the example we can conclude the following: listen carefully to the question, try to relax, and think before you answer!

Do not sit on the fence! If you avoid giving your opinions on controversial topics, it will be interpreted as indecision which is a negative trait for a prospective physician. You have a right to your opinions. However, you must be prepared to defend your point of view in an objective, rational, and informative fashion. It is also important to show that, despite your opinion, you understand both sides of the argument. If you have an extreme or unconventional perspective and if you believe your perspective will not interfere with your practice of medicine, you must let your interviewer know that.

For example, imagine a student who was against abortion under *any* circumstance. If asked about her opinion on abortion, she should clearly state her opinion objectively, show she understands the opposing viewpoint, and then use data to reinforce her position. If she felt that her opinion would not interfere with her objectivity when practising medicine, she might volunteer: "If I were in a position where my perspective might interfere with an objective management of a patient, I would refer that patient to another physician."

Carefully note the reactions of the interviewer in response to your answers. Whether the interviewer is sitting on the edge of her seat wide-eyed or slumping in her chair while yawning, you should take such cues to help you determine when to continue, change the subject, or when to stop talking. Also, note the more subtle cues. For example, gauge which topic makes the interviewer frown, give eye contact, take notes, etc.

Lighten up the interview with a well-timed story. A conservative joke, a good analogy, or anecdote may help you relax and make the interviewer sustain his interest. If it is done correctly, it can turn a routine interview into a memorable and friendly interaction.

It should be noted that because the system is not standardized, a small number of interviewers may ask overly personal questions (i.e., about relationships, religion, etc.) or even questions which carry sexist tones (i.e., *What would you do if you got pregnant while attending medical school?*). Some questions may be frankly illegal. If you do not want to answer a question, simply maintain your composure, express your position diplomatically, and address the interviewers real concern (i.e. *Does this person have the potential to be a good doctor?*). For example, you might say in a non-confrontational tone of voice: "I would rather not answer such a question. However, I can assure you that whatever my answer may have been, it would in no way affect either my prospective studies in medicine nor any prerequisite objectivity I should have to be a good physician."

2.4 Sample Questions

There are an infinite number of questions and many different categories of questions. Different medical schools will emphasize different categories of questions. Arbitrarily, ten categories of questions can be defined: ambiguous, medically related, academic, social, stress-type, problem situations, personality oriented, based on autobiographical material, miscellaneous, and ending questions. We will examine each category in terms of sample questions and general comments.

Ambiguous Questions:

• • *Tell me about yourself.*
How do you want me to remember you?
What are your goals?
There are hundreds if not thousands of applicants, why should we choose you?
Convince me that you would make a good doctor.
Why do you want to study medicine?

COMMENTS: These questions present nightmares for the unprepared student who walks into the interview room and is immediately asked: "Tell me about yourself." Where do you start? If you are prepared as previously discussed, you will be able to take control of the interview by highlighting your qualities or objectives in an informative and interesting manner.

Medically Related Questions:

What are the pros and cons to our health care system?
If you had the power, what changes would you make to our health care system?
Do doctors make too much money?
Is it ethical for doctors to strike?
What is the Hippocratic Oath?
Should fetal tissue be used to treat disease (i.e. Parkinson's)?
If you were a doctor and an under age girl asked you for the Pill (or an abortion) and she did not want to tell her parents, what would you do?
Should doctors be allowed to 'pull the plug' on terminally ill patients?
If a patient is dying from a bleed, would you transfuse blood if you knew they would not approve (i.e. Jehovah Witness)?

COMMENTS: The health care system, euthanasia, cloning, abortion, and other ethical issues are very popular topics in this era of technological advances, skyrocketing health care costs, and ethical uncertainty. A well-informed opinion can set you apart from most of the other interviewees.

Questions Related to Academics:

Why did you choose your present course of studies?

What is your favorite subject in your present course of studies? Why?

Would you consider a career in your present course of studies?

Can you convince me that you can cope with the workload in medical school?

How do you study/prepare for exams?

Do you engage in self-directed learning?

COMMENTS: Medical schools like to see applicants who are well-disciplined, committed to medicine as a career, and who exhibit self-directed learning (i.e. such a level of desire for knowledge that the student may seek to study information independent of any organized infrastructure). Beware of any glitches in your academic record. You may be asked to give reasons for any grades they may deem substandard. On the other hand, you should volunteer any information regarding academic achievement (i.e. prizes, awards, scholarships, particularly high grades in one subject or the other, etc.).

Questions Related to Social Skills or Interests:

Give evidence that you relate well with others.

Give an example of a leadership role you have assumed.

Have you done any volunteer work?

What would you do as Prime Minister with respect to the trade imbalance with China?

Is the monarchy a legitimate institution?

What are the prospects for a lasting peace in Afghanistan? Iraq? the Sudan? the Middle-East?

What do you think of the regional free-trade agreements?

COMMENTS: Questions concerning social skills should be simple for the prepared student. If you are asked a question that you cannot answer, say so. If you pretend to know something about a topic in which you are completely uninformed, you will make a bad situation worse.

Stress-Type Questions:

How do you handle stress?

What was the most stressful event in your life? How did you handle it?

The night before your final exam, your father has a heart-attack and is admitted to a hospital, what do you do?

COMMENTS: The ideal physician has positive coping methods to deal with the inevitable stressors of a medical practice. Stress-type questions are a legitimate means of determining if you possess the raw material necessary to cope with medical school and medicine as a career. Some interviewers go one step further. They may decide to introduce stress <u>into</u> the interview and see how you handle it. For example, they may decide to ask you a confrontational question or try to back you into a corner (i.e. *You do not know anything about medicine, do you?*). Alternatively, the interviewer might use silence to introduce stress into the interview. If you have completely and confidently answered a question and silence falls in the room, <u>do not</u> retract previous statements, mutter, or fidget. Simply wait for the next question. If the silence becomes unbearable, you may consider asking an intelligent question (i.e. a specific question regarding their curriculum).

MMI-Type Problem Situations:

A 68 year-old married woman has a newly discovered cancer. Her life expectancy is 6 months. How would you inform her?
A 34 year-old man presents with AIDS and tells you, as his physician, that he does not want to tell his wife. What would you do?
You are playing tennis with your best friend and the ball hits your friend in the eye. What do you do?
A 52 year-old female diabetic comes to your ER in a coma but dies almost immediately. You are the physician who must now inform her husband and daughter. Enter the room and talk to them.
Your best friend in med-school has a part-time job to support herself. She has been unable to make it to some compulsory seminars because of her job and has asked you to mark her name present on the roll. What do you do and why?

COMMENTS: Some programmes have a few MMI stations with an actor in the room or other students. As for the other questions,

listen carefully (or in the case of MMI, read the question posted on the door carefully) and take your time to consider the best possible response. Keep in mind that the ideal physician is not only knowledgeable, but is also <u>compassionate</u>, <u>empathetic</u>, <u>honest</u> and is objective enough to understand <u>both sides</u> of a dilemma. Be sure such qualities are clearly demonstrated.

Personality-Oriented Questions:

If you could change one thing about yourself, what would it be?
How would your friends describe you?
What do you do with your spare time?
What is the most important event that has occurred to you in the last five years?
If you had three magical wishes, what would they be?
What are your best attributes?

COMMENTS: Of course, most questions will assess your personality to one degree or the other. However, these questions are quite direct in their approach. Forewarned is forearmed!

Question Based on Autobiographical Materials:

COMMENTS: Any autobiographical materials you may have provided to the medical schools is fair game for questioning. You may be asked to discuss or elaborate on any point the interviewer may feel is interesting or questionable.

Miscellaneous Questions:

Should the federal government reinstate the death penalty? Explain.

What do you expect to be doing 10 years from now?

How would you attract physicians to rural areas?

Why do you want to attend our medical school?

What other medical schools have you applied to?

Have you been to other interviews?

COMMENTS: You will do fine in this grab-bag category as long as you stick to the strategies previously iterated.

Ending Questions:

What would you do if you were not accepted to a medical school?

How do you think you did in this interview?

Do you have any questions?

COMMENTS: The only thing more important than a good first impression is a good finish in order to leave a positive lasting impression. They are looking for students who are so committed to medicine that they will not only re-apply to medical school if not accepted, but they would also strive to improve on those aspects of their application which prevented them from being accepted in the first attempt. All these questions should be answered with a quiet confidence. If you are given an opportunity to ask questions, though you should not flaunt your knowledge, you should establish that you are well-informed. For example: "I have read that you have changed your curriculum to a more patient-oriented and self-directed learning approach. I was wondering how the medical students are getting along with these new changes." Be sure, however, not to ask a question unless you are genuinely interested in the answer.

2.5 The Interview: Questions, Answers and Feedback

Specific interview questions can be found online for free at futuredoctor.net. Dr. Ferdinand reproduced and captured the intense experience of a medical school interview on video to be used as a learning tool. "The Gold Standard Medical School Interview: Questions, Tips and Answers" was filmed live in HD on campus in front of a group of premedical students - most of whom were invited for medical school interviews. A volunteer is interviewed in front of the class and the entire interview is conducted as if it were the real thing. After the interview, an analysis of each question and the mindset behind it is discussed in an open forum format. If you are not sure that you have the interviewing skills to be accepted to medical school, then it is a must-see online video (GAMSAT-prep.com).

Whenever Dr. Ferdinand is conducting his live Medical School Interview seminar in Sydney, London or Dublin, the dates will be posted at GAMSAT-prep.com.

AUTOBIOGRAPHICAL MATERIALS AND REFERENCES

3.1 Autobiographical Materials

Autobiographical materials include resumes, CVs, personal statements, questionnaires and other written materials that may be required when applying to medical school or a graduate program. In general, these materials and letters of reference are required by almost all institutions in the US and Canada and some institutions in Australia, Ireland and the UK. Consult individual institutions regarding their requirements. Just in case the information can serve you well, we have included it. Autobiographical materials are a sort of *written interview*. Thus the same objectives, preparation, and strategies apply as previously mentioned for interviews. However, there are some unique factors.

For example, you can begin writing long in advance of the deadline. The ideal way to prepare is to use your computer or to have a few sheets of paper at home where you continually write any accomplishments or interesting experiences you have had anytime in your life! By starting this process early, months later you should, hopefully(!), have a long list from

which to choose information appropriate for the autobiographical materials. Your resume or curriculum vitae may also be of value.

Be sure to write rough drafts and have qualified individuals proofread it for you. Spelling and grammatical errors should not exist.

The document should be written on the appropriate paper and/or in the format as stated in the directions. Do not surpass your word and/or space limit. Usually the submission is online but if they require it on paper, ideally, it would be laser printed on business paper. The document should be so pretty that your parents should want to frame it and hang it in the living room! Handwritten or typed material with 'liquid paper' or 'white-out' is simply not impressive.

Your document must be clearly organized. If you are given directive questions then organization should not be a problem. However, if you are given open-ended questions or if you are told, for example, to write a 1000 word essay about yourself, adequate organization is key. There are two general ways you can organize such a response: *chronological* or *thematic*. However, they are not mutually exclusive.

In a **chronological** response, you are organized by doing a systematic review of important events through time. In writing an essay or letter, one could start with an interesting or amusing story from childhood and then highlight important events chronologically and in concordance with the instructions.

In the **thematic** approach a general theme is presented from the outset and then verified through examples at any time in your life. For example, imagine the following statement somewhere in the introduction of an autobiographical letter/essay:

My concept of the good physician is one who has a solid intellectual capacity, extensive social skills, and a creative ability. I have strived to attain and demonstrate such skills.

Following such an introduction to a thematic response, the essayist can link events from anytime to the general theme of the essay. Each theme would thus be examined in turn.

And finally, keep in mind the advice given for interviews since much of it applies here as well. For example, the appropriate use of an amusing story, anecdote, or an interesting analogy can make your document an interesting one to read. And, as for interviews, specific examples are more memorable than overly generalized statements.

3.2 Letters of Reference

Letters of reference (a.k.a. *assessments* which are written by *referees*) are required by most medical schools in North America. It provides an opportunity for an admissions committee to see what other people think of you. Consequently, it is often viewed as an important aspect of your application package.

Choose the people who will submit your letter of reference in accordance with instructions from the medical schools to which you are applying. If no such instructions are given, then construct a list of possible referees. Choose from this list individuals who: (i) you can trust; (ii) are reliable; (iii) can write, at least, reasonably well; (iv) understand the importance of your application; and (v) can present with some confidence attributes you have which are consistent with those of a good physician. A good balance would be to have one referee who is a professor, another a physician and a third who has experience with your social skills or achievements.

Often students either want or are told to have someone as a referee who they do not know well (i.e. a professor). In such a case choose your referee prudently. If they agree to give you a recommendation, give them your resume, curriculum vitae, or any other autobiographical materials you may have. Alternatively, you may ask to arrange a mini-interview. Either way, you would have armed your referee with information which can be used in a specific and personal manner in the letter of reference.

People are not paid to write you a letter of reference! Therefore, make it as easy as possible for them. Give them an ample amount of time before the deadline for submission. Also, supply them with a stamped envelope with the appropriate address inscribed. Besides being the polite thing to do, they may also be impressed by your organization. And finally, once the letter of reference has been sent, do not forget to send a "Thank-you" card to your referee.

$$\mathcal{A} + \mathcal{B} = ?$$

GAMSAT-Prep.com

UNDERSTANDING
THE GAMSAT
PART II

THE STRUCTURE OF THE GAMSAT

1.1 Introduction

The Graduate Medical School Admissions Test (GAMSAT) is a prerequisite for admission to participating graduate-entry professional programmes including medical and dental schools in Australia, Ireland and the UK. Each year thousands of applicants submit GAMSAT test results to medical, dental and graduate schools as well as other programmes (i.e. pharmacy, optometry, veterinary science, etc.). While the actual weight given to GAMSAT scores in the admissions process varies from school to school, often they are regarded in a similar manner to your university GPA (i.e. your academic standing).

The GAMSAT is available to any student who has already completed a bachelor's degree, or who will be enrolled in their penultimate (second to last) or final year of study for a bachelor's degree, at the time of sitting the test. The test is administered twice a year, in March and September, at test centres in Australia, the UK and Ireland. The March sitting and September sitting are no longer referred to as 'GAMSAT Australia/ Ireland' or 'GAMSAT UK,' respectively, since each sitting is now available in all three countries. Not all test centres are offered for each sitting. Additional test centres are available in Singapore, Washington D.C. (USA), and Wellington (NZ).

GAMSAT results are generally valid for 2 years. There is no restriction on the number of times you may sit the GAMSAT. Currently, results from sitting the GAMSAT in any one country can be used in applying to any other country that requires the GAMSAT.

To access the most up-to-date information, to register for the GAMSAT, and to purchase official GAMSAT practice materials, consider visiting the following website: gamsat.acer.org.

1.1.1 The new MCAT for International Applicants or for US/Canada

The new Medical College Admission Test (MCAT) is a prerequisite for admission to nearly all the medical schools in North America. Each year, over 50,000 applicants to American and English Canadian medical schools submit MCAT test results.

The MCAT is a computer based test (CBT) administered on a Saturday or a weekday, more than 20 times per year. To register for the MCAT, you should consult your undergraduate adviser and register online: www.aamc.org.

The MCAT can be used by international students applying to medical schools that accept GAMSAT scores. Only international students have the option of sitting the MCAT instead of the GAMSAT. Consult individual programmes for confirmation.

1.2 The Format of the GAMSAT

The GAMSAT aims to test your skills in problem solving, critical thinking, writing as well as mastery and application of concepts in the basic sciences. The exam is divided into three sections. All questions, save for Section II, are multiple choice with 4 options per question. Ten minutes reading time is given for Sections I and III, and five minutes for Section II. The following is your schedule for the test day:

Section I	
Reasoning in the Humanities and Social Sciences	
Questions	75
Time	100 minutes

Section II	
Written Communication	
Questions	2
Time	60 minutes
Lunch	60 minutes

Section III	
Reasoning in Biological and Physical Sciences	
Questions	110
Time	170 minutes

Biological and Physical Sciences collectively include biology, general and organic chemistry at the introductory university level, and A-Level/Leaving Certificate/Year 12 physics. Overall, the subject material is weighted as follows:

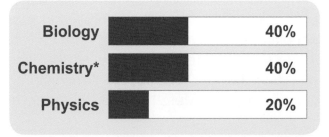

Biology	40%
Chemistry*	40%
Physics	20%

*Chemistry is equally divided between General (Inorganic) and Organic.

The layout of Section I and Section III are similar with separate "Units" containing stimulus material followed by multiple-choice questions. Section I may use excerpts from poems, novels, articles, a cartoon, etc. However, for Section III, the stimulus material can also include a passage, graph, equation(s), text, data, etc.

The MCAT's most recent incarnation began in 2015. Besides the subjects that the MCAT traditionally covered, which were the same as the GAMSAT, the new MCAT now includes biochemistry, psychology and sociology. It is a computer-based exam with 230 questions and there is no longer an essay section. The total test time is now about 7 h, 30 min. The value of understanding the differences and similarities between the two exams is as follows: (1) some students who are citizens of Australia, Ireland or the UK may choose to also sit the MCAT in order to apply to one of the majority of medical schools in the US and Canada that require the MCAT; (2) currently, international students have the option to sit either the GAMSAT or MCAT in order to submit applications to Australia, Ireland or the UK; some choose to sit the MCAT (or both tests) in order to

Table 1: Comparing the two standardized tests for medical school admissions.

	GAMSAT	MCAT (before 2007)	MCAT (2007-2014)
Testing method	Paper	Paper	Computer
Total test time	5½ hours	8 hours	5½ hours
Name of Verbal Section	Section 1	Verbal Reasoning	Verbal Reasoning
# Questions; Time	75 questions; 100 min.	65 questions; 85 min.	40 questions; 60 min.
Writing Section	Section 2	Writing Sample	Writing Sample
# Questions; Time	2 questions; 60 min.	2 questions; 60 min.	2 questions; 60 min.
Physical and Biological Sciences*	Section 3	1) Physical Sciences 2) Biological Sciences	1) Physical Sciences 2) Biological Sciences
# Questions; Time	110 questions; 170 min.	154 questions (total); 200 min. (total)	104 questions (total); 140 min. (total)
Breaks	• None between Section I and II • 1 hour for lunch	• 5 min. between sections • 1 hour for lunch	• 5 min. between sections • Lunch optional (max. 1 hour)
Countries	Australia, Ireland, UK	US, Canada	US, Canada
Test Frequency	Twice annually per country	Twice annually per country	More than 20 test dates annually
Official Practice Materials	4 booklets (e-books)	10 booklets	1 manual, 8 CBTs (practice tests #3 to #11)

* Physical Sciences includes physics and general or inorganic chemistry. Biological Sciences includes biology and organic chemistry. This table was used with permission from GAMSATtestpreparation.com.

also apply to North American medical programmes.

The 2 tests have both significant similarities and significant differences. The GAMSAT makes it possible for a student with little science background to learn independently and, with strong reasoning skills, succeed. Whereas, the MCAT requires formal training in the sciences because of the number of equations and facts that are considered 'presumed knowledge'.

Thus the GAMSAT leans on reasoning while the MCAT contains more memorization (though nowhere near as much memorization as required for an average introductory level university science course). It is the issue of presumed knowledge that makes some students say that the MCAT is more difficult but clearly that depends on your pre-exam reading history and learning experiences.

1.2.2 English as a Second Language (ESL)

Many ESL students will need to pay extra attention to Section I and Section II of the GAMSAT. Specific advice for all students will be presented in the chapters that follow. This advice should be taken very seriously for ESL students.

Having said that, GAMSAT scores are subjected to a statistical analysis to check that each question is fair, valid and reliable. Test questions in development are scrutinized in order to minimize gender, ethnic or religious bias, in order to affirm that the test is culturally fair.

Candidates whose native language is not English are permitted to bring a printed

bilingual dictionary on test day for use in Section I and Section II only. The pages must be unmarked and all paper notes removed. Any candidate using this option must submit the dictionary to the Supervisor for inspection before the test begins.

Depending on your English skills, you may or may not benefit from an English reading or writing summer course. Of course, you would have the option of deciding whether or not you would want to take such a course for credit. GAMSAT-prep.com also offers an online speed reading/comprehension program with extra practice questions.

1.3 How the GAMSAT is Scored

The GAMSAT is scored for each of the three sections individually. The sections consisting of multiple-choice questions

are first scored right or wrong resulting in a raw score. Note that wrong answers are worth the same as unanswered questions so

ALWAYS ANSWER ALL THE QUESTIONS even if you are not sure of certain answers. The raw score is then converted to a scaled score ranging from 0 (lowest) to 100 (highest). Essentially, the scores are scaled to ensure that the same proportion of individual marks within each section are given from year to year (using Item Response Theory). The scaled score is neither a percentage nor a percentile. It is not possible to accurately replicate this scoring system at home.

Section II is marked by three independent markers from each zone. A scale of 10 points is used. Should there be a difference of 5 or more in two scores then an additional marker will be used. Ultimately, the three closest scores are totaled for the Section II raw score which is then converted to a scaled score.

You will receive a score for each of the three sections, together with an Overall GAMSAT Score. The Overall Score is a weighted average of the three component scores.

The Overall GAMSAT Score is determined using the following formula:

Overall Score = (1 × Section I + 1 × Section II + 2 × Section III) ÷ 4

Standards for interviews or admissions may vary for both Sectional Scores and the Overall GAMSAT Score. For example, one particular medical school may establish a cut-off (minimum) of 50 for any given section and 60 for the Overall GAMSAT Score. Note that some programmes (e.g. USyd, UniMelb) calculate the Overall score differently - they do not weight Section III twice. Contact individual programmes for specific score requirements.

The GAMSAT may include a small number of questions which will not be scored. These questions are either used to calibrate the exam or were found to be either too ambiguous or too difficult to be counted or are trial questions which may be used in the future. So if you see a question that you think is off the wall, unanswerable or inappropriate for your level of knowledge, it could well be one of these questions so never panic! And of course, answer every question because guessing provides a 25% chance of being correct while not answering provides a 0% chance of being correct!

1.3.1 GAMSAT Scores in Different Countries

GAMSAT scores are interchangeable and can be used to apply to any university that requires the GAMSAT. You may sit the GAMSAT in the UK, Australia or Ireland to apply to universities in any of these countries. You must ensure that your scores have not expired if you are using a score from a previous sitting of the GAMSAT (i.e. GAMSAT scores cannot be more than two years old). Otherwise, you choose the GAMSAT score that you wish to submit for consideration for admissions.

Since there is no limit to the number of times you can sit the GAMSAT, you may even choose to sit the exam twice in one year. "Each year just under half of the questions in Sections 1 and 3 are new," according to *GAMSAT: A 10-year retrospective overview, with detailed analysis of candidates' performance* (BMC Med Educ. 2015; 15: 31; PMCID: PMC4351698). Despite the fact that over 50% of the multiple-choice questions are repeated, the study found a relatively small GAMSAT score increase (approx. 4/100, overall) with the first repeat, and little evidence of an upward trend thereafter. It seems clear that adequate preparation is more effective than constant repetition.

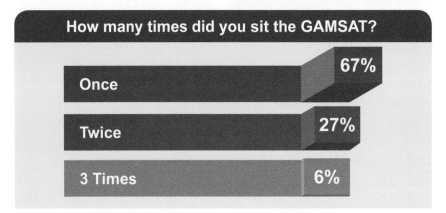

How many times did you sit the GAMSAT?

Once	67%
Twice	27%
3 Times	6%

2010 Gold Standard GAMSAT survey at the University of Sydney (Usyd Medical Science Society), n>100, average reported GAMSAT score (most recent): 62.2. Our study seems consistent with the upward trend reported by ACER: 31% of the cohort had repeated the GAMSAT in 2005, up to 45% in 2014.

1.3.2 Average, Good and High GAMSAT Scores

Please keep in mind that the percentile rank indicates your test performance relative to all the students who sat the same test on the same day. It records the percentage of students whose scores were lower than yours.

Score	Percentile	Score
56-58	50th	average
61-63	75th	usually good*
73 or higher	98th	very high

*Please note, a "good" score may be good enough for admittance to one particular medical school but below the cutoff of another. Consult the websites of the medical institutions to which you intend to apply. Click on your national icon at the following webpage to get a summary of scores required at institutions near you: www.gamsat-prep.com/GAMSAT-scores.

An average GAMSAT score is often around 56-58 and a high GAMSAT score is over 63. Please keep in mind when evaluating the statistics provided and the graphic: this data is meant to give you a general idea of the process. The numbers can vary some-what from one exam sitting to another. And as mentioned previously, you cannot repli-cate the scoring system at home since there is no formula provided to convert raw scores into official GAMSAT scores. Note that a score above 80 is very rare.

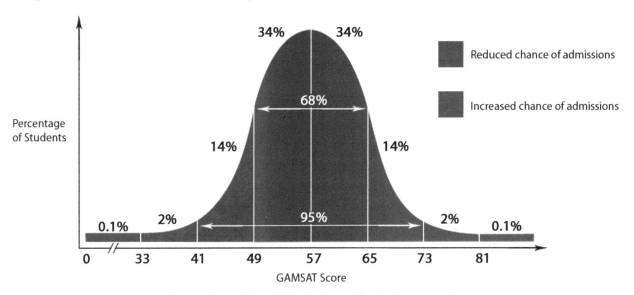

Figure 1: Typical Overall GAMSAT Score Distribution (Approx.)

1.3.3 When are the scores released?

GAMSAT is held twice a year, in March and September. GAMSAT results are released within 2 months of sitting the exam. Candidates are emailed login information to access their personal results report. Should there be any changes to the exam dates or any other modifications, get the up-to-date information online at gamsat.acer.org.

1.4 ACER

The GAMSAT has been developed by the Australian Council for Educational Research (ACER) with the Consortium of Graduate Medical Schools to help in the selection of students to graduate-entry programmes. ACER admin-isters the GAMSAT and publishes several important sets of materials which are avail-able on their website: i) GAMSAT Practice

Questions; ii) GAMSAT Sample Questions; and iii) GAMSAT Practice Test and GAMSAT Practice Test 2 which are released operational full-length tests. GAMSAT Practice Test 2 was released in 2010 for the very first time.

These materials can be obtained online at gamsat.acer.org.

Some students purchase commercially available simulated GAMSAT exams without ever having seen the materials from ACER. This is often a serious mistake. If you are looking to sit an actual GAMSAT, you go to the source. The source of the GAMSAT is ACER. Once you have been exposed to their style of questions and stimulus material, you will be in a better position to accurately assess other simulated practice material.

There are some students who feel that their experience with the real GAMSAT was not well represented by ACER's practice materials. Usually, this is not a problem with the materials; rather, it is a problem with the technique used in preparation. We will discuss this in detail in the next chapter.

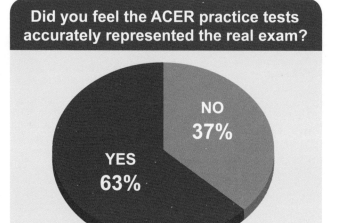

2010 Gold Standard GAMSAT survey at the University of Sydney (Usyd Medical Science Society), n>100, average reported GAMSAT score (most recent): 62.2.

1.5 Living a GAMSAT Life

Any discussion regarding the structure of the GAMSAT should end with a reminder of what the exam's structure means to you. Using your best reasoning skills with focus for an entire day is very challenging. Add to this the stress due to the importance of the exam, queues, nervous habits of other examinees, varying temperature/sounds/smells, etc., and you can quickly get a sense as to the unique nature of this exam.

We can give you the tools to get your mind ready. But, you must also get your body ready. For at least 2 weeks, every day prior to the real sitting of the exam, live your life like the exam's schedule. Wake up at the intended time, schedule similar meals, spend most of your waking hours intellectually engaged and, no naps! Ideally, your days would include practice tests followed by at least one full day to review the exam while taking very brief, top-level notes (*Gold Notes*). Your evenings could include exercise, hobbies and Gold Notes' review.

THE RECIPE FOR GAMSAT SUCCESS

2.1 The Important Ingredients

- Time, Motivation
- gamsat-prep.com/free-GAMSAT-study-schedule
- Read from varied sources
- The Gold Standard (GS) GAMSAT YouTube videos
- A review of the 4 basic GAMSAT sciences

GAMSAT-Specific Information
- The Gold Standard GAMSAT textbooks
- *optional:* The Gold Standard GAMSAT videos, apps, MP3s or online programs (GAMSAT-prep.com)
- *optional:* GS and/or ACER Essay Correction Service or GAMSAT University online.

- *optional*: YouTube Chemistry/Physics Crash Course or Khan Academy
- *AVOID:* uni. textbooks (too much detail), upper level courses for the purpose of improving GAMSAT scores

GAMSAT-Specific Problems
- Free GS chapter review problems
- The Gold Standard GAMSAT test (GS-1)
- Official ACER practice materials and full-length tests
- *optional:* Heaps of GAMSAT Sample Questions: 10 Full-length GAMSAT Practice Tests

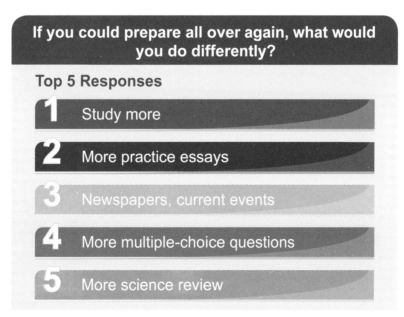

If you could prepare all over again, what would you do differently?

Top 5 Responses

1. Study more
2. More practice essays
3. Newspapers, current events
4. More multiple-choice questions
5. More science review

2010 Gold Standard GAMSAT survey at the University of Sydney (Usyd Medical Science Society), n>100, average reported GAMSAT score (most recent): 62.2.

2.2 The Proper Mix

1) Study regularly and start early. There is a lot of material to cover and you will need sufficient time to review it all adequately. Creating a study schedule is often effective. Consider going to gamsat-prep.com/free-GAMSAT-study-schedule and adapting our suggested, detailed study schedule to your own needs. Starting early will reduce your stress level in the weeks leading up to the exam and may make your studying easier. Depending on your English skills and the quality of your science background, a good rule of thumb is: 3-6 hours/day of study for 3-6 months. An avid reader with strong science-reasoning skills may require far less time, whereas someone with a non-science background (NSB) and little experience writing essays may require significantly more time.

2) Keep focused and enjoy the material you are learning. Forget all past negative learning experiences so you can open your mind to the information with a positive attitude. Given an open mind and some time to consider what you are learning, you will find most of the information tremendously interesting. Motivation can be derived from a sincere interest in learning and by keeping in mind your long term goals.

3) Section I and II preparation: Begin by reading the advice in this textbook as well as reviewing The Gold Standard GAMSAT YouTube videos. Time yourself and practice, practice, practice with various resources for Section I as needed at GAMSAT-prep.com and of course the ACER materials. You can also review free corrected Section II essays at GAMSAT-prep.com/forum.

For Section I, you should be sure to understand each and every mistake you make as to ensure there will be improvement. For Section II, you should have someone who has good writing skills read, correct, and comment on your essays. Have the person read Chapter 4 for guidance on what they should be evaluating. And finally, you also have the option of having your essays corrected, scored and returned to you with personal advice (GAMSAT-prep.com). ACER has introduced a program to automatically correct practice essays which you should seriously consider.

4) Section III preparation: The Gold Standard is not associated with ACER in any way; however, our GS science books contain each and every topic that you are responsible for in the Biological and Physical Sciences, as evidenced by past testing patterns. Thus the most directed and efficient study plan is to begin by reviewing - not memorizing - the science sections in those textbooks. While doing your science survey, you should take notes specifically on topics that are marked Memorize or Understand on the first page of each chapter. Your notes, we call them Gold Notes (!!), should be very concise (no longer than one page per chapter). Every week, you should study from your Gold Notes at least a few times.

As you are incorporating the information from the science review, do the Biological and Physical Sciences problems included in the free chapter review questions online at GAMSAT-prep.com. This is the best way to more clearly define the depth of your understanding and to get you accustomed to the most challenging of the questions you can expect on the GAMSAT.

5) Sit practice exams. Ideally, you would finish your science review in The Gold Standard text and/or the science review online videos at least a couple of months prior to the exam date. Then each week you can sit a practice exam under simulated test conditions and thoroughly review each exam after completion. Scores in practice exams should improve over time. Success depends on what you do between the first and the last exam. You can start with ACER's "GAMSAT Practice Questions" then continue with The Gold Standard (GS-1 at the back of this book) and *Heaps* practice exams, and then complete the practice materials from ACER.

You should sit practice exams as you would the actual test: in one sitting within the expected time limits. Doing practice exams will increase your confidence and allow you to see what is expected of you. It will make you realize the constraints imposed by time limits in completing the entire test. It will also allow you to identify the areas in which you may be lacking.

Some students can answer all GAMSAT questions quite well if they only had more time. Thus you must time yourself during practice and monitor your time during the test. On average, you will have 1.3 minutes per question in Section I and 1.5 minutes per question for Section III. In other words, every 30 minutes, you should check to be sure that you have completed approximately 23 questions (Section I) or 20 questions (Section III). If not, then you always guess on "time consuming questions" in order to catch up and, if you have time at the end, you return to properly evaluate the questions you skipped.

Set aside at least the equivalent of a full day to review the explanations for EVERY test question. Do NOT dismiss any wrong answer as a "stupid mistake." You made that error for a reason so you must work that out in your mind to reduce the risk that it occurs again. You can reduce your risk by testproofing answers (a technique first described in the Introduction to the GAMSAT video, GAMSAT-prep.com: spending 5-10 seconds being critical of your response). After your mock exam, you should consider the questions below.

1. Why did you get the question wrong (or correct)?
2. What question-type or passage-type gives you repeated difficulty?
3. What is your mindset when facing a particular passage?
4. Did you monitor your time during the test?
5. Are most of your errors at the beginning or the end of the test?
6. Did you eliminate answer choices when you could and actually cross them out?
7. For Section I, what was the author's mindset and main idea for each passage?
8. Was your main problem a lack of content review or a lack of practice?
9. In which specific science content areas do you need improvement?
10. Have you designed a study schedule to address your weaknesses?

6) Big on concepts, small on memorization: Remember that the GAMSAT will primarily test your understanding of concepts. The GAMSAT is not designed to measure your ability to memorize tons of scientific facts and trivia, but both your knowledge and understanding of concepts are critical.

Evidently, some material in the GS textbooks must be memorized; for example, some very basic science equations (i.e. weight $W = mg$, Ohm's Law, Newton's Second Law, etc.), rules of logarithms, trigonometric functions, the phases in mitosis and meiosis, naming organic compounds, and other basic science facts. Based on past testing patterns, we will guide you. Nonetheless, for the most part, your objective should be to try to understand, rather than memorize the biology, physics and chemistry material you review. This may appear vague now, but as you immerse yourself in the science review chapters and practice material, you will more clearly understand what is expected of you.

7) Relax once in a while! While the GAMSAT requires a lot of preparation, you should not forsake all your other activities to study. Try to keep exercising, maintain a social life and do things you enjoy. If you balance work with things which relax you, you will study more effectively overall.

2.3 It's GAMSAT Time!

1) On the night before the exam, try to get a good night's sleep. The GAMSAT is physically draining and it is in your best interest to be well rested when you sit the exam.

2) Avoid last minute cramming. On the morning of the exam, do not begin studying ad hoc. You will not learn anything effectively, and noticing something you do not know or will not remember might reduce your confidence and lower your score unnecessarily. Just get up, eat a good breakfast, consult your Gold Notes (the top level information that you personally compiled) and go do the exam.

3) Eat breakfast! It will make it possible for you to have the food energy needed to go through the first two parts of the exam.

4) Pack a light lunch. Avoid greasy food that will make you drowsy. You do not want to feel sleepy for the afternoon section. Avoid sugar-packed snacks as they will cause a 'sugar low' eventually and will also make you drowsy. A chocolate bar or other sweet highly caloric food could, however, be very useful during the last section when you may be tired. The 'sugar low' will hit you only after you have completed the exam when you do not have to be awake!

5) Make sure you answer all the questions! You do not get penalized for incorrect answers, so always choose something even if you have to guess. If you run out of time, pick a letter and use it to answer all the remaining questions. ACER performs statistical analyses on every test so no one letter will give you an unfair advantage so just choose your "lucky" letter and move on!

6)   Pace yourself. Do not get bogged down trying to answer a difficult question. If the question is very difficult, make a mark beside it, guess, move on to the next question and return later if time is remaining.

7)   Remember that some of the questions may be thrown out as inappropriate, used solely to calibrate the test or trial questions. If you find that you cannot answer some of the questions, do not despair. It is possible they could be questions used for these purposes.

8)   Do not let others psyche you out! Some people will be saying between exam sections, 'It went great. What a joke!' Ignore them. Often these types may just be trying to boost their own confidence or to make themselves look good in front of their friends. Just focus on what you have to do and tune out the other examinees.

9)   Do not study at lunch. You need the time to recuperate and rest. Eat, avoid the people discussing the test sections and relax! At most, you can review your Gold Notes.

10)   Before reading the "stimulus material" of the problem (the passage, article, etc.), some students find it more efficient to quickly read the questions first. In this way, as soon as you read something in the stimulus material which brings to mind a question you have read, you can answer immediately (this is especially helpful for Section I). Otherwise, if you read the text first and then the questions, you may end up wasting time searching through the text for answers.

11)   Read the text and questions carefully! Often students leave out a word or two while reading, which can completely change the sense of the problem. Pay special attention to words in italics, CAPS, bolded, or underlined. Underline or circle anything you believe might be important in the passage.

12)   You must be both diligent and careful with the way you fill out your answer document because you will not be given extra time to either check it or fill it in later.

13)   If you run out of time, just do the questions. In other words, only read the part of the passage which your question specifically requires in order for you to get the correct answer.

14)   Expel any relevant equation onto your exam booklet! Even if the question is of a theoretical nature, sometimes equations contain the answers and they are much more objective than the reasoning of a nervous pre-medical student! In physics, it is often helpful to draw a picture or diagram. Arrows are valuable in representing vectors.

15)   Consider having the following on test day: a watch (mobile phones are not permitted in the exam room) and layers of clothes so that you are ready for too much heat or an overzealous air conditioning unit.

16)   Solving the problem may involve algebraic manipulation of equations and/or numerical calculations. Be sure that you know what all the variables in the equation stand for and that you are using the equation in the appropriate circumstance.

In chemistry and physics, the use of **dimensional analysis** will help you keep track of units <u>and</u> solve some problems where you might have forgotten the relevant equations (we will next discuss this topic in GS Math Chapter 2). Dimensional analysis relies on the manipulation of units and is the source of many easy GAMSAT marks every year. For example, if you are asked for the energy involved in maintaining a 60 watt bulb lit for two minutes you can pull out the appropriate equations <u>or</u>: i) recognize that your objective (unknown = energy) is in joules; ii) recall that a watt is a joule per second; iii) convert minutes into seconds. {note that minutes and seconds cancel leaving joules as an answer}

$$60 \; \frac{\text{joules}}{\text{second}} \; \text{X} \; 2 \; \text{minutes} \; \text{X} \; 60 \; \frac{\text{seconds}}{\text{minutes}}$$

$$= 7200 \; \text{joules} \quad \text{or} \quad 7.2 \; \text{kilojoules}$$

17) The final step in problem solving is to ask yourself: *is my answer reasonable?* For example, if you would have done the preceding problem and your answer was 7200 kilojoules, intuitively this should strike you as an exorbitant amount of energy for an everyday light bulb to remain lit for two minutes! It would then be of value to recheck your calculations. {*'intuition' in science is often learned through the experience of doing many problems; if you do not have a science background, do not worry about the preceding points, we will be exploring dimensional analysis throughout the GS Biological Sciences and Physical Sciences textbooks including the online chapter review practice questions.*}

18) Whenever doing calculations, the following will increase your speed: (i) manipulate variables but plug in values only when necessary; (ii) avoid decimals, use fractions wherever possible; (iii) square roots or cube roots can be converted to the power (*exponent*) of 1/2 or 1/3, respectively; (iv) before calculating, check to see if the possible answers are sufficiently far apart such that your values can be approximated (i.e. $19.2 \approx 20$, $185 \approx 200$). Since 2012, calculators ceased being permitted for the GAMSAT. We added over 100 pages of GAMSAT Math to help you become quick and efficient with your calculations.

19) Are you great in biology and organic chemistry but weak in the physical sciences? Since biology and organic chemistry represent more than 1/2 your science score, you should attack those problems from the outset to ensure that you have fully benefitted from your strengths. Now you can go back and complete the physics and general chemistry. This is just an example of 'examsmanship': managing the test to maximize your performance.

20) Learn to relax or at least you must learn to manage your anxiety. Channel that extra energy into acute awareness of the information being presented to you. If you have a history of anxiety during exams to the extent that you feel that it affected your score, then you should start learning relaxation techniques now. You can search online regarding various methods such as visualization, mindfulness exercises, deep breathing and other techniques that can be used during the exam if needed.

The following is a closer look at your real GAMSAT exam day. Please try to simulate the schedule below when you sit the practice test GS-1 which is at the back of this textbook.

GAMSAT Exam Day: Schedule and Subjects

	Key Points	Event	Duration
Arrival and Sitting of Exam	In large testing centres, queues can be significant	Security, identification	45-60 minutes
Section 1: Reasoning in Humanities and Social Sciences	Interpretation and understanding of ideas in socio-cultural contexts based on stimulus material	Reading time	10 minutes
		75 MCQs*	100 minutes
Section 2: Written Communication	Produce and develop ideas in writing; this is the only written section of the exam	Reading time	5 minutes
		2 Writing tasks	60 minutes
Lunch	Consider packing your own lunch to avoid queues with nervous chatter	-	60 minutes
Section 3: Reasoning in Biological and Physical Sciences	40% Biology, 40% Chemistry (equally split between General and Organic); 20% Physics	Reading time	10 minutes
		110 MCQs*	170 minutes
Total Content Time	-	-	5 hours, 30 minutes
Total Test Time	-	-	6 hours, 55 minutes
Total Appointment Time	Success requires stamina; stamina improves with practice.	-	Approximately 7 hours 40 minutes**

*MCQs: multiple-choice questions, 4 options per question with 1 best answer

**A full day is needed to sit the GAMSAT test. It is not unheard of to spend 9 to 11 hours on exam day at the larger testing centres (i.e. Sydney, Melbourne, Brisbane, Perth, London, Dublin). Travel arrangements to and from the testing centre should be carefully considered, taking into account the likely added traffic on exam day at the larger testing centres.

GAMSAT-Prep.com

REASONING IN HUMANITIES AND SOCIAL SCIENCES

REVIEW FOR SECTION I

3.1 Overview

Section I of the GAMSAT is, for many applicants, the most difficult section to do well. This can be explained by the absence of an overall set of facts to study in order to prepare. Due to the lack of an official list of test content, some applicants either struggle or simply neglect to prepare for this section.

While the best preparation is regular reading from a variety of sources throughout your high school and undergraduate studies, it is also possible to improve your ability to do well in this section as you approach the test date. You should not neglect to prepare for this section as it accounts for one of your final GAMSAT numerical scores!

Section I is called "Reasoning in Humanities and Social Sciences". You are provided 10 minutes reading time at the beginning of this test section, then 100 minutes to answer 75 questions. This section consists of a number of "Units" where each Unit presents stimulus material and a number of multiple-choice questions (4 options per question).

The stimulus material in Section I can be anything from a poem, a cartoon, an extract from a play, novel, song, instructional manual or magazine. Essentially anything that involves words or symbols and thinking is fair game. There is no specific presumed knowledge required to answer any of the questions.

Reasoning, analysis, timing and pacing are all key components to success.

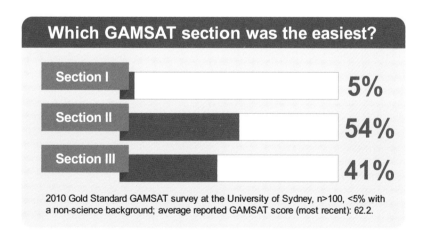

Which GAMSAT section was the easiest?

Section I	5%
Section II	54%
Section III	41%

2010 Gold Standard GAMSAT survey at the University of Sydney, n>100, <5% with a non-science background; average reported GAMSAT score (most recent): 62.2.

3.2 How to Prepare for Section I

3.2.1 One Year or More Before the GAMSAT

Read! Be known as a "voracious reader"! In the real exam, you will be presented with varying types of texts and language styles that range from literary, academic, instructional to numerical data and visual representations. You may encounter a few passages discussing unfamiliar topics or using convoluted language - or both! Additionally, you will have to deal with time pressure. Overcoming Section I, therefore, requires two interdependent reading skills: speed and comprehension.

Reading is fundamentally about language comprehension. If you aim to improve your reading speed, the best solution would be to read a repertoire of diverse materials in order to expand your vocabulary and in effect, increase your comprehension. Develop a "love" for reading. Read any novel that interests you. Read editorials from national, international and local newspapers (among your options: the reference section of the library or online).

If you have a short attention span, you can start with Ted.com. You will have powerful, easy-to-digest lectures on a great range of topics. Many of the videos will further develop your skills for learning new information and exercising the use of language through analogies, research, and stories spanning the globe as well as time. For the purpose of improving your language comprehension

skills for Section I, choose Ted.com topics that involve controversies related to social values and ethical dilemmas in the practice of medicine and health care.

Ted.com is a free website. We will always update further suggestions on GAMSAT-prep.com which you can find by clicking on FREE GAMSAT in the top menu. Please do note that Section I is not a test about pre-existing knowledge but about reasoning based on the given stimulus. Hence you should go through these materials with the purpose of identifying the main ideas, arguments, intents of the speakers or writers, any implicit meanings in the text, as well as expanding your vocabulary.

Ideally, you should spend an hour and a half daily reading a variety of written and visual pieces. Otherwise, you should endeavour to read at least once per week, for 1-3 hours, any of the following (many of which are available in a university library or online):

Our list is neither definitive nor exhaustive. These are merely suggestions to help develop your familiarity with the language styles and the typical pieces used in Section I passages. You are free to add other selections as part of your Section I reading library.

- **Articles from Medical Journals**

Many medical journals publish articles that are accessible online free of charge. Access to the full texts may require registration for a free user account. Look for articles on medical ethics, scientific studies that include graphs, tables and figures, sections on medicine and the arts, poetry, narratives and opinions from the doctors' as well as the patients' perspectives. The following are some of the most popular medical journals:

PubMed Central is a free access repository of scholarly articles published in the biomedical and life sciences journal literature at the U.S. National Institutes of Health's National Library of Medicine.

The Medical Journal of Australia has made all their MJA research articles published since 2002 open access and available free of charge online.

The BMJ (formerly the British Medical Journal) is an international peer-reviewed medical journal published by the BMJ Publishing Group Ltd, which is a wholly owned subsidary of the British Medical Association. It provides full access to journal articles in its online archive.

Irish Medical Journal is a free access general medical journal published by the Irish Medical Organisation, which features full-text scientific research, review articles, updates and reflections on contemporary clinical practices.

The Lancet Journals are produced by Elsevier Ltd and feature selected free full-text research articles and review content.

JAMA (Journal of the American Medical Association) is a peer-reviewed medical journal published by the American Medical Association with several free access texts covering original research, reviews, and editorials on various aspects of the biomedical sciences.

- **Creative Nonfiction**

This genre includes essays, memoirs, autobiographies, biographies, travel writing, history, cultural studies and nature writing with topics that span just about everything under the sun. The following selections will likely provide a good overview of typical subjects and writing styles found in some Section I Units.

- Charles Darwin (1859). *On the Origin of Species*

- Joan Didion (2006). *We Tell Ourselves Stories in Order to Live: Collected Nonfiction*

- Patrick Leigh Fermor (1977). *A Time of Gifts*

- Michel Foucault (1975). *Discipline and Punish*

- Sigmund Freud (1899). *The Interpretation of Dreams*

- Stephen Jay Gould (1977). *Ever Since Darwin: Reflections in Natural History*

- Catherine Hamlin *(2005). The Hospital by the River*

- Thomas Kuhn (1962). *The Structure of Scientific Revolutions*

- V. S. Naipaul (1999). *Between Father and Son: Family Letters*

- George Orwell (1961). *Collected Essays*

- Joseph Sacco (1989). *Morphine, Ice Cream, Tears: Tales of a City Hospital*

- Susan Sontag (1966). *Against Interpretation and Other Essays*

- Lionel Trilling (1950). *The Liberal Imagination: Essays on Literature and Society*

- Abraham Verghese (1994). *My Own Country: A Doctor's Story*

- Ludwig Wittgenstein (1953). *Philosophical Investigations*

- Virginia Woolf (1929). *A Room of One's Own*

- **Editorials and News Articles**

  The 'Opinions' section of reputable national newspapers tends to be argumentative, which is typical of Section I passages. Newspaper cartoons also use a style of humour and presentation that is fair game for the GAMSAT. Occasionally, news reports come with graphs and tables, which could help expose you to various types of graphical data. All of these make good sources for developing the reading speed and comprehension necessary for Section I.

- The Economist

- The Australian

- The Guardian

- The Irish Independent

- The New Yorker

- The Telegraph

Reviewing the novels, plays, and poems you encountered in Year 12 - or A Level - could help prepare you to tackle exam content featuring excerpts from literary works. Nevertheless, the following lists should be able to get you started with your literary reading. As a reminder, these are merely suggested titles and should not be taken as an official guide.

- **Novels**

  - Any Jane Austen novel

  - Julian Barnes (1980). *Metroland*

  - Karel Čapek (1936). *War With The Newts (a.k.a. War With The Salamanders)*

  - Charles Dickens (1861). *Great Expectations*

  - George Eliot (1871). *Middlemarch*

  - F. Scott Fitzgerald (1922). *The Beautiful and Damned*

  - Charlotte Perkins Gilman (1892). *The Yellow Wallpaper*

- Henry James (1881). *Portrait of a Lady*
- CS Lewis *(1942). The Screwtape Letters*
- Gabriel García Márquez (1967). *One Hundred Years of Solitude*
- Ian McEwan (1997). *Enduring Love*
- Patrick O'Brian (1972). *Post Captain*
- Brian O'Nolan (1939). *At Swim-Two-Birds*
- George Orwell (1949). *Nineteen Eighty-Four*
- Boris Pasternak (1957). *Doctor Zhivago*
- Leo Tolstoy (1869). *War and Peace*

- **Plays**
  - Euripides (412 BC). *Andromeda*
  - Christopher Marlowe (1592). *Dr Faustus*
  - William Shakespeare (1604). *Othello*
  - Sophocles (441 BC). *Antigone*

- **Poetry**
  - Any anthology book of poetry
  - Poems written by medical practitioners and medical students
  - Poems with subjects on medicine, science or in hospital settings
  - Some notable poets whose pieces make interesting reading for your Section I preparation are Dannie Abse, George Barker, Elizabeth Bishop, Emily Dickinson, Gwen Har-

wood, A. D. Hope, Elizabeth Jennings, John Keats, Philip Larkin, Sylvia Plath, William Shakespeare, Walt Whitman, and Virginia Woolf.

Again, your main goal in reading these materials is to increase your comprehension by becoming accustomed to the highly diverse themes and writing styles of Section I passages. Oftentimes, the difficulty of a specific Unit is subjective to an examinee. Someone who is not used to reading poetry and classic novels, for example, or dense articles from medical journals would find these passages very challenging to understand because of a limited exposure to such topics. Therefore, while no prior knowledge is required to answer any of the questions, your exposure to concepts involving creativity, culture, literature, current affairs, political cartoons and more will have a significant impact on your performance in Section I and even in Section II. The added benefit - which you may only appreciate later - will be your improved performance in the medical school interviews and possibly even less obvious at the moment - an increased well-roundedness.

In addition, active reading tends to improve comprehension and speed, so be sure that when you are reading, especially opinion pieces, you are continually asking questions:

1) How would you summarise or simplify what is being presented?

2) What are the main points of the author?

3) What types of evidence does the author employ to support a point?

4   How would you describe the author's attitude to the topic?

The following reading techniques may also prove helpful:

1. Skimming

This is a technique for spotting clues within the text itself. You run your eyes quickly through the content for an overview of what to expect in the material, occasionally slowing down on salient parts. As you skim over the words and the paragraphs, figure out which parts are essential and which are not. Using this technique will allow you to detect parts where you need to dedicate some attention for a better understanding of the material.

2. Paraphrasing

This reading technique is highly applicable to selections from the humanities and any text that demand inference. In order to test your general understanding of the reading material, restate the main idea of each relevant paragraph. By the end of the article, you will have a clearer outline of the author's central point. Taking the whole by its smaller parts is less overwhelming than having to swallow everything in a single glance.

3. Visualising

This technique usually works best with literary pieces such as poetry and novels. You mentally picture the colours and movements described in the different lines in order to capture the setting, the qualities and motives of a character, or the sentiment that the author wishes to express.

Section I typically consists of 14 to 18 units

| 1-2 units of philosophical texts | 2-3 units of cartoons | 2-3 units of excerpts from novels or plays | 2-3 units of a single poem or a group of poems | 2-3 units of tables and diagrams | 5 or more units of creative nonfiction |

3.2.2 One Year or Less Before the GAMSAT

Read RHSS 3.2.1 one more time! Even at this point in your preparation, being a voracious reader - with all that it entails - should remain your goal. This time, however, aim to develop a reading speed of at least 350 words per minute and an 80% comprehension rate. If you would like to check your current reading efficiency level, you may attempt the short test in RHSS 3.7.4.

It is important to note that your reading speed will likely fluctuate depending on the type of material you're perusing. For example, you might find that you can read and understand articles from newspapers much faster than those from medical journals; and yet, you have to re-read poems and classic novels several times before you can fully comprehend them. This is why familiarity with different types of texts is quite important. Besides improving your language comprehension, it allows you to gauge your timing and adjust your strategy for each type of passage in Section I. (Please see RHSS 3.2.3 for further discussion on this point.)

Contextual reading is another essential skill that you will need to develop for Section I, especially because almost 80% of the total units will have at least one question asking for the meaning of a word or its nuances in the passage's context. With contextual reading, you will learn how to make a logical guess about the meaning of an unfamiliar word based on the other words and phrases found within the immediate sentences in the paragraph. Writers themselves use this technique to make lucid points. Several cues easily offer probable definitions to uncommon terms:

1) Examples
Cue words: includes, consists of, such as

Equine animals, such as horses and zebras, have long been used not only to aid in man's work but also to assist in therapy.

Using the example clue (the use of "such as"), the word equine means:

A. *mammal.*
B. *reptile.*
C. *horse group.*
D. *dog.*

2) Synonyms
Cue words: is similar to, just as, also means

*Calling my cousin an "eccentric weirdo" is **tautologous**! It is similar to telling a ghost that he is dead twice.*

The cue word "is similar to" indicates that *tautologous* means:

A. repetitive.
B. alien.
C. scary.
D. ridiculous.

3) Antonyms and Contrasts

Cue words: unlike, contrary to/in contrast, on the other hand, as opposed to

*Contrary to the playwright's **euphemisms** about the King's corrupt leadership, the merchant was quite direct in criticising the latter's injustices.*

Based on the contrasting descriptions used in the sentence, the word *euphemism* refers to:

A. corruption.
B. indirect speech.
C. criticism.
D. politics.

Answers

1. C
2. A
3. B

4) Sense of the sentence

Oftentimes, you only need to observe how the words or phrases relate within the sentence in order to fairly conclude what the difficult word means. Take careful note of the descriptions in the paragraph. Use your logic to determine the most probable meaning of a newly-encountered term.

*March 21, 1894 marks a rare series of **syzygies** in the history of astronomical events. A few hours before Mercury transits the sun as seen from Venus, a partial lunar eclipse is witnessed from Earth. From Saturn, both Mercury and Venus could be seen simultaneously transiting the sun. Such planetary spectacles can also be observed by the naked human eye during full moons and new moons as the sun, our planet Earth, and the moon periodically align.*

Based on the context of the discussion in the paragraph, the closest meaning of *syzygies* could be:

A. planetary collisions.
B. lunar eclipses.
C. planetary alignments.
D. historical changes.

Answer

Descriptions in the paragraph mention "lunar eclipse," "Mercury transits the sun" and "the sun, our planet Earth, and the moon periodically align." These should serve as primary clues in determining a general definition of syzygies.

(D) Historical changes is obviously the least likely option. (A) Planetary collisions may sound related; however, nothing in the paragraph indicates a collision of the planets. This should now narrow down your choice between (B) lunar eclipses and (C) planetary alignments. Now common knowledge tells us that a lunar eclipse occurs when three celestial bodies such as the sun, the moon and the Earth align. On the other hand, a full moon or a new moon does not necessarily result to a lunar eclipse. This makes C the more logical answer!

5) Root Words, Prefixes, and Suffixes

Certain root words and word parts carry specific meanings. Being acquainted with these, combined with the other clues discussed earlier, helps you figure out the most probable meaning of an unfamiliar word.

If you have less than 6 months preparation time left, you should still try to read many of the selections in our suggested list. However, another approach that might improve your efficiency in tackling Section I units exploring creative nonfiction, novels and plays would be to read the synopsis of famous works on reputable 'Study Guide' websites such as SparkNotes.com and CliffsNotes.com. Again, your main objective in adopting this approach is to acquaint yourself with the plot, theme, characters, and symbolisms of as many literary pieces as possible. Attempt the chapter or study quizzes provided by these websites in order to increase your comprehension.

Besides reading, you need to practice. The best strategy is to take ACER's GAMSAT Practice Questions a.k.a red booklet (it is not a full-length test) and sit Section I as a timed exam and then review your mistakes. This should be done as soon as you commence your preparation. The ACER booklets are the closest that you will get to the real exam.

Using one of the shorter practice tests as a baseline of your test performance under timed conditions will help you understand what is expected. Take note of the type of passages and questions that give you the most difficulty (e.g., poetry, cartoon, prose, commentaries). This will enable you to slowly build on your weaknesses and target particular problem areas.

The full-length ACER practice exams should be completed later in the preparation process to further measure your performance while providing enough time to continually address your weaknesses.

If you performed well and understood the source of your errors then you will only require ACER and the Gold Standard (GS) GAMSATs in order to complete your preparation for Section I.

If, on the other hand, you struggled in the test or struggled to understand your mistakes then you may need additional work on strategies, practice or, as mentioned previously, a formal course with or without credit. An optional Section I GAMSAT program can be found at GAMSAT-prep.com, as well as 5 full-length GS GAMSAT practice tests and the GAMSAT Heaps book featuring 10 full-length mock tests.

Practice Problems
• ACER materials
• GS book and online

Practice Exams
• ACER materials
• GS book and online
• 5 GS Online GAMSAT Practice Tests
• GAMSAT Heaps: 10 Full-length Practice Tests for the GAMSAT (this includes the 5 GS tests)

3.2.3 Exam Strategies

Candidates have aced this section using different strategies. There is no "one size fits all" strategy to obtain a great score. The key is to be able to start early with your preparation so you can identify which strategy specifically works for you. A systematic approach with clear strategies – a 'game plan' – is vital in achieving an excellent Section I score.

Ideally, you should make a concerted effort to try the various strategies that we will discuss in this section during separate timed practice tests. Then you can compare the various scores which you have obtained. This will help you narrow down the specific strategies which give you your optimal performance. From that point onward, you should remain consistent.

• Time Management Strategies

One of your main aims in sitting timed practice exams is to gradually reach a speed where you have at least 10 minutes to spare. If you have time at the end, you can return to properly evaluate the questions you skipped or guessed. Start adopting the following time management strategies early in your preparation to master your exam speed.

1) Maximise the Reading Time

You will be allotted 10 minutes reading time before Section I begins. Though writing must not commence until signalled, you should use this time to begin working through questions and answering

them in your mind. If you 'browse', there should be a purpose; for example, you are identifying various types of passages to estimate and adjust your speed according to the difficulty levels of the texts, or you are seeking your favourite question type, like poetry or drama, to read and to mentally construct answers.

2) 'Examsmanship'

Play to your strengths. The following can be quite effective for both Section I and Section III:

During your reading time, identify the locations of your favourite content and begin to consider your answers. When the exam begins, answer all the question types that you are most comfortable with and then go back to answer the rest of the questions. Fill out your answer sheet as you go along but be very diligent to ensure you are always answering the correct question. As always, keep an eye on the time. By playing to your strengths, you can maximise your score.

3) Pace yourself

A major problem in this section is that, test takers run out of time. Read at a reasonable speed. You want to read carefully but quickly. You will have about 1.3 minutes per question in Section I. Every 30 minutes, you should check your watch to be sure that you have completed approximately 23 questions.

Of course, you can judge time in any way you want (20, 25, 30-minute intervals, etc.). But decide on a system when you are practising then stick to that system on exam day.

You should still prepare for any contingency in the actual sitting. After all, no one knows what specific topics and questions will appear on exam day. If you have not completed the desired number of questions in the interval that you have set for yourself, then you consistently guess on time-consuming questions in order to catch up; and if you have time at the end, you return to properly evaluate the questions you skipped or marked.

- **Exam Reading Strategies**

As much as possible, refrain from skimming through the stimulus material. Ideally, you only want to read through once in order to answer the questions correctly. If you deliberately focus on locating main ideas and important details, your speed and comprehension usually increase. This enables you to finish in the allotted time. Rereading lines in the passage interrupts the flow of comprehension and will only slow you down. Of course, referring back to material that you annotated is not the same as having to re-read a passage because you read too quickly the first time.

The following are only a few of the proven methods employed by past candidates. They vary in their attack of the passages and questions. The most logical means to find out which strategy - or which combination of strategies - would augment your test-taking skills is to practice. The more you practice, the more you are inclined to be comfortable with a particular strategy and to modify or even create a new technique to suit your own strengths or weaknesses.

1) Questions First, Passage Once
Some candidates like to get a glimpse of the questions prior to reading the text. Others read the questions but not the answer choices yet. Then they read the passage and answer questions as they read the information (usu. the questions are placed in the same order as you would find the answers in the passage). The point of doing this is to survey the kind of reading technique that will work best in attacking the passage and which other strategy to employ.

You may find it more efficient to work in this manner. Try one of the practice exams using this strategy and if you find it easier to answer the questions correctly, you should use the same method on the actual GAMSAT.

2) Passage First, Questions Next
Some examinees prefer to carefully read the passage once while noting the key details. You can take brief notes of the major ideas and concepts in each paragraph along with their keywords. You can use boxes or circles to categorise the important details and then, make meaningful connections between the main concepts and their supporting information by using arrows. This is also called "mapping".

This strategy allows you to mark significant information in specific paragraphs so that they are easier to locate when answering relevant questions later. At the same time, you can see where the discussion is going as you construct each part of the "map". Ideally, you should be able to make a reasonable conclusion of the author's central thesis once you complete the "map".

3) Read the Opening and Closing Paragraphs

In many cases, you would need to combine one or two of the preceding approaches in dealing with the passages. Going over the first and last paragraphs of a passage gives you a "bracket" to work within. Once you get an initial feel of the passage, you can decide on the appropriate strategy that will speed up your performance during the exam.

4) Read Carefully and Annotate

The test is yours. You paid for it so do not be afraid to underline words and important phrases as though you are preparing brief notes from which to study. Strikeout answer choices, circle or more rarely, make notes. Doing so keeps your attention from wandering and helps you to read actively so that later, you can find keywords or points without having to search aimlessly.

5) Identifying the main ideas

Many of the Units will have questions that require you to determine the central idea of the passage and distinguish opposing arguments. Therefore, always try to identify the main points of each paragraph, the idea behind the text and the structure of the passage as you read. Doing this will make it easier for you to answer the questions.

Some students find it helpful to do the following: just before you read from each Unit, imagine someone young that you know - for example, a younger brother, sister, cousin, etc. Imagine that once you finish reading the stimulus material, you will have to explain it to them in words that they understand. Keep that imagery during your evaluation of the material so you have a heightened sense of awareness and responsibility for what you are reading.

6) "Edutainment"

We have already established that reading diverse material in the period leading up to the exam will be useful since the stimulus material will be from a variety of sources. Use this reality to help you create a mindset that, in the exam, you are prepared for "edutainment".

You are ready to learn interesting, vibrant material which sometimes borders on a form of entertainment (novels, poems, cartoons, some articles, etc.). After completing a Unit, look forward to what you can learn and discover in the next Unit. Having properly prepared and then to sit the exam with the right attitude will give you an edge.

3.2.4 Question and Answer Techniques

Understanding the "science" of answering multiple-choice questions is another vital skill in dealing with not only the Reasoning in Humanities and Social Sciences section, but also with the GAMSAT exam as a whole. The following are general techniques used in answering test questions.

1) **Process of Elimination (PoE):** cross out any answers that are obviously wrong. Oftentimes, after crossing out clearly wrong answers, you will find yourself in a dilemma between two closely similar options. In this case, you should choose the more encompassing answer. For instance, if you cannot discriminate between options A and B, ask yourself: Does A include and speak for B? Does B include or speak for A? Choose the option that incorporates the idea of the other.

2) **Beware of the Extreme:** words such as always, never, perfect, totally, and completely are often (but not always) clues that the answer choice is incorrect.

3) **Comfortable Words:** moderate words such as normally, often, at times, and ordinarily are often included in answer choices that are correct.

4) **Mean Statements:** mean or politically incorrect statements are highly unlikely to be included in a correct answer choice. For example, if you see any of the following statements in an answer choice, you can pretty much guarantee that it is not the correct answer:

Parents should abuse their children.
Poor people are lazy.
Religion is socially destructive.
Torture is usually necessary.

5) **Never lose sight of the question:** by the time students read answer choices C and D, some have forgotten the question and are simply looking for "true" sounding statements; you can then fall into the next trap: choosing an option, which presents a statement that may be true but does not answer the question.

True but False and False but True: for example,

Answer Choice D: Most people are of average height. → This is a true statement.

However, the question was: What is the weight of most people?

Therefore, the true statement becomes the incorrect answer!
Continually check the question and check or cross out right and wrong answers.

6) Be on the lookout for qualifiers such as NOT: these may or may not be emphasised in the question stem or the options. They can also come in the form of double negatives in an attempt to confound you.

7) Verbatim Statements: a common decoy in most timed multiple-choice exams is presenting options with literal and direct quotes from the stimulus material. This is frequently an incorrect choice because of the context of the actual question.

3.3 Style of Questions

i) Knowledge: Simply put, you will not be asked questions based on prior knowledge. The very simplest of GAMSAT questions may ask you to recall information from a passage; however, this is rare. Most questions will require a higher level of reasoning and analysis.

ii) Comprehension: Identify key concepts and/or facts in a passage. This will require the candidate to infer, summarise and translate from the information presented.

iii) Application: Use the information presented in the passage to solve problems. This involves applying knowledge to new or existing problems presented in the stimulus/questions.

iv) Analysis: These types of questions require a holistic view of the stimulus and questions; they ask the candidate to organise ideas based on patterns and trends.

v) Synthesis: Use current information to create new ideas. Synthesis-style questions build further upon the inferences made in more basic comprehension questions, and often come after comprehension questions within a unit. These questions ask candidates to make greater, more difficult inferences.

vi) Evaluation: These are the most cognitively challenging questions and require candidates to evaluate, judge and consider ideas or facts at a much higher and nuanced resolution. Often, many of the answer options will appear correct thus higher logic must be used to develop the answer in a process of elimination. Look out for words such as 'least', 'closest', 'most' as they tend to be used in this style of question.

3.4 Online Help

As most of you will come to learn, this textbook has ample practice material with worked solutions to develop and hone your Section I skills. For those of you who need more, there are other options. You can get Section I help online including over 20 mini-tests through GAMSAT University at GAMSAT-prep.com. You can find general advice for written verbal skills at About.com.

To access our latest suggestions for all GAMSAT sections including Section I, go to GAMSAT-prep.com and click FREE GAMSAT in the top menu.

3.5 Types of Questions

Before we address the particular types of questions that you may be asked, it is useful to understand the nature of GAMSAT questions in general, and Section I questions in particular. Bloom's Taxonomy is an educational tool used to categorise questions that may be asked within an academic context. The levels of Bloom's model ascend according to the level of cognition required to answer particular questions. GAMSAT questions require candidates to exercise the levels leading towards the top of this model. Essentially, you will not be asked to simply recall or comprehend information you have read. Rather, the great majority of questions will require you to carry out complex cognitive tasks such as inferring, organising and evaluating.

Please note that the styles of questions discussed in RHSS 3.3 correspond to the different levels of thinking skills in Bloom's Taxonomy, namely:

▸ Knowledge
▸ Comprehension
▸ Application
▸ Analysis
▸ Synthesis
▸ Evaluation

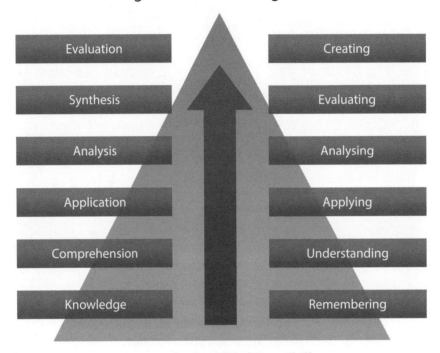

HOTS
Higher Order Thinking Skills

Evaluation	Creating
Synthesis	Evaluating
Analysis	Analysing
Application	Applying
Comprehension	Understanding
Knowledge	Remembering

Lower Order Thinking Skills
LOTS

Figure 2: Bloom's original taxonomy on the left and revised taxonomy on the right (Anderson, Krathwohl 2002; Adapted from Tangient LLC 2014).

The following is a list of typical question types you can expect to find as part of the Reasoning in Humanities and Social Sciences section of the GAMSAT. These questions may be asked within the context of different stimuli. As previously described, these stimuli include prose (extracts from literature, academic journals etc.), poetry and song lyrics, graphs and figures, cartoons and images, etc.

Main Idea Questions

These test your comprehension of the theme of the article. Questions may ask you for the main idea, central idea, purpose, a possible title for the passage, and so on. You may be asked to determine which statement best expresses the author's arguments or conclusions.

Inference Questions

These require you to understand the logic of the author's argument and then to decide what can be reasonably inferred from the article and what cannot be reasonably inferred. Occasionally, you will be asked to link like arguments/statements together into groups.

Analysis of Evidence Questions

These ask you to identify the evidence the author uses to support his/her argument. You may be required to analyse relationships between given and implied information. You may be asked not only to understand the way the author uses different pieces of information but also to evaluate whether the author has built sound arguments.

Implication Questions

You may be asked to make judgments about what would follow if the author is correct in his/her argument or what a particular discovery might lead to. You may be given new information and then asked how this affects the author's original argument.

Tone Questions

You may be asked to judge the attitude of the author towards the subject. The ability to understand tone also extends to comprehension of humour in its various guises including satire, lampoon, irony, hyperbole and parody among others (RHSS 3.5.5).

Hybrid Questions

Often more than one question type is used in the same instance. An "implication" question can be answered through the "tone" or "evidence" which is presented within the material. In addition, an assessment of material such as a "main idea" often includes "an analysis of evidence". There may be a number of "hybrid" type questions, which include one or more of all the question types discussed. In logically deducing and ruling out answers, two central ideas are very helpful: the most "encompassing" of the answers, and which of the answers has the most "explanatory power" in relation to the others. This will become more clear as we do some exercises.

3.5.1 Main Idea Questions

According to Bloom's Taxonomy, main idea questions ask candidates to utilise the intermediate skill of analysis which involves recognising and organising ideas into a hierarchy. These are therefore not the most difficult questions you will face in Section I, yet they are very important as they are quite prevalwent.

We will do some exercises to ensure that you can successfully deal with these question types. Please take a piece of paper (i.e. Post-it note) to cover the answers while you are responding to the questions. The worked solutions and/or answers are upside down when appropriate. To find the main idea, ask the following three questions.

1. What is this passage about (the topic)?
2. What is the most important thing the author says about the topic (the main idea)?
3. Do all of the other ideas in the passage support this main idea?

Read the following passage and find the main idea.

For most immigrants, the journey to America was long and often full of hardships and suffering. The immigrants often walked the entire distance from their villages to the nearest seaport. There the ships might be delayed and precious time and money lost. Sometimes ticket agents or ship captains fleeced the immigrants of all they owned.

The most important idea in this paragraph is:

A. immigrants had to walk long distances to get to seaports.
B. ship schedules were very irregular.
C. ship captains often stole all the possessions of immigrants.
D. the journey of immigrants to America was very difficult and often painful.

1. *What is this passage about?*

_____

_____

2. *What is the most important thing the author says about the topic (the main idea)?*

_____

_____

3. *Do all of the other ideas in the passage support this main idea?*

_____

_____

1. This paragraph is about the immigrants' journey to America. This is the topic of the paragraph.
2. The author says that the immigrants' journey "was long and often full of hardships and suffering." This is the main idea of the paragraph.
3. To be absolutely sure that this is the main idea, ask yourself: Do all of the other ideas in the passage support this main idea? There are other ideas in the paragraph, but each one is an example of some kind of hardship suffered by the immigrants. Thus, the correct choice is D.

The Main Idea at the Beginning of a Passage

Did you notice that the main idea was contained in the first sentence? Often the main idea is in the first sentence. The main idea may also be contained in the title of a passage.

Read the following passage and find the main idea.

Working conditions in the factories were frequently unpleasant and dangerous. A workday of 14 or 16 hours was not uncommon. The work was uncertain. When the factory completed its orders, the men were laid off. Often the pay was inadequate to feed a man's family. This meant that often an entire family had to work in factories in order to survive.

This paragraph is most concerned with:

    A. unfavourable and difficult working conditions in factories.

    B. the passage of child-labour laws.

    C. the lack of job security in early factories.

    D. the low pay scale of early factories.

1. *What is this passage about?*

_____

_____

2. *What is the most important thing the author says about the topic (the main idea)?*

_____

_____

3. *Do all of the other ideas in the passage support this main idea?*

_____

_____

1. The topic of the passage is working conditions in the factories.
2. Working conditions in the factories were frequently dangerous and unpleasant.
3. All of the other sentences give examples of dangerous or unpleasant working conditions. The correct choice is A.

Notice that all answer choices have an element of truth. However, the most encompassing, and therefore relevant, answer is A. Answer choices B, C and D are all specific examples of conditions included in A. In Section 1, you may often be able to narrow your answer choices to two options. In these cases, always ensure you choose the most encompassing answer.

The Main Idea in the Middle of a Passage

Sometimes the main idea is stated somewhere in the middle of a paragraph. That is why the three questions about the main idea are so helpful.

What is this passage about? → will help you focus on the main idea.

What is the most important thing the author says about the topic? → will point out the main idea.

Do all of the other ideas in the passage support this main idea? → will help you to be sure you have chosen the most important idea rather than one of the less important ideas.

If you can answer these three questions, you will find the main idea no matter where it is placed in the paragraph.

Read the following passage carefully and ask yourself the three key questions. Then answer the question following the passage.

Many who had left the Catholic Church during the Protestant upheaval eventually returned to their original faith. However, the religious struggle of the sixteenth century destroyed the unity of Western Christendom. No longer was there one Church, nor one people, or one empire.

The main point the author makes in this paragraph is that:

A. the Protestant Reformation destroyed the Catholic Church.

B. the Protestant Reformation did not affect the Catholic Church.

C. some Protestants rejoined the Catholic Church.

D. Western Christendom was never again unified after the Protestant Reformation.

1. *What is this passage about?*

   _____

   _____

2. *What is the most important thing the author says about the topic (the main idea)?*

   _____

   _____

3. *Do all of the other ideas in the passage support this main idea?*

   _____

   _____

The topic is the Protestant upheaval. The most important thing the author says about the Protestant upheaval is that it destroyed the unity of Western Christendom. The first sentence gives an example of unity. The second sentence points out that this example of unity was of minor importance compared to the disunity. The third sentence expands this idea of disunity and tells how extensive the disunity was. The main idea is contained in the second sentence. All of the other ideas support that sentence. Thus, the correct choice is D.

Answer choice A is close, however, it fails to address the specific notion of unity. Answer choice C is true, however, it is not the main idea. Answer choice B is simply incorrect.

The Main Idea in Several Sentences

The main idea is not always contained in a single sentence. Sometimes it takes more than one sentence to express a complex idea. Then you must piece together ideas from two or more sentences to find the main idea. The three questions are particularly helpful with paragraphs like this one:

Locke, of course, was no lone voice. The climate was right for him. He was a member of the Royal Society, and was thus intimately concerned with the work of the great seventeenth-century scientists. He argued that property, the possession of land and the making of money was a rational consequence of human freedom. This promise linked him to other great developments of the period: the formation of the powerful banks, the agricultural revolution, the new science, and the Industrial Revolution.

The main idea of this paragraph is:

A. John Locke believed that property was a product of human freedom.

B. John Locke was linked to the agricultural and industrial revolutions as well as to the new science and the formation of banks.

C. Property is the possession of land and the making of money.

D. John Locke's views on property linked him to all the other great developments of the seventeenth century.

1. *What is this passage about?*

   _____

   _____

2. *What is the most important thing the author says about the topic (the main idea)?*

   _____

   _____

3. *Do all of the other ideas in the passage support this main idea?*

   _____

   _____

You probably took a little more time to piece together the main idea. Notice that all of the choices are true statements. All of them are found in the passage. But now you are asked to judge which is the most important. The statement that includes all the main points of the passage should be the correct answer.

1. The topic is John Locke. More precisely, the passage is about how John Locke was linked to the great events of the seventeenth century.

2. What is the most important thing the author says about John Locke and the events of his time? Locke's idea that property was a natural result of human freedom linked him to the great developments of his period.

3. The first sentence says that Locke was not "a lone voice" which implies that his ideas were shared by many important people during his time. The second sentence complements this idea by saying that the "climate was right for him". These sentences support the idea that Locke was linked to the developments of his period. The third sentence states explicitly that Locke was "intimately concerned with the work of seventeenth-century scientists". The fourth sentence presents Locke's specific view on property (part of the main idea). The last sentence links Locke with the great developments of his period (part of the main idea) and it lists those developments. All of the sentences in the paragraph support the overarching idea that Locke's view on property linked him to several developments of his time. Answer choices A, B, and C support the main idea, but they do not state it completely. Choice D provides the most encompassing statement and is therefore correct.

The Main Idea in Several Paragraphs

So far, you have learned to find the main idea of paragraphs. To find the main idea of passages consisting of several paragraphs, first find the main idea of each paragraph. In the passage below, the main idea of each paragraph has been underlined.

Americans have long believed that George Washington died of injuries he received from a fall from a horse. We now know that his doctors killed him. Oh, it was no political assassination. They killed him by being what they were; physicians practicing good eighteenth-century medicine (which prescribed bleeding for every disease and injury). Washington was bled of two quarts of blood in two days.

It is commonly thought that the practice of blood-letting died with the eighteenth century, but even today leeches are sold in every major city in the United States. <u>These blood-sucking little worms are still used by ignorant people to draw off "bad blood,"</u> the old-world treatment for every disease of body and spirit.

The cities of America are infested with an even worse kind of bloodsucker than the leech. Like the leech, he is not a cure-all, but a cure-nothing. Like the leech, he transmits diseases more dangerous than those he is supposed to cure. And like his brother, the primordial worm, he kills more often than he cures. His name is "pusher". <u>His treatment is not blood-letting, but addiction.</u>

The purpose of the passage is to:

   A. explain how George Washington died.
   B. describe the eighteenth-century practice of using leeches to treat diseases.
   C. denounce the practice of blood-letting.
   D. make a comparison between leeches and drug pushers.

Re-read only the underlined portions of the passage. These sentences can be used to form a summary of the passage:

George Washington died of bleeding. Leeches are still used by ignorant people for treating diseases.

The cities of America are infested with an even worse kind of bloodsucker than the leech. His name is "pusher".

Now ask yourself the same questions you used to find the main idea of a single paragraph.

1. *What is this passage about?*

   _____

   _____

2. *What is the most important thing the author says about the topic (the main idea)?*

   _____

   _____

3. *Do all of the other ideas in the passage support this main idea?*

   _____

   _____

In addition to asking the three questions, you could also ask whether each of the answer choices is too narrow or too broad. For example, in the previous question choices A, B, and C are all too narrow to be the main idea.

The answer is D.

compares leeches and drug pushers and stresses that drugs are the more harmful.

ple. The second paragraph explains that ignorant people still use leeches. The third paragraph

3. The first paragraph explains that leeches were used in the eighteenth century and could kill peo-

2. Drug pushers are worse than leeches and do more harm than blood-letting.

1. The topic is leeches, blood-letting, and drug pushers.

3.5.2 Inference Questions

Some questions ask you to make inferences. An inference is a conclusion not directly stated in the text but implied by it.

Referring back to Bloom's Taxonomy, inferences is a high-level cognitive skill considered to be a component of Synthesis in the original taxonomy, and a component of Creating in the revised taxonomy. Inferring may also extend to extrapolating upon a particular idea, or sentiment. These types of questions can be complex.

Read the following passage. The topic is not directly stated, but you can infer what the paragraph is about.

Dark clouds moved swiftly across the sky blotting out the sun. With no further warning, great cracks of thunder and flashes of lightning disturbed the morning's calm. Fortunately, the deckhands had already tied everything securely in place and closed all portholes and hatches or we would have lost our gear to the fury of wind and water.

1. This passage most likely describes:

   A. a storm during an African safari.
   B. a storm at sea.
   C. an Antarctic expedition.
   D. a flash flood.

2. Which of the following statements is false?

   A. The storm was unexpected.
   B. The storm came suddenly.
   C. It was windy.
   D. It was cloudy.

The words dark clouds, thunder, lightning, wind, and water all suggest a storm. The words deckhands and portholes suggest a ship at sea. The answer to question 1 is B.

Nowhere in the paragraph are the words "sudden storm at sea" but, obviously, that is what the paragraph is about. Several other words give you the feeling of the suddenness of the storm. On the other hand, are you justified in concluding that the storm was unexpected? You know that things that happen suddenly are often unexpected. Was that the case with this storm? The last sentence tells you that the deckhands had already tied everything down and closed all portholes and hatches. That sentence indicates the storm, while sudden, was expected. The answer to question 2 is A.

Note that Answer A is a false statement and that's why it is the correct answer. Students often make mistakes with double negative questions (i.e. the question is asking for something false and the answer has "unexpected"). Process of elimination (3.2.4) and annotating your exam paper (i.e. putting Xs or check marks next to answer choices) will reduce the chance that you will make a mental error.

Read the following paragraph. You will be asked to examine the cause-effect relationships implied by it later.

Effect of Position on Valsalva Maneuver: Supine vs. 20-Degree Position

Blood pressure (BP) changes in response to the Valsalva manoeuvre (VM), which reflects the integrity of the baroreflex that regulates BP. Performing this manoeuvre in the standard supine position often prevents adequate venous preload reduction, resulting in a rise rather than a fall in BP, the "flat top" Valsalva response. We determined whether performing the Valsalva Maneuver (VM) at a 20-degree angle of head up tilt improves preload reduction, thereby reducing the frequency of flat top responses, improving reflex vasoconstriction, and increasing the Valsalva ratio (VR). 130 patients were evaluated in a prospective study. Each

patient performed the VM in both supine and 20-degree positions.

Flat top responses were present in 18% of subjects when supine. Twenty-degree position reduced the flat top response by 87%. The components of the response that are dependent on preload reduction also showed significant improvement with the 20-degree position.

A 20-degree angle of tilt is sufficient to reduce venous preload, decreasing flat top response rate and improving the VR and the morphology of the VM. We recommend this modification for laboratory evaluation of the VM, whenever a "flat-top" response is seen.
(PMC2729588; 2009)

3. The "flat top" response is triggered by:
   A. a high preload reduction.
   B. a rise in blood pressure.
   C. supine performance of the VM.
   D. performance of the VM with 20-degree head tilt.

In this case, there are many concepts that are likely to be foreign to the candidate. Rest assured, you do not require prior knowledge of such concepts to answer such questions. In this case, the correct answer is C. A is incorrect because it is actually a low preload reduction that causes the flat top response. B is incorrect as a rise in blood pressure is in fact what constitutes the flat top response. Finally, D is incorrect as the 20-degree head tilt is the method that the study shows reduces the prevalence of the "flat top" response.

Read the following paragraph. The question following it is concerned with the relationships between the main idea and supporting details.

Do we live in a revolutionary age? Our television and newspapers seem to tell us that we do. The late twentieth century has seen the governments of China and Cuba, among others, overthrown. The campuses of our universities erupted into violence; above the confusion of voices could be heard slogans of social revolution. We are constantly reminded that we live in a time of scientific and technological revolution. Members of militant racial groups cry for the necessity and inevitability of violent revolution. Even a new laundry detergent is described as "revolutionary!" Many causes, many voices, all use the same word.

4. Revolutionary ages are generally marked by:

   A. violence, slogans, science.
   B. violence, television coverage, governments overthrown.
   C. peace, science, technology.
   D. violence, confusion, governments overthrown.

Notice that the author does not answer his own question in the first sentence (the main idea). All of the other sentences give illustrations or examples of "revolution". The question asks you to make a generalisation about the nature of revolution from these examples. Choices A and B include examples from a particular revolution (if one does exist). They are not true generalisations. Choice C is patently contrary to the ideas of the passage. Choice D is correct.

3.5.3 Analysis of Evidence Questions

Some questions ask you to check back in the text to see if the passage confirms or refutes a particular detail. This is the easiest kind of question to answer. In fact, the answer may be so obvious, you may be tempted to feel that some kind of trick is involved. Relax! If you can find the answer in the passage, you are almost certainly right.

While it will not be as simple as just comprehending a particular fact, often only basic insight is required. The trick here may be to watch for double negatives, or the understanding of particular or sophisticated vocabulary.

Do not worry if you learn new words during your GAMSAT preparation. That's normal! The majority of students will learn many new words and expressions while studying for Section I. If you don't, then you are probably not practising enough (or you have unusually advanced English skills). Be sure to take notes for your Section I preparation just as you would for Section II and Section III. Review your notes often.

Attempt the following questions relating to the poem Beat! Beat! Drums! by Walt Whitman.

Beat! Beat! Drums! by Walt Whitman

Beat! beat! drums!—Blow! bugles! blow!
Through the windows—through the doors—burst like a force of armed men,
Into the solemn church, and scatter the congregation;
Into the school where the scholar is studying;
Leave not the bridegroom quiet—no happiness must he have now with his bride;
Nor the peaceful farmer any peace plowing his field or gathering his grain;
So fierce you whirr and pound, you drums—so shrill you bugles blow.

Beat! beat! drums! Blow! bugles! blow!
Over the traffic of cities—over the rumble of wheels in the streets;
Are beds prepared for sleepers at night in the houses? No sleepers must sleep in those beds;
No bargainers' bargains by day—no brokers or speculators. Would they continue?
Would the talkers be talking? would the singer attempt to sing?
Would the lawyer rise in the court to state his case before the judge?
Then rattle quicker, heavier drums—and bugles wilder blow.

Beat! beat! drums! Blow! bugles! blow!
Make no parley—stop for no expostulation;
Mind not the timid—mind not the weeper or prayer;
Mind not the old man beseeching the young man;

Let not the child's voice be heard, nor the mother's entreaties. Recruit! recruit!
Make the very trestles shake under the dead, where they lie in their shrouds awaiting the hearses.
So strong you thump, O terrible drums—so loud you bugles blow.

5. The poem relates an instance of which of the following?
    A. Conscription for war
    B. Propaganda dictated by authority
    C. Commercial infiltration of daily life
    D. Spawning of a social revolution

6. In the context of the poem, which of the following is closest in meaning to 'expostulation'?
    A. Confirmation
    B. Remonstration
    C. Exclamation
    D. Negotiation

7. The author uses many persons to emphasise his point. Which of these combinations is not used by the author?
    A. Clergy, fathers and children
    B. Mothers, children and those who perished
    C. Businessmen, farmers and physicians
    D. Brides, mothers and the judiciary

Question 5 clearly relates to war, thus the answer is A. The words bugle (the small trumpet often used for military signals), recruit and references to the dead on trestles (eventually, hearses) all support this notion. Note that the instruments are "loud" and "terrible" like war itself. Answer choices B, C and D could be assumed, but are not supported by evidence in the passage.

Question 6 asks you to define the term expostulation in context. Given the careless, relentless and advancing nature of the piece, B is the correct answer. Expostulation, or re-monstration in this context, refers to disagreeing or arguing about something. Answer choices A and D are close, but fail to encompass the sentiment of the use of the word. Answer choice C can be ruled out easily as incorrect.

Question 7 is a basic comprehension question. All combinations within answer choices A, B and D are used by Whitman in the poem. Answer choice C is the correct answer as the author makes no reference to physicians while stressing the undiscriminating recruitment drive for war.

3.5.4 Implication Questions

Sometimes you will have to apply one of the ideas in a passage to another situation. Sometimes this type of question takes a broad generalisation from the passage and asks you to apply it to a specific situation. In the context of Bloom's Taxonomy, this involves the higher cognitive skill of synthesis. Attempt the passage below.

In December 1946, full-scale war broke out between French soldiers and Viet Minh forces. The people tended to support the Viet Minh. Communist countries aided the rebels, especially after 1949 communist regime came to power in China. The United States became involved in the struggle in 1950, when the United States declared support of Vietnamese independence, under Bao Dai.

Finally, in 1954, at the battle of Dien Bien Phu, the French suffered a shattering defeat and decided to withdraw. The 1954 Geneva Conference, which arranged for a ceasefire, provisionally divided Vietnam into northern and southern sectors at the 17th parallel. The unification of Vietnam was to be achieved by general elections to be held in July 1956 in both sectors under international supervision. In the north, the Democratic Republic of Vietnam was led by its president, Ho Chi Minh, and was dominated by the Communist Party.

In the south, Ngo Dinh Diem took over the government when Bao Dai left the country in 1954. As the result of a referendum held in 1955, a republic was established in South Vietnam, with Diem as President.

8. A good title for this passage would be (main idea question):
   A. "The United States and Vietnam"
   B. "The Geneva Conference"
   C. "The Vietnamese Fight for Independence"
   D. "The Career of Bao Dai"

9. In the second paragraph, the word "provisionally" means (implication question):
   A. temporarily.
   B. permanently.
   C. with a large, outfitted army.
   D. helplessly.

10. Bao Dai was in 1950 (implication question):
    A. a possible Vietnamese independence leader.
    B. the leader of the French.
    C. the brother of Dien Bien Phu.
    D. the President of South Vietnam.

11. The tone of this passage is (tone question):
    A. objective.
    B. partial to the French.
    C. partial to the North Vietnamese.
    D. cynical.

12. From the passage, we might assume that in 1946, the Viet Minh were (implication question):
    A. South Vietnamese.
    B. Vietnamese rebels.
    C. North Vietnamese.
    D. French-supporting Vietnamese.

12. B
11. A
10. A
9. A
8. C

3.5.5 Tone Questions

An author may express his feelings or attitudes toward a subject. This expression of emotion imparts a tone to the writing. To determine the tone of a passage, think of the emotions or attitudes that are expressed throughout the passage. Below are some terms that can be used on the exam to describe tone.

Term	Meaning
Admiring	respectful, approving
Belittling	making small, depreciating

Term	Meaning
Cynical	unbelieving, sneering
Denigrating	blackening, defamatory
Didactic	instructive, authoritarian
Ebullient	exuberant, praising
Hyperbolic	overstated, exaggerating
Ironic	incongruous, contrasting
Lampooning	satirical, making fun of
Laudatory	praising

Term	Meaning
Mendacious	untruthful, lying
Objective	factual
Optimistic	hopeful
Praising	commending, laudatory
Reverential	exalted, regarding as sacred
Ridiculing	deriding, mocking, scornful
Saddened	sorrowful, mournful
Sanguine	confident, hopeful
Sarcastic	bitter, ironic
Sardonic	mocking, bitter, cynical
Satiric	ridiculing, mocking
Tragic	sad

A tragic tone reflects misfortune and unfulfilled hopes. A satiric tone mocks and ridicules its subject. An author may use an ironic tone to develop a contrast between (1) what is said and what is meant, (2) what actually happens and what appears to be happening, or (3) what happens and what was expected to happen. These are just a few of the emotions or attitudes that influence the tone.

Words themselves, statements and the general sentiment of the author all contribute to tone. Thus when attempting any Section I question, ensure you maintain awareness of the tone of the author. Even if there are no questions directly asking about tone, tone is likely to have a bearing upon how you approach other questions, especially when the stimulus is poetry, literature, or journalistic.

Attempt the questions below.

A certain rugby team won a regional championship for the first time in many years. Different people reacted differently.

13. "Wow! I can't believe it! This is the best thing that could have happened in this city!"
    The tone of this remark is:
    A. serious.
    B. excited.
    C. sarcastic.
    D. amazed.

14. "Ah! This is like it was when I was a boy. It makes my chest swell with pride again and brings tears to my eyes."
    The tone of this remark is:
    A. sentimental.
    B. excited.
    C. sarcastic.
    D. amazed.

15. "The team's manager and coach have had a lot of influence throughout the season. They deserve a lot of credit for this victory."
    The tone of this remark is:
    A. serious.
    B. excited.
    C. sarcastic.
    D. amazed.

16. "What!? They won!? And they started off so poorly this season. I just can't believe it!"

    The tone of this remark is:
    - **A.** serious.
    - **B.** excited.
    - **C.** sarcastic.
    - **D.** amazed.

17. "It couldn't have been skill since they don't have that. It couldn't have been bribery, since they don't have any money. The other team must all have been sick.

It's the only way they could have won."

The tone of this remark is:
- **A.** serious.
- **B.** excited.
- **C.** sarcastic.
- **D.** amazed.

17. C
16. D
15. A
14. A
13. B

3.6 Warm-up Exercises

These short, relatively easy passages will help consolidate the principles and techniques explained in RHSS 3.5.

Passage 12

As the mid-century approached, the women of America were far from being acclimated to their assigned dependent role. In fact, leaders of the growing suffrage movement were seeking equality under the law. Incredible as it seems now, in early nineteenth-century America a wife, like a black slave, could not lawfully retain title to property after marriage. She could not vote, and she could legally be beaten by her master.

18. One of the goals of the suffrage movement was:
    - **A.** dependence on a master.
    - **B.** equality with men.
    - **C.** recognition of divorce.
    - **D.** abolition of slavery.

19. Which sentence describes American women of the early 19th century?
    - **A.** They were against marriage.
    - **B.** They were satisfied with their role in society.
    - **C.** They were victims of a male-dominated society.
    - **D.** They had many slaves to do their work.

19. C
18. B

Passage 13

No dwelling in all the world stirs the imagination like the tipi of the Plains Indian. It is without doubt one of the most picturesque of all shelters and one of the most practical movable dwellings ever invented. Comfortable, roomy, and well ventilated, it was ideal for the roving life these people led in following the buffalo herds up and down the country. It also proved to be just as ideal in a more permanent camp during the long winters on the prairies.

20. What is a tipi?
    A. A buffalo
    B. An Indian
    C. A prairie
    D. A residence

21. What kind of life did the Plains Indians lead?
    A. They wandered with the buffaloes.
    B. They led comfortable and ideal lives.
    C. They spent their lives in one place.
    D. They lived in large, airy caves.

21. A
20. D

Passage 14

A dozen years ago, Thornton Wilder and I made the happy discovery that we were both invited to a White House dinner for the French Minister of Culture, Andre Malraux. We decided at once to go together. He was to pick up my wife and me at our hotel, and specified that I should have a double old-

fashioned ready for him. Thornton did justice to the drink. He also delighted my wife. She was nervous about the dress she was wearing, and he told her it reminded him of the black swan of Tasmania and was so graceful that it danced almost by itself. He illustrated in long, slow undulations, his arms waving. My wife was ham all evening.

22. Who is the narrator of the passage?
    A. Andre Malraux
    B. Thornton Wilder
    C. The passage does not say.
    D. Tasmania

23. What does "happy" mean in the expression "happy discovery"?
    A. Fortunate
    B. Contented
    C. Optimistic
    D. Clever

24. What delighted the narrator's wife?
    A. The invitation to the White House
    B. Wilder's compliment
    C. A double old-fashioned
    D. Attending the dinner with Wilder

24. B
23. A
22. C

Passage 15

Nobody knows with certainty how big a proportion of the world's population is suffering from the basic problem of chronic undernourishment. But the commonly quoted

United Nations estimate of 460 million sufferers is, if anything, on the low side. This represents 15 percent of the global population. Many more suffer from other deficiencies, making global totals even more difficult to calculate.

25. The paragraph indicates that:
A. malnutrition is the number one problem in modern society.
B. relatively few people suffer from malnutrition.
C. the United Nations is supplying food to those suffering from malnutrition.
D. it is not easy to count the number of people in the world who are under-nourished.

25. D

Passage 16

Another way to fight insomnia is to exercise every day. Muscular relaxation is an important part of sleep. Daily exercise leaves your muscles pleasantly relaxed and ready for sleep.

26. What is insomnia?
A. Muscular relaxation
B. Inability to sleep
C. Exercise
D. Sleep

27. According to the passage, daily exercise:
A. helps a person fall asleep more readily.
B. is harmful to the muscles.
C. prepares a person for fighting.
D. is unnecessary.

27. A
26. B

Passage 17

The decade was erected upon the smouldering wreckage of the 60's. Now and then, someone's shovel blade would strike an unexploded bomb; mostly the air in the 70's was thick with a sense of aftermath, of public passions spent and consciences bewildered. The American gaze turned inward. It distracted itself with diversions trivial or squalid. The U.S. lost a President and a war, and not only endured those unique humiliations with grace, but showed enough resilience to bring a Roman-candle burst of spirit to its Bicentennial celebration.

28. What image is used to describe the 70's?
A. A celebration
B. A race
C. A postwar period
D. A long movie full of passion

29. What is the author's attitude regarding the events of the 70's?
A. He is pessimistic.
B. He is bewildered.
C. He is optimistic.
D. He is afraid.

29. C
28. C

Passage 18

One bright spot in the U.S. economy in 1979 was the surprising decline in gasoline use. Rising fuel costs are finally prodding Americans to cut back on consumption, and the need for this becomes more acute all the time.

30. How does the author view the decline in gas consumption?
    A. He is indifferent.
    B. He thinks it is a good sign.
    C. He doesn't see the need for it.
    D. He is unhappy about it.

31. Why are Americans using less gasoline?
    A. The economy is good.
    B. They do not need as much.
    C. They want to spend more time at home.
    D. Gasoline is becoming very expensive.

31. D
30. B

Passage 19

During the early part of the colonial period, living conditions were hard, and people had little leisure time for reading or studying. Books imported from abroad were expensive and were bought mainly by ministers, lawyers, and wealthy merchants.

The only books to be found in most homes were the Bible and an almanac, a book giving general information about such subjects as astronomy, the weather, and farming.

32. The early colonists did not do much reading because:
    A. they did not know how to read.
    B. the Bible told them that reading was sinful.
    C. they did not have time.
    D. they were not interested in reading.

33. Books were bought primarily by:
    A. the nobility.
    B. professional and wealthy people.
    C. the lower class.
    D. sellers of almanacs.

33. B
32. C

Passage 20

Never before in history have people been so aware of what is going on in the world. Television, newspapers, radio keep us continually informed and stimulate our interest. The sociologist's interest in the world around him is intense, for society is his field of study. As an analyst, he must be well acquainted with a broad range of happenings and must understand basic social processes. He wants to know what makes the social world what it is, how it is organised, why it changes in the way that it does. Such knowledge is valuable not only for those who make great decisions, but also for you, since this is the world in which you live and make your way.

34. The passage chiefly concerns:
   A.   the work of a sociologist.
   B.   the news media.
   C.   modern society.
   D.   decision-makers.

35. It can be inferred that a good sociologist must be:
   A.   persistent.
   B.   sensitive.
   C.   objective.
   D.   curious.

36. According to the passage, modern society is more aware of world events than were previous societies because:
   A.   the news media keep us better informed.
   B.   travel is easier and faster.
   C.   there are more analysts.
   D.   today's population is more sociable.

36.   A
35.   D
34.   A

Passage 21

Whatever answer the future holds, this much I believe we must accept: there can be no putting the genie back into the bottle. To try to bury or to suppress new knowledge because we do not know how to prevent its use for destructive or evil purposes is

a pathetically futile gesture. It is, indeed, a symbolic return to the methods of the Middle Ages. It seeks to deny the innermost urge of the mind of men; the desire for knowledge.

37. The author believes that:
   A.   new ideas should not be encouraged.
   B.   we should return to the methods of the Middle Ages.
   C.   new knowledge is always used for evil purposes.
   D.   to suppress knowledge is a useless act.

38. What is the meaning of "no putting the genie back into the bottle"?
   A.   Once new discoveries have been made, it is impossible to deny their existence and to control the consequences which might result from them.
   B.   We cannot be sure that knowledge will be used for humanitarian purposes.
   C.   The desire for knowledge was not strong during the Middle Ages.
   D.   We cannot answer tomorrow's questions today.

39. According to the author, man's most basic desire is:
   A.   to know the future.
   B.   to prevent destruction and evil.
   C.   to become less ignorant.
   D.   to avoid useless activity.

40. The passage was written:
- **A.** to convince us that the Middle Ages contributed little to modern society.
- **B.** to inspire us to meet challenges wisely.
- **C.** to persuade us to mistrust new ideas.
- **D.** to show us what we can expect in the future.

37. D
38. A
39. C
40. B This answer remains after eliminating the others.

Passage 22

It is important to distinguish among communication, language, and speech. These terms may, of course, be used synonymously, but strictly speaking, communication refers to the transmission or reception of a message, while language, which is usually used interchangeably with speech, is here taken to mean the speech of a population viewed as an objective entity, whether reduced to writing or in any other form.

41. According to the author, which word could be best used to replace "speech"?
- **A.** Communication
- **B.** Transmission
- **C.** Language
- **D.** Reception

42. The author understands "language" to mean:
- **A.** the totality of the way a given people expresses itself.
- **B.** the giving or receiving of a message.
- **C.** the exchange of words between two people.
- **D.** the written works of a population.

41. C
42. A

Passage 23

The long, momentous day of John Glenn began at 2:20 a.m. when he was awakened in his simple quarters at Cape Canaveral's hangars by the astronauts' physician, Dr. William K. Douglas. Glenn had slept a little over seven hours. He shaved, showered, and breakfasted. Outside, the moon was obscured by fleecy clouds; the weather, responsible for four of the nine previous postponements, looked rather ominous.

43. At approximately what time did Glenn go to sleep?
- **A.** 5 p.m.
- **B.** 7 p.m.
- **C.** 9 a.m.
- **D.** 7 a.m.

44. Which statement about the weather is true?
- **A.** It was perfect for the occasion.
- **B.** It was cloudy and rainy.
- **C.** It had caused delays in the past.
- **D.** The passage does not say.

45. Who is John Glenn?
- **A.** A doctor
- **B.** A weatherman
- **C.** A spaceman
- **D.** A sailor

45. C
44. C
43. B

Passage 24

Freud wrote several important essays on literature, which he used to explore the psyche of authors and characters, to explain narrative mysteries, and to develop new concepts in psychoanalysis (for instance, *Delusion and Dream in Jensen's Gradiva* and his influential readings of the Oedipus myth and Shakespeare's *Hamlet in The Interpretation of Dreams*). The criticism has been made, however, that in his and his early followers' studies "what calls for elucidation are not the artistic and literary works themselves, but rather the psychopathology and biography of the artist, writer or fictional characters." Thus many psychoanalysts among Freud's earliest adherents did not resist the temptation to psychoanalyse poets and painters sometimes to Freud's chagrin. Later analysts would conclude that "clearly one cannot psychoanalyse a writer from his text; one can only appropriate him."

46. What would be the best title for this passage?
- **A.** Freudian Analysis of Literary Works
- **B.** The Interdisciplinary Work of Freud on Classical Literature
- **C.** Criticisms on the Psychoanalysis of Literature
- **D.** Pitfalls of Psychoanalysis in Art and Literature

47. With which statement would the author of the passage agree?
- **A.** Freud's work has been influential both in psychology and literature.
- **B.** One cannot always conclude about a writer's psyche based on his literary work alone.
- **C.** Many psychoanalysts were wrong in their findings of art and literature.
- **D.** Psychology and Literature can never go hand in hand.

48. Which of the following would Freud NOT be interested in analysing?
- **A.** painters
- **B.** writers
- **C.** psychological novels
- **D.** fictional characters

48. C
47. B
46. C

3.7 Short Test and Analysis

The multiple-choice Section I of the GAMSAT, as described before, is organised into Units. Now that you have worked through all the warm-up exercises, you can proceed to test yourself with GAMSAT-style Units with appropriate stimulus material. We will work through the answers when you are finished.

There are 7 Units with 15 questions: choose the best answer for each question. You have 20 minutes. Please time yourself.

> **BEGIN ONLY WHEN TIMER IS READY**

Unit 1

Questions 1–2

Marked by a rise of technology, the global economy can be thought of as a complex international system, interlinked through the flow of goods, services, and information. Geographically, there are spatial changes, in labour and production, and the global economy is marked by a lifting of trade barriers and restrictions. Globalisation has to some extent levelled out the competitive labour between major industrial countries and emerging countries. While prior to globalisation, the United States dominated the global economy to a great extent, with the advent of information technologies, such as computers, the internet and the Web, the relocation of jobs from high-wage to low-wage countries, the emergence of economic blocs, such as NAFTA, and the nascent beginning of industrialisation in Southeast Asia, the U.S. is purportedly dwindled to roughly one quarter of the global economy's flow of goods, services and information.

1. The best metaphor in describing the global economy in the passage would be:
   A. medium.
   B. river.
   C. network.
   D. hypertext.

2. One can make the inference that the spatial changes in labour and production are not only due to the lifting of trade barriers and restrictions but also because of:
   A. the production of goods and services in the US only.
   B. the advent of information technologies, such as the internet.
   C. the rise of the minimum wage in the United States.
   D. the displacement of labour due to economic factors.

Unit 2

Question 3

Oxymorons are literary devices, which bring two contradictory terms together to establish a nuance of meaning, or use, for effect. The rhetorical term oxymoron, made up of two Greek words meaning "sharp" and "dull", is itself oxymoronic. "Cheerful pessimist", "wise fool", and "sad joy" are all examples of oxymorons. This device is used in literary classics but also in everyday speech. "The true beauty of oxymorons," says Richard Watson Todd, "is that, unless we sit back and really think, we happily accept them as normal English." Todd illustrates his point in the following passage:

> It was an open secret that the company had used a paid volunteer to test the plastic glasses. Although they were made using liquid gas technology and were an original copy that looked almost exactly like a more expensive brand, the volunteer thought that they were pretty ugly and that it would be simply impossible for the general public to accept them. On hearing this feedback, the company board was clearly confused and there was a deafening silence. This was a minor crisis and the only choice was to drop the product line.

(Much Ado About English. Nicholas Brealey Publishing, 2006)

3. Given the description about oxymorons, which of the following phrases could LEAST be considered an oxymoron?
   A. Unbiased opinion
   B. Devout atheist
   C. Tough predicament
   D. Idiot savant

Unit 3

Questions 4–5

Morning at the Window

They are rattling breakfast plates in basement kitchens,
And along the trampled edges of the street
I am aware of the damp souls of housemaids
Sprouting despondently at area gates.
The brown waves of fog toss up to me
Twisted faces from the bottom of the street,
And tear from a passer-by with muddy skirts
An aimless smile that hovers in the air
And vanishes along the level of the roofs.

T.S. Eliot

4.   The images described by the speaker in the poem suggest:
    A.   poverty and dejection among the lower class.
    B.   hope despite misery among the lower class.
    C.   a juxtaposition of the lower class and the upper class.
    D.   a busy start of the day.

5.   Which of the following observations about T.S. Eliot's style of poetry best characterises the quality of "Morning at the Window"?

"Morning at the Window" presents:
    A.   an interpretation of a meditated experience.
    B.   a quiet yet involved desperation of sentiments.
    C.   images that describe the poet's sentiments toward a social condition.
    D.   an aggregation of images that evoke an emotional response in the reader.

Unit 4

Questions 6–10

Cyberterrorism, simply defined, is a convergence of computers, the internet, and terrorism. A specialist in cyberterrorism, Dorothy Denning, defines cyberterrorism as, "unlawful attacks and threats of attack against computers, networks, and the information stored therein when done to intimidate or coerce a government or its people in furtherance of political or social objectives". Further, to qualify as cyberterrorism, an attack should result in violence 5 against persons or property, or at least cause enough harm to generate fear.

To some extent, differentiation is made between cyber crimes, such as phishing and cyber sapping from cyberterrorism, but the line of demarcation becomes less accurate when major corporations are being hacked into.

The line between the two usually focusses on the "level of danger" or "threat" which is 10 usually not an individual hacker but a "premeditated use of disruptive activities, or the threat thereof, against computers and/or networks, with the intention to cause harm or further social, ideological, religious, political or similar objectives, or to intimidate any person in furtherance of such objectives." This definition is a merger of cyber and definitions of terrorism by the United States Department of Defense. The line between cyber crime and cyberterrorism becomes 15 quite arbitrary when considering that such a "cyber crime" as "identity theft" could be used by a terrorist to establish another identity or multiple identities. The use of bots, malware, spyware, viruses, and worms, provides another example in which one must distinguish whether the purported use on computer networks is by an alienated teenager or a terrorist.

Many countries (U.S., U.K., and India) will admit to "hacking" or internet intrusions from the 20 same suspects: China and/or Russia, and admit that the internet must be thought of as a utility, in the same manner as water, power, and possibly vulnerable to cyber-attack. There have been other "intrusions" in the past few years. The U.S. Power grid was invaded by software (by China or Russia), Estonia, Chechnya and Kyrgyzstan have all come under cyber attack, an estranged employee dumped massive amounts of sewage in Australia through a rigged computer program, 25 air control traffic in Alaska was hacked, causing a partial shutdown of the airport. These are notable examples that are quite real to those who would proclaim that cyberterrorism is a myth. "Hackers" theorise an attack on vulnerable businesses and corporations within the infrastructure of countries, instead of government "intrusions". One has to admit that the private sector and government sector are intertwined, interdependent, and possibly vulnerable to cyberterrorism. 30

6. According to the passage, the difference between "cyber crime" and "cyberterrorism" seems to be:
   A. congruous.
   B. tenuous.
   C. categorical.
   D. well-defined.

7. The author of the passage can be inferred to be:
   A. strongly opposed to hacking and cyber crime.
   B. indifferent towards the concept of cyberterrorism.
   C. opinionated yet professional on the issue of cyberterrorism.
   D. impartial towards the concept of cyberterrorism.

8. Which of the following can be inferred as the reason why the internet must be thought of as a public utility, much the same as water or power (lines 21-22)?
   A. It is run by both public and private companies.
   B. Governments and the internet are connected.
   C. It could be a likely target for terrorism.
   D. Most of the developed countries have access to the internet.

9. Which of the following arguments from the passage can be used to dispute the opinion that cyberterrorism is a myth?
   A. Real wars can be fought through the use of the internet.
   B. There is a difference between cyber crime and cyberterrorism.
   C. Cyberterrorism can blow up buildings and kill people.
   D. Cyberterrorism can cause public harm and fear.

10. What does the author mean by "infrastructure" in line 28?
    A. The vulnerable aspects of digital networks
    B. The digital networks of private enterprise
    C. The digital networks of private and public enterprise
    D. The digital networks of public enterprise

Unit 5

Question 11

A literary critic once remarked that the whole point of reading the works of Franz Kafka was to re-read. Indeed, Kafka presents an abstract world of images which almost seem to operate on their own volition.

The following are two very short stories by Franz Kafka.

The Wish to be a Red Indian

If one were only an Indian, instantly alert, and on a racing horse, leaning against the wind, kept on quivering jerkily over the quivering ground, until one shed one's spurs, for there needed no spurs, threw away the reins, for there needed no reins, and hardly saw that the land before one was smoothly shorn heath when horse's neck and head would be already gone.

The Trees

For we are like tree trunks in the snow. In appearance they lie sleekly and a little push should be enough to set them rolling. No, it can't be done, for they are firmly wedded to the ground. But see, even that is only appearance.

11. Which of the following terms would best describe the two stories, respectively?
    A. Initiation – Naturalisation
    B. Aspiration – Perception
    C. Alienation – Transformation
    D. Being - Becoming

Unit 6

Questions 12–14

12. Which of the following groups of subjects would most adequately represent the contentious ideas presented within the cartoon?
    A. Popular Media, Hypertextuality, File-Sharing
    B. Intellectual Property, The Internet, Piracy
    C. Corporate Greed, Data Transfer, Representation
    D. Human Rights, Copyrights, Media

13. The humour of the cartoon mainly rests on:
    A. exaggeration.
    B. understatement.
    C. irony.
    D. cliché.

14. Presenting a historical comparison of the use of the internet to other forms of media is a
form of argument that uses:
    A. definition.
    B. synthesis.
    C. induction.
    D. analogy.

Unit 7

Question 15

   The following aphorism from the philosopher Nietzsche presents two seemingly asym-
metrical concepts: chaos and creation. Given this odd pairing, one can make certain assumptions and inferences about Nietzsche's beliefs.

   "Without chaos, how could one create a dancing star?"

15. Which of the following would not be a likely inference to be drawn from the statement by
    Nietzsche?
    A. Chaos is not viewed with negative connotations.
    B. Creativity and chaos are interlinked.
    C. Chaos is necessary for creation.
    D. Chaos precludes creativity.

> If time remains, you may review your work. If your allotted time (20 minutes) is complete, please pro-
> ceed to the Answer Key.

3.7.1 Units 1–7 Answer Key and Explanations

1.	C	**4.**	A	**7.**	D	**10.**	C	**13.**	C
2.	B	**5.**	D	**8.**	C	**11.**	B	**14.**	D
3.	C	**6.**	B	**9.**	D	**12.**	B	**15.**	D

1. A controlling metaphor can be thought of as a "main idea" type of question in relation to RHSS 3.5. In addition, this metaphor must be inferred based on the logic presented in the paragraph. (C) A metaphor can be inferred through the main idea within the first sentence. In describing the global economy, it can "be thought of as a complex international system, interlinked through the flow of goods, services, and information." The two terms "interlinked" and "flow" particularly stand out, indicating the metaphor of a "network." While (A) "medium" and (D) "hypertext" are certainly related, they do not encompass the complexity of the global economy as described in the passage. The metaphor of (B) "river" indicates the general notion of a flow and the possibilities of interlinkage, but is limited by one direction – that is, a river is linear while a complex network would have a flow in many different directions.

2. This is most certainly an "analysis of evidence" type of question in relation to RHSS 3.5. We are asked to make logical connections in relation to the evidence, as an example is being presented and extended. The (B) advent of information technologies would affect the spatial redistribution of labour and production – communication and the flow of information could be accomplished with relative ease on a global level. This line of thought follows logically from the first sentence in terms of a "flow of... information" aside from the outsourcing of labour and production in different countries. Since information is also a commodity, in many instances, (B) would be the correct choice. (A) can be ruled out as a non-sequitur. Although (C) "the rise of the minimum wage" and (D) "the displacement of labour due to economic factors" may have consequential effects on the rise of the global economy geographically, the more encompassing influence adhering to the idea of "global" would most certainly be the advances in technology and digital communications.

3. The answer is (C). (A) is easily excluded since an opinion is, by definition, subjective and therefore biased. (D) is also easily excluded as a savant is defined as one with unusually high mental capacity. (B) is more difficult as it could be argued that an atheist is devout to their beliefs about nothing as a subject. However, (C) is least oxymoronic because to be in a predicament means to be in a tough situation.

4. The poem identifies its subjects as belonging to the working class - for example, "housemaids". It paints a picture of a typical morning of the working class and says nothing about the upper class, so this eliminates option (C). Answer choice (D) is too literal and general to be the correct answer. On the other hand, the poem is specific in describing the depressed state of the working class: "damp souls", "twisted faces", a passerby with tears in the eyes

and a smile that vanishes among the roofs - all suggesting sadness and dejection. "Basement kitchens", trampled or torn roads and "muddy skirts" depict a poor living condition. Nothing in the poem suggests (B) hope despite the miserable state of the subjects. In fact, the smile on one of the faces in the street is described as aimless and eventually vanishes, implying hopelessness. This leaves (A) as the best answer.

5. "Morning at the Window" presents a set of images of poverty, seen from the window of the speaker. It is not (A) an interpretation of someone's reflections on an experience. The poet, rather than expressing sympathies or feelings towards the working class' despondent state, chooses to merely describe various appearances and physical conditions of poverty. This eliminates options (B) and (C). The poet's impressions are then left for the individual reader to respond emotionally. This makes (D) the best answer.

6. Lines 15-19 provide the best clue in answering this question. The difference between "cyber crime" and "cyberterrorism" is often insubstantial, especially when the motive or the culprit of the crime is not clearly identified. Therefore, (B) is the correct choice, making (C) categorical and (D) well-defined the opposite and wrong answers. (A) Congruous means "in agreement". While both terms correspond one another, the question asks what the nature of the difference between the two terms is - not what the nature of their relationship is.

7. The author is striving to be impartial by presenting definitions and clarifying concepts related to cyberterrorism. Hence, the correct answer is (D). The author is not (C) very opinionated since generalisations concerning the subject are supported with evidence through the use of examples and testimony rather than mere opinion. Similar-

ly, while the author (A) may be possibly inferred to be against hacking and cyberterrorism, there are no calls to action for countermeasures nor is the language used emotionally-charged. The tone of writing may be rational, but it is neither disinterested nor (B) indifferent.

8. Even though (A), (B),& (D) are all true to some extent, the concepts do not necessarily relate to both of the ideas advanced in the question: the internet as a public utility within the context of terrorism; so by way of deduction, we find that (C) is the correct answer in that the internet shared by many, such as a public utility, is a likely, easily accessible, and vulnerable target to terrorist attacks. This is an "analysis of evidence" type of question as presented in RHSS 3.5. One makes assessments in a logical and deductive manner, by ruling out certain choices based on the evidence presented and its logical extension.

9. The correct choice is (D). Lines 5-6 state that "to qualify as cyberterrorism, an attack should result in violence against persons or property, or at least cause enough harm to generate fear". The examples provided in lines 23-26 indicate the extent of public damage and fear caused by cyber attacks in recent years. Options (A) and (C) require information outside of the passage in order to qualify the statements to be true or not. (B) is discussed as one of the main points in the passage, but this does not provide any evidence that will counter the idea that cyberterrorism is a myth.

10. The answer is (C). Although line 28 is non-specific, lines 29-30 go on to define an interdependency between both the private and public sectors. This is also implicit given the theme of interconnectivity throughout the stimulus. (A) is too specific and is implied in the other three options. (B) and (D) are also implied in (C).

11. (B) Aspiration – Perception is the correct answer. The first passage implies a "wish" (an aspiration into becoming something described in the story) that results in a sense of freedom and movement. Perception is quite correct in assessing the second passage since perception is interlinked with appearance. Answer (D) would be a close answer if the ratio was reversed to Becoming-Being to correspond to the order of the passages. There may or may not be an (A) initiation within the passage, but the term "naturalisation", albeit having connections to Nature – the tree, is vague, so this is not correct. (C) Alienation-Transformation is also very close, but the term "alienation" carries negative connotations. Undoubtedly, a transformation can be deduced to be occurring in the first passage but not in the second passage. This is a hybrid type of question, which presents abstract terms to define the main idea based on tone. So not only is the reader asked to relate an abstract term to a "main idea" type of question but also to review the "tone" of the passage by examining the dominant images.

12. All of the answer choices are at least partially correct. The most encompassing and specific in relation to the cartoon's contentions is (B). Through "an analysis of evidence" in assessing the main ideas presented within the material, this answer can be deduced. Again, we must determine what the most encompassing answer choice is while possessing the most explanatory power.

13. Options (B) and (D) can be readily eliminated among the answer choices. Nothing is (B) understated or (D) presented as an overused statement in the cartoon. It does seem like the rhetorical questions in the first set of images and the corporate character with the bags of money accusing the family to be stealing are (A) exaggerated assumptions. However, appreciating the humour of the cartoon requires looking at how the texts relate to the images. In the first set of images, 3 out of 4 technological representations do not appear to be threatening as described in the text. In the second set of images, the word "INTERNET" is written against a black, sinister-looking background and yet, the family viewing a video on the internet appears to be having fun. In the third image, while the corporate character labels the family's activity as stealing, he is portrayed to have a greedy agenda. The contrasts between what the texts are saying against what the pictures project indicate that the cartoon uses (C) irony to get its message across.

14. These comparisons are certainly an argument by (D) analogy by contrasting different forms of media throughout the years with the internet. (A) "Definition" is not correct because the internet is not being defined or interpreted as a specific media or medium. (C) An argument from "synthesis" would be a clash of ideas, in proper terms, dialectic and the result of this clash. This can be ruled out as well in relation to the cartoon. (C) "Induction" is close but not as encompassing as (D) analogy. As such, this question is "an analysis of evidence" type of question as referred to in RHSS 3.5.

15. All of the answers in relation to the Nietzsche quote can be inferred to some extent except (D), the correct choice. A certain degree of familiarity with vocabulary, particularly the term "precludes" is assumed and necessary to make the correct choice in (D). This phrase essentially would be antipodal – in opposition to the other assessments, meaning Chaos limits or rules out Creativity. This is an "inference" type of question, as presented in RHSS 3.5. We infer that all of the choices are correct, in relation, to the quote except for (D), which negates, instead of affirms a relation between the two: chaos and creativity.

3.7.2 Self-assessment

Consider your performance in the preceding short test and analysis:

- Did you finish answering all of the questions within 20 minutes?
- Were you able to answer most, if not all, of the questions correctly?

If you answered NO to at least one of these questions, then before proceeding to RHSS 3.8, we strongly advise that you access the Reading Speed and Comprehension Skill Builder Exercises in your online Section I lessons at GAMSAT-prep.com. Otherwise, you may start developing your reasoning skills for the Humanities and Social Sciences after your upcoming reading speed assessment.

3.7.3 Building Your Reading Speed and Comprehension Skills

The Gold Standard Reading Speed and Comprehension Skill Builder Exercises consist of at least five categories that each focusses on a particular type of text:

- ➤ Poems
- ➤ Excerpt From Novels
- ➤ Excerpts from Scientific Journals
- ➤ Philosophical Texts
- ➤ Visual Texts

Each exam category contains at least 10 separate timed Units that will test your speed and comprehension, and record your results. You may choose to attempt one Unit per category or just one category at a time in order to allow you to build your reading skills over time. Alternatively, you may attempt only those categories with which you have the most difficulty. Once you feel confident enough to tackle a particular type of passage in Section I, you may begin attempting one of the related mini tests.

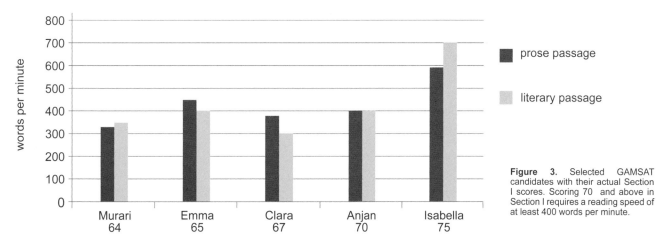

Figure 3. Selected GAMSAT candidates with their actual Section I scores. Scoring 70 and above in Section I requires a reading speed of at least 400 words per minute.

3.7.4 Reading Speed and Comprehension Test

If you already know your current reading speed, then you may choose to skip this section. Otherwise, the following test should be able to give you an idea of both your speed and comprehension rates. You will need a 'stopwatch' to perform this test. An online version with an automatic timer and instant score is also available when you log in to your GAMSAT-prep.com account.

Instructions:
1. Turn on your 'stopwatch' as soon as you read the first word of the passage. Turn it off as you read the very last word in the text.
2. Note down the number of minutes (rounded to the nearest minute) in the box provided at the end of the passage.
3. Proceed to answer the short quiz to check your comprehension.
4. Calculate your reading speed by dividing the number of words of the passage by the number of minutes it took you to read.
5. Check your comprehension rate by dividing the total number of correct answers by the total number of questions. Multiply the result by 100.

BEGIN ONLY WHEN TIMER IS READY

As early as February 21, 1775, the Provincial Congress of Massachusetts appointed a committee to determine what medical supplies would be necessary should colonial troops be required to take the field. Three days later, the Congress voted to "make an inquiry where fifteen doctor's chests can be got, and on what terms"; and on March 7, it directed the committee of supplies "to make a draft in favour of Dr Joseph Warren and Dr Benjamin Church, for five hundred pounds, lawful money, to enable them to purchase such articles for the provincial chests of medicine as cannot be got on credit".

A unique ledger of the Greenleaf apothecary shop of Boston reveals that this pharmacy on April 4, 1775, supplied at least 5 of the 15 chests of medicines. The account, in the amount of just over £247, is listed in the name of the Province of the Massachusetts Bay, and shows that £51 was paid in cash by Dr Joseph Warren. The remaining £196 was not paid until August 10, after Warren had been killed in the Battle of Bunker Hill.

The 15 medicine chests, including presumably the five supplied by Greenleaf, were distributed on April 18—three at Sudbury and two each at Concord, Groton, Mendon, Stow, Worcester, and Lancaster. No record has been found to indicate whether or not the British discovered the medical chests at Concord, but, inasmuch as the patriots were warned of the British movement, it is very likely that the chests were among the supplies that were carried off and hidden. The British destroyed as much of the remainder as they could locate.

Total Reading Time: _____ *minutes*

---

1. What is the name of the pharmacy from which the committee purchased the medicine chests?
    A. Massachusetts
    B. The Apothecary Shop
    C. Concord
    D. Greenleaf

2. In whose account were the medical supplies listed?
    A. Dr Joseph Warren and Dr Benjamin Church
    B. Dr Joseph Warren
    C. Province of the Massachusetts Bay
    D. Greenleaf

3. Which amount would approximately represent the price of one medicine chest?
    A. £334
    B. £51
    C. £247
    D. £500

4. Three of the medicine chests were distributed at which location?
    A. Sudbury
    B. Concord
    C. Greenleaf
    D. Bunker Hill

5. The Provincial Congress of Massachusetts decided to canvass for 15 medicine chests on which date?
   - **A.** February 21, 1775
   - **B.** February 24, 1775
   - **C.** March 7, 1775
   - **D.** April 18, 1775

Answers

(P stands for Paragraph, S stands for Sentence; the corresponding numbers point to the paragraph number and the sentence within that paragraph.)

| 1. | D | 2. | C | 3. | B | 4. | A | S1 |
| | P2 S1 | | P2 S2 | | P2 S2 | | P3 | |

5. B
   P1 S2
   The Provincial Congress of Massachusetts voted to "make an inquiry where fifteen doctor's chests can be got, and on what terms" three days after it appointed a committee for the medical supplies on February 21, 1775. February 21 plus 3 days makes February 24.

Score	Comprehension Rate
1	20%
2	40%
3	60%
4	80%
5	100%

What's my reading speed?

271 words / _____ minutes = _____ words per minute

3.7.5 Interpreting Your Reading Speed

The slowest form of reading, 'mental reading', involves sounding out each word internally, as if you are actually reading to yourself (average: 250 words per minute, wpm). This is a form of subvocalization, or silent speech.

'Auditory reading' can be optimised for GAMSAT Section I: Imagine hearing the read words (average: 450 wpm) but without subvocalization. Note from our small cohort in the previous section, a reading speed of 300-400 wpm can result in very good Section I GAMSAT scores.

The fastest process is 'visual reading' which requires extensive practice and/or talent in order to maintain high levels of comprehension. This technique locks into understanding the meaning of the word, rather than sounding or hearing (average: 700 wpm).

3.8 Section I Mini Tests

We work hard to continually improve each new edition of the Gold Standard GAMSAT. Adding brand new content to textbooks is always exciting because of the prospect of enhancing the learning experience; however, it can be a bit hazardous because the content has not had the same level of exposure as 'older' content.

Nonetheless, we have tested our practice questions with hundreds of students prior to publication. As with the entire book, we have carefully edited the content. However, if you have any questions or concerns about any content in these new sections, please go to gamsat-prep.com/forum to find the Gold Standard GAMSAT Textbook Section I thread.

The following sections contain 6 mini tests that are grouped according to specific types of passages:

- ▶ Verbal Reasoning Exercise 1 (Humanities and Social Sciences)
- ▶ Verbal Reasoning Exercise 2 (Science-based Passages)
- ▶ Doctor-Patient Interaction Test
- ▶ Poetry Test
- ▶ Cartoon Test
- ▶ Graphs and Tables Test

The objective is to help build your Section I reasoning skills one area at a time. We strongly suggest that you ALWAYS time yourself for every practice test. Otherwise, you would be eliminating one of the major components of your preparation making it more difficult to get a top GAMSAT Section I score. On the other hand, in the case that you are not pressured for time, do not assume that a specialty test is the same as a full-length exam. Just consider this experience as another step in your training.

At the end of each mini test, you should work through the answers and explanations. Keep notes of your wrong answers and then go back to the specific section(s) in this chapter, reviewing and analysing how you can still improve for your next attempts. Naturally, as you progress with your review, you should also consider full-length practice tests (i.e. Section I, Section II and Section III in one sitting) including those from ACER and Gold Standard (such as the complete mock exam GS-1 at the back of this book).

Olympic athletes go to the gym to improve strength and fitness. The gym is not the sport. These mini tests are part of your Section I gym. Train well and it will be reflected in your performance.

3.8.1 Verbal Reasoning Exercise 1 (Humanities and Social Sciences)

The following is a sample mini test, aimed at developing your skills in reading and answering passages that contain arguments within the humanities or social science context. There are 7 Units with 40 questions. Choose the best answer for each question. You have 50 minutes. Please time yourself.

BEGIN ONLY WHEN TIMER IS READY

Unit 1

Questions 1 - 6

Speech is so familiar a feature of daily life that we rarely pause to define it. It seems as natural to man as walking, and only less so than breathing. Yet it needs but a moment's reflection to convince us that this naturalness of speech is but an illusory feeling. The process of acquiring speech is, in sober fact, an utterly different sort of thing from the process of learning to walk. In the case of the latter function, culture, in other words, the traditional body of social usage is not seriously brought into play. The child is individually equipped, by the complex set of factors that we term biological heredity, to make all the needed muscular and nervous adjustments that result in walking.

Indeed, the very conformation of these muscles and of the appropriate parts of the nervous system may be said to be primarily adapted to the movements made in walking and in similar activities. In a very real sense the normal human being is predestined to walk, not because his elders will assist him to learn the art, but because his organism is prepared from birth, or even from the moment of conception, to take on all those expenditures of nervous energy and all those muscular adaptations that result in walking. To put it concisely, walking is an inherent, biological function of man.

Not so language. It is of course true that in a certain sense the individual is predestined to talk, but that is due entirely to the circumstance that he is born not merely in nature, but in the lap of a society that is certain, reasonably certain, to lead him to its traditions. Eliminate society and there is every reason to believe that he will learn to walk, if, indeed, he survives at all. But it is just as certain that he will never learn to talk, that is, to communicate ideas according to the traditional system of a particular society. Or, again, remove the newborn individual from the social environment into which he has come and transplant him to an utterly alien one. He will develop the art of walking in his new environment very much as he would have developed it in the old. But his speech will be completely at variance with the speech of his native environment.

Walking, then, is a general human activity that varies only within circumscribed limits as we pass from individual to individual. Its variability is involuntary and purposeless. Speech is a human activity that varies without assignable limit as we pass from social group to social group, because it is a purely historical heritage of the group, the product of long-continued social usage. It varies as all creative effort varies — not as consciously, perhaps, but none the less as truly as do the religions, the beliefs, the customs, and the arts of different peoples. Walking is an organic, an instinctive function (not, of course, itself an instinct); speech is a non-instinctive, acquired, "cultural" function.

- Excerpt from Edward Sapir, Language: An Introduction to the Study of Speech; 1921

1. What does the author most likely mean by the line "his speech will be completely at variance with the speech of his native environment" (paragraph 3)?
    A. The child will speak a language that is not understood in his adoptive country.
    B. The child will grow up speaking the language of his adoptive tribe or country.
    C. The child's way of speaking will anger and antagonise people in his native country.
    D. The child's way of speaking will shift between two sets of customs.

2. Which of the following pieces of information would support the author's claim that language is "the product of long-continued social usage"?
    A. A discovery proved that languages across the world share some features in common, such as nouns, verbs and similar grammatical structures.
    B. A deaf child raised without language input created her own gesture system that she used to form sentences.
    C. Two neighbouring tribes could not effectively communicate with each other because their languages contained untranslatable concepts.
    D. An extended family was found to have an average overall intelligence and normal upbringings but were congenitally unable to learn a language.

3. Which contrasting concepts does the author suggest to be important in understanding the difference between walking and speech, respectively?
    - **A.** Tradition vs innovation
    - **B.** Reflex vs purpose
    - **C.** Biology vs society
    - **D.** Growth vs function

4. Which of the following does NOT follow the author's line of reasoning when he states that "speech is a human activity which varies without assignable limit"?
    - **A.** Speech varies as we pass from one social group to another.
    - **B.** Speech varies based on the cultural heritage of a social group.
    - **C.** Speech varies based on a person's genetic capacity for complex grammar.
    - **D.** Speech varies more than the instinctive sounds and cries made by animals.

5. The linguist Noam Chomsky has argued that young children learn language surprisingly quickly from a relatively small amount of input, and that a "consideration of [the] narrowly limited extent of the available data [that children are exposed to] leave[s] little hope that much of the structure of the language can be learned by an organism initially uninformed as to its general character".

    If true, this claim would:
    - **A.** support the passage's argument because individual concepts are learned from a culture while a language's structure is innate.
    - **B.** contradict the passage's argument because people do not learn a language as thoroughly as the author argues they do.
    - **C.** support the passage's argument because babies are born without innate concepts for all the words they will eventually learn.
    - **D.** contradict the passage's argument because people would have to be born with some innate knowledge of a language's natural character.

6. According to the author, speech is often mistakenly perceived as a natural function because:
    - **A.** we rarely pause to define it.
    - **B.** speech is socially acquired.
    - **C.** it requires analysis to realise its purpose.
    - **D.** speech is an effortless daily activity.

Unit 2

Questions 7 - 12

To the romantic poets, poetry was an instrument of emotion and feeling intended to reconnect man with the natural world, and in general, the poet was viewed as a person uniquely equipped to guide the layman to this reconnection.

Romanticism as a movement appeared following a period in history when great importance was put on scientific discovery and formal education. In the eyes of the romantic poets, mankind had become so swept up in the pursuit of knowledge and innovation that they had disconnected from both the natural world, and their deeper, natural selves. Though the philosophies of the individual poets differed, in general, romantic poetry focussed on and lauded primitivism and emotion while minimising (but not discounting) the importance of reason and logic. The ultimate goal of romantic poetry was the attainment of the sublime, the ultimate, transcendental connection with the natural self.

Samuel Taylor Coleridge, one of the pioneers of the Romantic Movement, believed that the creative imagination was the key to man achieving his connection to the sublime. This caused much difficulty though, as the source of creative imagination was impossible to trace and because creative inspiration was quite fickle. Coleridge struggled with this conundrum throughout his life but felt that as a poet and as one who understood the importance of the creative imagination, it was his right and responsibility to better mankind through his poetry. William Wordsworth was, along with Coleridge, another leader in the early Romantic Movement.

Wordsworth believed that beauty and inspiration were to be found in the most rudimentary and common things and was not something that could only be found in the high and lofty. It was the role of the poet to extract and explain that beauty. In his preface to "Lyrical Ballads," Wordsworth describes a poet as a man speaking to men, but ensures that he differentiates the poet as a man ". . . endowed with more lively sensibility, more enthusiasm and tenderness, who has a greater knowledge of human nature, and a more comprehensive soul, than are supposed to be common among mankind. . ." Thus, while rustic man could be privy to the sublime, it took the unique soul of a poet to make the sublime accessible to all. Like Coleridge, Wordsworth believed that creative imagination was the source of poetry and the avenue to the sublime. He was also of the belief that poetry was the result of the "spontaneous overflow of powerful feelings."

Percy Shelley not only believed that poets were charged with reconnecting man with nature, he believed poets were the "unacknowledged legislators of the world." He stated as much in "A Defence of Poetry," an essay in which he explained the importance of poetry in reconnecting man with feeling and emotion, and the importance of the poet as a person who could influence the course of mankind through this reconnection. However, unlike Coleridge and Wordsworth who sought out recognition and importance, Shelley recognised the role of the poet as one who affects mankind from the shadows of obscurity.

Though Coleridge, Wordsworth and Shelley may have differed in their individual poetic philosophies, the three poets, along with their Romantic colleagues, each strove to the same end. Each of these poets recognised great value in the natural feelings and emotions of man, and the connection sparked by man's place in the natural world. Each strove to capture and explain that connection through creative imagination and ultimately, through poetry.

7. The author suggests that the Romantic poets:
    A. attempted to attain the sublime and ultimate connection with one's natural self.
    B. believed they had the unique task of showing and reconnecting man with the natural world.
    C. thought science was diminishing man's creative imagination.
    D. were against Victorian morals and ways of thinking.

8. According to the passage, the problem with creative inspiration was that it was:
    A. something that could only be found in the high and lofty.
    B. to be found in the most unsophisticated things.
    C. impossible to trace.
    D. capricious.

9. Which of the following assertions is NOT made in the passage regarding Romanticism?
    A. It was a reaction to the burgeoning trend towards scientific and formal knowledge.
    B. It sought to reconnect man to his natural self through creative imagination.
    C. It challenged the use of reason and logic over emotion.
    D. It emphasised feelings and emotions as the key to man's reconnection with the natural world.

10. What is the author's purpose for writing the passage?
    A. To point out the differences in the Romantic poets and their philosophies
    B. To show that despite differences in their philosophies, the Romantics had the same end in mind
    C. To illustrate Romantic tendencies in juxtaposition to the idealism of the poets involved
    D. To capture the essence of Romanticism through the eyes of the various philosophers

11. The "sublime" is a concept that many critics and scholars would generally refer as indescribable but can take various forms such as a mountain, a landscape, a poem, a good meal, a heroic deed or a state of mind. Given the information on Coleridge and Wordsworth's Romantic principles, the sublime is considered:
    A. a form of spontaneous powerful emotion.
    B. attainable through creative imagination.
    C. ephemeral in the natural world.
    D. an inspired connection with one's natural self.

12. The more popular notion of the word "romantic" is that which is associated with love or strong affection and at times, irrationality. Which of the following assertions in the passage would be confused to be the same concept as those advanced by the Romantic Movement?
    A. The works of the Romantic poets such as the lyrical ballads often dealt with love.
    B. Romantic poets are also known for their typical temper and passion.
    C. The Romantic poets emphasised the importance of natural feelings and emotions in preference to reason and logic.
    D. Wordsworth claims that poetry is a result of the "spontaneous overflow of powerful feelings".

Unit 3

Questions 13 - 18

Gauguin's attitude toward art marked a break from the past and a beginning to modern art. He was from the start preoccupied with suggestion rather than description. Gauguin considered naturalism an error to be avoided, and he sought to render images in their purest, simplest and most primitive form. He wanted to portray the essence of things rather than the exterior form, which could only be achieved through simplification of the form. The beginning of his modern tradition lay in his rejection of Impressionism. He firmly believed throughout his life that "art is an abstraction" and that "this abstraction [must be derived] from nature while dreaming before it." One must think of the creation that will result rather than the model, and not try to render the model exactly as one sees it. Like all Post-Impressionist artists, he passed through an Impressionist phase but became quickly dissatisfied with the limitations of the style, and went on to discover a new style that had the directness and universality of a symbol and that concentrated on impressions, ideas and experiences. It was the birth of "Synthetism" or rather Synthetist-Symbolic, as Gauguin referred to it, using the term "symbolic" to indicate that the forms and patterns in his pictures were meant to suggest mental images or ideas and not simply to record a visual experience.

Symbolism flourished around the period of 1885 to 1910 and can be defined as the rejection of direct, literal representation in favour of evocation and suggestion. Painters tried to give a visual expression to emotional experiences, and therefore the movement was a reaction against the naturalistic aims of Impressionism. Satisfying the need for a more spiritual or emotional approach in art, Symbolism is characterised by the desire to seek refuge in a dream world of beauty and the belief that colour and line in themselves could express ideas. Stylistically, the tendency was towards flattened forms and broad areas of colour, and features of the movement were an intense religious feeling and an interest in subjects of death, disease, and sin.

Similarly, "Synthetism" involved the simplification of forms into large-scale patterns and the expressive purification of colours. Form and colour had to be simplified for the sake of expression. This style reacted against the "formlessness" of Impressionism and favoured painting subjectively and expressing one's ideas rather than relying on external objects as subject matters. It was characterised by areas of pure colours, very defined contours, an emphasis on pattern and decorative qualities, and a relative absence of shadows.

Gauguin's new art form merged these two movements and succeeded in freeing colour, form, and line, bringing it to express the artists' emotions, sensibilities, and personal experiences of the world around them. His style created a break with the old tradition of descriptive naturalism and favoured the synthesis of observation and imagination. Gauguin sustained that forms are not discovered in nature but in one's wild imagination, and it was in himself that he searched rather than in his surroundings. For this reason, he scorned the Impressionists for their lack of imagination and their mere scientific reasoning. Furthermore, Gauguin used colour unnaturalistically for its decorative or emotional effect and reintroduced emphatic outlines. "Synthetism" signified for him that the forms of his pictures were constructed from symbolic patterns of colour and linear rhythms and were not mere scientific reproductions of what is seen by the eye.

13. Based on passage information, which of the following can you infer to be among the principles of Impressionism?
    A. Representing idealised versions of reality as they exist in the artist's mind
    B. Representing reality using technical tools such as photography to capture its appearance
    C. Representing the outward forms of things exactly as they appear to the naked eye
    D. Representing the feelings derived from an experience through vibrant colours and lines

14. According to passage information, what do Symbolism and Impressionism have in common?
    A. Both saw ideas as crucial to the impact of a work.
    B. Both focused on representing nature rather than man-made objects.
    C. Both considered the artist's subjective experience to be a key element to the work.
    D. Both thought art needed to express the idiosyncratic nature of the artist rather than pleasing society.

15. Which of the following hypothetical pieces of evidence would diminish the author's claims about the importance of Gauguin?
    A. Evidence that Gauguin's style of painting was based on work by van Gogh and other painters active during the 1870s and 80s
    B. Evidence that both Gauguin and the Impressionists rejected the more formal and conventional realism of the early 1800s
    C. Photographic evidence that some of Gauguin's works bear no apparent resemblance to the landscape they were supposedly based on
    D. Evidence that the Impressionists' works were considered just as shocking and revolutionary in their time as Gauguin's work would later be

16. Based on passage information, which of these quotes from fellow painters would Gauguin least likely agree?
   A. "Treat nature in terms of the cylinder, the sphere, and the cone." *(Paul Cezanne)*
   B. "Painting is a blind man's profession. He paints not what he sees, but what he feels, what he tells himself about what he has seen." *(Pablo Picasso)*
   C. "Paintings have a life of their own that derives from the painter's soul." *(Vincent van Gogh)*
   D. "There is only one true thing: instantly paint what you see. When you've got it, you've got it. When you haven't, you begin again." *(Édouard Manet)*

17. According to the passage, Gauguin rejected Impressionism for a number of reasons. Which of the following CANNOT be inferred to have been a motive of this rejection?
   A. Lack of flexibility within the style of Impressionism
   B. Lack of intense feelings and emotions in Impressionism
   C. Lack of beauty in Impressionism
   D. Lack of imagination in Impressionism

18. Elsewhere, it is said that Japanese art influenced Gauguin's work. Given the passage discussion of Synthetist-Symbolism, which of these features of Japanese painting can be reasonably assumed to characterise Gauguin's art form?
   A. Use of fluid curved lines
   B. Use of animals and landscapes as subjects
   C. Use of narrative elements to express ideas
   D. Use of strong colours and compositional freedom

Unit 4

Questions 19 - 25

Human conduct and belief are now undergoing transformations profounder and more disturbing than any since the appearance of wealth and philosophy put an end to the traditional religion of the Greeks.

It is the age of Socrates again: our moral life is threatened, and our intellectual life is quickened and enlarged by the disintegration of ancient customs and beliefs. Everything is new and experimental in our ideas and our actions; nothing is established or certain any more. The rate, complexity, and variety of change in our time are without precedent, even in Periclean days; all forms about us are altered, from the tools that complicate our toil, and the wheels that whirl us restlessly about the earth, to the innovations in our sexual relationships and the hard disillusionment of our souls.

The passage from agriculture to industry, from the village to the town, and from the town to the city has elevated science, debased art, liberated thought, ended monarchy and aristocracy, generated democracy and socialism, emancipated woman, disrupted marriage, broken down the old moral code, destroyed asceticism with luxuries, replaced Puritanism with Epicureanism, exalted excitement above content, made war less frequent and more terrible, taken from us many of our most cherished religious beliefs and given us a mechanical and fatalistic philosophy of life. All things flow, and we seek some mooring and stability in the flux.

In every developing civilisation, a period comes when old instincts and habits prove inadequate to altered stimuli, and ancient institutions and moralities crack like hampering shells under the obstinate growth of life. In one sphere after another, now that we have left the farm and the home for the factory, the office and the world, spontaneous and "natural" modes of order and response break down, and intellect chaotically experiments to replace with conscious guidance the ancestral readiness and simplicity of impulse and wonted ways. Everything must be thought out, from the artificial "formula" with which we feed our children, and the "calories" and "vitamins" of our muddled dietitians, to the bewildered efforts of a revolutionary government to direct and coordinate all the haphazard processes of trade. We are like a man who cannot walk without thinking of his legs, or like a player who must analyse every move and stroke as he plays. The happy unity of instinct is gone from us, and we flounder in a sea of doubt; amidst unprecedented knowledge and power, we are uncertain of our purposes, values and goals.

From this confusion, the one escape worthy of a mature mind is to rise out of the moment and the part and contemplate the whole. What we have lost above all is total perspective. Life seems too intricate and mobile for us to grasp its unity and significance; we cease to be citizens and become only individuals; we have no purposes that look beyond our death; we are fragments of men, and nothing more.

No one (except Spengler) dares today to survey life in its entirety; analysis leaps and synthesis lags; we fear the experts in every field and keep ourselves, for safety's sake, lashed to our narrow specialties. Everyone knows his part, but is ignorant of its meaning in the play. Life itself grows meaningless and becomes empty just when it seemed most full.

Let us put aside our fear of inevitable error, and survey all those problems of our state, trying to see each part and puzzle in the light of the whole. We shall define philosophy as "total perspective," as mind overspreading life and forging chaos into unity. Perhaps philosophy will give us, if we are faithful to it, a healing unity of soul. We are so slovenly and self-contradictory in our thinking; it may be that we shall clarify ourselves and pull ourselves together into consistency and be ashamed to harbour contradictory desires or beliefs. And through this unity of mind may come that unity of purpose and character which makes a personality and lends some order and dignity to our existence. Philosophy is harmonised knowledge making a harmonious life; it is the self-discipline which lifts us to security and freedom. Knowledge is power, but only wisdom is liberty.

Our culture is superficial today, and our knowledge dangerous, because we are rich in mechanisms and poor in purposes. The balance of mind which once came of a warm religious faith is gone; science has taken from us the supernatural bases of our morality and all the world seems consumed in a disorderly individualism that reflects the chaotic fragmentation of our character.

We move about the earth with unprecedented speed, but we do not know, and have not thought, where we are going, or whether we shall find any happiness there for our harassed souls. We are being destroyed by our knowledge, which has made us drunk with our power. And we shall not be saved without wisdom.

19. What could be inferred as the best title for this passage?
  A. What is Philosophy?
  B. The Age of Uncertainty
  C. The Dualities of Wisdom
  D. How We can Progress

20. The tone of the author is:
  A. bleak.
  B. hopeful.
  C. existential.
  D. cautious.

21. Which of the following statements would most likely contradict the author's thesis?
  A. Inconsistency is the key to flexibility.
  B. Values and morals are essentially socially-constructed.
  C. A given culture's development of wisdom in relation to the world's fragmentation is determined by symbolic behaviour.
  D. There is progress in technology in relation to a higher sense of spiritual development.

22. How does the author define philosophy?
    I.   As a "total perspective"
    II. As mind overspreading life and forging chaos into unity
    III. As the essential balance between mind and matter

    A. I only
    B. II only
    C. I and II
    D. I, II, and III

23. Based on passage information, philosophy is based according to which of the following notions?
    A. A synthesis of opposites
    B. A struggle for progress
    C. A reaching for goodness
    D. Harmony

24. In the passage, the author assigns knowledge and wisdom to particular representations. Which of the following best exemplifies this ratio?
    A. Power-Liberty
    B. Essence-Existence
    C. Being-Becoming
    D. Static-Active

25. The author claims that the movement from agriculture to industry gave people a fatalistic and mechanical view of life. Within the post-industrial age we currently live in, the movement to the digital world has given people a view of life, which is:
    A. disconnected and shallow.
    B. connected and hopeful.
    C. simultaneously interconnected yet disassociated.
    D. a network of linear lines of information affecting humanity globally.

Unit 5

Questions 26 - 32

The Sick Rose by William Blake

O Rose thou art sick.
The invisible worm,
That flies in the night
In the howling storm:
Has found out thy bed
Of crimson joy:
And his dark secret love
Does thy life destroy.

Here the title encapsulates the essential dynamic of the poem. The rose is an archetypal symbol, which means that it has been seized on by all cultures which have known roses as symbolising very much the same range of human experience, and is spontaneously recognised as doing so even by those who do not know what a symbol is.

Archetypes contain the ability to release a certain range of meanings with peculiar depth and power. Things become symbols because of characteristics evident in ordinary life, and these remain the primary elements in the symbol however much it might have been elaborated in the literary tradition. We are all aware of the rose as a queen of flowers, beautiful, rich in colour (especially the red rose), heady in perfume, sensuous in texture, incurved, enfolding erotic promise. The rose activates all the senses like the body of a desired woman. Rose metaphors are part of our common language. Rosy cheeks signify health; rosy lips are asking to be kissed. Few men have never sent a woman a bunch of red roses; and even when there is no verbal message, the woman has no difficulty knowing what that means. Burns wrote: 'My love is like a red, red, rose'. In giving a woman a red rose, a man is giving her an image of herself, or herself as he would wish her to be, rich with sexual passion.

As a primary female sexual symbol, the rose in the ancient world was attributed to Aphrodite/Venus, goddess of sexual love. The book which distilled and defined the courtly love invented by the medieval troubadours was called the Roman de la Rose, where the rose symbolises a woman's awakening to sexual love.

If we add together all the associations of the word rose, those we supply from our own experience, those common in our culture, and those we happen to be familiar with in the literary tradition, we have a very strong sense of youth, health, beauty and joy, of the feminine at its most desirable, of vitality and creativity, of the gratification of erotic desires. The last adjective we anticipate is 'sick'. Sickness, disease, corruption, are not only contrary to all the primary meanings of 'rose' but strike us as a violation of them, a sacrilege. The two words cancel each other out, leaving a void, a chaos. The title enacts linguistically the degradation of the rose the poem then dramatises. Blake was by no means the first poet to exploit this shock effect. In *A Midsummer Night's Dream* Shakespeare, needing to convey what happens when the natural progression of the seasons is violated and Great Creating Nature made sterile, writes: 'heavy-headed frosts / Fall in the fresh lap of the crimson rose'. And in Lycidas Milton wrote 'as killing as the canker to the rose'.

The poets Blake was most familiar with and most respected were Shakespeare and Milton, and he expected his readers to know them well. 'The Sick Rose' draws so heavily on both of them that it can hardly be read, or loses half its force, if the reader is unaware of the power and quite specific meanings flowing into this poem from *Twelfth Night*, *Hamlet* and *Paradise Lost*.

In Book IX of *Paradise Lost*, Satan, having crossed the howling storm of chaos, 'with meditated guile' flies 'as a mist by night' into Eden, where he enters the serpent, the fittest creature to communicate his 'dark suggestions' to Eve. (The first meaning of 'worm' in the Oxford English Dictionary is 'serpent, snake, dragon'.) Satan views Eve " . . . so thick the roses bushing round about her glowed" to which she is compared to, with a "storm so nigh" given as a background context from where Satan has come from. His avowed purpose is 'all pleasure to destroy' since he has lost his own capacity for joy. When Eve tells Adam what has happened, he describes her as 'deflowered': From his slack hand the garland wreathed for Eve, down dropped, and all the faded roses shed.

Nakedness and sex become for both of them a cause for shame, which they had never known before. This story, with its memorable imagery of the invisible tempter flying through a howling storm, becoming a worm, and desecrating the joy of the marriage bed for both man and woman, clearly looms behind 'The Sick Rose' and feeds it with potent suggestions. These suggestions mingle with others from Shakespeare. The worm which destroys the beauty of a young woman must remind us of Viola's story of an imaginary sister: She never told her love, But let concealment, like a worm i' the bud, Feed on her damask cheek: she pin'd in thought. The examples lend their credence that "The Sick Rose" is remarkably influenced by Milton and Shakespeare.

26. Given that the rose is an archetype recognised by all cultures as a symbol, it can be inferred that:
    A. poetry, as an aspect of culture, is an archetype which is created through symbolisation.
    B. the archetype is understood through language and interpretation of the referent.
    C. things are symbolised through evidentiary and ordinary characteristics representing the same elements.
    D. symbols are a generalised and universal aspect of all cultures as evidenced through archetypes.

27. By linking the contrary meanings of "sick and rose," the poem itself displays:
    A. an oxymoron throwing the reader into an abyss of chaos.
    B. a juxtaposition between romantic and destructive imagery.
    C. a tonality and effect which contradict each other linguistically.
    D. an explosion of multiple meanings and effects on the reader.

28. The author's attitude towards archetypes can be characterised as:
    A. telescopic.
    B. critical.
    C. focussed.
    D. encompassing.

29. The commentator refers to Milton in *Paradise Lost* in order to emphasise the beginning of:
    A. sin.
    B. the fall from Grace.
    C. shame.
    D. dualism.

30. Within the passage, it can be reasonably noted that the meaning of archetypes in culture have:
    A. profound reflections of man's common consciousness.
    B. associations with a certain range of intention.
    C. influences on the literary tradition.
    D. interrelations with linguistic structures.

31. Based on the author's discussions, if a reader is unfamiliar with Blake's allusions to Milton and Shakespeare:

    A. the rose will be overlooked as an essential archetype in the poem.

    B. the meaning of the poem loses half its force and power.

    C. the meaning of the poem will be lost in superficial interpretation.

    D. the worm will be misinterpreted within the scope of the poem's imagery.

32. The characterisation of Blake's poem with Milton can be reasonably described as:

    A. redundant.

    B. irrevocable.

    C. inharmonious.

    D. uncanny.

Unit 6

Questions 33 - 37

The "Theatre of the Absurd" is a term coined by Hungarian-born critic Martin Esslin, who made it the title of his 1962 book on the subject. The term refers to a particular type of play which first became popular during the 1950s and 1960s and which presented on stage the philosophy articulated by French philosopher Albert Camus in his 1942 essay, "The Myth of Sisyphus", in which he defines the human condition as basically meaningless. Camus argued that humanity had to resign itself to recognising that a fully satisfying rational explanation of the universe was beyond its reach; in that sense, the world must ultimately be seen as absurd.

Esslin regarded the term "Theatre of the Absurd" merely as a "device" by which he meant to bring attention to certain fundamental traits discernible in the works of a range of playwrights. The playwrights loosely grouped under the label of the absurd attempt to convey their sense of bewilderment, anxiety, and wonder in the face of an inexplicable universe. According to Esslin, the five defining playwrights of the movement are Eugène Ionesco, Samuel Beckett, Jean Genet, Arthur Adamov, and Harold Pinter, although these writers were not always comfortable with the label and sometimes preferred to use terms such as "Anti-Theatre" or "New Theatre". Other playwrights associated with this type of theatre include Tom Stoppard, Arthur Kopit, Friedrich Dürrenmatt, Fernando Arrabal, Edward Albee, N.F. Simpson, Boris Vian, Peter Weiss, Vaclav Havel, and Jean Tardieu. The most famous, and most controversial, absurdist play is probably Samuel Beckett's *Waiting for Godot.* The characters of the play are strange caricatures who have difficulty communicating the simplest of concepts to one another as they bide their time awaiting the arrival of Godot. The language they use is often ludicrous, and following the cyclical patter, the play seems to end in precisely the same condition it began, with no real change having occurred. In fact, it is sometimes referred to as "the play where nothing happens." Its detractors count this a fatal flaw and often turn red in the face fomenting on its inadequacies. It is mere gibberish, they cry, eyes nearly bulging out of their head - a prank on the audience disguised as a play. The plays supporters, on the other hand, describe it is an accurate parable on the human condition in which "the more things change, the more they are the same." Change, they argue, is only an illusion. In 1955, the famous character actor Robert Morley predicted that the success of *Waiting for Godot* meant "the end of theatre as we know it." His generation may have gloomily accepted this prediction, but the younger generation embraced it. They were ready for something new - something that would move beyond the old stereotypes and reflect their increasingly complex understanding of existence.

Whereas traditional theatre attempts to create a photographic representation of life as we see it, the Theatre of the Absurd aims to create a ritual-like, mythological, archetypal, allegorical vision, closely related to the world of dreams. The focal point of these dreams is often man's fundamental bewilderment and confusion, stemming from the fact that he has no answers to the basic existential questions: why we are alive, why we have to die, why there is injustice and suffering. Ionesco defined the absurdist everyman as "Cut off from his religious, metaphysical, and transcendental roots … lost; all his actions become senseless, absurd, useless." The Theatre of the Absurd, in a sense, attempts to reestablish man's communion with the universe. Dr. Jan Culik writes, "Absurd Theatre can be seen as an attempt to restore the importance of myth and ritual to our age, by making man aware of the ultimate realities of his condition, by instilling in him again the lost sense of cosmic wonder and primaeval anguish. The Absurd Theatre hopes to achieve this by shocking man out of an existence that has become trite, mechanical and complacent. It is felt that there is mystical experience in confronting the limits of human condition."

- Adapted from J. Crabb, Theatre of the Absurd; 2006

33. The author's tone in paragraph 6 discussing critics of Waiting for Godot can be described as:
    A. analytical.
    B. persuasive.
    C. mocking.
    D. definitional.

34. One can infer from passage information that "Theatre of the Absurd" plays:
    I. contain naturalistic dialogue based on the rhythms of speech.
    II. involve plots based on those of classical myths.
    III. alters viewers' perceptions of reality after they leave the theatre.

    A. I and III
    B. I, II, and III
    C. I only
    D. III only

35. Based on passage information, it can be inferred that in Samuell Beckett's play *Waiting for Godot*:
    A. the characters are mouthpieces for the author in accurately describing the absurdity of existence.
    B. the concept of waiting is given cosmic significance as both characters and audience wait for something that will never occur.
    C. the author provides an ambivalent statement on human existence because while the characters' lives do not improve, they also do not get any worse.
    D. Becket caricatures the ridiculous and shallow people of his time through the stilted words and actions of the characters.

36. Based on passage information, the playwrights under discussion in this passage used absurdity in order to:
    A. make viewers newly aware of the absurdity of human life.
    B. shock viewers who believed all theatre should reflect life realistically.
    C. provide a respite from the humdrum of normal life.
    D. express their real selves and the uniquely strange way they experienced life.

37. The author implies that the "Theatre of the Absurd" could be considered:
    A. a branch of realism.
    B. a step in the evolution toward today's artistic forms.
    C. a genre of literature.
    D. a template for producing artistic works.

Unit 7

Questions 38 - 40

At the present time, when women are beginning to take part in the affairs of the world, it is still a world that belongs to men – they have no doubt of it at all and women have scarcely any. To decline to be the Other, to refuse to be a party to the deal – this would be for women to renounce all the advantages conferred upon them by their alliance with the superior caste. Man-the-sovereign will provide woman-the-liege with material protection and will undertake the moral justification of her existence; thus she can evade at once both economic risk and the metaphysical risk of a liberty in which ends and aims must be contrived without assistance. Indeed, along with the ethical urge of each individual to affirm his subjective existence, there is also the temptation to forgo liberty and become a thing. This is an inauspicious road, for he who takes it – passive, lost, ruined – becomes henceforth the creature of another's will, frustrated in his transcendence and deprived of every value. But it is an easy road; on it, one avoids the strain involved in undertaking an authentic existence. When man makes of woman the Other, he may, then, expect to manifest deep-seated tendencies towards complicity. Thus, woman may fail to lay claim to the status of subject because she lacks definite resources, because she feels the necessary bond that ties her to man regardless of reciprocity, and because she is often very well pleased with her role as the Other.

- Excerpt from Simone de Beauvoir, Woman as Other; 1949

38. According to the author, the relationship that transpires between man and woman is that of:
    A. a master to his slave.
    B. a communal partnership.
    C. a provider and his dependent.
    D. a conspiracy.

39. The author suggests that the roles of men and women are dictated by:
    A. survival needs.
    B. male orientation.
    C. social preconditions.
    D. personal motives.

40. According to the author, the woman considers herself as:
   A. a dependent of man.
   B. a willing subordinate of man.
   C. an insecure social being.
   D. man's moral responsibility.

If time remains, you may review your work. If your allotted time (50 minutes) is complete, please proceed to the Answer Key.

3.8.2 Verbal Reasoning Exercise 1 (Humanities and Social Science) Answer Key and Explanations

1.	B	9.	C	17.	C	25.	C	33.	C
2.	C	10.	B	18.	D	26.	C	34.	D
3.	C	11.	B	19.	A	27.	B	35.	B
4.	C	12.	C	20.	C	28.	D	36.	A
5.	D	13.	C	21.	D	29.	C	37.	C
6.	D	14.	C	22.	C	30.	A	38.	C
7.	B	15.	A	23.	D	31.	B	39.	C
8.	D	16.	D	24.	A	32.	D	40.	B

1.   Correct Answer: B

This question asks what the author is claiming in his hypothetical scenario of an infant being transported to a different land. Sapir argues that the child would learn to walk in the same way regardless of which environment he was brought up in, but will learn a language in a specific way in the context of his new culture (rather than his native one). Thus he will speak the language of the adoptive land rather than the native one. This rules out answer choice (A). The example given in option (B) concerns someone who is transported to an adoptive land at a young age and thus learns its language. Therefore, it is the correct answer.

The context of this sentence assumes that the child has been permanently "transplanted" to the new social environment, so his language may no longer bear resemblance to his original (i.e., native) environment. The paragraph does not imply that when this happens, this will (C) anger the people in his native country. Likewise, the author uses "at variance" to suggest deep-seated difference rather than (D) changes or shifts in spoken language over time.

2.   Correct Answer: C

To answer this question, you must determine which hypothetical facts would support or weaken the passage's main argument, which states that language varies without limit - that languages are "a purely historical heritage of the group, the product of long-continued social usage". Thus the discovery that some languages contain culture-specific concepts and are vastly different would support the passage's claims. This makes (C) the best option.

(A) This discovery would weaken the claim that languages vary "without limit".

(B) The author states that language is not an innate function and that an individual learns to speak because "he is born... in the lap of a society that is certain, reasonably certain, to lead him to its traditions." Thus if a discovery was made that a person learned a language without being taught society's traditions of speech, this argument would weaken his claims.

(D) The fact that a family all suffered from a congenital condition would suggest it is hereditary. If people had enough intelligence to learn other information but were prevented from learning language by a hereditary condition, this would suggest that language has a biological aspect.

3. **Correct Answer: C**

This question asks what dichotomies are mentioned in the passage as separating speech from other human activities such as walking. Several instances in the excerpt emphasise biological development as a factor for walking as opposed to society's influence on an individual's speech development. This makes (C) the best answer.

(A) The author does mention tradition in the context of a culture, but it neither mentions innovation nor suggests that it is important to understanding speech.

(B) The author states that walking would eventually happen as a natural reflex but does not emphasise purpose as a factor in developing speech.

(D) The author states that walking will occur as an individual grows "if he survives at all". However, the author refers to walking and talking as - both - functions albeit instinctive and acquired, respectively.

4. **Correct Answer: C**

This question requires you to think about the implications of one of the author's main arguments. The claim that (C) speech varies based on genetics does not follow from the author's reasoning since a function that is genetically-based is innate and thus places a built-in limitation on how much it could vary (just as with human walking and running abilities).

(A) The author's notion of variation based on cultural differences means speech would vary between groups.

(B) The author states that "society... is certain, reasonably certain, to lead [a speaker] to its traditions" - in other words, the cultural heritage of the social group to which he belongs.

(D) The author states that speech varies according to culture; since animals lack culture, their communicative sounds would not vary as much.

5. **Correct Answer: D**

This question necessitates that you to think about the implications of a claim by another author (Chomsky) to the argument presented by the passage's author. Chomsky is saying that babies do not have access to as much data as they would need to learn an entire language from scratch. From the fact that people do eventually learn to speak their native languages, we can infer that people acquire language using not just cultural learning but some pre-existing information about a language's general character. This would contradict Sapir's claim that language is not an "inherent, biological function of man". The correct answer is (D).

(A) The passage never discusses a distinction between content and structure or suggests that any aspect of language is innate.

(B) Neither Chomsky nor Sapir expressed true doubt that people learn a language thoroughly.

(C) The quote from Chomsky suggests that young children are born with innate information about a language's general character in order to learn the structure of a language. This contradicts rather than supports Sapir's argument that language is only acquired through culture and social tradition, not by pre-existing information.

6. **Correct Answer: D**

Answering this question requires understanding the context of the author's premise that the "naturalness of speech is but an illusory feeling". This can be found in the first 3 sentences of the passage, which explains that speech, being part of our daily activities, is too familiar a function as breathing that we talk without requiring a deliberate effort to do so. This is the main reason why the author believes we often mistake speech as a natural function when it is actually socially acquired. The best option is (D).

(A) The author does state, "Speech is so familiar a feature of daily life that we rarely pause to define it." However, this is only part of his explanation as to the main reason why he deems speech to be an unnatural function. Also, please note that answer choices that are almost verbatim of a line from the passage are frequently used as a decoy and are thus incorrect.

(B) This is a true statement. The passage indeed argues that speech is acquired through one's social environment. However, this does not really answer the question, does it? (See RHSS 3.2.5 Technique Number 5.)

(C) The author says that "it needs but a moment's reflection" to realise that speech is not a natural function but does not mention about needing to realise the purpose of talking.

7. **Correct Answer: B**

This question requires differentiating the author's view and statements about the Romantic poets in general, from those of the three Romantic poets referred in the passage:

"To the romantic poets, poetry was an instrument of emotion and feeling intended to reconnect man with the natural world, and in general the poet was viewed as a person uniquely equipped to guide the layman to this reconnection." (P1)

"Each of these poets recognised great value in the natural feelings and emotions of man, and the connection sparked by man's place in the natural world. Each strove to capture and explain that connection through creative imagination and ultimately, through poetry." (Last paragraph)

(A) This option is a misreading of the information found in the last sentence of Paragraph 2 pertaining to the goal of Romantic poetry - not poets.

(C) This is another misreading of the idea that "In the eyes of the romantic poets, mankind had become so swept up in the pursuit of knowledge and innovation that they had disconnected from both the natural world, and their deeper, natural selves." The Romantic poets saw the scientific discoveries diminishing man's connection with the natural selves and the world – not creative imagination. In fact, they also valued reason and

logic as indicated in P2 S3:

"Though the philosophies of the individual poets differed, in general romantic poetry focussed on and lauded primitivism and emotion while minimising (but not discounting) the importance of reason and logic."

(D) This answer is an anachronism, i.e., the Victorian era comes after the Romantic age temporally.

8. **Correct Answer: D**

This is another question that calls for differentiating the concepts and perspectives presented in the passage. The trick in this question lies in the use of the terms "creative inspiration" and "creative imagination," which can get incorrectly interchanged and thus easily misinterpreted because they are being used in various details and concepts.

The answer can be readily found in P3 S2:

"This caused much difficulty though, as the source of creative imagination was impossible to trace and because creative inspiration was quite fickle."

This opposes Wordsworth's belief that inspiration is derived from the most basic and simplest of things:

"Wordsworth believed that beauty and inspiration were to be found in the most rudimentary and common things and was not something that could only be found in the high and lofty." (P4 S1)

(A) This is in contradiction to Wordsworth's view of beauty and inspiration.

(B) The passage does not imply that this is a problem of creative inspiration, as indicated in P4 S1.

(C) This refers to creative imagination - not inspiration.

9. **Correct Answer: C**

Although Romanticism as a movement was formed during the height of scientific discoveries, it did not essentially (C) challenge the use of reason and logic, but rather of man's tendency to be consumed by "the pursuit of knowledge and innovation" as indicated in P2:

"In the eyes of the romantic poets, mankind had become so swept up in the pursuit of knowledge and innovation that they had disconnected from both the natural world, and their deeper, natural selves. Though the philosophies of the individual poets differed, in general romantic poetry focussed on and lauded primitivism and emotion while minimising (but not discounting) the importance of reason and logic."

(A) The Romantic movement is thus in response, indeed, (though not necessarily a challenge) to the scientific and formal knowledge at that time. (P2 S2)

(B) This is supported in the last sentence of Paragraph 2 and the last paragraph. Beliefs of the three Romantic poets mentioned also emphasise this idea. (P3 S1, P4 S5, P5 S2)

(D) This is clearly stated in the second sentence of the last paragraph.

10. **Correct Answer: B**

The essay does not focus on just (A) differences, so this option can be ruled out. Nor does the essay focus on (D) "philosophers". (C) mentions "tendencies," which is ambiguous as this statement neither specifies poetic tendencies nor does the passage involve "juxtaposition" which implies a difference. This leaves (B) as the most inclusive of the answer choices.

11. **Correct Answer: B**

The question specifies an answer that involves identifying a common view between Coleridge and Wordsworth on to the "sublime". These can be found in the following lines:

"Samuel Taylor Coleridge, one of the pioneers of the Romantic Movement, believed that the creative imagination was the key to man achieving his connection to the sublime." (P3 S1)

"Like Coleridge, Wordsworth believed that creative imagination was the source of poetry and the avenue to the sublime." (P4 S5)

The rest are decoys that are meant to sound like commonly used terms in the passage and could be mistaken as relevant concepts. They are really just off-tangent concepts.

12. **Correct Answer: C**

This question requires recognising similarities between new information introduced and a significant concept discussed in the passage. The question specifies the ideas associated with the layman's term "romantic": love, affection, irrationality. These are then related to the concept that was developed by the Romantic Movement.

A and B are decoys that use outside knowledge and not discussed in the passage.

(C) This is discussed in the passage, particularly in P2 S3.

(D) This would sound highly relevant. However, this is only specific to Wordsworth's principle, not to Romanticism in general. Likewise, Wordsworth's claim does not address the concept of "irrationality".

13. **Correct Answer: C**

This question asks you to infer the qualities of an art genre that are not explicitly defined in the text. The passage defines Gauguin's work as a reaction against Impressionism, stating that "He wanted to portray the essence of things rather than the exterior form" and "not try to render the model exactly as one sees it". It also states that he reintroduced the outline to art. Thus the passage suggests that Impressionism was focussed on capturing reality exactly as it appeared to the eye. The correct choice is (C).

(A) The passage does not imply that Impressionist images were idealised, but that they were intended to represent things as they really appear.

(B) The passage emphasises representing an object "exactly as one sees it" and not as technical instruments show it to be.

(D) Although the passage does not explicitly exclude the use of bright and expressive colours and lines in Impressionist paintings, it clearly states that their subjects are literal representations of real objects and scenery. It is, therefore, safe to conclude that NO Impressionist painting is "a visual expression of emotional experiences".

14. Correct Answer: C

This question asks you to reason about possible similarities between two art movements that are described as opposites. The passage states that in Impressionism, one paints the work "exactly as one sees it" while in Symbolism, "painters try to give a visual expression to emotional experiences". Thus in both forms of painting, the artist tries to portray a subjective internal experience, whether sensory or emotional.

(A) This choice is incorrect because the passage never mentions ideas as a component of Impressionist works.

(B) The passage gives no reason to believe that all Symbolist paintings were based on observing nature.

(D) This choice is irrelevant because the passage never discusses the individual versus society.

15. Correct Answer: A

This question requires you to understand the author's main claims about Gauguin. The passage states that Gauguin's work "marked a break from the past" and describes him as a key originator of many aspects of Symbolism. If he instead borrowed these ideas and techniques from others, his influence and originality would be less, and his painting would represent less of a dramatic break from earlier work.

(B) This choice is irrelevant because the fact that both groups rejected an earlier style does not diminish the importance of the break between the two of them.

(C) This choice would reinforce the author's claims since the passage focusses on Gauguin's lack of interest in accuracy.

(D) This is also irrelevant because the passage does not imply that the Impressionists' work was never revolutionary.

16. Correct Answer: D

This question asks you to consider how quotes from artists relate to what we know about Gauguin's ideas. The quote from Manet suggests seeing the external world and capturing it immediately in a painting. This runs contrary to the ideas presented in the passage. The first paragraph says Gauguin was "preoccupied with suggestion rather than description" and that Symbolism is defined as the "rejection of direct, literal representation in favour of evocation and suggestion". This quote would thus align Manet with Impressionism, which Gauguin rejects.

(A) This quote from Cezanne presents another principle of simplification, which is consistent with the idea of the passage about Synthetism as well as Gauguin's reintroduction of "emphatic outlines".

(B) This quote is the exact antithesis of option (D) and suggests that painting should be based on expressing feeling, one of Symbolism's principles.

(C) This quote does not concern itself with the external world but the internal experience or soul of the artist.

17. Correct Answer: C

To answer this question, you have to look closely at what the passage says about Impressionism. The author never implies that Impressionist paintings were not beautiful.

(A) Paragraph 1 states that Gauguin abandoned Impressionism due to the limitations of the style.

(B) The passage states that Symbolists wanted paintings to "express the artists' emotions, sensibilities, and personal experiences of the world around them" (paragraph 4), suggesting that they would reject unemotional works.

(D) The Symbolists' "rejection of direct, literal representation" (paragraph 2) suggests they saw imagination as important.

18. **Correct Answer: D**

This question asks you to infer connections between Japanese painting and Gaugin's Synthetist-Symbolist art. Even without prior knowledge of Japanese art nor any discussions of it in the passage, the question itself implies that a reasonable assumption can be made using the descriptions provided in the passage about Synthetist-Symbolism.

Most of these descriptions are found in paragraph 4, particularly about how Gaugin used colours freely and "unnaturalistically for its decorative or emotional effect. . . the forms of his pictures were constructed from symbolic patterns of colour and linear rhythms". The correct answer is (D).

(A) The passage does state that Gauguin used outlines but does not suggest the importance of fluidity or curved versus straight lines.

(B) Paragraph 2 states that Symbolism, one of the two movements from which Gauguin formed his "new" art, has death, disease, and sin as its typical subjects. Gauguin similarly relates in paragraph 4 that "it was in himself that he searched rather than in his surroundings". This makes this answer choice incorrect.

(C) Gauguin was particularly interested in suggesting mental images and ideas in an art work as opposed to merely representing visual reality. Nothing in the passage mentions narrative as a factor in his artistic process or form.

19. **Correct Answer: A**

This type of question focusses on a general assessment of the passage as a whole and its main purpose. We must consider that all of the answers are partially correct, therefore the answer that is most inclusive will be correct. By doing this, we can assess that (A) encompasses all the others mentioned in (B), (C), and (D), as evidenced in the introductory sentence and Paragraph 7 in its entirety.

20. **Correct Answer: C**

This is a complex-sounding question, which requires a process of deduction. Again, we must look for the lateral distinction of inclusion to indicate the answer to this tone question. All the answers are partially correct, yet one will stand out from the others and include the other answers. There are passages which are (A) bleak, as well as (D) cautious, yet these are relatively too focussed to be general assessments of the "tone of the author." There are also indications of (B) some hope in the author's suggestions about wisdom and liberty, yet we cannot define the entire passage as "hopeful." (C) Existential is the most inclusive of the others because "existence will carry with it moments of caution, hope, as well as bleakness and despair." Despite its "absurdist" ring, the reflections of existential thought, found in Camus, Sartre, Ionesco, and others run the full range and gamut of human emotions and actions. The term existentialism has often been compared to a "tragic optimism" view of life, which this passage certainly suggests.

21. **Correct Answer: D**

This is a complex-sounding question and the answers are full of abstractions, which one must be very careful while ruling out answers.

(A) simply does not make sense – a created sort of joke and certainly does not go against the thesis.

(B) is a tangent and not really related to the author's thesis.

(C) is also a tangent and not really related to the author's thesis.

(D) would go against the author's "entropic" view of humankind. If this is considered to be true, even hypothetically, it would qualify as the best choice, given the other options

22. **Correct Answer: C**

This detail-oriented question can be answered by a close reading particularly in Paragraph 7: We shall define philosophy as "total perspective," as mind overspreading life and forging chaos into unity.

23. Correct Answer: D

This is a best-option type of question, in which all of the answers may be partially correct or inferred and/or implicative of passage information. Only (D) answers the question directly and can be found in Paragraph 7:

Philosophy is harmonised knowledge making a harmonious life.

24. Correct Answer: A

This is a detail-oriented question based on a distinction which the author makes within the passage. The best ratio is (A) while the other answers are created distractions. This idea is reflected in the following statement, from the passage:

Knowledge is power, but only wisdom is liberty.
(B) A distraction – philosophical babble of existentialism
(C) Babble of philosophy in general
(D) Never mentioned

25. Correct Answer: C

This is an inference question based on modern affiliations of people with the internet.
(A) is too generalised. We cannot proclaim we all feel disconnected and shallow.
(B) is also too generalised; we cannot all proclaim we feel connected and hopeful.
(C) When on the internet, we feel interconnected yet disassociated. This is a generalisation but also a bit of paradox because the context of face-to-face communication is not there.
(D) is too generalised, and the metaphor of a network is faulty. If there is a metaphor for the internet, the rhizome would be descriptive. Linear suggests one-way, we know that is untrue for the internet. There are multiple connections, going in multiple ways simultaneously constituting a quite complex assemblage of information and communication.

26. Correct Answer: C

Given the complexity of this question, which is based on detail and close reading or re-scan, one must be very careful because of the way terms are being emplaced together.
(A) This is too obvious and is somewhat tautological in reasoning (circular argument). If read carefully, it really does not answer the question.
(B) This is never really mentioned within the passage; this answer concerns linguistics.
(C) This is a summation of P2 S2 and answers the question.
(D) This is too obvious also and tautological, not really answering the question.

27. Correct Answer: B

This is an associative type of question where the answer must be the BEST choice or inference given the range of options:
(A) is partially true, yet "the abyss of chaos" is too extreme.
(B) This is the correct answer: the romantic imagery of the rose versus the destructive imagery of a worm flying through the storm making the rose sick.
(C) Linguistically, a real rose can be sick – infected with disease, bug-ridden, etc. This is an incorrect option.
(D) This answer is too general. Yes, there are multiple meanings and effects upon a reader, but that is a condition of most poetry.

28. Correct Answer: D

This question is another best-option type given the range of answers, in which one must deduce through a process of elimination (PoE) to arrive at the correct answer.
(A) Telescopic is vague and similar to (C), which is also incorrect. It suggests nothing of the author's attitude towards archetypes.
(B) Critical is also vague. This could be translated in a number of different ways – serious and analytical, which suggests more of an approach rather than an "attitude".
(C) This can be ruled out for a similar reason as

(A). (D) Archetypes as encompassing can be inferred to be correct because it is the theoretical framework of which the poem is analysed. Given the statements in P2, this idea can easily be supported.

29. **Correct Answer: C**
This is a detail-oriented question, which must be drawn from the passage itself because all of the answers may be implicative of the passage or inferred to be at least partially correct. Within the passage itself, (A) and (B) may be implied yet never directly mentioned as in (C) - Last Paragraph, S1. (D) is indicative of Blake yet overly complex and not mentioned within the passage.

30. **Correct Answer: A**
This type of question is also detail-oriented, which must be solved by close reading, rescan and deduction through the process of elimination (PoE).
(A) is implied in Paragraph 2.
(B) This answer is a created distraction – intention is never mentioned in the passage.
(C) and (D) are either too obvious or too literal to be correct yet lacks specificity.

31. **Correct Answer: B**
This type of question is also detail-oriented, which must be solved by close reading, rescan and deduction through the process of elimination (PoE).
(A) and (C) are tangential and unfocussed, therefore, incorrect. (D) is too specific yet likewise tangential and unfocussed. (B) can be affirmed by Paragraph 5 in general and thus correct.

32. **Correct Answer: D**
This complex-sounding question must proceed to be answered by the comparison of the poem with Milton:
(A) is partially true. The stories are the same, yet the language and style are quite different.

(B) is incorrect and a created tangent distraction amounting to nonsense, which means cannot be recovered(?).
(C) is also incorrect: the general theme of both poem and the Milton excerpt is quite similar.
(D) is correct. The similarities of the two almost border on weirdness given the general thematic, which is almost mirror-like based on the interpretation.

33. **Correct Answer: C**
Answering this question requires you to think about the author's tone. Crabb writes that critics of Godot "often turn red in the face fomenting on its inadequacies. It is mere gibberish, they cry, eyes nearly bulging out of their head". The passage aims to make these critics appear foolish by showing that their distaste for the play is exaggerated and overemotional. Thus his tone is mocking.
(A) This excerpt cannot be described as analytical since the language used is so emotionally weighted.
(B) The excerpt is based on describing a certain type of critic rather than persuading the reader of anything.
(D) This passage does not describe a concept or term.

34. **Correct Answer: D**
This question calls for an understanding of the passage's definition of a theatrical genre. According to a line quoted in the text, Absurd Theatre aims at "making man aware of the ultimate realities of his condition, by instilling in him again the lost sense of cosmic wonder and primaeval anguish. The Absurd Theatre hopes to achieve this by shocking man out of an existence that has become trite, mechanical and complacent." Thus this form of theatre intends to make viewers more aware of certain aspects of life, not just as they watch the play, but overall. The correct answer is (D).
I. The passage states that dialogue in *Waiting for Godot* is "ludicrous" and describes Theatre

of the Absurd as opposed to realism.

II. While the passage does define these plays as possessing mythic elements, it also describes Waiting for Godot as an almost plotless play that "seems to end in precisely the same condition it began". This suggests absurdist plays can have plots quite unlike those of traditional mythic narratives.

35. Correct Answer: B

This question asks you to make inferences from the author's description of an unusual play. The passage states that characters "bide their time awaiting the arrival of Godot, but that in the end, nothing happens, describing its message as "Change...is only an illusion." Thus we can infer that the event the characters are waiting for does not happen and that this has implied significance for human life overall.

(A) We are told the characters "have difficulty communicating the simplest of concepts to one another." Thus they do not eloquently voice the author's views.

(C) The overall message of the play is described as invoking absurdity and futility, so its message is negative, not ambivalent.

(D) The passage describes the play's message as focussed on life overall, not on a specific time period or type of person.

36. Correct Answer: A

This question is asking you to understand the absurdist playwrights' described motivation. The passage states that they "attempt to convey their sense of bewilderment, anxiety, and wonder in the face of an inexplicable universe". It goes on to discuss "instilling in [man] again the lost sense of cosmic wonder and primaeval anguish". Thus the main purpose is to make life's absurdity palpable to viewers.

(B) The passage does suggest the plays shocked people, but not that this was their main purpose.

(C) The passage does not suggest that the plays are a "respite" but a disturbing experience that reflects life's troubling qualities.

(D) The passage suggests that the playwrights were attempting to convey an experience, but one that they consider a truth about life, not unique to their worldview.

37. Correct Answer: C

This question is asking what type of literary phenomenon Theatre of the Absurd is. A genre is a category of artistic production in which works are grouped together based on similarities in subject matter, style and form. The passage describes Theatre of the Absurd as a type of play whose authors shared similar thematic concerns and means (such as static plots) of achieving them. This fits the definition of a genre.

(A) The passage describes Theatre of the Absurd as distinct from realism and rejecting the need to portray reality accurately.

(B) The passage never states Theatre of the Absurd had widespread influence on later forms of theatre.

(D) A template suggests a rigid set of instructions that would result in similar works while the passage describes a more loose set of interests and theatrical devices.

38. Correct Answer: C

In this question, candidates must be able to understand the author's overall concept of woman as the "Other". The passage describes man as one who "will provide woman-the-liege with material protection and will undertake the moral justification of her existence" implying that it is the man who takes the significant role of the provider while the woman settles for the convenience of being his dependent. This makes option (C) correct.

(A) This is a close answer because the author refers to the woman as a "liege" (which could either mean a slave or a dependent) who feels a "necessary bond that ties her to man". However, this is only because the woman's option of individuality is difficult that she chooses this role of subordination as indicated by the line: "But it is an easy road; on it, one avoids the strain involved in undertaking an authentic existence." In other words, a woman is not entirely a slave who is bound to obey without any choice but more of a willing dependent.

(B) A communal partnership is also close in the sense that the nature of this type of relationship is based on providing benefits and looking out for the welfare of the other person. However, the role of each person in the relationship is that of a partner - not as a sovereign to his subordinate as the passage author describes.

(D) Nothing is mentioned about conspiracy in the passage.

39. **Correct Answer: C**
The beginning of the paragraph places emphasis on change in the world as women are "beginning to take part in the affairs of the world" but makes reference to the pre-existing state of the world where it "belongs to men". This distinction between the status quo and the changes that are starting to occur in women's place in the world emphasises the existence of "social preconditions" that dictate the unequal

roles of men and women. (A) and (D) are some of the reasons implied in the passage why women submit to their subordinate role in society. The author describing society as (B) male-oriented only reinforces the fact that the importance accorded to the role of men is socially preconditioned.

40. **Correct Answer: B**
This question requires differentiating the author's concept of women as the (A) dependent "Other" from what she explains to be women's self-perception as (B) willing subordinates of men. The last line of the passage details the circumstances that lead women to conveniently acquiesce to their subordinate role in a male-oriented society. This question is asking candidates to determine how a woman considers herself based on passage information, and this is best answered by option (B). Answer choice (C) would require a subjective interpretation of the passage, which is incorrect. The passage briefly states that men "undertake the moral justification of [women's] existence" but this does not necessarily imply that women perceive themselves as (D) man's moral responsibility.

More GS Section I Mini Tests are available online at GAMSAT-prep.com.

3.8.3 Verbal Reasoning Exercise 2 (Science-based Passages)

The following is a sample mini test which is designed to aid in developing your skills in reading and answering passages that are related to science or medicine. These types of passages are known to appear in Section I of recent GAMSATs.

There are 7 Units with 40 questions. Choose the best answer for each question. You have 50 minutes. Please time yourself.

> BEGIN ONLY WHEN TIMER IS READY

Unit 1

Questions 1 - 5

Gold was first discovered at Summitville mine in Colorado in 1870. Significant gold production from underground workings occurred prior to 1900. In 1903, the Reynolds adit (entrance for access, drainage, and ventilation) was driven to drain the underground workings and serve as an ore haulage tunnel. Production occurred sporadically through the 1950s. The district received some exploration attention in the 1970s as a copper prospect, but no mining for copper was pursued.

Similar to many historic gold mining districts in the western United States, Summitville received renewed interest in the early 1980s due to technological advances that allow extraction of low-grade ores with cyanide heap leach techniques. In 1984, Summitville Consolidated Mining Company, Inc. (SCMCI), initiated open pit mining of gold ore from rocks surrounding the historic underground workings, where gold concentrations had been too low to be economic for the underground mining operations. Ore from the pit was crushed and placed on a heap leach pad overlying a protective liner. Cyanide solutions were sprinkled onto the heap and trickled down through the crushed ore, dissolving the gold. The processing solutions were then collected from the base of the heap leach pile, and the gold was chemically extracted from the solutions.

Environmental problems developed soon after the initiation of open-pit mining. Acidic, metal rich drainage into the Wightman Fork of the Alamosa River increased significantly from numerous sources on site, including the Reynolds adit and the Cropsy waste dump. Cyanide-bearing processing solutions began leaking into an underdrain system beneath the heap leach pad, where they then mixed with acid ground waters from the Cropsy waste dump. Cyanide solutions also leaked from transfer pipes directly into the Wightman Fork several times over the course of mining.

SCMCI had ceased active mining and had begun environmental remediation when it declared bankruptcy in December 1992 and abandoned the mine site. The bankruptcy created several immediate concerns. Earlier in 1992, the company had brought a water treatment plant on line to begin treating the estimated 150 to 200 million gallons of spent cyanide processing solutions remaining in the heap; however, treatment was proceeding so slowly relative to influx of snowmelt waters that the waters were in danger of overtopping a containment dike and flowing directly into the Wightman Fork. In addition, piping carrying the processing solutions to the treatment plant would have frozen within several hours, releasing cyanide solutions and stopping water treatment.

At the request of the State of Colorado, the U.S. Environmental Protection Agency (EPA) immediately took over the site under EPA Superfund Emergency Response authority and increased treatment of the heap leach solutions, thereby averting a catastrophic release of cyanide solutions from the heap. Summitville was added to the EPA National Priorities List in late May 1994. Ongoing remediation efforts include decommissioning of the heap leach pad, plugging of the Reynolds and Chandler adits, backfilling of the open pit with acid-generating mine waste material, and capping of the backfilled pit to prevent water inflow. The total cost of the cleanup has been estimated to be from US $100 million to $120 million.

The environmental problems at Summitville have been of particular concern due to the extensive downstream use of Alamosa River water for livestock, agricultural irrigation, and wildlife habitat. Increased acid and metal loadings from Summitville are suspected to have caused the 1990 disappearance of stocked fish from Terrace Reservoir and farm holding ponds along the Alamosa River. The Alamosa River is used extensively to irrigate crops in the southwestern San Luis Valley. Important crops include alfalfa (used for livestock feed), barley (used in beer production), wheat, and potatoes; there has been concern about potential adverse effects of the increased acid and metal loadings from Summitville on the metal content and viability of these crops. The Alamosa River also feeds wetlands that are habitat for aquatic life and migratory water fowl such as ducks and the endangered whooping crane; there are concerns about Summitville's effects on these wetlands and their associated wildlife.

- U.S. Department of the Interior | U.S. Geological Survey

1. What is the main idea of the passage?
   A. Open pit mining has disastrous effects.
   B. Open pit mining in Summitville has caused pending environmental hazards.
   C. There is a need for stricter controls and regulations governing open pit mining.
   D. Open pit mining typically affects the environment.

2. What is the author's purpose of the passage?
   A. To demonstrate and warn of the potential harmful effects left by Summitville mining to environment, particularly the Alamosa River
   B. To illustrate the environmental need for legislation for all open pit mining areas
   C. To demonstrate and suggest that similar efforts in other areas should follow the Summitville mining "cleanup" protocol and agenda
   D. To rally support for environmental groups and their political eco-green proposals and agenda

3. What evidence would MOST STRONGLY support the author's argument?
   A. Cyanide toxins can contaminate wetlands downstream in typical mining areas.
   B. The disappearance of certain species has been noted due to open pit mining.
   C. There are neither regulatory controls in place for monitoring of toxins nor clean-up planning in case of emergencies.
   D. Open pit mining threatens all life in as much as it threatens the general ecosystem of the area.

4. According to passage information, which of the following were NOT potentially affected by the runoff into the Alamosa River?
   I. Wildlife habitat
   II. Potable drinking water
   III. Livestock

   A. I and III
   B. II only
   C. III only
   D. II and III

5. What are the dominant kinds of evidence or support used by the author to strengthen his or her thesis?
   A. Real examples and statistics
   B. Hypothetical examples and statistics
   C. Expert testimony and current regulations
   D. Emotional appeals and green reasoning

Unit 2

Questions 6 - 11

Alfred Adler was a Viennese physician who founded Adlerian Psychology. He was the first in the fields of psychiatry and psychology to stress the importance of our perceptions and social relationships in affecting our emotional and physical health, as well as the health of our families and communities. The following passage discusses the main principles of Adlerian Psychology.

Adlerian Psychology holds that human beings are goal-oriented and choice-making by nature, not mechanistically victims of instinct, drives, and environment. As social beings, our basic goal is to belong. Although heredity and environment have strong influences, to a large extent, we make our own choices of how to belong.

Adlerian Psychology has a strong focus on prevention of mental disturbance and social distress through education and parenting. Much of Adler's work was with teachers and parents who wanted to replace traditional authoritarian styles of relating to children with more democratic—but not permissive—ways. One of Adlerian Psychology's claims to fame is the attribution to Adlerian Psychology of the concept that "separate is not equal" by an author of the social science brief for the US Supreme Court case on school desegregation. Today, many schools incorporate Adlerian-based approaches in teacher training and classroom work, and many parenting courses throughout the country are Adlerian-based.

Adler's concept of *Gemeinschaftsgefühl*, or a deep sense of fellowship in the human community and interconnectedness with all life, holds that human beings, as social beings, have a natural desire to contribute usefully for the good of humanity. According to Adler, a desire for social significance must focus on contribution, not on status-seeking, or one's social relationships and one's mental health will suffer.

Adlerian psychology is perhaps best known for the concept of the inferiority complex. Adler viewed some behaviour as overcompensation for perceived shortcomings. We sometimes make choices about how to belong on the basis of an often mistaken feeling of inferiority. Children, for example, sometimes seem to believe, mistakenly and not consciously, that they belong only when they are the centre of attention. Some adults act as if they believe, mistakenly, that they belong only when they can control others, or take revenge on others, or withdraw from others (and often such misperceptions developed in early childhood).

Both the inferiority complex and overcompensation indicated to Adler an exaggerated concern with self. This self-concern could be eased by nurturing one's innate abilities to cooperate and contribute through what Adler called the life tasks: work, intimacy, and friendship. Adlerian therapy helps to "liberate" clients by helping them move toward a clearer understanding of their unconscious, inferiority-based belief systems, or "lifestyles" and toward a clearer understanding of ways to incorporate cooperation and contribution and mutual respect in their relationships. Adlerians hope to let go of "private logic" and embrace dignity and respect in all relationships, thereby becoming emotionally and physically healthier and creating a more democratic culture.

- Adapted from Adlerian Psychology: An Overview (www.psasadler.org)

6. According to the passage, people's most important motive when interacting with others is to:
   A. make choices.
   B. perform tasks effectively.
   C. be accepted.
   D. overcome overcompensation.

7. Which of the following behaviours best exemplifies Adler's concept of *Gemeinschaftsgefühl?*
   A. A person going on a hunger strike in response to social injustice
   B. Running for political office to advance one's most important beliefs
   C. A teacher giving a lecture on social justice history to her students
   D. Ecological involvement with a local green group

8. It can be assumed from passage information that Adler's philosophies were in conflict with all of the following EXCEPT those of:
   A. Skinner, who argued that behaviour is determined by its consequence and will be repeated if it is positively reinforced.
   B. Freud, who argued that behaviour is shaped by drives and psychological features like the Oedipus complex.
   C. Maslow, who postulated that people have a hierarchy of needs ranging from basic survival to esteem and self-actualisation.
   D. Ayn Rand, who argued that people should consider their perceptions and logic the only true authority and their happiness the ultimate moral goal.

9. Based on passage information, one can ascertain that a person's mental health in Adlerian Psychology is primarily based on:
    A. overcompensation and inferiority complexes.
    B. innate abilities and the ability to achieve goals.
    C. fulfilment of instinctual desires.
    D. social outlook and interaction.

10. Based on passage information, what is typical of behaviour based on an inferiority complex?
    A. It displays an outsize need to impress others.
    B. It is self-deprecating and overly modest.
    C. It is designed to avoid attracting attention.
    D. It reveals the subject's paradoxical desire to prove their inferiority.

11. We might infer that according to Adler, ways to improve psychological health would include all of the following EXCEPT:
    A. undergoing psychotherapy to find out what false assumptions one is holding onto.
    B. undergoing testing to learn one's personality type to find a suitable job.
    C. practising productive ways to react when feelings of inferiority surface.
    D. finding ways to treat friends and loved ones with more respect.

Unit 3

Questions 12 - 16

In the natural sciences, enquiry is concerned with uncovering or discovering that which exists. "Invention" is not considered to be a feature of scientific enquiry and is perhaps not compatible with the dispassionate relationship with knowledge that scientists have traditionally claimed. Design, by contrast, claims invention (and personal ownership of it) as a central principle so it is difficult at first to see where the two traditions can overlap.

A central problem of science is how to recognise and define worthwhile subjects for investigation. For one thing, we may be faced with a myriad of opportunities and no means to decide which are going to be fruitful. On the other hand, our environment may limit our ability to recognise scientific problems and possibilities, especially the ones which could lead to significant changes in our understanding. To illustrate this second problem, philosophers have speculated on the science and culture of imaginary worlds which have fundamentally different and more restricted conditions than ours. If you and your environment consist of gases with no solid objects to reflect on, then you may not be able to conceive of geometry as we know it. If you lived in a 1- or 2-dimensional world you would have a very different set of concepts from us and, no doubt, people living in a 5-dimensional world would see us as conceptually impoverished in much the same way. Artists also engage with these issues, often in stimulating and accessible forms. For example, science fiction writers explore imaginary worlds which shape their civilisations in ways that may inform us about our own experience. Brian Aldiss described a world where each season lasted for many lifetimes, including a harsh winter which few people and institutions survived, effectively cutting people off from their history and most of the knowledge acquired during the previous summer. This fictional device provided a fresh perspective for the examination of individuals and societies confronted with difficult circumstances.

These abstracted questions have their parallels in everyday life and more mundane enquiries. Michael Polanyi describes the 'logical gap' between existing knowledge and any significant discovery or innovation. No matter how thorough our factual knowledge of the situation that we inhabit, the pursuit of logical reasoning or iterative development of existing concepts would not, on its own, allow us to cross this gap. There must be also some kind of leap of 'illumination' by which the scientist imagines a new concept and proposes it as a worthwhile subject for investigation. As Polanyi says, "Illumination....is the plunge by which we gain a foothold in another shore of reality. On such plunges, the scientist has to stake, bit by bit, his entire professional life."

Polanyi was concerned with what he called the "tacit dimension" in our knowledge. In particular, he wished to give proper value to the process of recognising, and making a commitment to, ideas or hypotheses, which may result from a rich understanding and knowledge but cannot be explained by explicit reasoning, in order to carry out the enquiry that will lead to them being more widely understood and accepted. I have used the term "accepted" rather than "proved" (itself shorthand for Karl Popper's concept of a falsifiable hypothesis that has proved so far to be reliable) because Polanyi held that all scientific knowledge is a question of "passionate belief" rather than dispassionate proof, requiring us to take account of the methods, competence, judgement and integrity of scientists, and the knowledge and principles that we already hold, before we accept the knowledge which they offer us. This seems much more reasonable today when more people appreciate the limitations of science than 50 years ago when Polanyi was developing his ideas.

12. The crux of the problem, which the author specifically focusses on is:
    A. developing protocol for what scientific endeavours are advisable to pursue.
    B. how scientific invention is related to discovery.
    C. the idea that scientific knowledge is a question of passionate belief.
    D. the idea that scientific knowledge is a question of dispassionate proof.

13. The relevance or significance of the passage, in relation to scientific invention and discovery, concerns:
    A. knowledge.
    B. criteria.
    C. instrumentation.
    D. measurement.

14. According to passage information, Polyani makes a distinction between tacit knowledge and what can be inferred as knowledge which is:
    A. socially constructed.
    B. hypothetically determined.
    C. explicit reasoning.
    D. deductively reasoned.

15. According to passage information, for Polyani, "illumination" is:
    I.   the key to invention and discovery in scientific endeavour.
    II. the bridge over the logical gap between theory and application.
    III. the connection between innovation and what is already known.

    A. I only   C. II and III
    B. II only   D. I and III

16. The author pursues the notion of which central problem that may limit our ability to recognise scientific problems and possibilities?
    A. Instrumentation designed to measure phenomena
    B. Knowledgeable processes involved in research
    C. Methodologies which are employed in measurement
    D. Environment or setting surrounding us

Unit 4

Questions 17 - 23

The politicisation of science is the manipulation of science for political gain. It occurs when government, business, or advocacy groups use legal or economic pressure to influence the findings of scientific research or the way it is disseminated, reported or interpreted. The politicisation of science may also negatively affect academic and scientific freedom. Historically, groups have conducted various campaigns to promote their interests in defiance of scientific consensus, and in an effort to manipulate public policy.

In August 2003, United States Democratic Congressman Henry A. Waxman and the staff of the Government Reform Committee released a report concluding that the administration of George W. Bush had politicised science and sex education. The report accuses the administration of modifying performance measures for abstinence-based programmes to make them look more effective. The report also found that the Bush administration had appointed Dr. Joseph McIlhaney, a prominent advocate of abstinence-only programme, to the Advisory Committee to the director of the Centre for Disease Control. According to the report, information about comprehensive sex education was removed from the CDC's website.

The Union of Concerned Scientists (UCS) also issued a report indicating that the Bush administration delayed for nine months an EPA report (eventually leaked) that indicated that 8 percent of women between the ages of 16 and 49 have blood mercury levels that could lead to reduced I.Q. and motor skills in their offspring. When new rules of mercury emissions were finally released by the EPA, at least 12 paragraphs were transferred, sometimes verbatim, from a legal document prepared by industry attorneys.

According to the Waxman Report, other issues considered for removal from government sponsored programmes included agricultural pollution, the Arctic National Wildlife Refuge and breast cancer; the report found that a National Cancer Institute website has been changed to reflect the administration view that there may be a risk of breast cancer associated with abortions. The website was updated after protests and now holds that no such risk has been found in recent, well-designed studies. In addition, proponents of "Intelligent Design" (ID) over "Evolution" have government-spearheaded efforts to be entered into the public schools and with success.

The overwhelming majority of the scientific community, which supports theories that are testable by experiment or observation, oppose treating ID, which is neither a scientific theory.

A 1999 report by the National Academy of Sciences states, "Creationism, intelligent design, and other claims of supernatural intervention in the origin of life or of species are not science because they are not testable by the methods of science." Public officials have supported public schools teaching intelligent design alongside evolution in science curricula.

In January 2007, the House Committee on Science and Technology announced the formation of a new subcommittee, the Science Subcommittee on Investigations and Oversight, which handles investigative and oversight activities on matters covering the committee's entire jurisdiction. The subcommittee has the authority to look into a whole range of important issues, particularly those concerning manipulation of scientific data at Federal agencies.

In an interview, subcommittee chairman Rep. Brad Miller pledged to "look into. . . scientific integrity issues under the Bush Administration. There have been lots of reports in the press of manipulating science to support policy, rigging advisory panels, and suppressing research by federal employees or with federal dollars. I've written about that here before, and you interviewed me a year ago about the manipulation of science. In addition to the published reports, the committee staff has been collecting accounts, some confidential, of interference by political appointees." Yet the promised reports were far from adequate (two educational reports) or not released completely to the public, quite possibly due to bipartisan politics and mutual scratch-back negotiations concerning other political agendas.

The issue is far from over. Patrick Michaels, as recently as April 2011, had written (CATO Institute), covering the climate change controversy, that "The conflation of political agendas with science is destroying the credibility of academia, with the complicity of the editors of our major scientific journals," noting a recent SCIENCE article which attempted to revive a 19th Century idea of "climatic determinism" - people do good things when things get warmer, bad things when cold – obviously, politically motivated.

17. What is the author's main argument in this passage?
    A. The Bush administration has been the worst offender in politicising science.
    B. Politicisation of science is common and a serious danger to evidence-based public policy.
    C. Accurate scientific information usually supports liberal policies, not conservative.
    D. It can be difficult to tell when a scientific claim by a politician or government agency is truthful.

18. "Abstinence-based programmes" (paragraph 2) refer to:
    A. information campaigns advocated by the people.
    B. ideological assumptions that promote reproductive choices.
    C. democratic agendas on preventing teen pregnancy.
    D. comprehensive sex education information campaigns.

19. Which of the following would count as a politicisation of science?
    A. Cherry-picking studies that suggest US nutrition guidelines are healthy and citing only those studies in a press release
    B. Using data from a new climate study to push for stricter environmental regulation
    C. Telling the public Iraq had weapons of mass destruction when it did not
    D. Conducting a study on the effects of welfare in an attempt to prove that more robust welfare programs benefit families

20. What of the following would the author likely NOT support to prevent the politicisation of science?
    A. Neutral oversight boards scrutinising the scientific claims of government agencies and political parties
    B. Less emphasis on science as a basis for political decisions
    C. Decisions about what to include in science curricula being based on the consensus among practising scientists
    D. New regulations that do not allow scientific reports from government agencies to be delayed or withheld from the public

21. The quoted statement by Rep. Brad Miller in paragraph 7 suggests that the passage author thinks it was:
    A. mendacious.
    B. unreliable.
    C. falsely-advertised.
    D. politically-motivated.

22. Which of the following does the author NOT state is a problem with intelligent design?
    A. The people promoting it have a political agenda.
    B. It cannot be proven true or false through scientific experiment.
    C. It is not supported as a valid theory by practising scientists.
    D. It is controversial and offends many people.

23. What does the passage imply to be a likely reason that reports by the Science Subcommittee on Investigations and Oversight were not fully released to the public?
    A. Politicians conspired to suppress reports containing information that was not flattering to anyone.
    B. No one understood the importance of the reports, so they were ignored.
    C. Democrats had little power during that time period and could not force Republicans to release them.
    D. Selected reports were concealed in exchange for political favours.

Unit 5

Questions 24 - 28

It has become more and more common to link together the once disparate concepts of biology and morality. One such way of doing this, which some sociobiologists have advocated, is by introducing the idea of "epigenetic rules". Epigenetic rules mean something like the following: there are certain genetically based processes that are realised in chemically and structurally similar ways in all (or most) humans. For example, there are specific patterns of neurotransmitters and organisational features of fibres and brain tissue that develop in more or less the same fashion in all humans, and this development is somehow regulated, though not determined, by our genes. By influencing and shaping the physical and consequently cognitive processes of the brain, genes affect, but do not determine, the range of possibilities humans possess. Epigenetic rules, then, are the sorts of processes that both constrain and predispose humans to behave and think within a certain range of options. Often cited as examples are certain phobias that transcend cultural boundaries; people tend to fear the dark, high places, snakes, etc.

These epigenetic constraints and dispositions are not limited to simple behaviours and perceptions, but also to our moral sense; epigenetic rules provide a boundary for what humans consider moral. For example, epigenetic rules may predispose us to consider altruism a virtue, since there is an evolutionary advantage (or so some geneticists claim) for altruism; from a genetic point of view, altruistic acts often involve sacrificing the genes of one organism for the furthering of the gene pool of the entire population.

While this is unquestionably a provocative perspective, there are many points with which to take issue. It first seems that this thesis runs the risk of claiming that any common behaviour that transcends cultures and time periods may now be easily attributable to epigenetic rules. As one opponent of this view proposed, there are certain truths about humans, such as 'all humans have a tendency to throw spears pointy-end first'. This behaviour is observed in most cultures ('spears' can be replaced with 'pointy-edged object'), yet it is not at all clear that such behaviour is evidence that humans are genetically predisposed toward this. Rather, it seems that given a certain amount of intelligence and interaction with our environment, many different cultures will reach similar conclusions about which end of a spear proves the most effective. At the least, it is a very open question why humans exhibit similar behaviour patterns. In some cases our intuitions side more with genetics, in others, such as the example above, it seems that other factors are at work.

Further, merely knowing that a particular moral inclination has a genetic basis does not indicate how wrong it is to kill innocent people, so even if it could be shown that this sentiment has a genetic basis, it is possible to override or at least temper it. To put it more generally, just because morality has a basis in our genes (if it in fact does), it does not follow that we should look to our genes to generate, or even help out with, a theory of morality. As the philosopher Friedrich Nietzsche pointed out, explaining the origin of something like morality does not explain why it is successful, nor does the origin necessarily hold the key to explaining or furthering or even affecting its success.

24. The central point of the passage is that:
     A. epigenetic rules exist, it is just a matter of carefully researching their content.
     B. epigenetic rules may exist, but sociobiologists have been too hasty in claiming that they do.
     C. epigenetic rules probably exist, but sociobiologists should focus on different behaviours to determine the content of the rules.
     D. epigenetic rules do not exist.

25. The author's statement, "epigenetic rules may predispose us to consider altruism a virtue, since there is an evolutionary advantage to altruism" (paragraph 2) assumes that:
     A. epigenetic rules favour evolutionary advantages.
     B. epigenetic rules are themselves evolutionary advantages.
     C. altruism is an evolutionary advantage.
     D. what was considered an evolutionary advantage in the past may not be considered to be one currently.

26. Based on the information in the last paragraph, the author would most likely agree with which of the following statements?
    A. The fields of science and morality should remain separate.
    B. The fact that most humans do not condone killing innocent people indicates the existence of epigenetic rules.
    C. Genetic discoveries should not be strongly relied on to provide solutions to moral dilemmas.
    D. Until research has unquestionably proven that there are relevant connections, we should not look to science to provide answers to moral dilemmas.

27. Which of the following is a claim made by the author but NOT supported in the passage by evidence, explanation, or example?
    A. Epigenetic rules transcend cultural and historical boundaries.
    B. Epigenetic rules influence conceptions of morality.
    C. Not all similarities between humans have a genetic basis.
    D. Explaining the origin of something does not explain why it is successful.

28. A recent study suggests that people living in rural areas fear snakes much more than gunshots while people living in urban areas fear gunshots more than snakes. These findings:
    A. support the author's views.
    B. support the sociobiologists' views.
    C. indicate that neither is correct.
    D. indicate that both are correct.

Unit 6

Questions 29 - 34

An "ethics of science" refers to ethical problems involved with scientific research, discoveries, and inventions. In scientific research and invention, experiments on humans, invention of biological weapons, etc., are scientific issues that assume ethical importance. In the field of medicine, ethical problems are associated with issues such as medical research, genetic manipulation, abortion, and euthanasia. In the field of environmental concerns, environmental ethics assumes an important place, as well.

The general issues that give rise to ethical questions concern scientific research and invention. In 1964, an experiment was carried out by the American psychologist Stanley Milgram that involved fooling people into thinking they were inflicting increasingly severe electric shocks on unseen but protesting victims. This experiment raised the ethical issue of whether it was morally right for a scientist to encourage people to inflict pain on others for experimental purposes. The issue of the invention of biological weapons that could affect civilians is an ethical one in the sense that it concerns the rightness or wrongness of harming civilians in war. The whole issue revolves around the concept of crime against humanity. One other issue related also to medicine is the issue of cloning, in which humans prescribe the genes of clones. How would a cloned child see his individuality after knowing that he was a clone? Wouldn't he feel his individuality as forever compromised? What if things go awry in the cloning process? Would that constitute a crime against a human? Who would be held responsible if things go awry?

Medical ethics is the study of moral standards in relation to the field of medicine. The ultimate issues underlying medical ethics are issues such as the definition of life and the value of life that are seen in the perspective of ethical theories regarding what differentiates good acts and principles from evil. Two of the problems, viz., medical research and embryo research will be discussed here. Research in medicine has the objective of alleviating human pain. However, this requires a study of how the human body works and what new drugs could be safely used to alleviate human pain. Things like experiments with embryos and test of drugs on humans assume ethical character when considering issues such as the value of life and the moral aim of medicine. For instance, during the 1980s there was a widespread debate about the ethics of research using human embryos. In such research, the embryos used were destroyed after 14 days from fertilisation. The argument that ended the debate in the UK leading to the legitimising of such research, up to the 14-day limit, was that a pre-14-day embryo was not in a state to be treated as an individual person since its cells were not differentiated to fulfil specific functions along with the possibility that the embryo was still in a condition to split into two identical twins. The 14-day limit assumed that since the nervous system begins to develop at about the 15th day from fertilisation, there was nothing ethically wrong with destroying it on the 14th day since the embryo doesn't know that it is a person. This also justifies abortion before the 14th day and provides a kind of ethical basis for research in human cloning.

The several assumptions behind the legalising of embryo research are that ethics is related to persons and not to potential persons, that personality is a matter of the nervous system and not the organism housing such a system, that humans are not accountable to anyone other than humans for what they do with any phenomenon of life; in other words, since God or some absolute judicial system doesn't exist, humans can decide what is to be done with humans. Such assumptions, however, cannot be accepted as axiomatic; they are philosophical issues, of course, but also crucial as pertaining to human life itself. In their ultimate development, such issues are settled according to the religious or anti-religious mindset of the political or judicial system in which the issues are raised.

29. According to the author, what was considered unethical about the Milgram experiment?
 A. Some of the subjects suffered physically because they suffered from electric shocks.
 B. The experimenters encouraged the subjects to behave cruelly by inflicting what they believed were electric shocks.
 C. Some of the subjects suffered fear because they believed they were going to be shocked.
 D. The experimenters were dishonest because they told the subjects beforehand that the electrical shocks were not real.

30. What would constitute a possible argument AGAINST anti-cloning arguments?
 A. The process is so fascinating on a scientific level that the pros outweigh the cons.
 B. Only a small number of people would have to be cloned to evaluate its effect on them.
 C. Twins and triplets have duplicate DNA, yet they do not suffer identity crises.
 D. Cloning is no different from other ways of scientifically creating life such as test tube babies.

31. What is the main idea the passage?
 A. An ethics of science concerns different disciplines and fields.
 B. Scientific ethics, particularly in the medical field, are marked by controversy.
 C. The ethics of science is a philosophical, not scientific, issue.
 D. Ethical questions basically concern research and invention.

32. What is a possible rationale for experimenting on embryos only before the 14-day limit?
 A. Because they cannot feel pain, they cannot be harmed.
 B. Because they do not have specific human organs, they are potential rather than actual humans.
 C. Because they do not have a personality and free will, they have no legitimate interest in life.
 D. Because they are not yet viable outside the womb, they are not autonomous human beings.

33. What does the term "axiomatic" (last paragraph) mean?
    A. Biased
    B. Redundant
    C. Needing further elaboration
    D. Taken for granted

34. In the second paragraph, the author uses rhetorical questions to emphasise cloning's ethical issues. How does this BEST function in terms of providing evidence?
    A. It lets the reader know that the questions are essentially unsolved.
    B. The questions propel the reader to contemplate certain issues and think about how ethical questions affect them.
    C. It stimulates the reader's emotions by showing that scientists are often shockingly unethical.
    D. The examples given have similar solutions suggesting that the author's preferred ethical philosophy is correct.

Unit 7

Questions 35 - 40

Some would argue that with capitalism came the notion that society is best understood as the autonomous actions of individuals. This idea has its biological correlate in Darwin's theory of natural selection where evolution takes place at the level of the reproduction of individuals in a species. In science, in general, we find it in the reductionist assumption that the whole is best understood in terms of its parts, and the more minute the level one goes to, the better the explanation.

This way of conceptualising the world also has the effect of breaking up the world into autonomous domains: internal and external. Views of causation are also affected in that causes become referred to as either internal or external. Internal factors (genes) cause organisms to be the way they are and the external environment causes some organisms to be selected for and thereby to survive into the next generation.

One might assert that this is the way in which biology has been conceived since Darwin, and that it is a terribly impoverished way of viewing biology, and that our understanding of nature would be richer if we moved away from our reductionist tendencies and instead recognised the complex interaction of the organism with the environment it creates. We would

GAMSAT-Prep.com
THE GOLD STANDARD

also be more effective in solving our problems if we moved away from the tendency to focus merely on the proximal physiological causes of disease, for example, focusing on the bacteria or viruses associated with disease instead of social factors.

These proposals to avoid pure reductionism and to take into account causes other than physiological ones are well founded. But by implying that the traditional focus on physiological causes is merely an intricate way of masking the social cause behind the disease, one ignores the more innocuous motivations for picking physiological causes before social ones.

First, it must be said that no legitimate medical scientist or physician would claim that there is merely one cause - the cause - for nearly any disease. When it is said in science textbooks that something is the cause of something else what is really being said is something is the proximal physiological cause of something else. It is proximal because it is the nearer to the effect (disease process) and physiological because it itself is some biological or chemical agent (i.e. not a social agent). People may be troubled by western medicine's overemphasis of these causes as opposed to social ones. However, there seem to be very good, socially unproblematic reasons for often choosing to put the emphasis on the proximal physiological causes of disease.

Second, there is a logical reason. Consider bacteria and viruses. Wherever there is tuberculosis there is tubercle bacillus bacteria. The bacteria are a necessary condition for someone having the disease. The same cannot be said of sweat shops or unregulated, industrialised capitalism. In fact, individuals in the upper class and rural areas, as well as individuals in nonindustrial Marxist countries have also become infected by tubercle bacillus bacteria and come down with tuberculosis. This is not to say that for something to be labelled a cause of disease it must be a necessary condition, but the logical relationship of necessity helps us understand the claim that something is the cause of something else.

In addition, giving a necessary condition of disease does not limit one to saying that the cause of disease must be a proximal physiological one. Chewing tobacco releases toxic chemicals, which may be the cause of a specific form of gum disease in the chewer. Wherever this form of gum disease is found so is a user of chewing tobacco. In this case, it would seem perfectly appropriate to say that chewing tobacco is a cause of the disease, although not the proximal physiological one.

Finally, a reformed orientation toward science and medicine will yield a more fruitful way of doing investigations. Short-sighted causal explanation allows for the social structure to go unexamined for its deleterious effects on the community, but physiological explanations are important in determining the cause and potential solutions, both physiological and social.

35. What does the author mean by "capitalism . . . has its biological correlate in Darwin's theory of evolution"?
   A. Both focus on complex relationships between groups of organisms and their surroundings.
   B. Both are of the opinion that the more detailed level one goes to, the better the explanation.
   C. Both hold a 'survival of the fittest' framework, e.g., the most successful organism will survive and reproduce.
   D. Both hold the view that explanations are most effective when looking at individual entities.

36. Based on paragraph 3, it appears that reductionist accounts of causation typically focus on which of the following causes?
   A. Social causes, because they are directly related to effects
   B. Physiological causes, more assignable to effects, in general
   C. Both social and physiological causes as simultaneous causes
   D. Either; the point is that reductionist accounts attempt to break down general causes into more specific ones

37. Based on the passage, an assumption made by those who argue against physiological accounts of causation is that:
   A. physiological accounts of causation tend to disregard the potential existence of harmful social agents.
   B. physiological accounts of causation are often incorrect by neglecting the social causes.
   C. social accounts of causation can replace physiological accounts of causation.
   D. explanations can be reductionist without being physiological.

38. The author mentions individuals in non-industrialised Marxist countries to make which of the following points?
   A. Post-industrial capitalism is not a necessary precondition for tuberculosis.
   B. Regardless of one's location, tubercle bacillus bacteria is the actual cause of tuberculosis.
   C. Living in an industrialised capitalist country is not a cause of tuberculosis.
   D. The best causal explanations are those which specify necessary conditions.

39. The central point of the passage is that:
   A. while the social accounts of causation are important, the physiological level provides better causal explanations.
   B. though some are suspicious, there are good reasons for including physiological accounts of causation along with social accounts of causation.
   C. people arguing against reductionist accounts of causation will most likely endorse the social accounts of causation.
   D. people arguing against physiological accounts of causation do not realise their importance.

40. Which of the following is NOT mentioned in the passage as a reason why proximal physiological explanations of causation are as desirable as social ones?
   A. They generally share more in an important logical relationship.
   B. They are important in determining both causes and potential solutions.
   C. They are, in some cases, necessary preconditions for a particular disease.
   D. They are more effective in getting at the actual cause of a disease than social explanations of causation.

If time remains, you may review your work. If your allotted time (50 minutes) is complete, please proceed to the Answer Key.

3.8.4 Verbal Reasoning Exercise 2 (Science-based Passages) Answer Key and Explanations

1.	B	9.	D	17.	B	25.	A	33.	D
2.	B	10.	A	18.	D	26.	C	34.	B
3.	A	11.	B	19.	A	27.	D	35.	D
4.	B	12.	A	20.	B	28.	A	36.	B
5.	A	13.	B	21.	B	29.	B	37.	A
6.	C	14.	C	22.	D	30.	C	38.	A
7.	D	15.	D	23.	D	31.	B	39.	B
8.	C	16.	D	24.	B	32.	B	40.	D

1. **Correct Answer: B**
(A), (C), and (D) are all too general and lack the specific focus of the passage, which is adequately expressed in (B).

2. **Correct Answer: B**
(A) and (D), similar to the preceding question are too general. (C) is a statement of policy - marked by the word "should" and a call to action, which is never addressed within the passage. This leaves (B), which possesses the specificity of "purpose" and reflects the passage information, as the best option.

3. **Correct Answer: A**
(D) is too encompassing and not really addressed adequately within the passage. (C) may or may not be true but also never addressed adequately within the passage, except for brief references to clean-up acts. (B) assumes a causal link not adequately established within the passage - there may be other factors involved. The statement needs more support within the passage to qualify as the best answer. (A) is specific enough to qualify as the best choice option in terms of significance and relevance, i.e. one can assume that cyanide toxins will have an "effect" on wildlife within a wetland. This would also be encompassing of the probability or possibility of (B).

4. **Correct Answer: B**
II is never mentioned within the passage while a rescan will confirm that I and III are addressed.

5. **Correct Answer: A**
(D) can quickly be ruled out due to the phrase "green reasoning," which is essentially meaningless. (B) can be ruled out, for there is little evidence which follows a hypothetical line of thought, such as "If this were to happen . . ." or "suppose that . . . then this would follow". (C) can be ruled out because there is no testimony used as support within the passage, such as "noted biologist Dr. Smith" or "the U.S. Geological Survey states that. . ." This leaves (A) as the correct answer, and both examples are used within the passage to support the main idea or thesis.

6. Correct Answer: C

This question is answered in paragraph 1: "As social beings, our basic goal is to belong."

(A) Although the passage states that Adlerian Psychology considers people to be choice-making by nature, this is not the most importantmotive in human interactions.

(B) This is not discussed in the passage.

(D) The passage suggests this should be a goal for many people but not that it is everyone's most basic goal.

7. Correct Answer: D

This question asks you to understand the author's definition of a term. Paragraph 3 tells us that the concept involves social involvement and a deep sense of belonging, so the option that involves working with others as equals is the best fit.

(A) Since this choice involves a person acting as an individual and not as a group, it is not the best example.

(B) Since *Gemeinschaftsgefühl* does not involve status-seeking, this is not the best choice.

(C) This choice involves a hierarchical relationship, which may not be conducive to a "deep sense of fellowship".

8. Correct Answer: C

This question compares different philosophies. Maslow's ideas emphasise the need for psychological health and overall self-esteem, making it compatible with Adler's interest in the need to avoid feeling inferior.

(A) This choice reduces human behaviour to instinct and impulses.

(B) This contradicts Adlerian psychology, which "holds that human beings are goal-oriented and choice-making by nature, not mechanistically victims of instinct, drives, and environment."

(D) This theory would be in conflict with Adler's beliefs against status-seeking and in favour of community involvement.

9. Correct Answer: D

This question asks you what would produce happiness according to Adler's theories. We are told that Adler was the first in the fields of psychiatry and psychology to note the importance of our perceptions and social relationships to our own emotional and physical health and to the health of our families and communities.

(A) The passage implies that this is a large factor in unhappiness but not that it is the greatest factor in mental health.

(B) The passage states that Adler's theories were based on humans making choices, not on innate qualities.

(C) According to Adler, people are not "mechanistically victims of instinct, drives, and environment".

10. Correct Answer: A

The answer to this question is answered in paragraph 4: "Adler viewed some behaviour as overcompensation for perceived shortcomings... Some adults act as if they believe, mistakenly, that they belong only when they can control others." This makes (A) the correct answer.

(B) This is the opposite of the best answer choice.

(C) This is not stated in the text.

(D) This is also not supported in the passage.

11. Correct Answer: B

This question asks you to think about solutions for the problems that interest Adler. The passage never mentions Adler as having an interest in different personality types or as focussed on work. The best choice is thus (B).

(A) The passage states, "Adlerian therapy helps to 'liberate' clients by helping them move toward a clearer understanding of their unconscious, inferiority-based belief systems."

(C) The passage points out the importance of "nurturing one's innate abilities to cooperate and contribute through what Adler called the life tasks: work, intimacy, and friendship". Hence, adopting productive ways to develop "one's innate abilities to cooperate and contribute" in order to deal with one's inferiority feelings wouldbe something that will interest Adler. This also includes (D) nurturing relationships with friends and loved ones.

12. **Correct Answer: A**

All answers (B) (C) and (D) are not "problems" per se, but theoretical issues - worth pursuing in their own terms, but not related to the question. (A) can be inferred to be the "crux" of the problem, indicated by the following passage information: "A central problem of science is how to recognise and define worthwhile subjects for investigation. For one thing, we may be faced with a myriad of opportunities and no means to decide which are going to be fruitful. On the other hand, our environment may limit our ability to recognise scientific problems and possibilities, especially the ones which could lead to significant changes in our understanding."

13. **Correct Answer: B**

(C) and (D) represent technological and/or verifiability issues in relation to theory, as such both answers can be deduced to be incorrect. (A) knowledge is too broad a subject to be warranted as the correct answer. One can infer (B) criteria - the means by which the two are assessed, to be the best choice option.

14. **Correct Answer: C**

This detail-oriented question can be answered as (C) from the following passage information: "Polanyi was concerned with what he called the "tacit dimension" in our knowledge. In particular he wished to give proper value to the process of recognising, and making a commitment to, ideas

or hypotheses, which may result from a rich understanding and knowledge but cannot be explained by explicit reasoning, in order to carry out the enquiry that will lead to them being more widely understood and accepted."

15. **Correct Answer: D**

Only I and III can be inferred to be correct in this detail-oriented question, these concepts are within the passage, particularly the discussion in paragraph 3.

16. **Correct Answer: D**

This is one of the main ideas (the second problem) of paragraph 2 and illustrated and expanded upon in paragraphs 3 and 4.

17. **Correct Answer: B**

This question requires candidates to find the main idea of the article. The author begins by defining politicisation of science, gives a number of examples in which the Bush administration and others misled the public about significant scientific issues, and concludes that "The issue is far from over." Thus the main point is that (B) this problem is widespread and causes harm.

(A) The author gives multiple examples involving the Bush administration but this may be because they are the most recent at the time of writing, not because the author believes they are the worst.

(C) The author cites examples of conservative-led politicisation but never argues that accurate science typically supports liberal ideas.

(D)The passage suggests that people are sometimes misled by these claims, but this is not the main point.

18. **Correct Answer: D**

This question requires understanding the contextual meaning of a term used in the passage. This is a comprehension type of question that ACER includes in several passages of their full-length practice exams (the Green and Purple e-books). To determine the correct answer, you need to consider the context of the paragraph or line (specified in the question) in which the term is used. Here, "abstinence-based programmes" is mentioned in the paragraph(paragraph 2) where the author discusses issues involving the politicisation of science and sex education during the Bush administration. The paragraph connects the term with the removal of "information about comprehensive sex education. . . from the CDC's website". This makes (D) the most relevant option.

(A) This context is not discussed in the paragraph.

(B) and (C) would require some extent of outside knowledge about the abstinence-based programme of the Bush administration. This is a knowledge skill that ACER will not test a candidate in the real exam.

19. Correct Answer: A

This question tests your understanding of the author's definition of a term and applying that contextual comprehension to hypothetical scenarios. The passage states: "The politicisation of science is the manipulation of science for political gain. It occurs when government, business, or advocacy groups use legal or economic pressure to influence the findings of scientific research or the way it is disseminated, reported or interpreted." In the given example in option (A), scientific findings are misrepresented in order to support a favoured idea. (A) is the best answer.

(B) Using scientific results to try to influence policy, as in this example, is not what the author means by "politicisation of science".

(C) This is an example of misleading the public, but the issue does not involve science.

(D) Conducting research with a goal in mind is not politicisation, according to the author, as long as the study is conducted and reported properly.

20. Correct Answer: B

This question asks you to seek out statements about the causes and enabling factors of politicisation. The author never suggests that basing political decisions on science is inherently bad but implies that the public should know the real scientific facts.

(A) The author writes approvingly of one such board: "the House Committee on Science and Technology announced the formation of a new subcommittee, the Science Subcommittee on Investigations and Oversight, which handles investigative and oversight activities on matters covering the committee's entire jurisdiction."

(C) This is implied in the discussion of Intelligent Design in paragraph 5: "The overwhelming majority of the scientific community, which supports theories that are testable by experiment or observation, oppose treating ID, which is neither, a scientific theory."

(D) This is implied in the discussion of paragraph 7 of reports being "not released completely to the public, quite possibly due to bipartisan politics."

21. Correct Answer: B

This is another type of question that ACER similarly introduces in their practice e-books in order to assess a candidate's ability to logically deduce the tone or attitude demonstrated in the text. In this particular question, it is crucial to take into account the relevant information provided in the paragraph where Rep. Miller's statement was quoted. In paragraph 7, the author states, "Yet the promised reports were far from adequate (two educational reports) or not released completely to the public, quite possibly due to bipartisan politics and mutual scratch-back negotiations concerning other political agendas." Although the passage author assumes Rep. Miller did not fully deliver what he promised due to politics, there is no evidence stating that Rep. Miller's previous statement was

(D) politically-motivated.

(A) The author is simply saying that "the promised reports were far from adequate... or not released completely to the public". HenceRep. Miller cannot be inferred to have been lying.

(C) The statement released by Rep. Miller was not part of an advertising.

This leaves (B) as the best answer choice.

22. **Correct Answer: D**

This question asks you to understand why a particular example of politicisation is considered troubling by the author. The discussion of ID states: "In addition, proponents of 'Intelligent Design' (ID) over 'Evolution' have government-spearheaded efforts to be entered into the public schools and with success. The overwhelming majority of the scientific community, which supports theories that are testable by experiment or observation, oppose treating ID, which is neither a scientific theory." The passage never suggests that simply being controversial is a reason to reject an idea since accurate scientific ideas could also offend people. The correct answer is (D).

(A) The passage gives ID as an example of an idea promoted by a group with a religious message.

(B)This is stated in the claim that "The overwhelming majority of the scientific community, which supports theories that are testable by experiment or observation, oppose treating ID, which is neither a scientific theory."

(C) This is also stated in the passage.

23. **Correct Answer: D**

This question asks you to seek out and make sense of specific information. The passage states that "the promised reports were far from adequate (two educational reports) or not released completely to the public, quite possibly due to bipartisan politics and mutual scratch-back negotiations concerning other

political agendas." Thus it is possible that the political favours were traded to suppress certain information.

(A) The passage never states that the reports were unflattering to anyone.

(B)The passage implies that those concerned did understand their significance.

(C)The reference to mutual back-scratch negotiations suggests that the two US political parties had some power. Also, this answer choice makes specific reference to Republicans and Democrats, which are not the focus of the passage.

24. **Correct Answer: B**

Options (A) and (D) cannot be correct because epigenetic rules are debated throughout the passage without a conclusion on their existence. Answer choice (C) is wrong because it is not the main idea of the passage to "focus on different behaviours to determine the content of the rules"; rather, the passage mentions specific behaviours to question the concept of such rules in the first place.

While the passage does not mention that the sociobiologists are hasty, the entire passage implies that the notion of epigenetics has been embraced even if there is, as yet, no evidence that it does. Epigenetics is simply an inference that sociobiologists have made since there are several behaviours that are common to most humans.

The passage begins with a premise: genes determine how our brains and neurotransmitters develop. Therefore, according to the socio-biologists, there are common behaviours among humans (fear of the dark, for example). The sociobiologists then jump to include 'morality' in the common behaviours (altruism, for example). From this, the sociobiologists argue that our genes determine our morality. This is a very wide jump from one point to another - it is too sweeping a generalisation. These all mean that the claim was made even before there is evidence for it. That is why it is 'hasty'. Option (B), which is the correct answer, is also found in the second sentence of paragraph 1.

25.   Correct Answer: A

Option (C) is true, but that is not the point being made by the author. Option (D) is an opinion, which is not part of the quote. Option (B) cannot be confirmed. This leaves (A) as the best option.

26.   Correct Answer: C

In the final paragraph, the author never objects to the linkage between science and morality. He seems to be suspicious at the linkage and then he objects strongly about using genes as a source of a theory of morality. However, he does not say that the genes, which may be linked, should not be sought.

On the other hand, consider the validity of the following statement given the author's assertions: "Genetic discoveries should not be strongly relied on to provide solutions to moral dilemmas." That makes (C) the best answer.

27.   Correct Answer: D

Option (D) expresses an idea of Friedrich Nietzsche, which is used in paragraph 4, to extend the author's view that merely knowing the genetic basis of something (or having its origin based on genetics) does not necessarily make the theories on genetics entirely true. This statement in option (D) only extends the main idea of the paragraph, but it is neither supported by an example nor does it serve as an illustration of the author's claim.

(A) This option is supported by the author's discussion in paragraph 1, in which examples of certain phobias are cited. Hence, this is a claim that was supported by examples in the passage.

(B) The claim stated in this option explained in paragraph 2's discussion about altruism. Again, this is a claim that was supported in the passage.

(C) This is a counterclaim cited by the author

in paragraph 3. Those who disagree with the theory of "epigenetic rules" highlighted the example of our tendency "to throw spears pointy-end first" as being dictated by human intellect and logic as opposed to being simply a genetic tendency. This counterclaim is, therefore, supported by an illustration in the passage.

28.   Correct Answer: A

This question requires differentiating the argument of the author from those of the sources or references cited in his or her article.

The author presents the sociobiologist perspective in the first 2 paragraphs (epigenetic rules, behaviour has a basis in our genes) and then in Paragraph 3, he begins to make his case for environment/experience being understated by epigenetic rules.

If, in the question, it stated that everyone in the world has a near equal fear of snakes, that would support the idea of a human gene (or genes) being responsible for behaviour. However, the question suggests that where you live has an impact on what you fear which is more in line with the (A) author's perspective.

29.   Correct Answer: B

This question asks you to carefully read an explanation of an experiment. Paragraph 2 states: "This experiment raised the ethical issue of whether it was morally right for a scientist to encourage people to inflict pain on others for experimental purposes." This suggests that the subjects' actions were unethical because they believed they were doing something cruel even though it was not real and thus the experimenters acted unethically in asking them to do it. This aligns with option (B).

(A) The passage states that there were no actual electric shocks.

(C) Since the passage states that the experimental subjects were fooled, we can guess that the "protesting victims" may have been in on the scheme from the start.

(D) Since the shocks were not real, this would not have been dishonest.

30. Correct Answer: C

This question calls for an understanding of the anti-cloning arguments the passage author presents. Paragraph 2 asks, "How would a cloned child see his individuality after knowing that he was a clone? Wouldn't he feel his individuality as forever compromised?" Since both clones and twins are people who share DNA with someone else, the existence of twins who are content with their identity suggests that this is not necessarily a source of angst.

(A) The passage overall suggests that science must always conform to ethical principles even if it is otherwise beneficial.

(B) The passage suggests that causing suffering to even one person would violate medical ethics.

(D) The passage suggests that cloning is fundamentally different because it duplicates an identity.

31. Correct Answer: B

The passage begins by defining an ethics of science, continues by discussing the type of issues that cause ethical debate, gives examples and concludes that they will be difficult to resolve. Thus the main point is that (B) scientific and medical ethics are contentious.

(A) This is true but a trivial point, not the author's main argument.

(C) The author never suggests that ethics be confined to just philosophical or just medical discussion.

(D) This is not stated in the passage.

32. Correct Answer: B

The answer to this question can be found in paragraph 3: "The argument that ended the debate in the UK leading to the legitimising of such research, up to the 14-day limit, was that

a pre-14 day embryo was not in a state to be treated as an individual person since its cells were not differentiated to fulfil specific functions along with the possibility that the embryo was still in a condition to split into two identical twins." Thus (B) the lack of certain basic physiological traits separates these embryos from human beings.

(A) The passage never mentions pain.

(C) The passage does not discuss personality and free will.

(D) This is irrelevant since embryos much older than 14 days are also not viable outside the womb.

33. Correct Answer: D

This type of vocabulary question is common in ACER practice exams. Answering this question requires a reading comprehension skill called contextual reading as discussed in RHSS 3.2.2. Hence, you can answer this question by logically guessing from the context of the last paragraph: "Such assumptions, however, cannot be accepted as axiomatic; they are philosophical issues, of course, but also crucial as pertaining to human life itself." The author is saying they cannot be assumed without debate and reasoning, so (D) "taken for granted" works well.

(A) and (B) are irrelevant to the context of the sentence.

(C) The author is saying that they DO need further elaboration.

34. Correct Answer: B

This question asks you to think about a type of rhetorical device in the passage and its overall effects. Examples include:

- "How would a cloned child see his individuality after knowing that he was a clone?"

- "Wouldn't he feel his individuality as forever compromised?"

- "What if things go awry in the cloning process?"
- "Would that constitute a crime against a human?"
- "Who would be held responsible if things go awry?"

The profusion of questions implies both that there are more of them than people may realise and that using this technology is more difficult than it may seem (for instance, since something could go awry). (B) The reader is prompted to think about the questions and realise that they are difficult to answer.

(A) The passage aims not just to state which questions are unsolved but to make the reader think about why they are unsolved.

(C) Many of the examples do not portray scientists as unethical, so this is not the main point.

(D) The author suggests that these questions do not have easy answers - not that the ethical philosophy behind them is correct.

35. Correct Answer: D

The answer to the question can be deduced from the following: "This idea has its biological correlate in Darwin's theory of natural selection where evolution takes place at the level of the reproduction of individuals in a species."

Option (B) gives the definition of reductionist thinking but it does not state what capitalism and Darwinism have in common - which is, (D) both go down to the level of the individuals.

36. Correct Answer: B

The answer to the question can be deduced from the following:

"We would also be more effective in solving our problems if we moved away from the tendency to focus merely on the proximal physiological causes of disease, for example, focusing on the bacteria or viruses associated with disease instead of social factors."

37. Correct Answer: A

The answer to this question is briefly implied in the last paragraph of the passage: "Short-sighted causal explanation allows for the social structure to go unexamined for its deleterious effects on the community. . ." This makes (B) somewhat inaccurate. At the most, the author would simply consider that focusing on physiological causes alone is "a terribly impoverished way of viewing biology," but not entirely incorrect. After all, "physiological explanations are important in determining the cause and potential solutions."

(C) is out scope.

(D) can be a tempting option. However, this statement would imply that even explanations within a social context is reductionist as well.

38. Correct Answer: A

This is a question of why and then an example is used. The answer to this question can be found in paragraph 6:

"In fact, individuals in the upper class and rural areas, as well as individuals in nonindustrial Marxist countries have also become infected by tubercle bacillus bacteria and come down with tuberculosis. This is not to say that for something to be labeled a cause of disease it must be a necessary condition, but the logical relationship of necessity helps us understand the claim that something is the cause of something else."

(A) is why industrialisation is mentioned at all - to illustrate how it is not required. This is the correct answer.

(B) would be mistakenly selected if one does not get the point of the author.

(C) is the opposite of the point being made.

(D) is a vague and irrelevant choice that could be tempting.

39. Correct Answer: B

Option (C) is found in paragraph 4. It is a true statement, but it is not the main argument of the passage. (D) is slightly discussed in paragraph

5 but it is not a valid argument. (A) is also wrong because the whole passage talks about both social and physiological accounts; not about how one is better than another. This leaves (B) as the correct answer.

The central point of the passage can be followed this way: First, it explains what it means when we say that something causes disease. The passage asserts that when doctors say that a bacteria causes disease, the doctor is simply saying that the immediate physiological cause is the presence of the bacteria. It is the most precise and measurable way of finding out what causes disease.

The passage also asserts that these physiological causation do not take into account social agents that may cause disease. Because it is difficult to precisely and accurately pinpoint which social agents cause disease, people are suspicious about social agents causing disease.

40. **Correct Answer: D**

This question asks you to choose which of the options was NOT mentioned in the passage. Option (D) is the best answer because it states that physiological causes are more effective in determining the actual cause of the disease that social causes. This is NOT mentioned in the passage. What the passage actually states is that we would be more effective if we focussed not only on the physiological causes but also on the social causes.

This part of the passage directly contradicts statement (D):

"We would also be more effective in solving our problems if we moved away from the tendency to focus merely on the proximal physiological causes of disease, for example, focussing on the bacteria or viruses associated with disease instead of social factors."

More GS Section I Mini Tests are available online at GAMSAT-prep.com.

3.8.5 Doctor-Patient Interaction Test

Candidates who have sat recent GAMSAT exams reported having encountered Units with doctor-patient scenarios. Most of the questions in these passage types require candidates to infer tone and purpose in a conversation. Before attempting the following questions, it might be a good idea to review the discussion and short exercises in RHSS 3.5.5 (Tone Questions).

Please choose the best answer for each question. You have 13 minutes. Please time yourself.

> **BEGIN ONLY WHEN TIMER IS READY**

Unit 1

Questions 1 - 4

The following passage is an interaction between Emma and her general practitioner about her son James. Emma has brought her son to the doctor because of a rash.

Doctor: Emma, I don't want to alarm you but because of James' rash and how long he's been unwell, I would recommend that you take him to the hospital immediately.

Emma: The hospital? I don't think he's that sick; I thought he'd just need some antibiotics.

Doctor: At the moment, I don't think antibiotics will be helpful for James. Hopefully, all the investigations at the hospital will just be routine and he won't have to be admitted; but we need to be sure.

Emma: I guess we can take him to the hospital. I'll get my husband to drive us when he gets home from work and I've finished doing my errands.

Doctor: Actually, he needs to go as soon as possible. I can arrange for an ambulance to pick him up immediately.

Emma: Ok, if that's what you think is necessary.

1. Which best describes the tone of the doctor in the above statement?
   A. Tactful
   B. Anxious
   C. Incredulous
   D. Relaxed

2. Emma's initial reaction to the news about her son can be best described as:
   A. confused.
   B. incredulous.
   C. infuriated.
   D. accepting.

3. Consider the following sentence from the given scenario.

   Doctor: Emma, I don't want to alarm you but because of James' rash and how long he's been unwell, I would recommend that you take him to the hospital immediately.

   What type of response from Emma would the doctor expect at this point in the conversation?
   A. Relaxed
   B. Concerned
   C. Stolid
   D. Angry

4. Consider Emma's final statement to the doctor.

   Emma: Ok, if that's what you think is necessary.

   Emma's final response is best described by which of the following?
   A. She is now concerned about her son's health.
   B. She doesn't care about what happens to her son.
   C. She is annoyed that her plans have been interrupted.
   D. She is willing to do what her doctor has recommended.

Unit 2

Questions 5 - 7

An elderly woman is sitting next to a male medical student on a plane as he reads a medical textbook. She notices the textbook and, after realising he is a medical student, she begins to relate concerns about her health. She relates that has fallen twice in the past few months. She continues by telling the student about her multiple surgeries and the significant list of medications. Despite all of this, she claims her GP brushes away her concerns.

5. The woman appears to be:
    A. perturbed.
    B. beside herself.
    C. disturbed.
    D. distraught.

6. The medical student would most likely respond to the woman by:
    A. politely rebuffing the woman, explaining the need to study.
    B. asking her if she could further explain some of her illnesses.
    C. explaining to the woman that many people her age fall down and she should not worry.
    D. None of the above.

7. Near the end of the plane journey, the woman asks the student for advice.

    What is the most appropriate response the student could give?
    A. Ask the woman to repeat herself as he was not sure what the problem could be.
    B. Give her the number of the local hospital and tell her to see a doctor as soon as possible.
    C. Explain that he is a medical student and should not give her any medical advice.
    D. Explain to the woman that many people her age fall down so she should not worry.

Unit 3

Questions 8 - 10

Bacon was inadvertently given to a Muslim patient for his breakfast meal. Due to a previous surgical procedure, the patient did not realise until his father saw the half-eaten meal when he visited him at lunch. The father became very angry and began shouting for a nurse and demanded to see someone in charge.

8. What is the best way to describe the father's reaction?
    A. Appropriate
    B. Audacious
    C. Incensed
    D. Indignant

9. What would be the most appropriate action to take for a healthcare professional who responds first to the patient's father?
   A. Acknowledge the mistake and apologise
   B. Refer the father to their supervisor
   C. Assure the father that the employee responsible will be reprimanded
   D. Inform the head nurse and the health workers who distributed the meals

10. Medical students are considered 'part of the hospital' and must be amiable when interacting with patients.

    Given the same given scenario, how would a first-year medical student initially respond to the patient's father?
    A. Acknowledge the mistake and apologise
    B. Guide the father to their supervisor
    C. Assure the father that the employee responsible will be made accountable
    D. Inform the head nurse and the health workers who distributed the meals

3.8.6 Doctor-Patient Interaction Test Answer Key and Explanations

1.	A	3.	B	5.	A	7.	C	9.	A
2.	B	4.	D	6.	D	8.	C	10.	A

1. **Correct Answer: A**
   In this conversation, the doctor is able to make Emma understand the urgency of bringing her son to the hospital by providing medically sound reasons. The doctor remains calm and diplomatic despite insisting that James is brought to the hospital for proper evaluation. This rules out (B) anxious and (C) incredulous as possible options. The doctor cannot be inferred to be (D) relaxed since he continues to urge Emma to act immediately. The best answer is (A).

2. **Correct Answer: B**
   Emma's response upon hearing the doctor's advice to bring her son to the hospital can be inferred as that of (B) disbelief. Her statement denotes she expected the doctor to merely prescribe a medication for James. If she was confused, she would have asked more clarificatory questions. This makes option (A) incorrect. Her tone changed to being (D) accepting only in the latter part of the conversation. Nothing in the conversation indicates that Emma expressed (B) anger.

3. **Correct Answer: B**
   The answer to this question can be deduced from the beginning of the doctor's statement: "I don't want to alarm you". Had the doctor expected Emma to be (A) relaxed or (C) composed, the doctor would have told Emma straight away that James should be admitted to the hospital. On the other hand, expecting someone to get angry would require a different tone such as, "I want you to stay calm".

4. **Correct Answer: D**
   Emma's last line implies trust that the doctor will act in the best interest of her son's health. Hence, a tone of (D) willingness can be inferred. Nothing in the statement proves that she was (A) annoyed or (B) did not care. It can be reasonably assumed that she has become (A) concerned, but that is the reason why she was willing to follow the doctor's advice.

5. **Correct Answer: A**
   The candidate should identify that the woman in this scenario is feeling anxious (via her concern, relating her multiple surgeries and her significant list of medications). In this instance, the word (A) perturbed (meaning anxious, unsettled or upset) is most analogous. The general behaviour of the woman does not imply she was antsy (agitated or impatient). (C) Disturbed, in this instance, is analogous to upset and does not match the anxiety shown by this woman. Both (B) "beside herself" and (D) "distraught" would imply she is overly sad or angry about her experience and medications rather than anxious and worried.

6.   Correct Answer: D

It is important for the candidate to remain compassionate as it is obvious the woman is anxious or perturbed. To understand why option (D) is the correct answer, the candidate should know that the best response would be to calm the woman and point her in the direction of a medical professional. A further conversation could explain how getting a second opinion is a great option, and any concerns she has should be raised with a medical professional. This answer shows that (A) rebuffing would be insensitive as the woman is clearly distressed and you could easily point her in the direction of someone who could help her. It could be interesting to (B) hear the woman elaborate on her illnesses; however, this is not the best response as a medical student is not qualified to give any advice, even if it is taken directly from a textbook. (C) is not correct because a medical student's bearing could influence her decision not to seek professional medical advice, which could be detrimental to her health. Option (D) is true in that many elderly people fall down, but there is definitely cause to worry about her safety.

7.   Correct Answer: C

It is important for candidates to identify that only licensed medical professionals should give medical advice. This makes (C) the correct answer. Following this, option (A) should not be considered as it might encourage the woman to continue asking the medical student for advice on her illnesses. (B) could instil a sense of panic in an already anxious woman and is not correct. (D) As already stated, the woman may have a serious condition that needs attention.

8.   Correct Answer: C

In this instance, it was clear that the father reacted angrily. It could be said the father acted (A) appropriately to the situation. However, in this instance, the BEST word to describe the father should be analogous exhibiting anger, which is (C) incensed. (B) An impudent lack of respect could again be argued. However, no direct untoward disrespect shown to any member of the staff is mentioned in the passage. (D) Indignant is close; however, it conveys a more annoyed tone than the anger and passion shown by the father.

9.   Correct Answer: A

The first and most logical action to take during conflict resolution is to (A) acknowledge the mistake on the part of the hospital staff. Option (B) is a good option and will certainly come later. However, it would still come after apologising. Option (C) would come from someone who manages the ward/hospital. It is not the role of the first responder, which is to calm the aggrieved party and acknowledge the conflict. Option (D), in a similar vein to option (B) will come later. However, the father is of priority and communication with him is most important.

10.   Correct Answer: A

The best option in this situation is exactly the same as the previous question for similar reasons: the patient needs to be calmed down first. A medical student is part of the hospital, and it would still be appropriate to (A) apologise on behalf of the hospital. Options (B) and (D) would be the ensuing actions while option (C) is wholly inappropriate for a medical student to say.

More GS Section I Mini Tests are available online at GAMSAT-prep.com.

3.8.7 Poetry Test

Units with poems or song lyrics appear two to three times in Section I of most GAMSAT exams. Recent sittings would include Poetry Units that consist of a set of three or more poems sharing a similar subject or theme.

This Poetry mini test is composed of 5 units, each with one poem as the stimulus. They are designed to get you used to interpreting themes, patterns, and symbolisms in poems and songs, among others. If you wish to attempt Poetry Tests with more than one poem in a single set, you may access them in our full-length practice tests.

GAMSAT Poetry Tips:
➢ Read at least one poem a day.
➢ Learn common literary devices and symbolisms.
➢ 3 months before the exam, do poetry mini tests regularly.
➢ 4 weeks before the exam, attempt full-length GAMSAT practice tests, feeling comfortable with poetry questions in Section I.

There are 20 questions in this mini test. Please choose the best answer for each question. You have 25 minutes. Please time yourself.

? Guide Questions for Understanding Poetry

• What is the central idea of the poem?

• What images are described in the poem?

• How do the images relate to each other?

• Is there an overarching image, character or mood that the poem emphasises? Does it form a unified pattern throughout the poem?

BEGIN ONLY WHEN TIMER IS READY

Unit 1

Questions 1 - 4

Chemin De Fer

Alone on the railroad track
I walked with pounding heart.
The ties were too close together
or maybe too far apart.

The scenery was impoverished: 5
scrub-pine and oak; beyond
its mingled gray-green foliage
I saw the little pond

where the dirty old hermit lives,
lie like an old tear   10
holding onto its injuries
lucidly year after year.

The hermit shot off his shot-gun
and the tree by his cabin shook.
Over the pond went a ripple   15
the pet hen went chook-chook.

"Love should be put into action!"
Screamed the old hermit.
Across the pond an echo
Tried and tried to confirm it.   20

Elizabeth Bishop

1. The emotions expressed by the speaker walking with a "pounding heart" (line 2) and the
    dirty old hermit "holding onto its injuries" (line 11) suggest that:
    A. both characters suffer from insecurity.
    B. the speaker is in a state of flight while the hermit, of entrapment.
    C. both characters are experiencing pain.
    D. the speaker's present mood is positive while the hermit's, negative.

2. "Chemin De Fer" is a French word for railroad. The title of the poem and the meaning evoked by the last two lines represent:
   A. indifference.
   B. an unwelcomed rebound.
   C. stagnation.
   D. an inescapable cycle.

3. The poet's use of the image of the pond (line 8) and her reference to the echo (lines 19 - 20) imply that:
   A. the hermit represents the pond; and the speaker, the echo.
   B. both characters similarly feel isolated.
   C. the hermit is an outcast and the speaker is a fugitive.
   D. the speaker and the hermit represent one and the same person.

4. Which of the following insights about Elizabeth Bishop's poetic style best describe the quality of "Chemin De Fer"?
   A. Too much intellectualisation of the poetic images results to obliquity.
   B. Heavily using extended metaphors creates a mask of the poet's persona.
   C. Using an outsider's perception to view another outsider's circumstance is an effective means of identifying perceptions and consciousness.
   D. To identify one's self as an outcast and to try to live, and love, in two worlds, is to dream of the impossible safe place.

Unit 2

Questions 5 - 7

Driving to Town Late to Mail a Letter

It is a cold and snowy night. The main street is deserted.
The only things moving are swirls of snow.
As I lift the mailbox door, I feel its cold iron.
There is a privacy I love in this snowy night.
Driving around, I will waste more time.   5

Robert Bly

5. Based on the images described in the first 3 lines, what is the atmosphere of the poem?
   A. Melancholic
   B. Austere
   C. Stark
   D. Desolate

6. The irregular rhythm and metre of the poem help create which effect that accurately suggests the poem's overall scenario?
   - **A.** An attempt to break away from monotony
   - **B.** An aimless disposition
   - **C.** A relaxed atmosphere
   - **D.** Disinterest in important matters

7. The last 2 lines of the poem imply that the speaker:
   - **A.** perceives life as lacking in purpose.
   - **B.** considers solitude to be a waste of time.
   - **C.** ends his ambivalent mood with a final choice to "waste more time".
   - **D.** welcomes the chance to commune with nature and the self.

Unit 3

Questions 8 - 12

The Waking

I wake to sleep, and take my waking slow.
I feel my fate in what I cannot fear.
I learn by going where I have to go.

We think by feeling. What is there to know?
I hear my being dance from ear to ear.   5
I wake to sleep, and take my waking slow.

Of those so close beside me, which are you?
God bless the Ground! I shall walk softly there,
And learn by going where I have to go.

Light takes the Tree; but who can tell us how?   10
The lowly worm climbs up a winding stair;
I wake to sleep, and take my waking slow.

Great Nature has another thing to do
To you and me, so take the lively air,
And, lovely, learn by going where to go.   15

This shaking keeps me steady. I should know.
What falls away is always. And is near.
I wake to sleep, and take my waking slow.
I learn by going where I have to go.

Theodore Roethke

8. The line "I wake to sleep, and take my waking slow. . ." has generated various interpretations from several critics, the most predominant of which is in reference to "dying". Which of the following lines would reinforce this interpretation?
   A. Light takes the Tree; but who can tell us how?
   B. This shaking keeps me steady.
   C. Great Nature has another thing to do. . .
   D. I learn by going where I have to go.

9. Which tone do the repeating, heavily end-stopped lines of the poem create?
   A. Shortness of breath
   B. Cycle and Stability
   C. Interrupted thoughts
   D. Emphasis and Confidence

10. The paradox introduced in the first line is further reinforced in several succeeding lines of the poem (lines 2, 11, 16, 17) in order to:
   A. emphasise the contrast between life and death.
   B. indicate a peaceful acceptance of the inevitable.
   C. illustrate opposing forces in life.
   D. reflect the speaker's confusion.

11. Another interpretation of the poem is that the theme revolves around its rejection of the intellect as the way to "enlightenment". What would support this interpretation?
   A. The repeated use of words based on feelings rather than reason
   B. The poem's constant use of paradoxes
   C. The poet's romantic references to Nature
   D. The predominance of irrational lines

12. "What falls away is always. And is near" suggests:
   A. resignation to one's fate.
   B. a fast approaching death.
   C. the inseparability of life and death.
   D. fear of the uncertain.

Unit 4

Questions 13 – 16

One Flesh

Lying apart now, each in a separate bed,
He with a book, keeping the light on late,
She like a girl dreaming of childhood,
All men elsewhere - it is as if they wait
Some new event: the book he holds unread,   5
Her eyes fixed on the shadows overhead.

Tossed up like flotsam from a former passion,
How cool they lie. They hardly ever touch,
Or if they do, it is like a confession
Of having little feeling - or too much.   10
Chastity faces them, a destination
For which their whole lives were a preparation.

Strangely apart, yet strangely close together,
Silence between them like a thread to hold
And not wind in. And time itself's a feather   15
Touching them gently. Do they know they're old,
These two who are my father and my mother
Whose fire from which I came, has now grown cold?

Elizabeth Jennings

13. What does "chastity" mean in the second stanza?
    A. Abstinence   **C.** Virtue
    B. Isolation   **D.** Mortality

14. The different meanings of "touch" in lines 8 and 16, respectively, equate:
    A. truth and evanescence.   **C.** passion and time.
    B. youth and old age.   **D.** action and imagination.

15. The thread (line 14) signifies:
    A. union.   **C.** absence of communication.
    B. spiritual isolation.   **D.** lifeline.

16. "Flotsam" (line 7) symbolises:

    A. spent passion.

    B. incapacity.

    C. uselessness.

    D. deterioration.

Unit 5

Questions 17 - 20

Gift

O my love, what gift of mine
Shall I give you this dawn?
A morning song?
But morning does not last long -
The heat of the sun   5
Wilts like a flower
And songs that tire
Are done.

O friend, when you come to my gate.
At dusk   10
What is it you ask?
What shall I bring you?
A light?

A lamp from a secret corner of my silent house?
But will you want to take it with you   15
Down the crowded street?
Alas,
The wind will blow it out.

Whatever gifts are in my power to give you,
Be they flowers,   20
Be they gems for your neck
How can they please you
If in time they must surely wither,
Crack,
Lose lustre?   25
All that my hands can place in yours
Will slip through your fingers
And fall forgotten to the dust
To turn into dust.

Rather,   30
When you have leisure,
Wander idly through my garden in spring
And let an unknown, hidden flower's scent startle you
Into sudden wondering-
Let that displaced moment   35
Be my gift.
Or if, as you peer your way down a shady avenue,
Suddenly, spilled
From the thick gathered tresses of evening
A single shivering fleck of sunset-light stops you,   40
Turns your daydreams to gold,
Let that light be an innocent
Gift.

Truest treasure is fleeting;
It sparkles for a moment, then goes.   45
It does not tell its name; its tune
Stops us in our tracks, its dance disappears
At the toss of an anklet
I know no way to it-
No hand, nor word can reach it.   50
Friend, whatever you take of it,
On your own,
Without asking, without knowing, let that
Be yours.
Anything I can give you is trifling -   55
Be it a flower, or a song-

Rabindranath Tagore

17. The beginning stanza of the poem depicts:

    A. sadness.   **C.** a quest.

    B. confusion.   **D.** affection.

18. "Displaced moment" (line 35) means:

    A. a rare moment.   **C.** a gift.

    B. an unexpected chance.   **D.** random.

19. "Shady avenue" (line 37) connotes:

    A. danger.   **C.** desperation.

    B. obstacle.   **D.** chaos.

20. The speaker regards the "gift" as something that is:

    A. trifling.

    B. elusive.

    C. spontaneous.

    D. surprising.

If time remains, you may review your work. If your allotted time (25 minutes) is complete, please proceed to the Answer Key.

3.8.8 Poetry Test Answer Key and Explanations

1.	B	6.	B	11.	A	16.	B
2.	D	7.	D	12.	C	17.	D
3.	D	8.	D	13.	D	18.	B
4.	C	9.	B	14.	C	19.	B
5.	D	10.	B	15.	A	20.	C

1.   Correct Answer: B

This poem is often identified by various critics as one of Bishop's medium in obliquely expressing her own fears and feelings of alienation in reference to her gender identity.

The poet successfully portrays two polarised emotions in this piece: fear resulting to an urge to escape, and frustrations resulting to a refusal to move on. In line 2, being alone on a railroad track and having unstable perceptions of one's path with "ties (being) too close together or... too far apart" connote a sense of danger and of fear. On the other hand, an image of seclusion in the character of the hermit and an echo that bounces back to the hermit's point suggest containment.

This is a "hybrid" type of question that can be answered through a correct interpretation of the emotions depicted in the poem and the evidence found within their contexts.

(A) refers to a likely common feeling experienced by the two characters. The question stem specifically points at two emotions cited in the poem. In (C), pain is apparent in the hermit's character but not necessarily in the speaker's. (D) is a misreading of the tones presented in the poem.

2.   Correct Answer: D

This question specifically refers to "Chemin De Fer" (railroad) and the last two lines of the poem: "Across the pond an echo / Tried and tried to confirm it." Railroads operating on a recurring schedule is common knowledge. The same recurring action is stated in the repeated sound of the echo. Recurrence denotes a cycle. In addition, the general atmosphere of isolation suggests something inescapable.

(A) is an out-of-context interpretation of the title and the final lines of the poem. (B) is a misinterpretation of the final lines of the poem and is not congruent with a railroad's symbolism. (C) is another aspect of the poem's imagery. However, this is more appropriately represented by the pond – NEITHER the railroad NOR the echo.

3.   Correct Answer: D

This question requires analysis and relating concepts to the following "pieces of evidence" provided in the poem: (1) Pond contains water. Water mirrors whatever is placed parallel to it; (2) An echo reflects sounds. The poem starts with a premise of escapism. The speaker, therefore, avoids facing his/her own issues by reflecting these on an "invented" character.

(A) is too direct yet does not provide a substantial answer. (B) describes what the two characters may possibly feel but does not answer what the images of the pond and the echo imply. (C) seems plausible; however, this is not the best answer. The question asks: which among the options can identify what is being implied by the poet's use of the image of the pond and her reference to the echo? This requires an answer that will present an insight into the poem's symbolism. (D) is the best option because it offers a considerable interpretation parallel to what the question asks.

4. **Correct Answer: C**

This is an implication question that requires determining two things: the overall idea that the poet tries to communicate in her poem; and, the means or technique that the poet employs in order to get her thoughts across to the readers. This poem speaks about fear and frustration, and flight and confrontation on love. The poet uses images that symbolise the "act of mirroring".

(A) is wrong because the poem is emotionally charged rather than objective or "intellectualised". (B) is halfway true in stating that the extended metaphors hide or indirectly portray the truth. However, the term "persona" distorts the concept of the statement. "Persona" refers to a person's facade, not the inner personality or thinking. (C) is more accurate in presenting an insight into the poem's quality. (D) states the poem's possible theme, NOT an insight about the poem's quality.

5. **Correct Answer: D**

This is a tone question that entails a careful consideration of specific images presented in the poem's first 3 lines. "Swirls of snow" (line 2) calls to mind some sort of a ghost town or deserted place. "Deserted (street)" (line 1) sets such an atmosphere. These two images are powerful enough to connote a desolate –

solitary - mood in the first part of the poem.

(A) Although sadness is a possible aspect that comes with a desolate atmosphere, it is not established in the first 3 lines. (B) or apathy is usually associated with "cold", but this option takes the interpretation of the poem out of context. (C) offers a synonym of "laziness", which can likewise be associated with cold weather. Again, this option takes the mood of the poem out of context.

6. **Correct Answer: B**

This is another tone question that involves recognising the overall attitude or mood of the poem's speaker in relation to the poem's structure. The irregularity in poetic structure combines with the images in depicting a scenario of being adrift or aimless: "swirls of snow" suggests a movement without a definite direction; so does "driving around" with the intention of wasting time.

(A) is an out-of-context interpretation. (C) is a more general view of the poem's atmosphere compared to (B). (D) is not established in the poem. In fact, the speaker has just performed an errand of mailing a letter amid the difficult weather.

7. **Correct Answer: D**

This implication question requires judging the attitude projected by the speaker of the poem in lines 4 and 5. Line 4 reveals the speaker's outlook towards the rather unfriendly weather by stating, "There is a privacy I love in this snowy night." "Wasting time" then, in the poem's essence is not a negative endeavour but an opportunity to enjoy one's private moment.

(A) is an incomplete interpretation of the poem that disregards the speaker's remark in line 4. (B) is a misreading of lines 4 and 5. (C) is wrong because there is no indication in the poem where the speaker is expected to decide or choose.

8.   Correct Answer: D

In order to understand this seemingly complicated poem, careful consideration of the accompanying details of each line is required. (D) "I learn by going where I have to go" is repeated in the first and last stanzas, as well as every twostanzas in the poem as though it is a reminder of something inevitable - just as death is an inevitable destination. This is, therefore, the correct answer.

(A) Line 10 implies enlightenment rather than death. The image following the line depicts the "lowly worm" climbing to take the light.

(B) Line 16 is a paradox of finding stability out of chaos.

(C) Line 13 is ambiguous. If taken within the context of its stanza, it could mean that the author tells the reader to enjoy what Nature has to offer.

9.   Correct Answer: B

The lines "I wake to sleep, and take my waking slow" and "I learn by going where I have to go" are alternately repeated in every stanza, either linking the thought of the preceding lines or reasserting a dominant idea of the poem. In effect, this (B) cycle keeps the general context of the poem within the perspectives of these 2 lines.

(A) is not possible because all the lines have complete thoughts. Shortness of breath could have comprised unrelated, broken thoughts.

(C) is also wrong because no separate idea is inserted in between the sentences within a single stanza. (D) Emphasis is a possible effect of the repetitions. Confidence, however, is not obvious in the poem.

10.   Correct Answer: B

In order to arrive at the best answer, the specified lines must first be interpreted.

Line 2: "I feel my fate in what I cannot fear." Instead of fearing the unknown, the line suggests a brave acceptance of one's fate.

Line 11: "The lowly worm climbs up a winding stair." The UPWARD action of climbing to take the light, in contrast to the LOWLY state of a small worm, indicate a slow and quiet determination to elevate ones' self from the "dark" despite the twists ("winding") of life.

Line 16: "This shaking keeps me steady. I should know." Shaking implies the uncertain and unforeseen in life. It can also indicate a sign of a fatal illness. In any case, the speaker expresses a calm ("steady") acknowledgement of such circumstances.

Line 17: "What falls away is always. And is near." This line recognises the fact that "falling away", i.e. opposing forces, is always a part of life.

Lines 2, 11, 16, and 17 altogether convey a positive recognition about certain facts of life. The question calls for a correlation of this shared idea to the first line of the poem, "I wake to sleep, and take my waking slow." Sleeping is as essential as waking, and vice versa. As indicated by the speaker's statement to "take" i.e. "accept" his waking slow, the opposing states of waking and sleeping do not signify a contrast but of inevitability. Hence, it can be inferred that paradoxes are used in the poem to reconcile seemingly unlike states – to be more specific, to accept the inevitable (line 2), the ironies (lines 11 and 17), and the uncertain (line 16) in life.

(A) and (C), therefore, are wrong. (D) is a misinterpretation.

11.   Correct Answer: A

The answer to this question can be deduced from the following:

"I FEEL my fate in what I cannot FEAR." (line 2);

"We think by FEELING." (line 4);

" LIVELY air" (line 14); and,

"LOVELY, learn by going where to go." (line 15)

Feel, fear, feeling, lively and lovely are subjective words spread in the different stanzas of the poem. In lines 4 and 15, the subjective words are used as a means to thinking and learning, as opposed to using the mind.

(B) is wrong because paradoxes are mainly used in this poem in order to illustrate the innate but inevitable contrast of life, not a rejection of intellect. (C) is debatable because although "Nature" is regarded in romanticism as a contrast to scientific rationalism, "Nature" isusually presented as a work of art itself.

(D) The lines are seemingly irrational at initial reading. However, further analysis reveals that these are meant to show the inherent duality of life.

12. Correct Answer: C

"What falls away is always" indicates a condition that lingers. The fact that it "is near" means that it is inescapable too. In other words, death will always come with life.

(A) does not point to the essence of the line being referred in the question. (B) is only applicable to the second statement: "And is near." However, a fast approaching death happens only once, not "always". (D) is not implied in the line or within the context of the stanza.

13. Correct Answer: D

The message of this poem is best understood by the logical interpretation of the symbolisms and expressions presented in the poem. These can be inferred from the context of the lines or stanzas specified.

The second stanza alludes to the lack of marital relations between the old couple. The death of sexual desire accompanying old age can be said to equate (D) death, which is everyone's destination and part of life's preparation.

(A) Abstinence and (B) isolation are not exactly regarded as things that everyone prepares for in later life. (C) Virtue may be hoped for but this necessitates being morally good or righteous. This is neither implied anywhere in the poem nor is the poem about morality. This leaves (D) as the correct answer.

14. Correct Answer: C

This question is specifically confined to lines 8 and 16. Touch is mentioned in the respective contexts of "a former passion" and time being fleeting. This makes (C) correct.

(A) is literal but does not correctly answer the question. (B) and (D) are mentioned in other parts of the poem but not in response to the lines specified.

15. Correct Answer: A

The meaning of this word is taken from the following: "Strangely apart, yet strangely close together, / Silence between them like a thread to hold / And not wind in. And time itself's a feather / Touching them gently." This implies that despite the absence of spoken communication, the couple is still connected by their marital union and by the memories of the time that they have spent together.

(B) and (D) are not implied in the stanza. (C) is a literal reference to the "silence" mentioned in the same line.

16. Correct Answer: B

The symbolism of this word can be derived from the following: "Tossed up like flotsam from a former passion, / How cool they lie. They hardly ever touch, / Or if they do, it is like a confession / Of having little feeling - or too much." The general thought of these lines directs to the incapacity of the couple to effectively demonstrate passionate feelings or sexual desires. This makes (B) as the correct answer.

(A) is wrong because the question asks what the word symbolises, not what it means in the context of its sentence or line. (C) would refer to the general function of weak, old people. However, "flotsam" was referred in the poem in relation to passion; hence, (C) is a remote option. (D) is also wrong because the word is not associated with just a failing capacity but a sexual INcapacity.

17. Correct Answer: D

The reference to a loved one in the beginning line suggests that the poem has an affectionate tone. Therefore, (D) answers this simple inference question. (A) is wrong because the succeeding lines must not be misinterpreted to be depressing but the speaker's way of showing that material things fade through time. (B) is also a misinterpretation. (C) may sound like a possible option because of the line, "what ... / Shall I give you this dawn?" However, the speaker is able to rationalise and answer his own question in the succeeding lines. Therefore, (C) is a weak choice.

18. Correct Answer: B

This question calls for an "analysis of evidence", which can be construed from: "...let an unknown, hidden flower's scent startle you" (line 33). This means that a "displaced moment" is unexpected and extraordinary in its occurrence.

Although (A) is true, this answer is encompassed by (B).(C) is what "displaced moment" is being paralleled with by the speaker. The question asks for what the phrase means, NOT to what it is being equated. (D) is not explicitly mentioned in the stanza.

19. Correct Answer: B

This is an inference question that requires contextual interpretation of the stanza. The answer can be deduced from lines 37 to 41. The speaker's reference to a darkness enlightened by a realisation of a dream indicates that "shady avenue" implies the hardships or "obstacles" undergone by a person.

(A) and (C) are not suggested in the stanza. (D) is wrong because the stanza does not mention a circumstance too forceful to constitute chaos.

20. Correct Answer: C

The speaker details his idea of a "gift" in the last stanza. He regards gifts that are material and man-made to be insignificant. Instead, he mentions of "displaced moment" and "whatever you take of it, / on your own, / without asking, without knowing" - things and instances that come at the spur-of-the-moment – to be the "truest treasures". This makes C as the most apt choice.

(A) refers to the material gifts. (B) is wrong because the speaker only mentions the "unexpected" gifts among everyday matters, not those that are hard to find. (D) is a component of being spontaneous, but this choice offers a limited response compared to (C).

For more Poetry practice tests and free resources, go online at GAMSAT-prep.com.

3.8.9 Cartoon Test

Units with cartoon interpretation usually appear once or twice during the real exam. This mini test presents 11 units with 20 questions. Choose the best answer for each question. You have 25 minutes. Please time yourself accordingly.

BEGIN ONLY WHEN TIMER IS READY

Unit 1

Questions 1 - 2

Cartoon 1

RUBES®   By Leigh Rubin

"I don't care what all the other kids are doing,
you're *not* getting your lip pierced!"

Reprinted with permission from Creators Syndicate.

1. The humour portrayed in the cartoon mainly relies on:
    A. satire.
    B. analogy.
    C. double meaning.
    D. juxtaposition.

2. The dialogue in the cartoon can be paralleled to real-life situations wherein:
   A. adolescents tend to imitate fashion trends to the dislike of their parents.
   B. parents constantly nag on their children about being too radical.
   C. parents and children tend to be at odds when it comes to social conformity.
   D. the young generation often ignores the wisdom of the elders.

Unit 2

Questions 3 - 4

For questions 3 and 4, consider the following quotation and analyse the cartoon.

The Internet will help achieve "friction free capitalism" by putting buyer and seller in direct contact and providing more information to both about each other.

Bill Gates

Cartoon 2

"Thanks pal, let me put you on my mailing list."

Cartoon by P.C. Vey. Reproduced with permission.

3. The statement of Bill Gates is MOST suggestive of:
   A. a growth in commerce due to digital technology.
   B. a positive development in information systems.
   C. good leadership in E-Commerce.
   D. the important role of information technology in business trade.

4. This cartoon speaks about:
    A. the impoverished working class trying to 'beat the system'.
    B. a shift in social stereotypes.
    C. the ironic humour of everyday life.
    D. the sad plight of homeless people.

Unit 3

Questions 5 - 6

For questions 5 and 6, consider the following comment and analyse the cartoon.

Global warming is too serious for the world any longer to ignore its danger or split into opposing factions on it.

Tony Blair

Cartoon 3

Cartoon by Nicholson from "The Australian" www.nicholsoncartoons.com.au.
Printed with permission.

5. The comment of Tony Blair connotes:
    A. an appeal to emotions.
    B. an appeal for immediate action.
    C. a warning against passivity.
    D. a contempt for passivity.

6. The statement in the cartoon signifies a:

    A. positive vision of the future.

    B. bleak vision of the future.

    C. remote possibility.

    D. warning against an impending threat.

Unit 4

Questions 7 - 8

Cartoon 4

Printed with permission from Jonathan P. Jurilla

7. The cartoon is humorous because:

    A. of the analogy between individuality and the audience in the cartoon.

    B. of the irony expressed in both the textual and graphical messages.

    C. as a matter of fact, individuality is difficult to attain.

    D. of the way the message is delivered by the speaker.

8. The cartoon is an example of:
    A. graphic art with an erroneous text.
    B. a social commentary.
    C. irony.
    D. a witty remark.

Unit 5

Questions 9 - 11

For questions 9 to 11, consider the following quotation and analyse the cartoon.

A soul mate is someone who has locks that fit our keys, and keys to fit our locks. When we feel safe enough to open the locks, our truest selves step out and we can be completely and honestly who we are; we can be loved for who we are and not for who we're pretending to be. Each unveils the best part of the other. No matter what else goes wrong around us, with that one person we're safe in our own paradise.

Richard Bach

Cartoon 5

Printed with permission from Cathy Thorne.

9. The statement of Richard Bach describes:
    A. a universal truth about love.
    B. a lesson learned in finding true love.
    C. an aspiration to find true love.
    D. an ideal view of romantic love.

10. The statements in the cartoon express:
   A. a disbelief in soul mates.
   B. a disenchantment with soul mates.
   C. the truth about soul mate.
   D. an accismus*.
      *Accismus: expressing the want of something by denying it.

11. The cartoon could be best described as:
   A. a metaphorical illustration of the quotation.
   B. a satirical interpretation of the quotation.
   C. a trite interpretation of the quotation.
   D. an alternative interpretation of the quotation.

Unit 6

Question 12

Cartoon 6

Printed with permission from Grea Korting www.sangrea.net

12. The joke in the cartoon mostly stems from:
   A. the similarity in the characters' situations.
   B. the juxtaposition of the characters' concerns.
   C. the paradox in the speaker's situation.
   D. the irony of the characters' situations.

Unit 7

Question 13

The following relates to the importance of good communication skills.

Communication is said to be a vehicle for transferring knowledge and fostering cooperation and understanding in society. Of course, this is not limited to the verbal medium. Nonverbal expressions such as gestures, facial reactions, and signs all form part of the communication process.

Cartoon 7

Printed with permission from Kevin Kallaugher.

The following are views of famous writers about communication:

I.   I quote others only in order the better to express myself.
                                                     - Michel de Montaigne
II.   When people talk, listen completely. Most people never listen.
                                                     - Ernest Hemingway
III. After all, when you come right down to it, how many people speak the same language even when they speak the same language?
                                                     - Russell Hoban
IV.   It seemed rather incongruous that in a society of supersophisticated communication, we often suffer from a shortage of listeners.
                                                     - Erma Bombeck

13. Which of the four views coincide with the way communication is portrayed in the cartoon?
- **A.** I and II
- **B.** III and IV
- **C.** II, III and IV
- **D.** II and IV

Unit 8

Question 14

Cartoon 8

"That's a crazy idea but it might work."

Printed with permission from CartoonStock Ltd.

14. The cartoon reflects a commentary about certain scenarios that resulted from the anti-smoking bans.

Study the following comments:

I.   Tobacco companies have sought new and creative ways of getting "around the law" as advertisements have been increasingly regulated with certain bans in print, radio and television media.

II. Health warnings will remain as part of anti-smoking campaigns.

III. Tobacco companies use alternative campaigns that do not necessarily look like tobacco advertisements but have an effect of promoting smoking.

IV. Anti-smoking laws leave tobacco companies with limited marketing alternatives.

Which of these comments would apply to the cartoon?
- **A.** Comment I only
- **B.** Comments II and IV only
- **C.** Comment IV only
- **D.** Comments I and III only

Unit 9

Questions 15 - 16

Cartoon 9

Printed with permission from Grea Korting www.sangrea.net

15. The thought expressed by the wife in the cartoon is an example of:
    A. subliminal perception.
    B. denial.
    C. psychological repression.
    D. a metaphor.

16. Based on the cartoon, the best advice on marriage would then be:
    A. "A successful marriage requires falling in love many times, always with the same person." (Mignon McLaughlin, The Second Neurotic's Notebook, 1966)
    B. "In every marriage more than a week old, there are grounds for divorce. The trick is to find, and continue to find, grounds for marriage." (Robert Anderson, Solitaire & Double Solitaire)
    C. "Never feel remorse for what you have thought about your wife; she has thought much worse things about you." (Jean Rostand, Le Mariage, 1927)
    D. "I have learned that only two things are necessary to keep one's wife happy. First, let her think she's having her own way. And second, let her have it." (Lyndon B. Johnson)

Unit 10

Questions 17 - 18

In February 2008, former Prime Minister Kevin Rudd read an apology that particularly addressed the "stolen generations" of Aborigines in Australia. Part of the momentous speech was the Parliament's recognition that the indigenous people were indeed mistreated in the past, and that the families suffered severe impacts from the forced removal of the children.

Compensation claims followed and were filed in the courts. However, not all claims were granted because many of the removals were done with consent and in accordance to specific legal acts of the Australian law.

Cartoon 10

Cartoon by Nicholson from "The Australian" www.nicholsoncartoons.com.au.
Printed with permission.

17. The statement of the speaker in the cartoon:
  A. shows that the Aborigines doubted the sincerity of the government's apology.
  B. stresses that the Aborigines should be entitled to a monetary compensation from the government.
  C. shows that some Aborigines possibly did not understand the legal conditions of deserving a payout.
  D. stresses that the Aborigines expected a compensation to accompany the verbal apology.

18. The word "apology" is used in the cartoon to equate:
  A. hypocrisy.
  B. vindication.
  C. indemnity
  D. profit.

Unit 11

Questions 19 - 20

Cartoon 11

Printed with permission.
(Copyright 2004) Dennis Draughon & The Scranton Times (PA)

19. The cartoon is a reaction to:
    A. an economic depression.
    B. the unbearable rising prices of petrol.
    C. a pretentious lifestyle.
    D. social indifference towards the needy.

20. The type of humour found in the cartoon is:
    A. a pastiche.
    B. an understatement.
    C. a parody.
    D. a hyperbole.

If time remains, you may review your work. If your allotted time (25 minutes) is complete, please proceed to the Answer Key.

3.8.10 Cartoon Test Answer Key and Explanations

1.	C	6.	D	11.	B	16.	B
2.	C	7.	B	12.	D	17.	C
3.	D	8.	C	13.	C	18.	C
4.	B	9.	D	14.	D	19.	A
5.	B	10.	B	15.	B	20.	D

1. Answer: C

Choices (A) and (D) are similar to each other in their use of contrasts. (A) Satire uses irony as a form of contrast in order to achieve humour with the intent of criticising society. However, irony in satires must be strongly charged to the point of being socio-political. Clearly, the dialogue in the cartoon merely connotes a joke on everyday family life issues.

(D) A juxtaposition is also a form of contrast by placing two elements, which could be objects or texts in an art form, next to each other. In the cartoon, the parent-fish is portrayed to be asserting a parental rule against the child-fish who has already committed the "violation" of this same rule. It would, then, seem that the possible answer to this question would be (D). However, while there is a clear contrast here, another option – (C) – also poses a more appropriate representation of the cartoon's humour.

(C) The cartoon can be interpreted as either a joke about the plight of fishes or as a creative comparison of parent-child conflict in real-life. (C) then becomes the best choice of answer.

(B) An analogy must be expressed in a statement that compares two things. For example, "Her face was a perfect oval, like a circle that had its two sides gently compressed by a ThighMaster." The dialogue in the cartoon does not come close to this form of humour.

2. Answer: C

Choice (A) offers a literal interpretation of what the cartoon may be trying to portray.

Choices (B), (C), and (D) are closely similar. However, (B) mentions the word "radical". The term mostly connotes political leanings. The cartoon only shows a fashion trend among youngsters. (D) requires a much profound dialogue or illustration. The best choice is (C) because it embraces a more general interpretation of both the text and the cartoon illustration by using the term "social conformity".

3. Answer: D

Although choices (A), (B), and (D) all have something to do with information or identity management, (D) makes an inclusion of the effect of information technology on businesses. Bill Gates' quote uses the term buyer and seller, and these are clearly common terms used on businesses. (C) merely speaks of Bill Gates' status in the internet industry.

4. Answer: B

The cartoon satirises a reversal of attitudes and a duality of roles between the beggar and the middle class. In a way, the cartoon does distort the way society generally perceives these two stereotypes. The correct answer is (B).

(A) is easily negated as the correct answer

because, as already mentioned, the cartoon tends to create a duality of roles between a beggar (i.e. accepts a donation) and a member of the working class (i.e. wears an office suit). One couldn't really tell for sure unless the cartoon would be given a literal interpretation.
(C) The cartoon may be portraying an "everyday life" scenario, but the joke doesn't necessarily qualify as an irony of daily life.
(D) There is nothing sad about a homeless beggar who can afford a computer!

5. **Answer: B**
"Too serious for the world any longer to ignore" provides the clue that the comment is not just a statement of (C) warning or (D) opinion but a call for (B) urgency of action. (A) would be a contentious choice.

6. **Answer: D**
(A) is wrong because the cartoon shows the earth on its final days. "The last person to leave the planet" suggests an exodus, which is not exactly a positive thing. (B) Although the cartoon projects humour and witticism, the idea being hinted is rather unwelcoming and terrifying. The statement likewise requests an involvement ("please turn off the power") from the reader ("the last person"), this makes the cartoon, not just a mere presentation of the artist's vision of the future but, more of a (D) warning of a fast coming reality. In other words, option (D) includes the idea in option (B). (C) The accompanying quotation provides the idea of a serious threat or reality, not an impossibility.

7. **Answer: B**
Answering this question requires evaluating the relevance of the text to the graphical illustration. (A) and (D) mislead the examinee to pay primary attention to the image. (C) is a profound interpretation of the cartoon but it is not the device used to make the cartoon humorous. This leaves (B) as the best answer.

8. **Answer: C**
(A) and (B) are the farthest choices because no obvious errors in spelling and grammar can be found nor is there any reference to social or political justice.
(D) The cartoon is more sarcastic than witty.
(C) is the best choice because both the illustration and the textual message expresses subtle mockery and contrasts.

9. **Answer: D**
The quotation simply describes the author's model of a compatible partner in a relationship referred as soul mate. "Soul mates" are what many hope to find as expressed in (C). However, the kind of relationship described in the quotation does not always apply in every relationship. Therefore, it is not (A) a universal truth. Obviously, it is not (B) a lesson or wisdom being imparted either. This leaves (D) as the best answer.

10. **Answer: B**
(A) is incorrect as the cartoon acknowledges the existence of soul mates. The second statement, "Your soul mate will bring up every one of your unresolved issues", is just the artist's opinion about soul mates - not a (C) universal truth. (D) is a red herring – there is no evidence to suggest the author of the cartoon/statements is demonstrating a desire for a soul mate via repression. Therefore, (B) is the correct answer.
A little more about answer choice (D): do not expect to find a definition among answer choices during the real GAMSAT, nor during your practice full-length exams. We were just trying to be polite during your training!

11. Answer: B

Since the cartoon portrays an opposite view of the quotation, (A) and (D) can be eliminated from the choices. (B) Taking the quotation into context, it should be noted that there is mention of the line: "Each unveils the best part of the other." One should recall that satire uses humour by highlighting the irony or contrast of a situation or, in this case, the quotation. This is the correct answer. (C) is quite subjective depending on the reader's point of view.

12. Answer: D

The cartoon shows both a (A) similarity and (B) a contrast between the beggar and the passerby. Both characters are in a depressed situation. The beggar seeks financial help yet the passerby overlooked his plight. Ironically, the passerby expresses a need for emotional attention and feels too aggrieved by his own problem that he fails to see the beggar's worse condition. Therefore, the answer is (D) as it encompasses choices (A) and (B). (C) is a ruse: the paradox would have applied to the two characters' situations - not in the speaker's situation.

13. Answer: C

The cartoon is about the distortion of information as words get passed on to the next receiver. In general, the cartoon depicts miscommunication and its source is a failure to listen fully. Quote I is about improving one's communication skills through imitating others. Quote II is an advice to listen and focus as poor listening can be a cause of miscommunication. Quote III implies that miscommunication is common even among people who speak the same language - they don't listen to each other. Quote IV also implies miscommunication even with advanced technology - again, the source is not listening. Choice (C) is the correct answer.

14. Answer: D

Comment I: The line, "That's a crazy idea but it might work", implies entertaining an idea that has not been thought of before – therefore new and creative - but is hoped to pass a certain scrutiny (e.g., an anti-smoking regulation).
Comment II: "Good health isn't everything" is not a health warning.
Comment III: "Good health isn't everything" is another way of saying that there are benefits in vices that cannot be found in a healthy lifestyle. In a way, this is the kind of advertisement described in Comment III.
Comment IV: The cartoon shows a presentation of a novel idea in an advertising campaign. This doesn't show a limitation of options.

15. Answer: B

Of the four choices, (D) metaphor is the easiest to eliminate. A metaphor is an analogy or a parallelism of the resemblance of two things. The statement of the wife expresses a contrast between her situation and those of "the people on the internet".
(A) Subliminal perception requires a stimulus that is unnoticeable but perceived anyway. In the illustration, the wife may look like she doesn't notice her husband falling asleep, but her thoughts in the cartoon tell that she chooses not to recognise it either.
(B) Denial and (C) repression are both forms of defence mechanism. Their main difference is that denial is a refusal to accept a pressing or unbearable problem while repression, against a desire that might result to a problem or cause a suffering if that desire is satisfied. The wife is clearly refusing to recognise a lack of "together"-ness with her husband despite spending their time in the same place.

16. Answer: B

(A) can be easily confused as the correct answer. The advice would relate more to extra-marital temptations as opposed to falling in love "with the same person". This situation is not illustrated in the cartoons.

(C) proposes an advice from a husband's standpoint only. The cartoon, however, presents only the wife's perspectives.

(D) This cartoon does not depict a power struggle between husband and wife. Hence, advice (D) is not applicable.

This leaves (B) as the best answer: the wife is finding a way to cope - albeit in an unfavourable light - with their failing communication.

17. Answer: C

(A) The line "It's an apology all right..." indicates that the speaker does acknowledge the apology. What he is only suspicious of is having been cheated in the monetary proceeds due him.

(B) This tone of suspicion in the speaker's statement, however, does not necessarily echo an assertion or a call to grant the compensation.

(C) What can be conveyed from the cartoon is the speaker's expectation of receiving some monetary benefit. This expectation hence illustrates his misunderstanding that all Aborigines will receive a claim. As stated in the descriptive paragraph, NOT ALL Aborigines were granted a payout because others were taken into government guardianship under reasonable circumstances.

(D) Indeed, the cartoon clearly implies that the Aborigines expected to be automatically compensated. This expectation, therefore, high-lights the reason why (C) is the correct answer.

18. Answer: C

(A) is not implied anywhere in the cartoon. (B) and (D) sound plausible but not accurate enough in relation to the graphic illustration as well as to the given descriptive paragraph. (C) Indemnity refers to a payment made to someone in order to compensate for damages. This is indicated by the speaker's immediate reaction upon receiving an envelope.

19. Answer: A

While there is an absence of sympathisers and donors in the cartoon, such lack fails to show a discernible portrayal of social indifference either. (D) can be therefore eliminated as the answer.

Having two cars indeed speaks of a high-profiled lifestyle. However, resorting to begging does not necessarily show pretence as it does a decline in one's financial state. Therefore, (C) is not a definite answer.

The cartoon indeed shows either poverty or economic scarcity. The sign bearing the words "2 cars to feed" specifically pinpoints the cause of poverty. (B) The context of rising petrol prices is a little oblique. The correct answer is thus (A) - economic depression.

20. Answer: D

(A) Pastiche is a form of a lampoon. The cartoon is not taken from a famous work. Hence, it does not qualify for a pastiche.

(B) An understatement is an extreme diminution of an otherwise important characteristic or topic in order to achieve humour. The cartoon does not reduce the problem implied by the cartoon but rather exaggerates it. A hyperbole exactly does that. The answer is (D).

(C) is wrong because it is not an imitation of another art work.

More practice questions and free resources are available in your Section I online lessons at GAMSAT-prep.com.

3.8.11 Graphs and Tables Test

The following mini test aims to help you focus on interpreting graphs and tables. These types of stimuli usually appear in two to three Section I Units of the GAMSAT.

One of the initial steps in understanding graphs and tables is reviewing the Math chapters of the Gold Standard GAMSAT Maths, Physics & General Chemistry book. Math is the basis of graphs and tables and must be understood before moving on to GAMSAT-level practice.

The difference between Section I and Section III is that Section I graphs and tables questions are heavily based on qualitative data gathered from social science research (for example, social values and preferences, marriage systems) or theories (for example, socialism, evolution). Knowing what each type of diagram, graph, flowchart, table, and quadrant is used for in social science research can prove beneficial in your preparation.

There are 6 units with 20 questions in this mini test. Please choose the best answer for each question. You have 25 minutes. Please time yourself.

BEGIN ONLY WHEN TIMER IS READY

Unit 1

Questions 1 - 4

Study the following abstract on medical consultation and the computer, and the accompanying consultation (hermeneutic) circle.

Abstract

Objective: Studies of the doctor–patient relationship have focussed on the elaboration of power and/or authority using a range of techniques to study the encounter between doctor and patient. The widespread adoption of computers by doctors brings a third party into the consultation. While there has been some research into the way doctors view and manage this new relationship, the behaviour of patients in response to the computer is rarely studied. In this paper, the authors use Goffman's dramaturgy (theatrical approach: scene, actor, stage, script, act) to explore patients' approaches to the doctor's computer in the consultation and its influence on the patient–doctor relationship.

Design: Observational study of Australian general practice. 141 consultations from 20 general practitioners were videotaped and analysed using a **hermeneutic framework.***

Results: Patients negotiated the relationship between themselves, the doctor, and the computer demonstrating two themes: dyadic (dealing primarily with the doctor) or triadic (dealing with both computer and doctor). Patients used three signalling behaviours in relation to the computer on the doctor's desk (screen watching, screen ignoring, and screen excluding) to influence the behaviour of the doctor. Patients were able to draw the doctor to the computer and used the computer to challenge doctor's statements.

Conclusion: This study demonstrates that in consultations where doctors use computers, the computer can legitimately be regarded as part of a triadic relationship. Routine use of computers in the consultation changes the doctor–patient relationship and is altering the distribution of power and authority between doctor and patient.

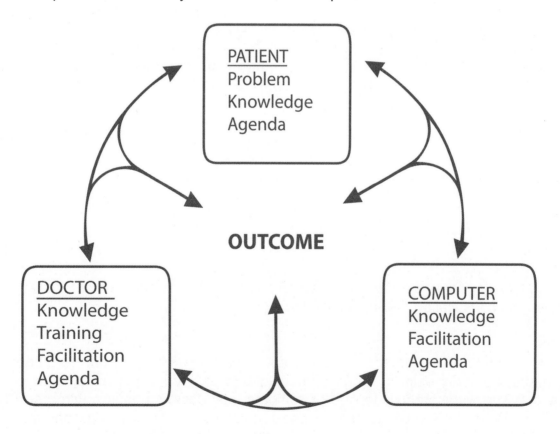

*****Hermeneutics** is an old term which refers to the interpretation of biblical, literary, and mythical texts. This process of interpretation (assigning meaning) gathered more momentum in philosophical and social science studies particularly, as how meaning is developed between the text and the subject – that each mutually defines the other. In as much as we question a given text, it will question or influence us in a co-creation of meaning.*

1. The main focus of the study is:
    A. to document the influence of the computer on the dyadic patient-doctor relationship.
    B. to understand the patient's influence on the doctor's use of the computer in medical consultations.
    C. to explore the patient's behaviour in response to the influence of doctors' use of a computer.
    D. to assess the use of computers in the triadic doctor-patient-computer relationship.

2. Based on the given textual and graphical information, which statement can be said to be the least congruent with the meaning of "hermeneutic"?
    A. The use of a computer in consultations transforms doctor-patient relationships and interactions.
    B. The outcome of the consultation is created by mutual interactions between doctor, patient, and the use of a computer.
    C. The patient's perception of the doctor-computer usage influences the outcome of the consultation.
    D. Doctor-patient relationships and interactions are facilitated by a computer in the consultation.

3. The commentary and graph imply that interactions between patient, doctor, and computer comprise a:
    A group relationship with a mutual definition.
    B. triadic relationship with a mutual facilitation.
    C. dyadic relationship with a mutual agendas.
    D. processual relationship with a mutual knowledge.

4. The metaphor used to approach this research is a:
    A. network.
    B. theatre.
    C. system.
    D. machine.

Unit 2

Questions 5 - 8

When viewing the chart below, assume that the first score (Judge's) is correct. **There are errors in the chart in the other ordinal scores.** *First, find the inconsistencies in the scores to answer the questions.*

CHART (with errors)

	Judge's score x	Score minus 8 $x-8$	Tripled score $3x$	Cubed score x^3
Alice's cooking ability	10	2	300	1000
Bob's cooking ability	9	1	27	792
Claire's cooking ability	8.5	0.5	25.5	614.125
Dana's cooking ability	8	0	24	521
Edgar's cooking ability	5	3	15	150

5. From the cooks in the chart, who has a correct score in all representational summaries?
   - **A.** Edgar
   - **B.** Bob
   - **C.** Dana
   - **D.** Claire

6. The order of the scores, if calculated correctly, can be described to decrease:
   - **A.** steadily.
   - **B.** exponentially.
   - **C.** parsimoniously.
   - **D.** regressively.

7. If there were any discrepancies in the tripled score, and they were corrected, the average correct tripled score would be:
   - **A.** 24.3
   - **B.** 135.3
   - **C.** 13.53
   - **D.** 23.4

8. What would be the cubed score of the average judge's score?
   - **A.** 664.125
   - **B.** 531.441
   - **C.** 596.025
   - **D.** 614.125

Unit 3

Questions 9 - 11

The following are charts measuring oil production and consumption from the years of 1990 – 2009 for both countries: Australia and the U.K. Take note that certain numerical estimates or assumptions are listed below the graphical representations. Study these carefully for certain questions will be based on these estimates.

Australia and UK Oil Production and Consumption

Australia's Oil Production and Consumption, 1990-2009

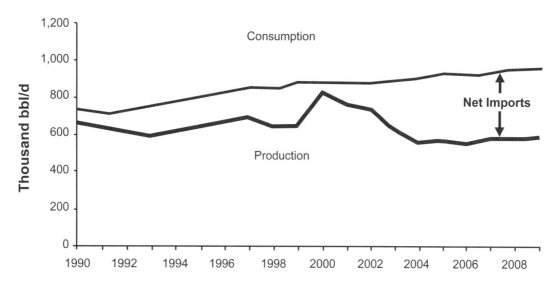

Source: EIA

bbl/d = barrels per day

Estimates and assumptions based on graphical data:
Population – Australia (2000) – 19,153,000 +/-
Consumption Assumed 820,000 (2000)
23.35 barrels per day per citizen (2000)

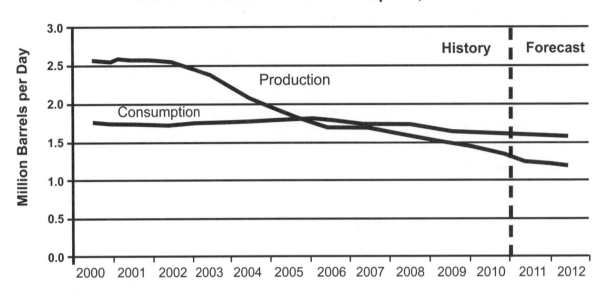

U.K. Oil Production and Consumption, 2000-2012

Source: U.S. Energy Information and Administration

Estimates and Assumptions based on graphical data:
Population – UK (2000) – 58,893, 000 +/-
Consumption Assumed 1,750,000 (2000)
33.65 Barrels per day per citizen (2000)

9. Assuming in 2000 that the consumption level of oil per barrel per day for the UK was 1,750,000 and Australia was 820,000, based on the population for that year, what is the rough difference of bbl/d per citizen between each country in that year?
   - **A.** 33
   - **B.** 23
   - **C.** 10
   - **D.** 13

10. The net imports in Australia in 2008 were roughly:
    - **A.** 300,000 bbl/d.
    - **B.** 400,000 bbl/d.
    - **C.** 350,000 bbl/d.
    - **D.** 450,000 bbl/d.

11. What has been the most consistent variable from both graphs?
    - **A.** Production
    - **B.** Net Imports
    - **C.** Consumption
    - **D.** Barrels per day

Unit 4

Questions 12 – 15

Carefully read the following commentary and study the accompanying graph.

The PRECEDE-PROCEED planning system or framework is from the National Cancer Institute for communication strategies in health education.

Once health communications planners identify a health problem, they can use a planning framework such as the two described: social marketing and PRECEDE-PROCEED. These planning systems can help identify the social science theories most appropriate for understanding the problem or situation. Thus planners use the theories and models described below within the construct of a planning framework. Using planning systems like social marketing and PRECEDE-PROCEED increases the odds of program success by examining health and behaviour at multiple levels. Planning system perspectives emphasise changing people, their environment, or both.

The PRECEDE-PROCEED framework is an approach to planning that examines the factors contributing to behaviour change. These include:

- Predisposing factors - the individual's knowledge, attitudes, behaviour, beliefs, and values before intervention that affect willingness to change

- Enabling factors - factors in the environment or community of an individual that facilitate or present obstacles to change

- Reinforcing factors - the positive or negative effects of adopting the behaviour (including social support) that influence continuing the behaviour

These factors require that individuals be considered in the context of their community and social structures, and not in isolation, when planning communication or health education strategies.

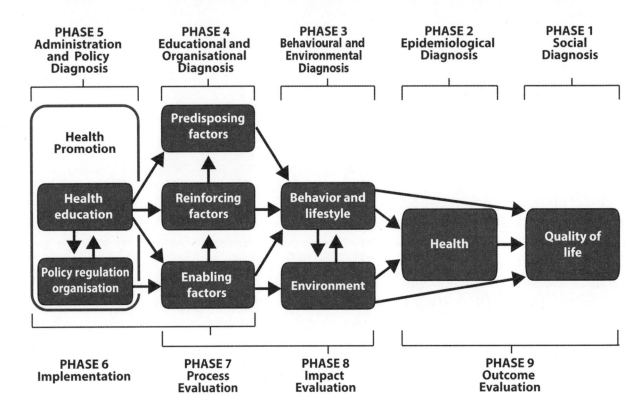

12. The most crucial phases as illustrated in the diagram are phases:
   A. 3 and 8.
   B. 4 and 7.
   C. 5 and 6.
   D. 1 and 5.

13. How are phases 3 and 8 related (Behavioural and Environmental Diagnosis and Impact Evaluation, respectively)?
   A. Through predisposing, reinforcing and enabling factors
   B. Through process evaluation and educational diagnosis
   C. Through examining impact evaluation and behavioural/environmental diagnosis
   D. Through implementation of the process and epidemiological diagnosis

14. The relationship between phases 5 and 6 can be described as:
   A. linear orientation.
   B. mutual reciprocity.
   C. branching influence.
   D. symbiotic or commensal.

15. Based on the information from the text and diagram, why are the three factors considerably important?
    A. They are the foundational basis for behavioural change.
    B. They are interlinked with impact modification.
    C. They are the hub of activity within the graph itself.
    D. They are the required phase or level for changes in administration and policy.

Unit 5

Questions 16 - 17

Venn diagrams or set diagrams are diagrams that show all possible logical relations between finite collections of sets (aggregation of things). Venn diagrams were conceived around 1880 by John Venn. They are used to teach elementary set theory, as well as illustrate simple set relationships in probability, logic, statistics, linguistics and computer science. The number of shared areas, according to symbolic logic, is represented by n. These shared areas are logical connections.

Intersections of the Greek, Russian, and English Alphabets –Venn Diagram.

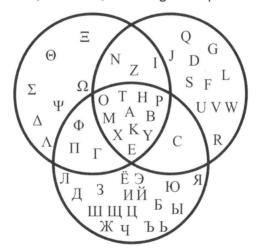

16. Which of the following conclusions cannot be supported by the Venn diagram?
    A. The Greek alphabet does not share C with English and Russian.
    B. Z is shared only by Greek and English alphabets.
    C. Greek, Russian, and English alphabets share more vowels than consonants.
    D. R is exclusively English.

17. Which pair of words can be made using the combination of Greek-English alphabets, but not the combination of Russian-English alphabets?
    A. Home, path
    B. Ozone, cable
    C. Bait, biome
    D. None of the above

Unit 6

Questions 18 - 20

Geert Hofstede is known for having empirically developed, with the help of IBM employees, a multidimensional model of cultural differences. Until the 2000s, it characterised nations along five main dimensions: Power Distance Index (PDI, or the acceptance that power is unequally distributed in organisations and that there are organisational hierarchies that must be respected); Individualism vs Collectivism (IND–COL, or the valuing of tight in-group social networks vs extended family networks); Masculinity vs Femininity (MAS-FEM, or the acceptance of the division of men and women's emotional roles, and the valuing of assertiveness, competitiveness, and material goods acquisition over quality of life and caring relationships); Uncertainty Avoidance Index (UAI, or the lack of tolerance and tendency to normalise and legislate every uncertain situation); and Long-term-Short-term orientation (LTO, or the holding of future-oriented values such as persistence and thrift vs past- and present-oriented values such as respect for tradition and fulfilling social obligations).

Figure 1 plots several nations alongside two of these dimensions, and Figure 2 shows the scores obtained with employees from Australian, United Kingdom (UK) and United States of America (USA) across five domains.

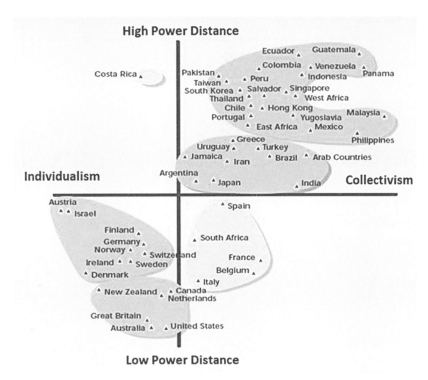

Figure 1. Worldwide nations along IND-COL and PDI dimensions.

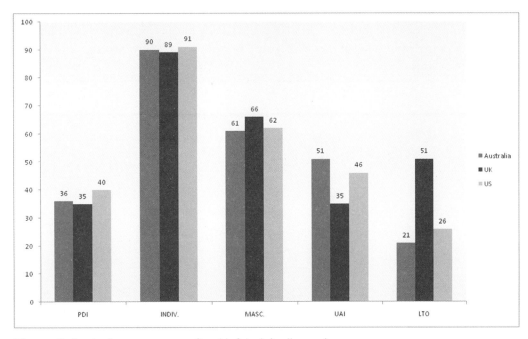

Figure 2. Australia scores over five Hofstede's dimensions.

Sources: G. Hofstede, G. J. Hofstede, & M. Minkov. "Cultures and Organizations, Software of the Mind",
Third Revised Edition, McGrawHill Eds, ISBN 0-07-166418-1. Copyright 2010 Geert Hofstede B.V. Printed with permission.

18. If the majority of citizens of a nation disliked following superiors' orders and nurtured extended family ties, in which quadrant of Figure 1 would it likely be placed?
    A. Bottom left
    B. Upper left
    C. Bottom right
    D. Upper right

19. An employee from a different country feels offended because never once have colleagues asked about his personal life and state of mind. According to Hofstede's model, such cultural clash likely relates to which of the following dimensions?
    A. Power distance
    B. Uncertainty Avoidance
    C. Individualism-Collectivism
    D. Masculinity vs Femininity

20. In Figure 2, the main difference between Australia and the UK is that:
    A. Australians are more individualist.
    B. Australians are more assertive.
    C. Australians hold more traditional values.
    D. Australians are better able to deal with unstructured processes.

If time remains, you may review your work. If your allotted time (25 minutes) is complete, please proceed to the Answer Key.

3.8.12 Graphs and Tables Test 1 Answer Key and Explanations

1.	C	5.	D	9.	C	13.	C	17.	C
2.	D	6.	A	10.	C	14.	B	18.	C
3.	B	7.	A	11.	C	15.	A	19.	D
4.	B	8.	B	12.	B	16.	C	20.	C

1. **Correct Answer: C**
   As stated in the abstract objective: "to explore patients' approaches to the doctor's computer in the consultation and its influence on the patient–doctor relationship" this clearly confirms (C) as the correct answer.

2. **Correct Answer: D**
   This question asks you to choose the LEAST correct option. The diagram demonstrates that (A) doctor-patient relationships are certainly influenced by the use of computers. The note and diagram explain that (B) hermeneutics are based on a mutual definition. The abstract results explain why (C) agrees with the meaning of hermeneutics.

   The answer is (D). The use of a computer was part of the study's methodology and the doctor-patient interaction can be said to have been facilitated by a computer to a certain extent. However, this statement does not coincide with the concept of hermeneutics, which concerns the co-creation of meanings (i.e. the facilitation needs to be reciprocal).

3. **Correct Answer: B**
   "Patients negotiated the relationship between themselves, the doctor, and the computer demonstrating two themes: dyadic (dealing primarily with the doctor) or triadic (dealing with both computer and doctor)." This quote from the results overview confirms (B) as the correct answer.

4. **Correct Answer: B**
   The reference to Goffman's dramaturgy indicates (B) theatre as the correct answer: *"In this paper, the authors use Goffman's dramaturgy (theatrical approach: scene, actor, stage, script, act) to explore patients' approaches to the doctor's computer in the consultation and its influence on the patient–doctor relationship."*

5. **Correct Answer: D**
   First, using a scratch pad, this would represent the corrected table - corrected scores are highlighted.

   There are no errors in Claire's scores, indicating (D) as the correct answer.

	Judge's score x	Score minus 8 $x-8$	Tripled score $3x$	Cubed score $x3$
Alice's cooking ability	10	2	30	1000
Bob's cooking ability	9	1	27	729
Claire's cooking ability	8.5	0.5	25.5	614.125
Dana's cooking ability	8	0	24	512
Edgar's cooking ability	5	-3	15	125

6. **Correct Answer: A**

The scores decrease steadily with Alice's scores to be the highest and Edgar's scores to be the lowest, indicating (A) as the correct answer. (B) Exponentially is incorrect because the decrease of scores would be in large quantitative amounts. (C) Parsimoniously is nonsense, while (D) regressively refers to best fit, smallest size decreases of numerical relations, more properly suited to statistical analysis techniques – this answer is a bit of a red herring or distraction. Also, the question stem already states that the scores are supposed to decrease (i.e. regress).

7. **Correct Answer: A**

To find the average, total the 5 scores and divide by 5. 30 + 27 + 25.5 + 24 + 15 = 121.5/5 = 24.3 This indicates (A) as the correct answer.

8. **Correct Answer: B**

First, find the average judge's score:
10 + 9 + 8.5 + 8 + 5 = 40.5
40.5/5 = 8.1 (Average Judge's Score)

To find the cubed score x3 (8.1 x 8.1 x 8.1). This results to 531.441 indicating (B) as the correct answer.

9. **Correct Answer: C**

A quick scan of the estimates and assumptions based on graphical data (33.65 bbl/d per citizen in the UK in 2000 and 23.35 bbl/d per citizen in Australia in 2000) indicates a rough difference of 10 bbl/d confirming (C) as the correct answer.

10. **Correct Answer: C**

Net imports refer to the difference between consumption and production. A trick for these kinds of questions is using a straight edge, like a ruler or piece of paper aligned across the graph. This alignment will roughly show the difference between 600,000 and 950,000 indicating (C) 350,000 bbl/d as the correct answer.

11. **Correct Answer: C**

A quick glance will affirm that (C) consumption has varied the least - making it the most consistent variable.

12. **Correct Answer: B**

(B) Phases 4 and 7 are central hubs of activity within the diagram connecting 3 and 5, as well as 6 and 7. The whole gist of the last paragraph, concerning the factors, stresses this importance in terms of behaviour change and its relation to health education strategies.

13. **Correct Answer: C**

This easy detail-oriented quick scan question is transparently (C).

14. **Correct Answer: B**

One can infer within the rubric of Health Promotion, of which both phases 5 and 6 are associated with. There is mutual dynamism occurring between "health education" and "policy regulation and organisation". The arrows are pointing to each other indicating a mutually defining, modifying or changing process. For these reasons, (B) mutual reciprocity is the correct answer. The other answers are incorrect because (A) linear orientation stresses a one-way, unidirectional flow of information. (C) applies to the arrows moving into phases 4 and 7, yet this does not address the internal relationship between 5 and 6 while (D) is simply irrelevant.

15. **Correct Answer: A**

Considering that the commentary and diagram are essentially concerned with health education in relation to behavioural change, (A) is the correct answer. The other answers are holistically related to the diagram itself but do not reflect the essential focus of behavioural change. Without these contextually defining factors, the diagram would be meaningless. The whole framework of the analysis is based on the factors as can be inferred from the commentary excerpt:

The PRECEDE-PROCEED framework is an approach to planning that examines the factors contributing to behaviour change. . . These factors require that individuals be considered in the context of their community and social structures, and not in isolation, when planning communication or health education strategies.

16. **Correct Answer: C**

    A quick perusal of the Venn diagram will confirm that all propositions (A), (B), and (D) are true while (C) the correct answer cannot be supported by the Venn diagram.

17. **Correct Answer: C**

    (A) HOME and PATH can be formed at both intersections.

    (B) While OZONE can be formed in Greek-English alphabets, CABLE cannot be formed at either of the intersections.

    (C) Only at the intersection of Greek-English alphabets can BAIT and BIOME can be formed. This is because the letter "I" is exclusive at the Greek-English intersection. Of course, this makes option (D) wrong.

18. **Correct Answer: C**

    The acceptance that power is unequally distributed and hierarchies must be respected are assessed via PDI. Those with low scores on this scale do not easily accept that their place in organisations is unquestionable and defined by their place within the organisational hierarchies.

For a country with high PDI, this is understood as a lack of respect for superiors' orders. This would thus likely be associated with the bottom quadrants of Figure 1. The valuing and nurturing extended family ties, rather than the emotional bonds with a small set of individuals who may or may not belong to one's family, is associated with collectivism. This places the country to the right of Figure 1. Then, the nation should be placed on the bottom right side of the quadrant in Figure 1.

19. **Correct Answer: D**

    The offended individual expected co-workers to establish an intimate, personal relationship with him/her. When colleagues failed to do so, they demonstrated how such line of querying and relating was not a cultural norm regulating their behaviour. That is, they clash in regards to the dimension MAS-FEM. This dimension taps into values such as the establishment of caring relationships (Femininity) vs the establishment of competitive, materialistic, and assertive relationships (Masculinity).

20. **Correct Answer: C**

    According to Figure 2, the three nations are similar in terms of PDI, IND-COL, and MASC-FEM. They differ more in terms of UAI and LTO. Australians score slightly higher on UAI and lower on LTO. That is, they experience more of the need to regulate every interaction and procedure and thereby avoid the uncertainty of situations (UAI). They also, and more markedly, hold on to cultural/national traditions and mores.

GAMSAT-Prep.com

WRITTEN
COMMUNICATION

REVIEW FOR SECTION II

4.1 Overview

GAMSAT Section II, or "Written Communication," is comprised of 2 writing tasks, which should be completed within a 60-minute time limit. Each writing task has four to five quotations - listed as "Comments" - that appertain to a common theme.

Additionally, candidates will be given 5 minutes to read through the instructions and quotations before the actual test begins. This short reading time should allow you to start examining the two writing tasks carefully and begin to plan a response to each. Take note that you are not allowed to write or make any notes during your 5 minutes reading time. Also note that the reading time allotted to Section I and Section III is 10 minutes, each.

Why write an essay?

In the early 1990s, the essay was included in the MCAT following complaints from the deans of various medical schools concerning the communication skills of medical students. Subsequently, it was included in the inaugural GAMSAT in 1995 and, of course, has continued to this day. Ironically, the new MCAT no longer has an essay section.

Section II will measure your ability to:
1) articulate your perspective on a given topic

2) synthesise ideas and concepts
3) express ideas in a logical and cohesive way
4) write clearly, using standard English and appropriate grammar, spelling and punctuation.

Being the only non-multiple choice section of the GAMSAT, this section requires two handwritten essays that must respond to two different themes. The first essay "Task A" is supposed to address a socio-cultural theme and the second essay "Task B", personal and social themes. You may use 1 or more of the given quotations as the basis for your written response. In selecting topics, ACER makes an effort to minimise factors which might disadvantage candidates from non-English speaking backgrounds.

You are not expected to write a short polished essay of final draft quality. The people grading your exam are aware that you only had 60 minutes to write two essays.Nevertheless, you will be expected to come up with a 'good' essay expressing your well-considered view of the ideas or themes presented in each writing task. Please refer to WC 4.7 for a scoring key. You may also consult WC 4.8 and GAMSAT-prep.com for examples of what a 'good' essay is in the eyes of the markers.

Real GAMSAT Exam Section II Topics Reported in Public Forums

YEAR	Writing Task A	Writing Task B
2017	• state of politics and public fear • multiculturalism	• celebrity culture • past vs present
2016	• freedom of speech • experience vs knowledge	• pets / animals • dreams / fame
2015	• human nature • cooperation • government	• imagination / fantasy • self-identity
2014	• cultural diversity • modern communication and technology	• happiness • art and its impact on society
2013	• meritocracy • government • superstition vs science	• marriage • work / play • idleness / procrastination
2012	• nanny state • technology	• love • life goals
2011	• affirmative action • space exploration	• happiness • humour
2010	• censorship • political correctness	• self-confidence • competition
2009	• intelligence • the role of government	• age and wisdom • media and its impact on society
2008	• past, present, future • racism	• wisdom and knowledge • optimism
2007	• human nature • nationalism / identity	• humour • work

Note: Themes are usually different in the March and September sittings and, sometimes, in different testing locations. This explains the numerous themes in a single exam year.

Several years ago, ACER suggested a different writing format of response to the socio-political theme of Task A as compared to the personal theme of Task B. However, in recent years, no mention of a particular essay style has been made in any of ACER's official materials, and many candidates have scored well using the same writing style in both Tasks A and B. In fact, some candidates find it much easier to practice and follow one format.

Of course, those who possess significant skills in prose should work to their strengths. A word of caution, though: personal essays can be difficult to control at times, and can attract the disapproval of essay markers if they become ill-structured or overly sentimental. In this case, using the more objective style of argumentative-persuasive would be a better option.

Either way, an organised structure and ideas that display sound reasoning, supported by relevant examples, are central to a high-scoring Section II written response.

4.1.1 General Pointers for Section II

While you do not need any specific knowledge to do well in this section, you should read from varied sources (see RHSS 3.2.1) to familiarise yourself with current political and social concerns.

You are expected to write a first-draft quality essay. A few grammatical, punctuation or spelling errors will not affect your mark greatly. However, a large number of such errors to the extent that your ideas become difficult to follow will harm you. You are allowed to cross out words, sentences or passages. Do not try to recopy your essay. You are not expected to and you will not have the time to do this. However, please be sure that your writing is legible.

A title is not mandated but it could be helpful especially if it were catchy or intriguing. A good title should grab the reader's attention and - having crystallised the essay's thesis - orient the reader to the literary feast that is about to unveil. Both tasks must have at least 3 paragraphs: an introduction, the body and the conclusion.

The use of creativity can be great. For example, some students choose to write the essay (especially Task A) as though it is a conversation between two people. Other students use metaphors. For example, you can use a video camera as a metaphor of an objective observer that switches from scene to scene. In the final scene (the conclusion or resolution), one could begin by saying: "And now, the camera is truly in focus" as one describes how the conflict is resolved.

Though such creative expressions can be quite powerful, they cannot make up for the following basic fact: you must address the needs of the essay. You must clearly deal with the concerns of ACER which includes: (1) addressing the central theme clearly; (2) applying at least one of the quotations to your essay; (3) demonstrating logical thinking; (4) communicating your ideas in a clear and organised manner; and to a lesser extent, (5) technical issues.

Of course, being "overly" creative could have its own risks (i.e. inappropriate distraction). Creativity is best left to those with significant literary ability. It is crucial that candidates become expert at their essay structure and develop a strong body of knowledge and arguments for GAMSAT-style issues. Without a practiced writing style, strong structure, and an eclectic body of knowledge, no amount of gloss or ingenuity will score well – markers will see your essays for the mere veneer they are.

For Writing Task A, since this is formal writing, minimise your use of contractions as well as first-person and second-person pronouns ("I," "me," "you"). For both tasks, consider avoiding using contracted words such as "can't", "don't" or "won't". Finally, attempt to expand your vocabulary by avoiding the use of negating prefixes such as 'not', 'in' or 'un'.

For example, instead of saying "not complete" use the positive form of the word, which is "partial". Another example might be using the word "vague" instead of 'unclear'. The use of positive terms will elevate the quality of your essay.

Specific examples can be powerful from history or from current affairs. Both will be greatly bolstered with the advice in RHSS 3.2.1 and RHSS 3.2.2 of the previous section - irrespective of your academic background.

Either way, an organised structure and ideas that display sound reasoning, supported by relevant examples, are central to a high-scoring Section II written response.

Typically, the most interesting ideas will get the most marks.

4.2 Key Skills to Develop for Section II

It must be noted that assessment in Section II largely focusses on a candidate's ability to form an educated opinion and validate it using logic and reason. In other words, you are to write about what you think, NOT how much knowledge you have, about the topic. The ideas that you will discuss must be highly relevant to what the quotations are talking about, and they must demonstrate careful reasoning. Your ideas must be supported by evidence. You cannot simply state an idea without detailing supporting examples and theory; or in the case of personal essays, relevant anecdotes. Keep in mind that your essay will not be marked for having the most correct idea but for having a logical point of view. Having said that, you must still keep in mind that a real person is marking your essay. Unsavoury or politically incorrect ideas are unlikely to score well. While remaining objective, generally distasteful ideas will likely have negative implications for how this person views your work.

A Section II response:
- must be relevant to the theme of the writing task
- must express a well-thought-out opinion
- must demonstrate sound reasoning
- must be supported by evidence
- must be well-structured

4.2.1 Generating the Response

Forming a response for a Section II writing task starts with two important skills - identifying the theme and stating your thesis.

- Identifying the Theme

While you will be asked to generate a written response to one or more of the given quotations - referred in the exam as "comments" - a particular set will noticeably talk about a common topic. Some comments will offer contradicting views; hence, the theme is presented as a debatable issue. In other cases, the comments will convey varying definitions of the same subject.

Your initial task is to determine what the comments, when taken together, are trying to say about an idea. This is different from merely identifying the topic. Finding the theme means answering the question: "What is it about this topic that the comments are saying?"

Even if you choose to develop an essay based on just one or two comments, you still need to consider the general context within which an idea is discussed.

Still, some students make the mistake of either reacting to the topic alone or choosing one of the comments and discussing a point that may be true within the quotation's context but so far off from the main idea (i.e. the theme) of all the comments. Let's take the following as an example:

* * * * *

Comment 1

Justice is justly represented blind, because she sees no difference in the parties concerned.

William Penn

* * * * *

Comment 2

Justice cannot be for one side alone, but must be for both.

Eleanor Roosevelt

* * * * *

Comment 3

It is better that ten guilty persons escape than one innocent suffer.

William Blackstone

* * * * *

Comment 4

It is more important that innocence be protected than it is that guilt be punished, for guilt and crimes are so frequent in this world that they cannot all be punished.

John Adams

* * * * *

Comment 5

> Justice consists not in being neutral between right and wrong, but in finding out the right and upholding it, wherever found, against the wrong.
>
> Theodore Roosevelt

As an aside, it is recommended that you learn about important historical figures such as William Blackstone or Theodore Roosevelt. Although the recent GAMSATs have not credited the sources of their quotes in the stimulus, this has been common practice in the past. If you understand the biography of a famous figure, you are likely to have a better insight into his or her statement. In general, historical biographies are great repositories of ideas and can serve as evidence for your arguments.

Going back to our sample quotations, the word "justice" is mentioned repeatedly, so this must be the topic. Now here's an example of an incorrect response: you recognise that the topic of this writing task is justice, so you open your essay with another quote by Abraham Lincoln: "I have always found that mercy bears richer fruits than strict justice." Then you proceed to cite the arguments between strictly enforcing justice and balancing it with mercy.

Or, you pick the fourth comment and talk about how punishment can leave a negative mark on a person's life. Then you cite an example about a young offender who was sent to prison for shoplifting. While in prison, he was exposed to cruelty and violence. This traumatic experience became an impetus for him to resent the justice system and become a ruthless criminal.

While the discussion in both cases may be very interesting, the general topic of this writing task does not really pertain to justice vs mercy or crime and punishment, but to justice being nondiscriminatory. So how can you mine the five comments for a main idea?

Here is a good procedure that you can follow to determine a theme:

First, read all the comments and note the words or phrases that are often mentioned. Repetition of words and phrases means that these are being emphasised. In our example, the words "justice", "guilt" or "guilty" and "innocence" or "innocent" are mentioned the most.

Second, observe how each comment either discusses the repeated words in a positive or a negative light. Note that the comments highlight facets of meaning or aspects of a given topic.

The first two comments speak of justice as making no distinction between different parties or sides. The next two comments place more importance in the protection of the innocent rather than punishing the guilty. The last comment views justice as upholding what is right.

Third, synthesise the ideas from all the comments. This is what you should react to. Your essay will either support or contradict this idea in the comments.

Again from our example, we were able to sift three ideas: that justice does not discriminate between two parties; that justice can only be achieved if the innocent is protected; and justice should always seek for what is right. We can then phrase this as a debatable issue: Should justice remain impartial or should justice ensure that the innocent is protected and uphold what is right?

Now you can decide which side to take and defend. The stand you choose will help formulate your thesis statement.

Let's take another set of quotations and apply the three-step approach that we just discussed:

* * * * *

Comment 1

Parents are always more ambitious for their children than they are for themselves.

* * * * *

Comment 2

We never know the love of a parent till we become parents ourselves.
Henry Ward Beecher

* * * * *

Comment 3

Parents can only give good advice or put them on the right paths, but the final forming of a person's character lies in their own hands.
Anne Frank

* * * * *

Comment 4

Some mothers are kissing mothers and some are scolding mothers, but it is love just the same, and most mothers kiss and scold together.
Pearl S. Buck

Comment 5

A father's goodness is higher than the mountain, a mother's goodness deeper than the sea.

Japanese Proverb

First, the most repeated word in this writing task is "parents".

Second, the first comment says that parents want their children to have a better life or future than their own. The second comment says children will only appreciate their parents when they become one. The third comment says parents can only guide their children but their children will still decide for themselves. The last two comments basically express the same view - every parent shows his or her love in different ways.

Third, we are now aware that while there are four thoughts on "parents" in this writing task, they all have to do with how parents show love or provide guidance to their children. This should now become the backdrop of your essay's discussion.

You can choose to agree or disagree with the idea that no matter the parenting style, parents want what's best for their children. Alternatively, you can expound on the issue of parents being overprotective and whether or not this is justifiable. Whichever perspective you choose, it needs to be expressed in the form of a thesis statement.

- Stating the Thesis

Whether your essay takes the form of a discursive or a reflective piece, the thesis statement has to be apparent. The thesis statement serves as your main response because it embodies the overall point of your essay. It answers the question, "What is it that I will try to prove in this piece?" Now, there are important points that you should take into account when composing your thesis statement.

1. **The thesis statement should be ideally written within the first paragraph; it is usually placed in the last sentence.** Because you are writing a 30-minute piece, you will not have the luxury of time to beat around the bush. Communicate the premise of your essay early on.

Of course, there are essays where the thesis statement is declared in the last paragraph. Should you take this path, you have to ensure that you will hold the interest of your reader all throughout the piece or that your arguments are organised to fit this kind of structure. Nevertheless, this is only advisable if you are a skilled writer who has used this technique effectively in many practice attempts.

2. **The thesis statement should be clearly stated in the declarative format.** In some cases, an essay might pose a question; for example, "Should justice stay blind and impartial in all instances?" This is not exactly a thesis statement. The answer to this question IS the thesis

statement. Hence you need to present your thesis in the declarative (e.g., "Justice cannot remain blind if the protection of the innocent is compromised.")

Again, because this is a (more or less) 30-minute writing task, you cannot waste time posing several questions because you will need to answer all of them. Otherwise, your essay will feel unresolved and indecisive. Remember that your task is to provide a definite standpoint - not just raise questions.

3. **A thesis statement should be a debatable claim to be proven using logical reasoning.** It should not be a statement about a generally accepted idea or fact. If you choose to make a generally accepted idea, your essay will fail to be a dialectic as you will likely struggle to present a sound antithesis. A failure to do so will naturally lead to a lower mark.

4. **A good thesis statement should cover a narrow scope of the topic.** If you embark on a very broad premise such as justice or parenting in general, you will either run out of time or overwhelm yourself with a plethora of evidences to offer in order to persuade your reader that your position is valid. The narrower the scope of your thesis, the more effective your argument will be. Again, the more general your thesis, the more difficult it will be to develop and respond to an antithesis.

Example of a factual statement: It is every parent's duty to guide his or her children onto the right path.

Example of a debatable and narrow thesis: Parents should refrain from becoming too close with their children if they want to develop emotionally resilient and responsible adults.

4.2.2 Writing an Interesting Introduction

"The beginning is the most important part of the work," according to Plato. How you write your essay's introduction is indeed critical. You either impress and arouse the markers' interest or you forewarn them that this is going to be a difficult read. This makes beginning the essay quite intimidating for some candidates. For others, generating the initial ideas itself is a struggle.

The good news is that you can remedy a scriptophobia of introductions by following an outline for writing your first paragraph. You can choose to adopt a logical introduction or a creative and catchy one.

● The Logical Introduction

Most discursive essays follow this type of introduction. Your main aim will be to set a logical connection between the main idea, which the comments express and the viewpoint you are taking.

It is also important to introduce the quote at this stage. This may seem redundant, however, it will give you an opportunity to demonstrate that you understand the idea being quoted. You will also be required to define the key term/s, especially if you are responding to them through a particular assumption. Do not be scared to address any parameters in the initial paragraph. For instance, you may decide to limit the discussion about justice to a particular area. By doing this, you are demonstrating to the marker that you have recognised the breadth of the theme, and you are choosing to thoroughly examine one aspect.

Sentence 1: state your interpretation of the comments' theme.

You can choose to write a summation of the comments' core idea or a paraphrase of one or two of the given comments. Alternatively, you can interlace a restatement of your selected quote.

Example:

A point of debate about the essence of justice is whether justice should remain unbiased or advocate for what is right.

Sentences 2 to 3: introduce the quote, and then define what the theme means in this context. Alternatively, expound the idea of the first sentence by citing the two sides of the argument.

A good formula to use for these two sentences would be to write something to this effect: *"Some say that . . . (quote or paraphrase one of the comments). Others say that . . . (quote or paraphrase another one of the comments)."*

Example 1:

Some say that justice cannot choose who it should favour. Others say that it should prompt one to always choose the right thing to do.

Example 2:

As Eleanor Roosevelt once said, "Justice cannot be for one side alone, but must be for both." On the other hand, proponents against this view will argue that justice cannot sacrifice the truth and the protection of the innocent.

Sentence 4: state which point of view you are taking. This is essentially your thesis statement.

Example:

Justice needs to be dispensed by going through the process of the legal system even if the end result does not suit everyone's ideal of justice.

Now let's put everything together and see if the introduction makes sense:

A point of debate about the essence of justice is whether justice should remain unbiased or advocate for what is right. Some say that justice cannot choose who it should favour. Others say that it should prompt one to always choose the right thing to do. Nevertheless, I believe that justice needs to be dispensed by going through the process of the legal system even if the end result does not suit everyone's ideal of justice.

● The Catchy Introduction

Another way to open your essay is by making it unique or striking. In an exam where thousands of papers are being marked, novelty and freshness of ideas can give your piece an edge. Uniqueness may also refer to presentation style. There are several creative devices to help you bait the markers' attention. We will discuss five of the most effective ones, namely: <u>surprising facts or statistics, dramatic anecdotes, analogies or metaphors, thought-provoking questions, and powerful quotations.</u>

However, please keep in mind that no matter which style you choose, you should not deviate from the the two main purposes of your introduction: to link the ideas between the comments and your own, and to articulate your point of view through a clear thesis statement.

1. Surprising fact or statistics

This approach requires adequate research and reading from various sources such as history, published research and the news.

Example 1:

In 16th century England, an otherwise loyal subject of Henry VIII uttered, "I like not the proceedings of this realm". For this, he was imprisoned.

Example 2:

On June 11, 1963, a Vietnamese Mahayana Buddhist monk named Thích Quang Duc burned himself to death in Saigon to protest the predominantly Catholic South Vietnamese government's persecution of Buddhists.

Example 3:

An article in The Economist in 2013 reported that ten people were killed in a fire in a factory used by famous foreign clothes retailers in the Bangladeshi capital. Bangladesh is the world's second largest supplier of clothes, yet three-fifths of its factories are far from being a risk-free work environment.

Example 4:

It takes 2400 litres of water to make one hamburger.

Example 5:

Every year, three times as much garbage is being dumped in oceans as the weight of fish caught.

2. Dramatic anecdote

If you perceive yourself as someone with unique stories to tell, then this style might work for you. Basically, you begin your essay with an engaging narrative. It could be about a personal experience or an imagined scenario that depicts the essence of your response to the writing task.

If you do decide to adopt this introductory device, make sure to expose yourself to as many creative narrative styles. Practice regularly so that you develop the following key skills:

- Use of vivid, descriptive language
- Keeping the narrative concise yet entertaining

Creative introductions still follow the conventions of a standard introductory paragraph.

Example 1:

By the time I was five years old, I learnt all of The Beatles songs as my parents would always play their albums at home. One song particularly stood out to me - "Help!" In times of need during my five years in the world, I always had my friends to lend a helping hand, whether it be help to colour in my new art book or help to keep me from boredom when I played alone with my Barbie dolls. I could not imagine my life without help from my friends. After listening to John Lennon's song longing for friendship, I took it upon myself to respond. I proceeded to write an appealing letter to John letting him know that I would be delighted to be his friend - I would help him with his interest in music and he could voice my Ken dolls when we played my favourite game.

Example 2:

As I laid eyes on the tray of fresh fruits on our breakfast table this morning, I imagine a not-so-distant future when fruits take the form of morning shots instead. Natural food consumption would have become a luxury, reserved only for the privileged and moneyed. Farms and plantations would have all dried up and devoid of soil nutrients. Rain would have been only spoken in fairy tales. Earth would have been deprived of its once abundant blessings from Mother Nature; and so we have to create an artificial environment somewhere in space for plants to grow. Such are possibilities that I envision as I look at my morning fruits with global warming in the background.

3. Analogy, metaphor, simile

Analogies and metaphors are creative tools for thinking about a concept. They are usually effective in making a complicated idea or a very broad theme simpler to understand. You may also use this stylistic device if you want to give an old and tired concept a fresh treatment.

Basically, you have to choose a symbol or an equivalent situation that will embody the central point of your essay. Then you discuss it with an "as if" perspective. The trick is to use this symbol as a main reference throughout your paper. Refer back to it in the body as well as in the conclusion of your essay.

Reading creative literature frequently is a great way of honing the skillful use of analogies, metaphors and similes in an essay.

Example 1:

People attempt love like climbers attempt Mt. Everest. You struggle upward and end whenever and wherever you grow weary. If you do make it to the top to see the view, it is amazing; but most people will die trying. Love's dual nature . . .

Example 2:

A democratic government is like a boarding school. The lawmakers and public officials take the role of housemasters or mistresses in keeping the house and in overseeing its day-to-day running while you go on with your personal endeavours. You pay your taxes just like you would pay the boarding school fees; otherwise, the services will cease to fully operate. Citizens are also called to vote much like parents would be invited in a meeting for consultations on key issues. If you fail to show up in such a referendum, then you forfeit your opportunity to be heard. The balancing system in a democratic government is such that . . .

4. Thought-provoking question

Sometimes, an idea becomes all the more powerful when you inject some intrigue or controversy into it. This is what you intend to do when you pose a thought-provoking question at the start of your essay. But as already discussed, make sure to provide a clear answer to your own question during your main discussion. Remember that a question is only used here in order to emphasise a point. It is not up for the markers to answer or think about.

Examples:

Would you break the law to keep your country safe?

What will you say at your parents' funeral?

Is doing something wrong acceptable if no one is harmed anyway?

If money cannot buy happiness, can you be truly happy even without money?

5. Powerful quotation

"I quote others only in order to better express myself," DeMontaigne once said. A properly placed quotation can have a powerful effect on your Writing Task. If used improperly, you will have inadvertently confirmed that you misunderstood the statement provided.

You can choose to use a quotation to support your position or to provide the opposite point of view. But remember: the quotation must parallel the theme of the writing task, and a quote must be written word for word. Markers will not be impressed if you misquote John F. Kennedy or The Constitution. If you only forgot the name of someone who is not well-known, you can get away with saying something like: "It has been said that..."

Don't forget that even with creative introductions, responding to the comments' theme is still the central objective. You may also still need to expound on the idea brought forward by the surprising fact, the dramatic anecdote, the analogy, the thought-provoking question or the powerful quotation that you used. Basically, all of the ingredients of the logical introduction must remain while you add the extra creativity using the latter methods. Finally, the introductory paragraph must also be concluded by a strong thesis statement.

Here is an example of an introduction, which employs a dramatic anecdote in response to our previous quotes on parents:

My mother and I never really got along. I think it started when I was about five. My mother was suffering from palpitations and she kept telling me that my misbehaviours would aggravate her condition. Whenever she saw me, she noticed something wrong with what I wore or with what I was doing. She never told me she loved me, and she never hugged or kissed me - and to think that I was an only child. Surprisingly, the events following my mother's death would prove that parents do need to distance themselves from their children if it means teaching them to be emotionally resilient and to live responsibly.

The next sample introduction uses one of the interesting historical facts that we featured earlier. It is a response to the following comments:

* * * * *

Comment 1

A people which is able to say everything becomes able to do everything.

Napoleon Bonaparte

* * * * *

GAMSAT-Prep.com
THE GOLD STANDARD

Comment 2

Freedom of Speech is ever the Symptom, as well as the Effect of a good Government.

Cato's Letters

* * * * *

Comment 3

To have a right to speak about something is not the same as to be in the right mind and position in saying it.

* * * * *

Comment 4

Free speech includes the right to not speak.

Jimmy Wales

* * * * *

Comment 5

Freedom of speech is a principal pillar of a free government.

Benjamin Franklin

In 16th century England, an otherwise loyal subject of Henry VIII uttered, "I like not the proceedings of this realm". For this, he was imprisoned. It is hard to imagine a time when people can be put to death for speaking their minds. Yet history has taught us that despite adverse consequences, free speech proves to be one of the most powerful indicators of democracy and a vehicle of positive change. Therefore, for a country like Australia to be considered a truly free society, it must amend its constitutional declaration of rights to include free speech or the freedom to express one's opinion publicly without fear of censorship or punishment.

If you want to practice formulating your own initial paragraph in response to a given set of comments, you can jump to the end of this chapter (WC 4.11) to find the Section II practice worksheet for writing an introduction.

4.2.3 Supporting Your Thesis

After you have established your view on the overall idea of the various comments, your next task is to provide reasons why you are choosing a particular stand (thesis). Each reason must be discussed in one paragraph and supported by an evidential example.

Consider the markers to be educated yet skeptically, neutral readers. They may not be hostile to your point of view. They may not also agree with all your assumptions and conclusions; but they certainly need to be convinced that your claim has logical bases. You must be able to show them that you can very well defend your views in an intelligent and systematic manner.

Hence the primary purpose of using examples is to strengthen your point. Do not enumerate an aimless list of events and all sorts of examples just to interpret a quote or define the theme. Every assertion you make in the essay must be substantiated, placed in concrete scenarios and logically argued in defence of your main thesis. **The key is in sifting the strongest and most relevant supporting examples.**

● Qualities of Effective Examples

The following is a list of factors to consider when choosing which examples to use in your supporting arguments.

1. Relevance

Everything you include in your essay should be about backing up the thesis statement. Stay on track. Always keep that thesis statement in mind when you discuss your examples. In addition, remember that whatever points you make in the body of your essay are meant to be synthesised in the concluding paragraph. If you discuss a number of unrelated ideas, this will result in a conclusion which is disorganised or characterised by redundant statements.

2. Balance

The evidence you present must include a full range of opinions about the issue. Your argument must not only be convincing but must also be well-rounded. Choose the strongest possible refutation to your thesis. However, do not say outright how the opposing views are wrong. Rather, examine one or two counterpoints and explain why you disagree with them. It could be because those views are biased or outdated. Be firm but maintain tact.

When done properly, including a counterargument gives your paper credibility. It means that you have thoroughly considered all possible assertions about the subject before arriving at an informed decision. It may seem counter-intuitive to detail arguments in refutation of your thesis; however, there exists sound reason to do so. Inclusion of an antithesis demonstrates critical thinking; it shows that you have thought about the weaknesses of your thesis, and it then allows you to defend your thesis in a new context. It is not enough to state your thesis and supporting examples, nor is it enough to simply discuss the "for" and "against" of your argument – the best essays will address one or more arguments in support of the thesis, an argument supporting the antithesis and then also address the shortcomings of this antithesis.

3. Accuracy

If necessary, cite data that are accurate and up-to-date. Include your sources. These will make your claims all the more real and valid.

● Different Types of Supporting Examples
There are several types of examples that you can use to build your argument, but it is important to understand how you can use them in conjunction with the three levels of appeals in reasoning:

Logos - is an appeal to the reader's mind and sense of reason because it employs factual and quantifiable evidence. Examples are drawn from research and wide reading hence they are predominantly objective. They become even more convincing when interpreted in the light of your thesis. This is the most common appeal used in argumentative essays.

The following are forms of factual evidence:

> **Real examples** drawn from history or current events

> **Statistics** such as those cited in surveys and case studies

> **Published research** from reputable journals and books

> **News Report**

Ethos - makes use of the writer's credibility or 'ethical appeal'. For example, if the theme speaks about environmental issues and you happen to have experience working in a climate change organisation, you might want to mention it in your essay. Just make sure that it is highly relevant in your discussion.

A usual form of evidence used in this level of appeal is an expert testimony:

> **Expert testimony** or opinion coming from a reputable source in a specialised field

In this case, the quality of evidence is just as important as the credibility of the source. Would you believe information cited in The Economist rather than from a student newsletter?

Ethos can also be achieved through the use of an authoritative tone, as well as sophisticated language.

Pathos - appeals to the reader's emotions and imagination. One of the most effective means to convey pathos is through a narrative in which the reader can sympathise and even identify with the writer's point of view. It should be evident by now that an argument can take the form of a narrative or a reflective essay if your main objective is to prove a point. Pathos, when appropriately used in conjunction with ethos, can be quite powerful.

> **Narrative** drawn from first-hand experience

Take note that a personal example is only material in an argumentative piece if it is able to illustrate the main assertion that you want to make. Moreover, this type of justification would be ideal to use when more objective and more logical sources of evidence are not available. In this instance, the validity of an argument cannot be easily questioned because it is based on a "lived experience". Further, a personal narrative must be emotionally, psychologically or spiritually poignant.

● Forming Opinions

The importance of reading a wide range of topics cannot be stressed enough. Your choice of reading materials should include opinion articles from reputable newspapers and magazines, books on political theories and even philosophical essays. However, do not just take note of possible supporting examples, which you can get from these sources. Aside from reading for the purpose of exposing yourself to different issues and concepts, you also need to develop the habit of forming your own judgement based on what the writers are saying. This second purpose is the essence of the Section II writing tasks.

Some successful candidates in the past reveal that they engage in journal writing as part of their Section II preparation. If you have the time to emulate this strategy, you can keep a notebook where you can write out your thoughts about certain events, debates, and other writer's opinions on current issues. Do you agree with them? Why or why not? What do these issues mean to you? How do these issues affect you or members in your community?

4.2.4 Organisation and Structure

Keeping a logical organisation of your thoughts is another important element in building an argument. It allows the marker to have a clear vision of your reasoning process. Moreover, an orderly, sound explanation of each argued point adds weight to your claims.

It is also essential to keep in mind that Section II is a timed writing test. Following a prepared format for your writing tasks will save you time in planning what to do. Instead, you can just focus on developing quality content and still maintain coherence throughout the piece. We will discuss this further in the next sections.

Of course, you have to practice using an essay template as many times as you can prior to the actual sitting. The earlier you practice using a certain template, the better chance for you to get so used to writing in an organised manner such that you would become confident enough to experiment injecting your own style.

Nevertheless, do not forget that structure precedes style. A reader will be less likely to appreciate a stylish but disorganised essay. One idea must flow smoothly to the next. You have to be able to indicate properly if you are about to shift your line of argument or extend it with a detailed discussion.

There are "transitional cues" that you can use depending on your purpose in the different paragraphs. The following usually apply, although they are not limited to the first paragraph and its supporting paragraphs:

To place what you just said in a particular context: in this connection, in relation to, in this perspective

To give an example or an illustration: for example, for instance, in this case, to illustrate, as an illustration, take the case of, to take another example, namely, that is, as shown by, as illustrated by, as expressed by

To offer a similar point: similarly, in other words, likewise, in a similar manner, like, in the same way

The following are commonly found in the paragraph that offers a counterargument:

To show contrast: however, nevertheless, rather, whereas, on the other hand, on the contrary, but, yet, although, conversely, meanwhile, in contrast, otherwise, one may object that . . .

To compare: by comparison, compared to, balanced against, vis a vis, alternatively

The next transitional cues are mostly used towards the concluding paragraphs:

To refer back to an earlier point: as I have said, in brief, as I have noted, as indicated earlier, as has been noted

To refer back to an earlier point: as I have said, in brief, as I have noted, as indicated earlier, as has been noted

To express a resolution: granted, naturally, of course, in any case

To prove your point: for the same reason, obviously, evidently, indeed, in fact

To show cause and effect: as a result, consequently, hence, therefore, due to, for this reason

To conclude: on the whole, to sum up, to conclude, in conclusion, as I have shown, as I have said

The next list of transitional cues are used in any part of an essay as deemed necessary:

To add something: further, furthermore, equally important, moreover, in addition, not only . . . but also

To introduce a new idea: furthermore, moreover, in addition

To emphasise an idea: indeed, definitely, extremely, undeniably, absolutely, obviously, surprisingly, without a doubt, certainly

The last paragraph is your last shot at convincing the markers that your essay deserves a high score. Summarise the major points discussed in the preceding paragraphs so that your ideas follow a logical conclusion. Never introduce any new ideas or another example. Instead, address any questions posed in the essay. Then restate your thesis using different words and in the light of the various arguments presented.

The next two sections will now focus on the format of the two writing tasks (A and B).

4.2.5 Focussing on Task A

Let "A" be Argumentative!

In the current GAMSAT, there is no strict imposition coming from ACER that candidates should adhere to a certain style. However, the argumentative (thesis – antithesis – resolution) or discursive (pro – con – resolution) formats prove to be the most effective in dealing with socio-cultural topics.

Moreover, as a candidate seeking admission to a medical education (a science-based degree!), you should be able to display an ability to be objective in weighing the pros and cons of various arguments.

An argumentative essay has three tasks. These tasks are summarised below:

Gold Standard Structure for Writing Test A

1   **Thesis:** the first paragraph should provide an explanation or an interpretation of the theme. You may also include one or two quotations that you have chosen, followed by an expression of your position on the point of issue. The second paragraph (and sometimes a 3rd) provides an example, real or hypothetical, that supports your thesis.

2   **Antithesis:** the next paragraph or paragraphs evaluate opposing views to the one presented in the Thesis.

3   **Synthesis:** the final paragraph concludes with a way for the conflict between the viewpoint expressed in the Thesis and the one presented in the Antithesis to be reconciled.

These three tasks should keep you quite busy for approximately 30 minutes that you have to write the essay. The tasks, however, once you are familiar with them, will help you by structuring your essay automatically.

Alternatively, you can follow a detailed outline, which can serve as either a Writing Task A template or a checklist to make sure that the essay meets all the requirements. In any case, having a framework of presentation allows you to actually think of the substance as the form has already been prepared.

Gold Standard Detailed Structure (Test A)

Paragraph 1: Open with a thesis statement.

a. Paraphrase the comment you are responding to. You can state it as a regular statement or you may use a creative device.

b. Explain what the comment means to you in light of the overall theme.

c. State your agreement or disagreement with this main idea. This is your expression of the thesis statement.

Paragraph 2: Provide support for your thesis.

a. Give the reason why you agree or disagree with the comments.

b. Explain what your argument is and provide an example or examples to support them.

c. Explain how the examples relate to the arguments.

Paragraph 3: Discuss an antithesis to your main idea.

a. Cite the strongest argument against your main idea.

b. Discuss it so that you can show the marker that you are capable of 'reasoning' through objections and observations that may put your arguments in jeopardy.

c. Provide an illustration of the counterargument.

Paragraph 4: Explain why you stay firm with your thesis.

a. Demolish the antithesis by showing its weaknesses against your arguments in support of the thesis.

b. Alternatively, you can cite situations in which your thesis best applies and in which instances the antithesis can be appreciated.

Paragraph 5: Conclude your essay.

a. Tie up all the ideas and present it for the consideration of the reader.

b. You may propose a plan of action or a course of action so that the reader can act upon your ideas.

c. You can also invite the reader to agree with you.

You may also want to use Section II Practice Worksheet III (Task A Template) found in WC 4.11 as a guide every time you practice writing your Task A responses.

Why not the expository format?

The Written Communication section assesses your thinking process in forming your views on the given themes. An expository essay simply explains an idea, a theme or an issue. Explanations may show your vast knowledge on a subject but not necessarily your ability to form judgments.

An argumentative or discursive essay, on the other hand, involves the process of establishing a claim (your thesis statement) and then proving it with the use of logical reasoning, examples, and research.

The following are two sample responses to the quotations on justice. The sample responses were both written by students within the prescribed time limit. Just as an additional exercise, after reading the instructions and quotations, you should try completing an essay in 30 minutes prior to reviewing the two sample responses.

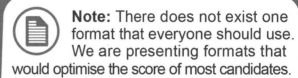

Note: There does not exist one format that everyone should use. We are presenting formats that would optimise the score of most candidates.

Confidence and skill level may lead you to apply your own approach with or without creativity. The key is to practice your chosen approach and improve with time.

Writing Task A

Read the following statements and write a response to any one or more of the ideas presented.

Your essay will be evaluated on the value of your thoughts on the theme, logical organisation of content and effective articulation of your key points.

* * * * *

Comment 1

Justice is justly represented blind, because she sees no difference in the parties concerned.

William Penn

* * * * *

Comment 2

Justice cannot be for one side alone, but must be for both.

Eleanor Roosevelt

* * * * *

Comment 3

It is better that ten guilty persons escape than one innocent suffer.

William Blackstone

* * * * *

Comment 4

It is more important that innocence be protected than it is that guilt be punished, for guilt and crimes are so frequent in this world that they cannot all be punished.

John Adams

* * * * *

Comment 5

Justice consists not in being neutral between right and wrong, but in finding out the right and upholding it, wherever found, against the wrong.

Theodore Roosevelt

Sample Response 1 (Discursive Essay)

The Net of Justice: Selective or Unselective?

Even if guilty men walk free, justice is done provided the innocent avoid punitive measures. This was the notion expressed by judge and author of the Commentaries on the Laws of England William Blackstone when he declared, "It is better that ten guilty persons escape than one innocent suffer." From this perspective one can define justice to be served only when the guilty are punished, and the innocent unaffected. While some proponents of Blackstone's view argue that this is the only way justice can be achieved, there are those who advocate that justice necessitates castigating some of the innocent. The following dialectic will urge that justice can only be achieved if the innocent remain unscathed in the pursuit of justice.

When the guilty and innocent fail to be differentiated, injustice occurs. It is reasonable to hold this view because the innocent are necessarily punished for crimes that they have not committed. If society does not discriminate between the guilty and the innocent, it either grants freedom to all or freedom to none, and it is clear that both situations fail to amount to justice. For example, the sexual abuse scandals in the Catholic Church over the last few decades have been cause for great communal debate. Initially the heinous crimes against children had been ignored by senior figures from within the church. At this point, justice was not affected upon the individual perpetrators, and this has primed the contemporary state. Today, it has become very difficult to prosecute the perpetrators of sexual abuse due to the amount of time that has passed. The result of this injustice and constant revelation of new scandal from the past has led to an undercurrent of hatred and anger for the Catholic Church that is perhaps unwarranted when one considers that only very few of their congregation actually committed crimes. This notion is also evident in the newly enacted laws restricting the associative activities of motorcycle clubs in Queensland. Though members may not be criminals themselves, they are treated as such due to their association with gangs labelled 'outlaws'. In these instances, one can see that the failure to sequester the guilty and the innocent can lead to great injustice as either the guilty are free, or the innocent are punished.

Conversely, there exists merit for countervailing arguments, especially given the complexity of the subject that is justice. Some argue that in some instances it is necessary to prosecute both the guilty and the innocent in pursuit of justice. This notion might be exemplified in areas such as sport where athletes are forced to endure mandatory drug testing at any hour of the day or night. In this situation, all are considered guilty before they have even laid step onto their respective sporting arenas. Though this view is understandable, the example of drugs in sport is more an anomaly than a rule, and the damages to the innocent are rather insignificant when the higher purpose is considered. The invalidity of this greater argument becomes apparent when one applies this rule to subjects such as the mandatory detention of asylum seekers. All asylum seekers whether legitimate or fraudulent are processed through the same means: off shore, within a dangerous penitentiary and with a long wait. Asylum seekers legitimately seeking refuge from the flames and bullets of their homelands find no sanctuary due to these inappropriate processes and the plight of those afflicted by this unjust process exemplifies the shortcoming inherent in the notion that it is acceptable to punish the innocent in the pursuit of the guilty.

Thus, justice can only be achieved when the guilty are differentiated and prosecuted. When this fails to occur, so does justice as exhibited by the current plight of the Catholic Church and Queensland motorcycle clubs. Though there are anomalous instances where it may be acceptable to net the innocent with the guilty, this rule usually applies to instances where the imposition is insignificant and is not applicable across greater society. Therefore, it is difficult to find difference with Blackstone's view.

Sample Response 2 (Persuasive Essay)

The Justice System

Justice depends upon fallible humans applying imperfect laws, thus, justice is imperfect. But without the justice system, without the laws and the rules, society will break down and anarchy will reign.

We call it a "system" because dispensing justice involves several steps, several procedures and several people. There are legislators who make laws that define what behaviours are deemed to be criminal acts. There are police officers who enforce these criminal laws and apprehend persons thought to be violating the law. Then there are prosecutors who weigh the availability of evidence as well as the admissibility of the evidence gathered by the police. The prosecutors decide if there is enough evidence to obtain a conviction and file indictments based on the evidence gathered. The accused are afforded the right to retain their own lawyer so that they can put up a defence. The accused are given their day in court to face their accusers. The judge decides what pieces of evidence can be considered by the court or by the jury. The jury decides if the evidence presented gives them a moral certainty that a crime was indeed committed by the person accused of it.

Justice is not simple. There are concepts such as "innocent until proven guilty" and the "right against self-incrimination" that ensure that each accused person is afforded due process of law before he is found guilty. Ultimately, justice is practical: is there enough evidence to prove that a crime has been committed and that the accused committed the crime? This is all that should matter.

Of course, it is also true that when the accused is poor, he has not the resources to hire a lawyer of his choice. He usually is assigned a lawyer by the court. Because he is poor, he does not have money to ensure that he obtains all the evidence and all the expert testimony necessary to present a credible defence. When the accused is rich, he has all the resources to hire the best lawyers, and he has the money to challenge every piece of evidence presented by the prosecution.

Justice under the law is not true justice. It is judicial justice. It is not unheard of that a person who truly committed a crime has been acquitted because there was no sufficient evidence to convict him beyond reasonable doubt. It is not unheard of either that a person who has not committed a crime has been found guilty of having committed one. Justice often boils down to the impression made on the jury. It is the perception of the jury that matters whether or not a person will be found guilty or not guilty.

A jury consists of ordinary men and women who swear to hear evidence and evaluate it according to set rules and to determine if the evidence presented is enough to find the accused guilty. If any member of the jury has any mental reservation at all, then there can be no conviction. This is the rule of reasonable doubt. If any member of the jury has any doubt as to the probable guilt of the accused, then, the accused will have to be acquitted.

Justice is lofty not in the result but in the effort with which we ensure that it is carried out. Yes, occasionally, a guilty man may be acquitted and yes, an innocent man may be convicted. This does not mean that there is no justice. Justice cannot always be done, but justice must be served by going through the process of the justice system even if the end result does not suit everybody's sense of justice.

4.2.6 Focussing on Task B

Let "B" be Bersonal? OK, it does not exactly spell "personal" but it's close enough! The important point is to understand that you may attempt a different approach in the second writing task. But then again, nothing stops you from utilising the argumentative style in Task B.

Why so different?

Consider some of the criticisms aimed at young doctors: impressive "book knowledge" and technical ability but lacking skills in listening, communicating and empathising. Is it a fact that younger people are less empathetic because of a lack of experience? Can interpersonal skills - including empathy - be the focus of a section of a standardised exam? How does one evaluate empathy?

Ideas and imagination

They need to know whether you can imagine someone else's perspective. This does not mean that you need to write a creative story using the imagination of Isaac Asimov! It simply means that you have to be able to visualise and explain how other people may be feeling and experiencing life; thus the personal-interpersonal and social theme.

Introspection and Reasoning

The logical presentation of your views on the theme (i.e. your reasoning process) will still be part of the marking criteria in Task B. You can also demonstrate empathy using the discursive format. On the other hand, you may find that using pathos through personal reflection would be more effective in supporting your thesis.

A personal reflection is a narrative about a remarkable event in your life. It can be your own experience or one that involved a close friend or a family member. It must be recounted with enough details in order to help the readers understand where your perspectives are coming from. However, it should neither read like a confession nor a diary. Rather, it should serve as an example from which you can extract life-lessons that are germane to the theme.

Unlike a pure narrative or a creative non-fiction, you have to be explicit in your realisations, perceptions, and opinions. This personal example is your proof, taken from first-hand experience, to validate a point that you are trying to make. In addition, it should highlight a shift in perspectives or a fresh insight into a prevalent interpersonal-social problem such as bullying, domestic violence, discrimination and the likes.

Extending your personal realisations to a social issue exhibits another aspect of reasoning ability: the ability to be mentally resilient. When you can learn from an experience, take a personal truth and apply it to a novel situation, you are showing that you can continue to educate yourself outside formal teaching, adapt ideas and make them work under different circumstances.

The Personal and Social Relevance

When discussing the social issue part in your essay, it might help to imagine as if you are talking to a patient or a relative of a patient who is in a challenging condition. The person may be feeling frustrated, discriminated, or starting to lose self-esteem because of a debilitating disease. In this case, you would like to share your story as a possible source of inspiration.

The conversation can go something like "I (or my friend) once was. . . But I came to realise that . . . so then I decided to . . . and now I feel that (state a possible solution based on your personal triumph). . ." Of course this is just one strategy. An alternative would be to pick a quote from the given comments that easily pose a personal-social significance. This way, both themes can be interwoven in a single thread of discussion.

The organisation of the Task B essay can be summarised as follows:

Gold Standard Structure for Writing Test B

1   **Introduction:** the first paragraph should acquaint the reader with the topic. In addition, it should give the markers a glimpse of what to expect from the body of your text, which you can do by clearly stating your specific assertion and point of view. Make sure your introduction is written in an active tone, with strong verbs and powerful statements.

2   **The body:** the second paragraph (and sometimes a 3rd and/or 4th) should focus on one main idea that supports your assertions in the Introduction. Dissect that main idea into three distinct parts: the main assertion, a specific supporting example or examples, and a summary (each could be one paragraph depending on how much you can write effectively in the limited time).

3   **Conclusion:** the last paragraph summarises the main point(s), reasserts your view and ends the essay with impact. This will be the last thing markers will get from your essay, so make sure it ties everything together succinctly as well as creates a lasting impression in their mind.

Remember to write your Task B with feeling.

The following is a more detailed outline in writing a personal reflection:

Gold Standard Detailed Structure (Test B)

Paragraph 1: Begin with a thesis statement.

a. Paraphrase the comments. Explain what they mean to you in light of the overall theme.

b. State whether you agree or disagree with the main idea in the comments and why.

c. Briefly discuss one argument that supports your stance. This is the transitional sentence for you to introduce your narrative. Your personal experience of an event or a condition will be your main argument.

Paragraph 2: Begin the narrative.

a. This is your personal illustration thus it must be written in your own point of view (avoid the third person).

b. It must be a story of something that happened to you or to someone very close to you and which you experienced vicarious pain or joy, stress, discomfort or fear.

c. You must choose an event that is rich with emotion and one that is pivotal in your life.

Note: Sometimes, the narrative can take several paragraphs.

Paragraph 3: Reflect upon the narrative you just described.

a. You must say what you learned from the narrative or experience.

b. Describe how you felt, how you thought and what made you change your mind or your perspective.

c. There must be a 'before-and-after' description of your state of mind and state of heart.

Paragraph 4: Apply the reflection or life-lesson you learned.

a. Find a problem that is relevant to the problem you described in your narrative.

b. The problem must be something that affects a large segment of society.

c. Your life-lesson can be an insight you can share with those people who may be similarly situated; it could be a source of inspiration or a challenge for them.

Section II Practice Worksheet IV found in WC 4.11 corresponds to a Task B Template. You can use it as a guide when attempting your Task B essays. We have placed two sample responses to the quotations on parenting or parents' love. They were both written within the prescribed time limit. Consider attempting the 30-minute essay before reviewing the sample responses.

Writing Task B

Read the following statements and write a response to any one or more of the ideas presented.

Your essay will be evaluated on the value of your thoughts on the theme, logical organisation of content and effective articulation of your key points.

* * * * *

Comment 1

Parents are always more ambitious for their children than they are for themselves.

* * * * *

Comment 2

We never know the love of a parent till we become parents ourselves.

Henry Ward Beecher

* * * * *

Comment 3

Parents can only give good advice or put them on the right paths, but the final forming of a person's character lies in their own hands.

Anne Frank

* * * * *

Comment 4

Some mothers are kissing mothers and some are scolding mothers, but it is love just the same, and most mothers kiss and scold together.

Pearl S. Buck

* * * * *

Comment 5

A father's goodness is higher than the mountain, a mother's goodness deeper than the sea.

Japanese Proverb

Sample Response 1 (Reflective Essay)

Every time I saw my father, I saw disappointment in his eyes. And why should he not be disappointed? He spent for my education through grade school, high school, university and post graduate studies in law. I was a lawyer and I left my law practice to tend to my sick son. It was once said that "parents are always more ambitious for their children than they are for themselves." However, I believe that the way I live my life, raise my own family and define success is still up to me.

My son developed jaundice on the second day of his life because there was bile sludge in his bile duct. He needed surgery and after the successful surgery, he needed follow-up. I was at the peak of my career, but I made the difficult decision to concentrate on nursing my son back to health instead of going to court everyday and leaving my sick son in the care of strangers.

I was a full-time and hands-on kind of mother. I breastfed the baby, changed him, cleaned him, played with him and rocked him to sleep. I read to him, sang to him and talked to him. We were inseparable. I was with him to every doctor's appointment. I held him and comforted him through every inoculation and every blood test. This was militant mother's love – the kind that is untiring in promoting and ensuring the health and well-being of her child.

I did this 24/7. I wanted to go back to work when he was about a year old but I found myself pregnant with my second child. I thought to myself that it was unfair to mother my son militantly and then leave my daughter to be raised by strangers. I did it all over again. Instead of having one child to care for, I had two. I did it every day for years that it became second nature to think of my children first before thinking of myself.

My own mother told me that I was cruising for a major disappointment because I was pouring myself into my children. She said that if I poured my entire being into my children, imprinting into them my very person, I would exhaust myself and then there would be no strength left for me. My mother said that someday, these children I had loved so intensely will grow up and leave and then, where would I be? I'd be left empty with no sense of achievement that I can proudly share with my own family.

I did not say a word when my mother said that. I did not argue with her. It made me understand her – that is why my mother was always stand-offish. All the while I was growing up, I felt that she was keeping something back from me, pulling from me each time we could be close. I thought she didn't really like me. Now I know. She loved me, but she just couldn't pour herself into me because she was afraid I would leave her one day. The result was that I had gotten accustomed to turn to myself for comfort and affection because I did not get sufficient comfort, attention or affection from my mother. I grew up without her, and I learned to fend for myself without her. Now that she is old, she reaches out to me, she wants us to hang out but there is just no love or affection between us - there is just nothing there on which to build a meaningful relationship upon.

My mother may be right – now that my kids are grown up, they go to school on their own, they go out with friends more often, and I'm left on my own again. I feel like my world is shaking – I am beginning to feel orphaned and naked. My children were like leaves on my tree and flowers on my bush. When they leave, I would be purposeless and meaningless. My life would be without prettiness because I think that my children made my life pretty. I like having them around, and I think they like having me around, too. They tell me things they wouldn't tell others. They ask me things they do not dare ask others. When they leave my nest, my nest will be empty.

So what should I do then? I've already done it – I got myself a dog. Dogs cannot take the place of my children, but they do fill the space and the hours when my kids are away. The dogs are there so that I'd have something to keep me occupied while I wait for my kids to come home. They really can't stay away too long – they are sure they will get love and attention here from me. I realise that I didn't take care of my children because they were mine and I was their mother. I took care of my children because that is who I am – I am a person who derives pleasure and meaning from taking care of others. In taking care of them, I was effectively actualising myself.

Mothering was what I was meant to do, this was what I was meant to be – I am a mother. And a mother's job is to raise kids so strong that they can survive without her. My mother and I just went about raising our kids in different ways: I would like to think that we both raised kids so strong they can survive without us. The only difference is, my kids would rather not survive without me. I have made their lives pretty just as they made mine pretty. That is the only difference.

Sample Response 2 (Discursive Essay)

Parenting As a Social Responsibility

Would you starve your own daughter until she masters a very difficult lesson? This is what American lawyer, book author, and Yale Law School professor Amy Chua almost did to her younger daughter. In her book **Battle Hymn of the Tiger Mother**, Amy Chua confesses having a highly authoritarian parenting style. In one extreme situation, she did not allow her daughter, Lulu, to get up - not even for water or for bathroom breaks - until Lulu perfected playing a difficult piano piece. Professor Chua justifies her methods, claiming it is all about believing in your child more than they believe in themselves and making them realise their own potentials.

On the other hand, we've also heard of parents adopting a more positive and affectionate child-rearing style and advocates the same aspirations that Professor Chua hopes to achieve. Certainly, parents often have to use "carrot and stick" in order to instill discipline and values in a child. In any case, they are driven by one common reason: they love their children hence they will do whatever it takes to turn them into better and successful individuals. However, I do not agree that parenting should just be about developing your child's full potential and securing his or her bright future. Parenting should also be about raising children who will eventually become positive contributions to society.

Open communication and reasoning - explaining to a child the reasons why he or she is being pushed to the limits and at times punished - are quite important in developing individuals who are not merely focussed on self-improvement but also on the welfare and the rights of others. An example of this inductive approach is when a child - let's name him Andy - is found taking his classmate Ben's lunch without permission and worse, he does not own up to the misdemeanour. As his punishment, Andy is not allowed to watch TV and play video games for a month. But his parents also discuss crucial questions with him ranging from "How could have Ben possibly felt when he didn't have anything to eat during lunch?" to "How would your classmates and teachers feel now that they have someone in class whom they can no longer trust?"

Of course, the next time Andy feels like committing a similar misconduct, he would not only remember the punishment but also the uncomfortable thoughts and feelings attributed to the act: "I'd feel bad if someone did that to me. . . I don't want to lose their trust again. . . Our family does not take what's not ours." Hence Andy would discourage himself from misbehaving again. The benefits of inductive discipline for developing pro-social behaviour is further supported by a study conducted by Krevans and Gibbs in 1996. Their case study shows that parents who explain to their children the reasons and consequences of bad behaviour tend to develop empathy early in a child. These children also exhibit more self-control, moral reasoning, and consideration of how others feel.

The same approach can be employed when encouraging a child to excel in a skill. Instead of using pressure and threats, the parent draws from positive reinforcement and reasoning: "If you practiced real hard today, you'll be able to perfect your piano piece very shortly. We'll have time to go to the beach this weekend, and you'll still be all set for a superb performance next week! Everyone's happy." Or better yet, a socially responsible parent would be able to reinforce his or her teenager's decision to take up a health-related course that will help treat a disabled sibling and others with the same affliction.

Nonetheless, some child psychologists believe that moral reasoning may not always work with children who either have stronger and fearless temperament or too weak and fearful. Children who take on an adventurous outlook on life will take risks in repeating their offences. In this case, discipline may take more than explanations and simple punishment. Even emotional support may have to be in the form of firm rules and ultimatums. This is probably what drove Amy Chua to resort to extreme measures with her daughter, Lulu, who she described as a "real fireball".

Another danger of moralising and reasoning especially to a young child is when an act of punishment is not properly processed. Parents are by no means developmental experts and may use words and situations that are not age-appropriate. For example, a five-year-old girl caught taking her friend's favourite toy without permission may be made to think of the consequences of stealing. The concept of stealing may not even be fully clear at this age. This could result to confusion and unwarranted guilt on the part of the child.

Despite these contrary opinions on inductive parenting, open communication remains an effective tool in shaping socially and morally responsible children - and families. Even Amy Chua admits that her need to reach out to her daughter Lulu, who was rebelling at the time, served as the impetus to her (in)famous book. Showing the manuscript of her book to her husband and her daughters was cathartic to their family and saved their relationships. In the same manner, a parent who constantly talks and reasons with his or her child would know the most appropriate types of punishment and motivation to carry out. Hence, the argument against over-moralising would be more of a few exceptions than the rule.

In the end, it all boils down to a parent's sense of purpose. If one is to merely mould a self-actualised individual and overlook the social responsibility that comes with raising a child, then any parenting method would do as long as the results are achieved. On the other hand, if one is to inculcate moral and social sensibility in a child, then open communication and moral reasoning should be a significant component of a family. The hope is that, as a child grows to adulthood, and as the presence of an authority figure correspondingly fades, he or she will develop a sense of internal moral compass to reason his or her way through life's dilemmas rather than be on the lookout for any external promise of reward or threat of punishment.

Notes on Writing Task B Sample Response #2

The second essay reflects upon a personal issue that the writer feels strongly about. Using the third person (instead of the first person point of view) does not diminish the strong personal conviction of the writer that underlies each and every single idea expressed. While the essay is about child rearing, it cannot be overlooked that the author is actually formulating an opinion on child discipline based upon strongly-held personal beliefs which the author then measures up against the standards of psychological theories. It is implied that the author is actually reacting to the extreme form of child rearing that s/he not only heard about or read about, the author may actually be reacting to the insensitive and inattentive parenting that he or she witnesses all around.

The essay also works (despite its argumentative stance) because it highlights the social responsibility of parenting. That is to say, the author's ideas on how children should be raised is extrapolated to the way we, as a society, is equipping the next generation to learn discernment and circumspection in choosing how we behave and how we make decisions. This is (obliquely) a commentary on a social issue that confronts us: undisciplined children who grow up to be lawless adults; the lack of standards of behaviour that allow our children to conclude that they can do whatever they wish without thought of consequences.

Over all, this essay works because it is an educated opinion that is logically presented and organised. The control of language is superb even if there are a few grammatical errors. It has a clear message, and it conveys that message quite forcefully. It paints a good picture for the marker to take away after reading the essay. It shows a picture of us as a society, and it lays the accountability for our failure, as parents, to ensure reason and reasonableness in our children. The examples may not be gleaned from the writer's actual life experiences for it to be potent but because the examples are so commonplace, we see it every day; and therefore, readers can relate to the examples.

4.2.7 Timing

Timing skills should be developed during the early stages of your Section II preparation. Be careful not to get too engrossed in developing your great ideas that you might neglect containing those thoughts within a limited time. You need to be able to get used to writing two legibly handwritten and well-organised essays on two different themes within 60 minutes.

Getting used to writing within the time limit will teach you to include only the most pertinent and strongest arguments in your essays. Also, please note that several past candidates report being given full 60 minutes to complete the two writing tasks - that is, you can spend 20 minutes on Task A while 40 minutes on Task B.

Indeed, some students can generate ideas easier on issues involving socio-cultural concerns and can thus finish Task A in less than 30 minutes. Others can be quite persuasive using a narrative. Still, others are more efficient discussing a well-balanced presentation of pros and cons. You will learn which essay format or style will be the easiest for you to control if you have practiced writing in a timed setting way beforehand.

Speed Writing

Remember that GAMSAT is a paper-based exam, which means that your Section II responses will be written by hand.

Even if you have a clear penmanship, there are still other factors that can affect its readability. Time pressure tends to bring about anxiety, causing you to constantly misspell and erase several words. This can make your paper look untidy and some parts difficult to read. If you are used to typing, writing fast by hand might be challenging as well and can even affect your thinking process.

It is therefore important that you practice writing by hand regularly within a maximum of 30 minutes per task. Just like any skill, timed writing can be done in small stages. The trick is to do it consistently.

At first, do not worry about whether or not you'll be able to come up with an excellent piece. Just get yourself used to thinking spontaneously and then wrapping up your main points within the limited time. To help keep your thoughts organised, use the practice worksheets found in the last section of this chapter.

Next, review your writing and identify your weaknesses. Analyse what could be the causes. Is it a lack of exposure to current news? Could it be because you are uncomfortable with the format? Perhaps, you have problems arranging your ideas. It might also help to have someone check if your handwriting is readable enough.

Once you know what your weaknesses are, you can address them one at a time. Continue to practice writing essays on a regular basis but aim to improve at least one aspect for every attempt.

Finally, if you still have ample time for preparation, practice, practice, and practice to a point when you can almost tell how many minutes have elapsed as you get to Paragraph 1, to Paragraph 2, and so forth. Most candidates arrive to sit the test having completed around 10-20 essays. While this may sound significant, there is much to be gained by writing and rewriting up to fifty essays. By doing so, you will arrive with a much greater body of knowledge and a strong faith in your structures.

4.2.8 The Gold Standard Five Minute, Five Step Plan

Another important component of your Section II strategy, which is quite related to timing, is pre-planning. We know that while it is possible to write a structured, complete essay in 30 minutes, this requires practice for most students. This is because normally, an essay would be written over a considerable period of time. You would think about your essay, plan what you would write, actually write, correct and polish your essay, and perhaps rewrite sections.

However, a timed essay is not normal. It is a situation where your thoughts have to be ordered, structured and organised straight out of your head! You have to plan what you will write quickly and efficiently. This is what the Gold Standard Five Minute, Five Step Plan is all about. The objective is for you to take 5 minutes to prepare and 5 steps to finish the essay.

<u>Step 1</u>: Read the instructions and the stimulus material.

This may seem obvious, but you would be surprised by the number of students who misread or misinterpret what is expected of them. Carefully read the quotations in both Writing Task A and Writing Task B during the 5-minute reading time given at the start of this section.

Since you are not yet allowed to do any writing at this time, you can just mentally note keywords from the quotations. Then look at the relationships of each idea in the different comments. Actively ask yourself the following questions: How does this particular idea relate to the other ideas? Do they contradict or support each other? If they contradict each other, what is the debatable issue that must be addressed? If they all agree with each other, what is the unifying theme that ties them all together? Earlier, we mentioned having completed as many essays as possible. By doing so, you will increase your chances of being able to use material from one of your practice essays.

Consider the following quotations and create an essay in response to one or more of them.

Example of a quotation that could be chosen from stimulus material in Writing Task A:

The government is best that governs least.

Henry David Thoreau

Now, in your mind, you should be thinking of writing a comprehensive essay in which you accomplish the following objectives. Explain what you think the statement means. Describe a specific example in which the government's powers should be increased. Discuss the basis for increasing or decreasing the government's powers. The preceding outlines the structure of the 'classic' argumentative essay (WC 4.2.5).

Step 2: Prewrite your Thesis (Task 1), Antithesis (Task 2) and Synthesis (Task 3).

Once the actual testing time starts, you should jot down notes in the margin of your test booklet or below the quotation (you will not be permitted "scrap" or "scratch" paper). Alternatively, a one-page notes section is provided in each booklet. You can write your rough outline for Task A on the notes page of the second booklet, and then for Task B on the first booklet. This way, you don't have to keep flipping the pages when you are composing your essay.

Generating ideas at this early stage will have the greatest impact on your final score.

Task 1: Usually, you will have to explain a statement which will not be simply factual or self-evident. For example, the statement, "The government is best which governs least," has to be explained and terms have to be defined. Make notes as the information comes to mind:

Ex.: Government: *-federal, state, provincial, municipal*
-authority, power -a ruling body

Governs: *- rules, delegates, guides*
-creates laws
-exerts control, authority

When it comes time to write (Step 4), you will formulate a statement which clearly addresses Task 1: "Explain what you think the statement means ." You should choose one clear definition from amongst the possibilities. You may also want to use an example to further illustrate the point of view you are presenting:

The ideal ruling body would strive to maintain, at a minimum, its exertion of authority over the population. Clearly, a government representing the people should not have the right to indiscriminately curb the freedom of an individual. The consequence would be a contradiction of democratic principles. Thus a government should avoid extending its powers; rather, government should use its authority prudently.

There are many different interpretations and examples which can be used to explain what the statement means. One possibility is to suggest that 'big' government produces excessive 'red tape' or bureaucracy which eventually may lead to higher taxes and a greater deficit. Also consider using a quotation about government (e.g., from John F. Kennedy).

Another possibility would be to mention that 'big' government leads to too much power, and "absolute power corrupts absolutely." There are an endless number of possibilities. The key is to choose one line of thinking and present it in a clear manner. {Note how the structure and length of the sentences vary in the example.}

Task 2: Follow a similar approach for tasks two and three. Write down any points you may want to include in your essay which contradict the statement even if you completely agree with it. You should be able to see the other side. If you cannot think of something to challenge the statement, try to think what someone who actively disagrees with the statement would say.

Ex.: i> *Rights of one person begins where another person's rights end: government ensures that happens.*
      ii> *National crisis*
      iii> *War/draft*

Choose one specific example and elaborate. Take (iii) as a case in point. The writer may use World War II as a specific example. The fact that the government increased its powers by legislating that certain members of the population must go to war (= draft) could be explored. The war prevented the Nazi government from becoming an even greater destructive force and its reign of terror ended. Thus the government expanded its powers for the greater good.

Task 3: For the third task, look back at the ideas you wrote down to address the first two tasks. You should then be able to reconcile the two opposing views. Write down what you think is the key component of your answer to the third task. Remember that you are not expected to solve all the problems in the world. Simply try to find the best way you know to solve the dilemma outlined by the first two tasks. There are no right or wrong answers for this assignment. What is being graded is your reasoning and your ability to express your thoughts.

Ex.: i> *When the survival of the community is endangered*
      ii> *Government should govern for the benefit of its citizens*

Prewriting the tasks is not like writing a formal outline. It is simply a way to structure your ideas in order to enable you to write a well-organised essay in 30 minutes. While prewriting might seem like a waste of time, it is the key to helping you complete all three tasks in the time allowed.

<u>Step 3</u>: Organise your notes

Once you have completed the three tasks, you will want to organise and clarify your ideas. This will allow you to review your ideas before you write and to see how they fit together. You may want to remove some ideas and reformulate others. At this stage, you will decide in which order you will address the three tasks (normally, however, you will keep the order as Tasks 1, 2, 3, respectively). Once you have done this, you will be ready to write the essay. At this point, you will have spent five or six minutes prewriting the tasks. In doing so, you will have created a structure for your essay which will make writing it much easier.

Step 4: Write

When you write, pace yourself. This will be much easier as your notes will provide a framework to work with in writing. You will want to ensure you have a few (about five) minutes to review your masterpiece! Make sure that your essay flows. Use transition words and phrases between your paragraphs. Pay attention to your spelling, punctuation and grammar. Be sure to vary the structure and length of the sentences in your text.

Do not assume that the reader can read your mind! Be explicit in your presentation. Providing a specific, well-illustrated example can impress the marker. And finally, be sure to not digress from the theme of your essay.

Step 5: Proofread

Reread your text. You want to spend your last five minutes proofreading your essay. Look for and correct mistakes and ensure you followed the plan you established as you prewrote the tasks. At this point you want to simply polish your essay.

4.3 Building Your Vocabulary

Clarity of expression makes a GAMSAT Section II essay an easy read. On the other hand, it also helps to make an impression on the marker by interweaving words that will add a "wow" factor in your writing. Of course, you don't use "big words" just for the sake of it. You have to make sure that they make sense within the sentence's context. Simply using one or two of these words in your essay will elevate it above many others. Consider making flashcards or an mp3 with the words you like most to help with repetition.

One way to improve or strengthen your vocabulary skills is to keep a "beautiful words" notebook. You can build your list by writing down a new word in this notebook every time you find a term that you feel would make your sentences sound more elegant in an essay. The following list is meant to help get you started.

Accoutrement - *(noun)* additional clothing or equipment; accessories

> *The Freedom of Information Act is the perfect **accoutrement** to the Bill of Rights.*

Affectation - *(noun)* a display of behaviour or attitude that is artificial or pretentious but meant to impress others. This is different from affection which is a feeling of liking or caring for another person

> *The daughter-in-law held her mother-in-law's hand and touched it to her cheek: clearly an **affectation** intending to convey fondness for the old lady who held the family's purse.*

Allegory - *(noun)* the representation of abstract ideas or principles by characters, figures, or events in narrative, dramatic, or pictorial form

> *The book, Animal Farm, is an **allegory** of communism and the pitfalls of having a common identity.*

Altruism - *(noun)* a selfless commitment to the service of others

> ***Altruism** is a rare gift, exemplified by the likes of Mother Teresa and Princess Diana.*

Aphorism - *(noun)* a brief statement containing a general truth or opinion; an adage

> *He is the master of Shakespearean **aphorisms**.*

Apocryphal - *(adjective)* of doubtful authority or authenticity but widely made out to be the truth

> *Historians are always faced with the challenge of distinguishing authentic happenings from **apocryphal** stories.*

Arcane - *(adjective)* understood by a select few who have the knowledge or interest; mysterious; concealed

> *Only real poets can speak the **arcane** language of poetry.*

Bellwether - *(noun)* someone who leads the flock; a person or entity at the forefront of a trend, profession, industry or any other endeavour; trendsetter

> *Our biology professor is a **bellwether** of practical science.*

Bifurcate - *(verb)* to divide into two separate branches; forked

> *The end of the road **bifurcates**, leading you into two different directions.*

Caveat - *(noun)* a warning or word of caution; specific limits

*As comprehensive and eloquent as this policy is, there is still one **caveat**: it fails to mention where jurisdiction resides.*

Chicanery - *(noun)* the use of tricks to deceive someone (usually to extract money from them)

***Chicanery** made him rich and so will be his downfall.*

Circumlocution - *(noun)* an indirect way of conveying one's thoughts and ideas; excessive use of words to express a simple meaning

*Laws have become a series of **circumlocutions**, disconnecting the people from the government and marginalising the poorest of the poor.*

Circumvent - *(verb)* to evade or avoid using strategic or deceptive means; to bypass or go around; to entrap

*Individuals who **circumvent** the law are regarded by society as deviants.*

Conundrum - *(noun)* a serious problem with some degree of difficulty; a puzzle, riddle or question asked for the sake of amusement

*Through unity and cooperation, social institutions can combat this **conundrum**.*

Conviviality - *(noun)* a quality marked by good cheer, liveliness and friendliness

*His **conviviality** and trustworthiness brought him to the heights of success.*

Cupidity - *(noun)* overwhelming desire (to the point of greed); the excessive urge to possess or covetousness

*Human **cupidity** has been subject to much contention in the field of sociology.*

Cynosure - *(noun)* the center of attention because of its beauty; a guide

*An uncompromising policy against corruption is the **cynosure** of the new government.*

Demagogue - *(noun)* a leader who tries to stir up people by appealing to their emotions and prejudices for the purpose of gaining power

*Adolf Hitler was the greatest **demagogue** of all time as history itself certifies this claim.*

Discombobulate - (verb) to upset, disconcert; to provoke feelings of confusion or frustration

*If you try to **discombobulate** me, I will stop talking to you for months.*

Ebullient - (adjective) energetic, enthusiastic or in high spirits; in a boiling state

*His **ebullient** personality made a lot of people weary except me.*

Eclectic - (adjective) adopting, made up of or combining elements from varying sources; acceptance of or adherence to more than one system of thought, belief, culture or practice

*My friend embraces an **eclectic** way of life, being a Buddhist, a Christian and a Muslim all at the same time.*

Egalitarian - *(adjective)* an assertion and manifestation of or belief in the equality of all people especially in political and socio-economic matters; favouring equality in all aspects

*The French Revolution was a prime example of an uprising fueled by **egalitarian** sentiments.*

Egregious - (adjective) outstandingly bad; notorious

*Such an **egregious** mistake should never be committed again.*

Enfranchise - *(verb)* grant freedom to, as from slavery or servitude; to afford rights or privileges that were previously withheld

*This new system could **enfranchise** and empower women in the labour sector, who feel underrepresented and voiceless.*

Ephemeral - *(adjective)* a temporary condition, situation or state of being; short-lived

*The passing of Princess Diana shows us that no matter how brightly she shined, her glow was still **ephemeral**.*

Epistemology - *(noun)* a system, method or manner of learning; a theory on human knowledge and the process of learning

*From this **epistemology**, he arrived at the conclusion that knowledge and consciousness are distinct entities.*

Equanimity - *(noun)* exuding grace under pressure; composure even in the face of tension

*For the quick delivery of relief services, both public servants and victims must practice **equanimity**.*

Erudite - *(adjective)* characterised by extensive reading or knowledge; well instructed; highly educated or learned

*An **erudite** person like you should go to medical school.*

Excogitate - *(verb)* to devise a plan or think something through; to understand something by carefully studying it

*During the meeting, we **excogitated** the best solution to the problem at hand.*

Existential - *(adjective)* relating to or affirming existence; grounded on existence or the experiences of existence; empirical (can be apprehended by the five senses of man, thus, capable of being measured)

*Bruno Bettelheim believed that fairy tales that have been passed generation to generation are society's way of helping children deal with **existential** anxieties.*

Expurgate - *(verb)* to omit or modify parts considered indelicate or inappropriate

*Economic policies are thoroughly **expurgated** prior to publication.*

Facetious - *(adjective)* characterised by wit and pleasantry; no serious or literal meaning

*His **facetious** remarks entertained the crowd.*

Fait accompli - *(noun)* an accomplished and presumably irreversible deed or fact; a done deal

*For this bill to be made into law is **fait accompli**.*

Fatuous - *(adjective)* devoid of intelligence; mindless or foolish

*Use your head if you don't want to be a **fatuous** victim of love.*

Gasconade - *(noun)* excessive boasting; a boastful manner of talking

*You can actually tell the difference between a sincere memoir and one that's full of **gasconade**.*

Gerrymander - *(verb)* to divide unfairly and to one's advantage; to manipulate boundaries, as in voting districts, for self-serving reasons

*Politicians found guilty of **gerrymandering** will face legal charges and be made to answer to the court of law.*

Halcyon - *(adjective)* pertaining to peaceful, tranquil, undisturbed and happy

*The **halcyon** days are gone, replaced by war and strife.*

Hegemony - *(noun)* the dominance or leadership of one social group or nation over others; the pursuit of world domination through aggressive or expansionist acts

*Imposing one's political beliefs on other people is a manifestation of **hegemony**.*

Hubris - *(noun)* an excess of pride or self-confidence

*He who falls prey to **hubris** shall fail to see the real meaning of life.*

Hyperbole - *(noun)* a deliberate exaggeration; a figure of speech characterised by extravagant expressions

*To say that Helen of Troy's beauty can launch a thousand ships is nothing more than a **hyperbole**.*

Iconoclast - *(noun)* one who attacks and seeks to overthrow traditional or popular beliefs and ideas of institutions under the assumption of error or irrationality

*During the Byzantine era, **iconoclasts** from the Eastern Orthodox faith destroyed religious statues and images that belonged to the Roman Catholic Church.*

Idiosyncratic - *(adjective)* an unusual way in which a particular person behaves or thinks; may also refer to an eccentric feature of something

*Dishevelled and unruly hair is **idiosyncratic** of Albert Einstein as purple socks are idiosyncratic to my grandmother.*

Inchoate - *(adjective)* partially but not fully in existence or operation; underdeveloped or incomplete; still at the initial stages

*According to the principles of International Law, unless you fully occupy a piece of land, merely discovering it will only give you an **inchoate** title.*

Incognito - *(can be used as a noun, an adjective or an adverb)* without revealing or concealing one's identity in order to avoid notice

*The monarch of a 19th century superpower country traveled **incognito** to Australia.*

Irony - *(noun)* an amusing or comical situation that arises from the contradiction of things, especially when expectations are at odds with the resulting reality

> *Note: **Irony** is also used in debate and in cross-examination (Socratic irony: where a person who seems to be ignorant, asks questions of someone who appears to be smart only to expose that the "smart' person is anything but smart). It is also used in drama (When the sequence of events leads the audience to expect a particular ending but the ending does not conform to expectations, the ending is said to be one of dramatic irony).*

> *It is **ironic** that the prankster slipped and fell as he was setting up a prank on someone else.*

Jejune - *(adjective)* not of interest; not distinctive or remarkable in any way; insipid
> *The **jejune** lecture caused me to doze off.*

Ken - *(noun)* understanding, perception or knowledge (of an idea or circumstance); to comprehend, recognise or discern

> *Math is a subject that has always been beyond my **ken**.*

Lexicon - *(noun)* a stock of terms used in a particular profession, subject or style; a vocabulary list or a record, collection or inventory of words and terms

> *Adorbs and clickbait are now part of the global **lexicon**.*

Magnanimous - *(adjective)* refers to a person's generous and kind nature; may also refer to a lofty and courageous spirit; suggests nobility of feeling and generosity of mind

> *Bill Gates was **magnanimous** in his contributions to charity.*

Milieu - *(noun)* social or cultural environment; backdrop or setting

> *Our definition of marital union is often dictated by the standards of a particular **milieu**.*

Moiety - *(noun)* one of two (approximately) equal parts; a part of something

> *Ethnic tribes comprise one **moiety** of the whole nation.*

Myopic - *(adjective)* lack of discernment or long-range perspective in thinking or planning; inability to act with prudence or foresight; narrow-minded

> *Racists and chauvinists have a **myopic** mindset, which can be corrected through immersion in and constant exposure to a pluralist community.*

Nefarious - *(adjective)* wicked in the extreme; promulgates injustice

*I knew he was plotting something **nefarious** when I saw him enter the warehouse.*

Nihilism - *(noun)* complete denial or outright rejection of all established authority, systems and institutions, be it political, economic or social; a preference for anarchy, revolution or absolute destruction

*The Holocaust was a clear manifestation of **nihilism**.*

Obviate - *(verb)* to prevent or eliminate by interception; to render unnecessary

*Studying will **obviate** the risk of getting a low score.*

Oligarchy - *(noun)* a political system governed by a few people, usually of significant wealth and influence; pertains to any other system (economic or social) or institution whereby power is concentrated in the hands of a select group of people

***Oligarchy** is the reason why 75% of our country's population continues to live below the poverty line.*

Ostentatious - *(adjective)* a display of wealth or knowledge that is meant to attract attention admiration or envy; also refers to a fondness for conspicuous and vainglorious and pretentious display

*A peacock, displaying his multicoloured tail feathers to attract a peahen, is not really being **ostentatious**; it assures the peahen that their offspring will be likely as strong and attractive as the peacock, thus ensuring the propagation of their species.*

Paragon - *(noun)* a perfect example of; a model of excellence

*This government is no longer a **paragon** of transparency and accountability.*

Parsimonious - *(adjective)* of or having a thrifty, frugal or stingy disposition

*Experiencing financial failure taught our family to be more **parsimonious**.*

Patrician - *(noun)* a highly educated person of refined upbringing, manners and taste; an aristocrat or someone from a noble or privileged lineage

*The upper echelons of society house individuals with a **patrician** background.*

Pecuniary - *(adjective)* relating to money or monetary transactions

> *All **pecuniary** concerns must be directed to the finance officer.*

Pedantic - *(adjective)* learning in an attempt to impress others; bookish or excessively concerned with tiny details

> *There's nothing **pedantic** about me joining the Ivy League Debaters Club.*

Pejorative - *(adjective)* has a disparaging, belittling or derogatory impact

> *Not to be **pejorative** about it, but the lesson was simply uninteresting.*

Perfidy - *(noun)* intentional treachery or breaking off of trust; any treacherous or dishonest act

> *Officials found guilty of **perfidy** should answer for their crimes.*

Pernicious - *(adjective)* results to harm or injury; deadly

> *This **pernicious** beast must be tamed before he swallows us all.*

Perspicacious - *(adjective)* having a sharp mental perception; discerning

> *Choosing the right candidate requires **perspicacious** judgement.*

Plenary - *(can be used as an adjective or a noun)* fully constituted or complete; a gathering characterised by the presence of all qualified members

> *The **plenary** session of the Senate will not start until a quorum is formed.*

Pragmatism - *(noun)* a reasonable and logical way of doing things or thinking about problems that is based on dealing with specific situations instead of on ideals and theories

> *Choosing to work from home as a blogger shows the **pragmatism** of a stay-at-home mom of three toddlers: she can earn money while keeping an eye on her children.*

Prevaricate - *(verb)* to create false truths or impressions with the intention to mislead or deceive; to deviate from the truth

> *The proletariats believe that the bourgeoisie **prevaricate** their way to the top.*

Probity - *(noun)* honesty, uprightness; with integrity

*Citizens are encouraged to vote for political candidates with a proven reputation for **probity** and fairness.*

Proclivity - *(noun)* a natural inclination

*The dentist's receptionist has a **proclivity** for discussing trivial details.*

Proficuous - *(adjective)* useful, profitable, advantageous

*A **proficuous** turn of events propelled the economy to full recovery.*

Puerile - *(adjective)* displaying a lack of maturity or child-like characteristics; relating to children or youthfulness

*What a **puerile** way of looking at things.*

Pusillanimous - *(adjective)* lacking in courage; faint-hearted or cowardly

*A person with a **pusillanimous** nature will have a hard time in the military.*

Quotidian - *(adjective)* daily; ordinary; the usual; a common or mundane occurrence

*I don't understand why you're so excited when it's just a **quotidian** event.*

Rancor - *(noun)* consumed by bitterness or resentment for a long time

*The moment her sister asked for forgiveness, the **rancor** she felt all those years began to melt.*

Renege - *(verb)* to revoke a given promise or commitment

*Find another supplier if this one tries to **renege** or demand an unreasonable sum.*

Res Ipsa Loquitur - *(noun)* a legal doctrine referring to situations where an injury was obviously caused by negligence; a legal jargon for "what you see is what you get"

*This accident is a case of **res ipsa loquitor**, seeing that there is not one warning device found anywhere in the vicinity.*

Sangfroid - *(noun)* composure or coolness of mind, sometimes excessive, as shown in dangerous situations or under trying circumstances

*To commit a crime with **sangfroid** is far from normal.*

Sanguine - *(adjective)* confidently optimistic or cheerful; relating to blood or the color red

*What a **sanguine** face this baby has.*

Sardonic - *(adjective)* bitterly sarcastic; mocking or sneering

*I want to wipe that **sardonic** grin off his face.*

Satire - *(noun)* humour derived from poking fun at social issues and human follies in general

*George Orwell's novel, Animal Farm, is a good example of a political **satire** as it exposes the folly of our notions of equality and sums it up in one phrase: "Everyone is created equal, but some are more equal than others."*

Scintilla - *(noun)* a minute amount; an iota or trace

*Not even a **scintilla** of my fortune will go to that scheming relative.*

Soliloquy - *(noun)* a speech you make or a long diatribe to yourself; a monologue

*She delivered a **soliloquy** in an empty auditorium just to make herself feel better.*

Suffragist - *(noun)* an advocate of the extension of voting rights (especially to women); one who promotes or supports the idea that everyone has the right to vote

*Louisa May Alcott, the author of Little Women, was a famed **suffragist**.*

Susurrus - *(noun)* whispering, humming or rustling sounds; soft murmurs or mutters

*The **susurrus** of leaves was like a lullaby that brought my baby to sleep.*

Tautological - *(adjective)* unnecessary repetition of the same sense in different words; redundant use of words, statements or ideas to the point of vagueness

*This book often makes **tautological** conclusions.*

Temperament - *(noun)* typical behaviour, condition or disposition

> *Though he does not have a pleasant **temperament**, he still wins friends wherever he goes.*

Touche - *(interjection)* an expression used to acknowledge a striking point or a clever remark made by another person in a discussion

> ***Touche**! Your suggestion hit the nail on the head.*

Ubiquitous - *(adjective)* universal, omnipresent or being everywhere; accepted by all

> *His name became **ubiquitous** in the current news because of the atrocities exposed during his leadership.*

Unctuous - *(adjective)* unpleasantly and excessively suave; insincere

> *Even her charitable works were perceived to be **unctuous** by her disgruntled constituents.*

Usufruct - *(noun)* the right or privilege to enjoy the use and advantages of a property owned by another, not including the destruction or misuse of its substance

> *They may not have ownership rights but tenants have **usufruct** rights over their landlord's territory.*

● **Helpful Latin Expressions**

The Western world owes much to the classical language of Latin. Some expressions we use today are borrowed from Latin. Even the terms and concepts that serve as basis for our current systems of government, education, science and philosophy are derived from Latin. For this reason, although no one speaks this language nowadays, Latin lives on as part of English expressions. Here are some of them that might come handy when you write your Section II essays. You can choose to use one up to a maximum of two of these phrases in your essay:

A priori - *(adjective)* means something assumed or known even without experience; self-evident

> *The analysis provided by the speaker mostly stems from* **a priori** *discernment of one's moral values.*

Ad hoc - *(adjective)* means something that is set up only for this one instance, to address a singular and particular set of circumstances, problem or situation and not as something permanent

> *The President formed an* **ad hoc** *committee to assess the rehabilitation needs of places affected by the supertyphoon Haiyan.*

Ad infinitum - *(adverb)* means "endless"; to remember the meaning of this phrase, you only have to remember Buzz Lightyear as this is his catchphrase: "To infinity and beyond."

> *The nagging wife made it a point to rehearse her husband's faults to his face* **ad infinitum**.

Ad nauseum - *(expression)* signifies a boring and tedious repetition

> *The doting mother extolled,* **ad nauseam**, *the virtues of her beloved son, to anyone who cared to listen.*

Barba tenus sapientes - *(expression)* A man described as barba tenus sapientes is literally said to be "wise as far as his beard". In other words, he might look intelligent but he's actually far from it. This is just one of a number of phrases that show how the Romans associated beards with intelligence, alongside barba non facit philosophum, "a beard does not make a philosopher," and barba crescit caput nescit, meaning "the beard grows, but the head doesn't grow wiser."

> *Robert doesn't shave off his beard; he thinks it makes him look* **barba tenus sapientes**.

Bona fide - *(adjective)* means something genuine, honest, authentic and sincere; especially without any intention to deceive or beguile

> *As per his client's wishes, and against the better judgment of the stockbroker, he made a* **bona fide** *offer to buy the shares of stock of Enron.*

Brutum fulmen - *(noun)* a harmless or empty threat; literally means "senseless thunderbolt"

> *When a man who is swaying on his feet from drunkenness tells you he is going to beat you up, you can be sure it's just* **brutus fulmen**.

Carpe diem - *(expression)* literally means "to seize the day"; conveys the same meaning as "make hay while the sun shines" meaning, seize the opportunities that present themselves. In the movie Dead Poets' Society, the actor Robin Williams played the role of a professor in a prep school who urged his students to "carpe diem" - seize the day.

> *My 70 year-old grandmother, wishing to tick-off items on her bucket list, went bungee jumping – the last thing she said before jumping off was* ***"Carpe diem!"***

Caveat emptor - *(noun)* a doctrine in both law and business that someone who wishes to buy anything must be aware of the conditions, circumstances and consequences of the purchase as the seller cannot be held responsible unless expressed in a warranty

> *When buying a second-hand car, always look for the car's registration papers and insurance; check that the chassis and engine numbers which appear on the car match the numbers on the registration. After all, this is due diligence because of* ***caveat emptor****.*

Cogito ergo sum - *(expression or idea)* literally means **"I think, therefore, I am."**; the conclusion reached by the person who wonders whether he exists. In the work by Rene Descartes, the phrase was in French ("Je pense donc je suis."). This phrase became the basis for Western philosophy. For Rene Descartes, existence is self-awareness and self-awareness presumes existence.

Compos mentis - *(adjective)* literally means "of sound mind" ; this phrase usually appears in the negative "non compos mentis" which means "not of a sound mind"; this phrase is often used to describe people who are incompetent to stand trial, to act with legal effect in entering binding contracts

> *The heirs of the 90-year old billionaire went to court asking that he be declared "****non compos mentis****" and therefore, put into their guardianship.*

Coup de grace - *(French expression)* means the final touch or decisive stroke; In art, it is the last brushstroke to a masterpiece. In murder novels, it is the "last strike or the last stroke" meaning, the death blow.

> *The fencer lunges with a* ***coup de grace*** *- his foil hits the mark near the heart of his opponent. It was his winning move.*

Cui bono - *(expression)* literally means "Who benefits?"; a rhetorical Latin legal phrase used to imply that whoever appears to have the most to gain from a crime is probably the culprit. More generally, it is used in English to question the meaningfulness or advantages of carrying something out.

*The police detective, all dressed up in the fashion of Sherlock Holmes, turned around most theatrically and said to the relatives of the victim: "**Cui bono**? He who has the most to gain from the crime probably had the strongest motive to commit it."*

De facto - *(noun)* In law and business, it means to exist as a fact even without legal sanction or legal right.

*In Australia, when a man and a woman live together sharing domestic life, they are considered a **de facto** couple and are entitled to the same rights given to married couples.*

De jure - *(noun)* according to law; by legal right

*Adultery is illegal, **de jure**, in many states, but the laws are never enforced.*

De novo - *(adverb)* used in English to mean "anew" or "afresh"

*When one appeals a lower court decision, the appellate court usually reviews the evidence **de novo**.*

Dum spiro spero - *(expression or motto)* literally means, "While I breathe, I hope."; the English equivalent is "Hope springs eternal."

*My grandmother, on a hospital bed after suffering a stroke, said to the doctor who told her that she might not be able to drive a car anymore: **"Dum spiro spero."***

E pluribus unum - *(expression or motto)* literally means "out of many, one"

*The Latin phrase "**E pluribus unum**" appears on the seal of the United States as it is the official motto of the United States of America, signifying the federal system of government.*

Errare humanum est - *(expression)* literally means "to err is human"; It means that it is expected for mortal men to make mistakes. This harks back to the Biblical story of the first man, Adam, and how he and his wife, Eve, fell into sin. The rest of humanity which was begotten of them, therefore inherited the tendency to err, to make mistakes and to sin. The entire phrase is: "Errare humanum est, et ignoscere divinum." (Translated: To err is human, and to forgive, divine.")

Félix cupla - *(noun)* literally a "happy fault"; an apparent mistake or disaster that actually ends up having surprisingly beneficial consequences

> *Losing my job when I was laid off, although quite a stressful experience, turned out to be a **félix culpa** since I started a business, which is now quite profitable.*

Imperium in emperio - *(noun)* meaning "an empire within an empire"; can be used literally to refer to a self-governing state confined within a larger one; or to a rebellious state fighting for independence from another; or, more figuratively, to a department or a group of workers in an organisation who, despite appearing to work for themselves, are still answerable to an even larger corporation.

> *The IT Department at our office is an **imperium in imperio**: it is made up of techie geeks who work independently, often ignoring the office dress code and the designated office hours.*

Je ne sais quoi - *(noun)* This is actually French phrase which literally means "I don't know what"; its English equivalent is 'a certain something'; refers to an innate quality of a person or thing that makes them attractive but which cannot be quantified, articulated, or put into words

> *To be a supermodel, it is not enough to be merely tall or beautifully proportioned; one also needs to have a presence, a certain **je ne sais quoi**.*

Mea culpa - *(expression)* literally means "the fault is mine"; it is the Latin equivalent of a plea of guilty in court; also a form of apology

> *The witness exclaimed, "**Mea culpa!**" when the opposing lawyer showed her a discrepancy in her recollection of events.*

Modus operandi - *(noun)* often used to describe a signature move or signature moves of criminals

*Most internet scammers have the same **modus operandi**: they send you an email informing you that you have won several thousand dollars but in order to receive the entire amount, you are to deposit a certain smaller amount to "verify" your account and whereabouts.*

Non sequitur - *(noun)* an illogical conclusion; the opposite of "et sequitur" which means "and so on and so forth"; usually indicates that there is a logical gap between two propositions

*Just because I agreed to go out on one date with you, it doesn't mean I love you or I want to marry you – that is **non sequitur**.*

Panem et circensēs - *(noun)* means "bread and circuses"; refers to the basic needs and desires - i.e., food and entertainment - to keep a person happy

*In order to keep the Roman citizens from becoming an unruly mob, the emperors took it as their political duty to provide them with **panem et circensēs** to keep them quiet and compliant.*

Persona non grata - *(noun)* literally means "an unwelcome person"; the term is primarily used of diplomatic officials from other countries when they have committed crimes in a host country and are expelled from that host country

*Even when he was accused of sexually harassing his personal assistant, the attaché could not be criminally charged but he was declared "**persona non grata**" and he left for his home country.*

Quid pro quo - *(noun)* literally means "this for that"; the original phrase signifies an exchange of things with equivalent value; the English equivalent is "tit for tat" signifying an equivalent retaliation;

*The serial killer Hannibal Lester refused to answer the FBI agent's questions unless the FBI agent herself answers his questions regarding her personal life; he told her "**Quid pro quo**, Clarisse."*

Semper Fi - *(noun)* This is the motto of the US Marines which means "Always faithful" or "Always keep the faith". This motto comes with a twin "Marines leave no man behind." This signifies the camaraderie in arms of the Marines that in battle, at great risk to themselves, they will bring home the men with whom they fought side by side, be they dead or alive. It also signifies that Marines will always be faithful to their oath to uphold their nation's defense.

Sine qua non - *(noun)* something you cannot do without; in law, it is an absolute condition, that is, it is a condition that must be met before entering into a privilege or a right

> *When Sara's grandmother bequeathed to her one million dollars in her will, she made Sara's marriage a* **sine qua non** *to the inheritance.*

Status quo - *(noun)* In law, this phrase is used as "status quo ante" which means, the status or state of affairs prior to the present controversy; in everyday language, the term "status quo" means the actual state of affairs in the present. The best way to remember this phrase is by calling to mind the Disney movie High School Musical:

> *The popular girl, Sharpe Adams, was opposed to the basketball athletes and Math wizards joining the drama club and the musical so she sang, "stick to the* **status quo.**"

Tempus fugit - *(expression)* literally means "time flies"; in English, the phrase "time flies when you're having fun" comes from the Latin phrase 'tempus fugit'.

Veni, vidi, vici - *(expression or motto)* This is what Julius Ceasar said when he reported to the Roman Senate after he conquered the Gauls (of France) "I came, I saw, I conquered."

Verbatim - *(can be used as adverb or adjective)* means "word for word"; a precise and exact quote of what someone said

> *The senator said to the reporter who was interviewing him: "You can quote me on that, in fact, quote me* **verbatim**, *why don't you?"*

Veto - *(can be used as noun or verb)* the political power to single-handedly stop or make void a law

> *The new immigration bill passed by a slim margin in Congress, but the President is likely to* **veto** *it.*

Vox populi - *(noun)* literally means "the voice of the people"; refers to public opinion

> *When elected viva voce by the Roman mob, this is what the elected official says when he accepts the elected position "***vox populi**, *vox dei" which means, God has spoken through the people.*

4.4 Practice Materials

It is great to know the structure, as previously described, for Task A and Task B. However, you must practice generating ideas and expressing yourself.

Practice Problems
• Brainstorm using famous quotes (WC 4.5)
• Generate thesis statements using sets of quotes (WC 4.6)
• ACER's Automatic Scoring for Written Communication
• Gold Standard (GS) Essay Correction Service

Full-length Practice Tests
• 5 GS Online GAMSAT Practice Tests
• GAMSAT Heaps: 10 Full-length Practice Tests for the GAMSAT (this includes the 5 GS tests)
• ACER Materials

If you want to find out how you would fare according to ACER's marking guide, ACER offers a paid, automated essay scoring service. On the other hand, if you are very concerned about your performance and feel that you need personalised comments from an expert, you can find an essay correcting service available at GAMSAT-prep.com.

4.5 Advice on How to Generate Ideas

Many candidates struggle in generating their initial ideas for an essay. One possible root cause may be a difficulty in comprehending the idea expressed in a quotation. In most cases, you will simply not know enough about the topic. By writing a timed essay, and then revising it by doing research outside of exam conditions, you will grow your body of knowledge. This body of knowledge is what separates the very high achievers from the median in Section II.

As your knowledge builds, you may still experience issues attempting to piece together your arguments and evidence. One way to address this problem is by having a ready set of guide questions that you can actively ask yourself while you consider a given quotation. The following are some of these possible questions:

Main idea/Introduction:

1. What is the quotation talking about?

2. What is its main point?

Thesis/Body:

1. What is my immediate thought or reaction to the quotation?

2. What is the significant issue / first-hand experience that I can relate to my thesis?

3. Check for focus and relevance: How does it connect to the view reflected by the quotation?

Antithesis/Body:

1. What opinion or situation can I recall, based on knowledge or experience, that will counter my initial view in the thesis?

2. Check again for focus and relevance: How does it connect to the central idea presented in the quotation?

Synthesis/Conclusion:

1. How do I reconcile the two opposing views with my thesis?

2. How do I connect these views in my present socio-cultural or interpersonal context?

We have placed 50 quotations for you to work through. Half for Writing Task A and the other half for Writing Task B. Please consider re-reading WC 4.2.5 and WC 4.2.6. Your aim is to quickly key in on the idea being presented and generate ideas in point form in less than 5 minutes. Frankly, your efficiency should increase in the last 10 essays in each section. Do not try to complete all the exercises in one sitting.

You can discuss the way you structured your essay with other students in our Forum.

4.5.1 Writing Task A Quotations

1. Let us never negotiate out of fear. But let us never fear to negotiate.

   John F. Kennedy

   Thesis _____
   Antithesis _____
   Synthesis _____

2. We live in a moment in history where change is so speeded up that we begin to see the present only when it is already disappearing.

   R.D. Laing

   Thesis _____
   Antithesis _____
   Synthesis _____

3. All diplomacy is a continuation of war by other means.

   Chou En-Lai

   Thesis _____
   Antithesis _____
   Synthesis _____

3. All diplomacy is a continuation of war by other means.

   Chou En-Lai

   Thesis _____
   Antithesis _____
   Synthesis _____

4. It is better that ten guilty persons escape than one innocent suffer.

   William Blackstone

   Thesis _____
   Antithesis _____
   Synthesis _____

5. Money is like the sixth sense without which you cannot make a complete use of the other five.

   W. Somerset Maugham

   Thesis _____
   Antithesis _____
   Synthesis _____

6. That man is richest whose pleasures are the cheapest.

    Henry David Thoreau

    Thesis _____
    Antithesis _____
    Synthesis _____

7. The technologies which have had the most profound effects on human life are usually simple.

    Freeman Dyson

    Thesis _____
    Antithesis _____
    Synthesis _____

8. The great growling engine of change - technology.

    Alvin Toffler

    Thesis _____
    Antithesis _____
    Synthesis _____

9. Ability is a poor man's wealth.

    John Wooden

    Thesis _____
    Antithesis _____
    Synthesis _____

10. The mother of revolution and crime is poverty.

    Aristotle quotes

    Thesis _____
    Antithesis _____
    Synthesis _____

11. It is better to be defeated on principle than to win on lies.

    Arthur Calwell

    Thesis _____
    Antithesis _____
    Synthesis _____

12. Those who make peaceful revolution impossible will make violent revolution inevitable.

    John F. Kennedy

    Thesis _____
    Antithesis _____
    Synthesis _____

13. Injustice anywhere is a threat to justice everywhere.

    Martin Luther King, Jr.

    Thesis _____
    Antithesis _____
    Synthesis _____

14. ...government of the people, by the people, for the people, shall not perish from the earth.

Abraham Lincoln

Thesis _____

Antithesis _____

Synthesis _____

15. In the long-run every Government is the exact symbol of its People, with their wisdom and unwisdom.

Thomas Carlyle

Thesis _____

Antithesis _____

Synthesis _____

16. The cost of liberty is less than the price of repression.

W. E. B. Du Bois

Thesis _____

Antithesis _____

Synthesis _____

17. I have to follow them, I am their leader.

Alexandre-Auguste Ledru-Rollin

Thesis _____

Antithesis _____

Synthesis _____

18. I would rather be exposed to the inconveniences attending too much liberty than those attending too small a degree of it.

Thomas Jefferson

Thesis _____

Antithesis _____

Synthesis _____

19. Those who expect to reap the blessings of freedom, must, like men, undergo the fatigues of supporting it.

Thomas Jefferson

Thesis _____

Antithesis _____

Synthesis _____

20. The only way to make sure people you agree with can speak is to support the rights of people you don't agree with.

Eleanor Holmes Norton

Thesis _____

Antithesis _____

Synthesis _____

21. I disapprove of what you say, but I will defend to the death your right to say it.

Voltaire

Thesis _____
Antithesis _____
Synthesis _____

22. He that would make his own liberty secure must guard even his enemy from oppression.

Thomas Paine

Thesis _____
Antithesis _____
Synthesis _____

23. War settles nothing.

Dwight D. Eisenhower

Thesis _____
Antithesis _____
Synthesis _____

24. You can't hold a man down without staying down with him.

Booker T. Washington

Thesis _____
Antithesis _____
Synthesis _____

25. Men prize the thing ungained, more than it is.

Shakespeare

Thesis _____
Antithesis _____
Synthesis _____

4.5.2 Writing Task B Quotations

1. It is amazing how complete the delusion that beauty is goodness.

Leo Tolstoy

Introduction _____
Body _____
Conclusion _____

2. Whether you think you can or think you can't - you are right.

    Henry Ford

    Introduction _____
    Body _____
    Conclusion _____

3. From the deepest desires often come the deadliest hate.

    Socrates

    Introduction _____
    Body _____
    Conclusion _____

4. The error of youth is to believe that intelligence is a substitute for experience, while the error of age is to believe that experience is a substitute for intelligence.

    Lyman Bryson

    Introduction _____
    Body _____
    Conclusion _____

5. Conform and be dull.

    James Frank Dobie

    Introduction _____
    Body _____
    Conclusion _____

6. You can stay young as long as you can learn, acquire new habits and suffer contradictions.

    Marie von Ebner-Eschenbach

    Introduction _____
    Body _____
    Conclusion _____

7. Hatred is the coward's revenge for being intimidated.

    George Bernard Shaw

    Introduction _____
    Body _____
    Conclusion _____

8. The young always have the same problem – how to rebel and conform at the same time. They have now solved this by defying their parents and copying one another.

    Quentin Crisp

    Introduction _____
    Body _____
    Conclusion _____

9. Youth is the best time to be rich, and the best time to be poor.

    Euripides

    Introduction _____

    Body _____

    Conclusion _____

10. Some people say they haven't yet found themselves. But the self is not something one finds; it is something one creates.

    Thomas Szasz

    Introduction _____

    Body _____

    Conclusion _____

11. My youth is escaping without giving me anything it owes me.

    Ivy Compton-Burnett

    Introduction _____

    Body _____

    Conclusion _____

12. You can't get rid of poverty by giving people money.

    P.J. O'Rourke

    Introduction _____

    Body _____

    Conclusion _____

13. Nobody can make you feel inferior without your consent.

    Eleanor Roosevelt

    Introduction _____

    Body _____

    Conclusion _____

14. Youth is something very new: twenty years ago no one mentioned it.

    Coco Chanel

    Introduction _____

    Body _____

    Conclusion _____

15. There are three things extremely hard: steel, a diamond, and to know one's self.

    Benjamin Franklin

    Introduction _____

    Body _____

    Conclusion _____

16. Comedy is the last refuge of the nonconformist mind.

Edward Albee

Introduction _____
Body _____
Conclusion _____

17. When she stopped conforming to the conventional picture of femininity she finally began to enjoy being a woman.

Betty Naomi Friedan

Introduction _____
Body _____
Conclusion _____

18. When you can't remember why you're hurt, that's when you're healed.

Jane Fonda

Introduction _____
Body _____
Conclusion _____

19. Laughter is the shortest distance between two people.

Victor Borge

Introduction _____
Body _____
Conclusion _____

20. In prison, those things withheld from and denied to the prisoner become precisely what he wants most of all.

Eldridge Cleaver

Introduction _____
Body _____
Conclusion _____

21. People travel to wonder at the height of mountains, at the huge waves of the sea, at the long courses of rivers, at the vast compass of the ocean, at the circular motion of the stars, and they pass themselves by without wondering.

St. Augustine

Introduction _____
Body _____
Conclusion _____

22. Ask the young. They know everything.

Joseph Joubert

Introduction _____

Body _____

Conclusion _____

23. A sense of humor is a major defense against minor troubles.

Mignon McLaughlin

Introduction _____

Body _____

Conclusion _____

24. If the misery of the poor be caused not by the laws of nature, but by our institutions, great is our sin.

Charles Darwin

Introduction _____

Body _____

Conclusion _____

25. They can't hurt you unless you let them.

Multiple attributions

Introduction _____

Body _____

Conclusion _____

4.6 Exercises for Developing a Logical Response

Other candidates may not have much of a problem understanding quotations. But they do find difficulty in identifying the central theme or issue of the different quotations. We have prepared 20 sets of 5 comments each as supplementary exercises - 10 for Writing Task A and the remaining 10 for Writing Task B.

You may want to review WC 4.2.1 before going through these exercises. You may also use the templates found in WC 4.11 as guides for developing your essays.

4.6.1 Writing Task A Exercises

Exercise 1:

Comment 1

> Without censorship, things can get terribly confused in the public mind.
>
> William Westmoreland

* * * * *

Comment 2

> I don't believe in censorship, but I do believe that an artist has to take some moral responsibility for what he or she is putting out there.
>
> Tom Petty

* * * * *

Comment 3

> If you have to be careful because of oppression and censorship, this pressure produces diamonds.
>
> Tatyana Tolstaya

* * * * *

Comment 4

> The most dangerous untruths are truths moderately distorted.
>
> Georg Christoph Lichtenberg

* * * * *

Comment 5

> To forbid us anything is to make us have a mind for it.
>
> Michel de Montaigne

Topic:_____

Socio-cultural Theme/Issue: _____

Thesis Statement:_____

Exercise 2:

Comment 1

Only when the last tree has died and the last river been poisoned and the last fish been caught will we realise we cannot eat money.

Indian Cree Proverb

* * * * *

Comment 2

Environmentally friendly cars will soon cease to be an option . . . they will become a necessity.

Fujio Cho

* * * * *

Comment 3

I would feel more optimistic about a bright future for man if he spent less time proving that he can outwit Nature and more time tasting her sweetness and respecting her seniority.

Elwyn Brooks White

Comment 4

Every human has a fundamental right to an environment of quality that permits a life of dignity and well-being.

* * * * *

Comment 5

After one look at this planet any visitor from outer space would say "I want to see the manager".

William S. Burroughs

Topic:_____

Socio-cultural Theme/Issue: _____

Thesis Statement:_____

Exercise 3:

Comment 1

My personal opinion (not speaking for IBM) is that DRM [Digital Rights Management] is stupid, because it can never be effective, and it takes away existing rights of the consumer.

David Safford

* * * * *

Comment 2

Digital files cannot be made uncopyable, any more than water can be made not wet.

Bruce Schneier

* * * * *

Comment 3

Trusted systems presume that the consumer is dishonest.

Mark J. Stefik

* * * * *

Comment 4

Hoaxes use weaknesses in human behavior to ensure they are replicated and distributed. In other words, hoaxes prey on the Human Operating System.

Stewart Kirkpatrick

* * * * *

Comment 5

It's baffling to me that the content industries don't look at the experience of the software industry in the 80's, when copy protection on software was widely tried, and just as widely rejected by consumers.

Tim O'Reilly

Topic:_____

Socio-cultural Theme/Issue: _____

Thesis Statement:_____

Exercise 4:

Comment 1

> If the past cannot teach the present and the father cannot teach the son, then history need not have bothered to go on, and the world has wasted a great deal of time.

Russell Hoban

* * * * *

Comment 2

> The best of my education has come from the public library . . . my tuition fee is a bus fare and once in a while, five cents a day for an overdue book. You don't need to know very much to start with, if you know the way to the public library.

Lesley Conger

* * * * *

Comment 3

> He who opens a school door, closes a prison.

Victor Hugo

* * * * *

Comment 4

> Education is an ornament in prosperity and a refuge in adversity.

Aristotle

* * * * *

Comment 5

> Education... has produced a vast population able to read but unable to distinguish what is worth reading.

G. M. Trevelyan

Topic:_____

Socio-cultural Theme/Issue: _____

Thesis Statement:_____

Exercise 5:

Comment 1

Technology makes it possible for people to gain control over everything, except over technology.

John Tudor

* * * * *

Comment 2

Humanity is acquiring all the right technology for all the wrong reasons.

R. Buckminster Fuller

* * * * *

Comment 3

If it keeps up, man will atrophy all his limbs but the push-button finger.

Frank Lloyd Wright

* * * * *

Comment 4

The real danger is not that computers will begin to think like men, but that men will begin to think like computers.

Sydney J. Harris

* * * * *

Comment 5

It has become appallingly obvious that our technology has exceeded our humanity.

Albert Einstein

Topic:_____

Socio-cultural Theme/Issue: _____

Thesis Statement:_____

Exercise 6:

Comment 1

Government, even in its best state, is but a necessary evil; in its worst state, an intolerable one.

Thomas Paine

* * * * *

Comment 2

The worst thing in this world, next to anarchy, is government.

Henry Ward Beecher

* * * * *

Comment 3

Freedom is when the people can speak, democracy is when the government listens.

Alastair Farrugia

* * * * *

Comment 4

Good government is no substitute for self-government.

Mahatma Gandhi

* * * * *

Comment 5

Every civilised society needs a government that will protect the people's lives and rights to liberty and property.

Topic:_____

Socio-cultural Theme/Issue: _____

Thesis Statement:_____

Exercise 7:

Comment 1

> Globalization has changed us into a company that searches the world, not just to sell or to source, but to find intellectual capital – the world's best talents and greatest ideas.

> Jack Welch

* * * * *

Comment 2

> It has been said that arguing against globalization is like arguing against the laws of gravity.

> Kofi Annan

* * * * *

Comment 3

> Globalization means we have to re-examine some of our ideas, and look at ideas from other countries, from other cultures, and open ourselves to them.

> Herbie Hancock

* * * * *

Comment 4

> Globalization has created this interlocking fragility. At no time in the history of the universe has the cancellation of a Christmas order in New York meant layoffs in China.

> Nassim Nicholas Taleb

* * * * *

Comment 5

> Globalization by the way of McDonald's and KFC has captured the hearts, the minds, and from what I can see through the window, the growing bellies of the folks here.

> Raquel Cepeda

Topic:_____

Socio-cultural Theme/Issue: _____

Thesis Statement:_____

Exercise 8:

Comment 1

Capitalism is an organised system to guarantee that greed becomes the primary force of our economic system and allows the few at the top to get very wealthy and has the rest of us riding around thinking we can be that way, too.

Michael Moore

* * * * *

Comment 2

I am opposing a social order in which it is possible for one man who does absolutely nothing that is useful to amass a fortune of hundreds of millions of dollars, while millions of men and women who work all the days of their lives secure barely enough for a wretched existence.

Eugene V. Debs

* * * * *

Comment 3

Capitalism tries for a delicate balance: It attempts to work things out so that everyone gets just enough stuff to keep them from getting violent and trying to take other people's stuff.

George Carlin

* * * * *

Comment 4

Today's consumers are not opposed to companies making a profit; they want more empathic, enlightened corporations that seek a balance between profit and purpose.

* * * * *

Comment 5

You cannot help the poor by destroying the rich. . . You cannot lift the wage earner by pulling the wage payer down . . . You cannot help people permanently by doing for them, what they could and should do for themselves.

Abraham Lincoln

Topic:_____

Socio-cultural Theme/Issue: _____

Thesis Statement:_____

Exercise 9:

Comment 1

> People demand freedom of speech as a compensation for the freedom of thought which they seldom use.
>
> Soren Kierkegaard

* * * * *

Comment 2

> Freedom of speech means freedom for those who you despise, and freedom to express the most despicable views.
>
> Alan Dershowitz

* * * * *

Comment 3

> The Internet's like one big bathroom wall with a lot of people who anonymously can say really mean things.
>
> Zooey Deschanel

* * * * *

Comment 4

> If liberty means anything at all, it means the right to tell people what they do not want to hear.
>
> George Orwell

Comment 5

> Freedom of speech does not protect you from the consequences of saying stupid shit.
>
> Jim C. Hines

Topic:_____

Socio-cultural Theme/Issue: _____

Thesis Statement:_____

Exercise 10:

Comment 1

Helping those who have been struck by unforseeable misfortunes is fundamentally different from making dependency a way of life.

Thomas Sowell

* * * * *

Comment 2

Dependency is death to initiative, to risk-taking and opportunity. It's time to stop the spread of government dependency and fight it like the poison it is.

Mitt Romney

* * * * *

Comment 3

We must promote upward mobility, starting with solutions that speak to our broken education system, broken immigration policy, and broken safety net programs that foster dependency instead of helping people get back on their feet.

Paul Ryan

* * * * *

Comment 4

Once you go on welfare, it changes you. Even if you get off welfare, you never escape the stigma that you were a charity case.

Jeannette Walls

* * * * *

Comment 5

I do not believe that the power and duty of the General Government ought to be extended to the relief of individual suffering which is in no manner properly related to the public service or benefit.

Grover Cleveland

Topic:_____

Socio-cultural Theme/Issue: _____

Thesis Statement:_____

4.6.2 Writing Task B Exercises

Exercise 1:

Comment 1

A man's growth is seen in the successive choirs of his friends.

Ralph Waldo Emerson

* * * * *

Comment 2

Friendship is a single soul dwelling in two bodies.

Aristotle

* * * * *

Comment 3

I have friends in overalls whose friendship I would not swap for the favor of the kings of the world.

Thomas Edison

* * * * *

Comment 4

The bird a nest, the spider a web, man friendship.

William Blake

* * * * *

Comment 5

True friends stab you in the front.

Oscar Wilde

Topic:_____

Personal/Social Issues: _____

Thesis Statement:_____

Exercise 2:

Comment 1

In every man's heart there is a secret nerve that answers to the vibrations of beauty.

Christopher Morley

* * * * *

Comment 2

I see beauty as the grace point between what hurts and what heals, between the shadow of tragedy and the light of joy. I find beauty in my scars.

* * * * *

Comment 3

What makes the desert beautiful is that somewhere it hides a well..

The Little Prince, Antoine de Saint Exupery

* * * * *

Comment 4

When you have only two pennies left in the world, buy a loaf of bread with one, and a lily with the other.

Chinese Proverb

* * * * *

Comment 5

We ascribe beauty to that which is simple; which has no superfluous parts; which exactly answers its end; which stands related to all things; which is the mean of many extremes.

Ralph Waldo Emerson

Topic:_____

Personal/Social Issues: _____

Thesis Statement:_____

Exercise 3:

Comment 1

Where love rules, there is no will to power; and where power predominates, there love is lacking. The one is the shadow of the other.

Carl Jung

* * * * *

Comment 2

Contrary to Pascal's saying, we don't love qualities, we love persons; sometimes by reason of their defects as well as of their qualities.

Jacques Martain

* * * * *

Comment 3

Love is like racing across the frozen tundra on a snowmobile which flips over, trapping you underneath. At night, the ice-weasels come.

Tom Robbins

* * * * *

Comment 4

If somebody says, "I love you", to me, I feel as though I had a pistol pointed at my head. What can anybody reply under such conditions but that which the pistol-holder requires? "I love you, too".

Kurt Vonnegut, Jr.

* * * * *

Comment 5

They do not love that do not show their love. The course of true love never did run smooth. Love is a familiar. Love is a devil. There is no evil angel but Love.

William Shakespeare

Topic:_____

Personal/Social Issues: _____

Thesis Statement:_____

Exercise 4:

Comment 1

Experience is not what happens to you. It is what you do with what happens to you.

Aldous Huxley

* * * * *

Comment 2

It is not only for what we do that we are held responsible, but also for what we do not do.

Moliere

* * * * *

Comment 3

Experience is a hard teacher because she gives the test first, the lesson afterward.

Vernon Law

* * * * *

Comment 4

Life teaches none but those who study it.

V. O. Kliuchevsky

* * * * *

Comment 5

Experience is a great advantage. The problem is that when you get the experience, you're too damned old to do anything about it.

Jimmy Connors

Topic:_____

Personal/Social Issues: _____

Thesis Statement:_____

Exercise 5:

Comment 1

The road of excess leads to the palace of wisdom.

William Blake

* * * * *

Comment 2

One's first step in wisdom is to question everything - and one's last is to come to terms with everything.

Georg Christoph Lichtenberg

* * * * *

Comment 3

Wisdom begins at the end.

Daniel Webster

* * * * *

Comment 4

The wisest mind has something yet to learn.

George Santayana

* * * * *

Comment 5

He who devotes sixteen hours a day to hard study may become at sixty as wise as he thought himself at twenty.

Mary Wilson Little

Topic:_____

Personal/Social Issues: _____

Thesis Statement:_____

Exercise 6:

Comment 1

Heroes are ordinary people who make themselves extraordinary.

Gerard Way

* * * * *

Comment 2

Anyone who does anything to help a child in his life is a hero to me.

Fred Rogers

* * * * *

Comment 3

I would describe a hero as a person who has no fear of life, who can face life squarely.

Alexander Lowen

* * * * *

Comment 4

Those who say that we're in a time when there are no heroes, they just don't know where to look.

Ronald Reagan

* * * * *

Comment 5

The real hero is always a hero by mistake; he dreams of being an honest coward like everybody else.

Umberto Eco

Topic:_____

Personal/Social Issues: _____

Thesis Statement:_____

Exercise 7:

Comment 1

Forgiveness is a virtue of the brave.

Indira Gandhi

* * * * *

Comment 2

It is easier to forgive an enemy than to forgive a friend.

William Blake

* * * * *

Comment 3

You can make up a quarrel, but it will always show where it was patched.

Edgar Watson Howe

* * * * *

Comment 4

To err is human; to forgive, divine.

Alexander Pope

* * * * *

Comment 5

There is no revenge so complete as forgiveness.

Josh Billings

Topic:_____

Personal/Social Issues: _____

Thesis Statement:_____

Exercise 8:

Comment 1

> The worst loneliness is not to be comfortable with yourself.

> Mark Twain

* * * * *

Comment 2

> Solitude is the profoundest fact of the human condition. Man is the only being who knows he is alone.

> Octavio Paz

* * * * *

Comment 3

> Loneliness is a barrier that prevents one from uniting with the inner self.

> Carl Rogers

* * * * *

Comment 4

> At the innermost core of all loneliness is a deep and powerful yearning for union with one's lost self.

> Brendan Francis

* * * * *

Comment 5

> To dare to live alone is the rarest courage; since there are many who had rather meet their bitterest enemy in the field, than their own hearts in their closet.

> Charles Caleb Colton

Topic:_____

Personal/Social Issues: _____

Thesis Statement:_____

Exercise 9:

Comment 1

If you want creative workers, give them enough time to play.

John Cleese

* * * * *

Comment 2

There is a time for work and there is a time for play. Don't ever mix both.

* * * * *

Comment 3

This is the real secret of life - to be completely engaged with what you are doing in the here and now. And instead of calling it work, realise it is play.

Alan Wilson Watts

* * * * *

Comment 4

There is virtue in work and there is virtue in rest. Use both and overlook neither.

Alan Cohen

* * * * *

Comment 5

You can discover more about a person in an hour of play than in a year of conversation.

Plato

Topic:_____

Personal/Social Issues: _____

Thesis Statement:_____

Exercise 10:

Comment 1

Attitude is a little thing that makes a big difference.

Winston Churchill

* * * * *

Comment 2

Excellence is not a skill. It is an attitude.

Ralph Marston

* * * * *

Comment 3

Our attitude towards others determines their attitude towards us.

Earl Nightingale

* * * * *

Comment 4

You cannot change what has already happened - but your attitude can.

* * * * *

Comment 5

Weakness of attitude becomes weakness of character.

Albert Einstein

Topic:_____

Personal/Social Issues: _____

Thesis Statement:_____

4.7 The Scoring Key

Your score in the Written Communication section will mostly be based on how you present your ideas. Although technical issues - like occasional grammar and spelling errors - essentially influence the quality of your writing, these are only assessed relative to the effectiveness of your general response. Your personal stand and attitude towards the subject matter will not be part of the assessment. The following are two primary criteria on which Section II is assessed: thought and content, and organisation and expression.

Thought and content refers to the substance of your ideas in response to a text. The GAMSAT gives emphasis on generative thinking, which is basically about generating values and innovative ideas in your writing within the thirty minutes per essay time limit. The way you effectively carry out your thoughts and feelings as responses to the task give weight to this criterion.

Organisation and expression is how you develop those fresh ideas in a logical and coherent manner. Control of language, i.e., grammar and fluency, is an inherent consideration in the assessment. However, your skills in this area will only be secondary to the overall content of your response.

Most papers are evaluated on common scoring descriptions. It is advisable that you ask someone to correct your essay to get a general idea. Have this person go through the following guide. Please be reminded that this is not endorsed by ACER and should only be considered as a guide to provide you with a general idea of the process.

Typical Essay Grade	Characteristics of a Paper	Estimated Conversion to a GAMSAT Score
6/6	Thought and content shows clear and coherent transitions of ideas. The writer stays focussed on the subject or issue. There is evidence of a logical build-up of arguments (i.e., normally just Task A but possibly Task B) or reflective discussion (i.e., Task B). Command of the language is excellent.	≥ 72
5/6	Writing shows clarity of ideas with a certain extent of complexity. The argument stays focussed on the issue while main ideas are well-developed. Control of the language is strong.	65–71

Typical Essay Grade	Characteristics of a Paper	Estimated Conversion to a GAMSAT Score
4/6	The essay observes clarity of thought and some depth in ideas. There is also a development of major points and some focus. Control of the language is adequate.	58–64
3/6	There is evidence of some problems with integration and transition of ideas. Major ideas need to be organised and discussed clearly. Errors in grammar and mechanics are evident.	51–57
2/6	Thought and content are disorganised and unclear. There is a lack of logical organisation of main ideas. There are numerous errors in grammar, usage and structure.	44–50
1/6	The essay shows a lack of comprehension about the writing task. There is no development and organisation of ideas. Poor handling of the language prevents the reader from following the points of the writer.	≤ 43

In the next section (WC 4.8), you will find a couple of corrected Section II essays and later, in WC 4.9, we will present some excellent essays for your perusal. Also, we have placed dozens of Section II essays online that were corrected using the Gold Standard (GS) Essay Correction Service. You can access all these essays by logging in to your GAMSAT-prep.com account and clicking on Lessons in the top menu. Of course, you can also leave comments at GAMSAT-prep.com/forum.

4.8 Sample Corrected Essays

In this section, you will find two response essays with corresponding comments. If you wish, use this as yet another exercise. Get a pen and some lined paper. Time yourself (30 minutes) and create an essay in response to the instructions below. Subsequently, compare your response to the graded essays that follow.

WRITING TASK A

Consider the following comments and develop a piece of writing in response to one or more of them.

Your writing will be judged on the quality of your response to the theme; how well you organise and present your point of view, and how effectively you express yourself. You will not be judged on the views or attitudes you express.

* * * * * *

"Laws made by common consent must not be trampled on by individuals."

George Washington

"The final test of civilization of a people is the respect they have for law."

Lewis F. Korns

"In matters of conscience, the law of the majority has no place."

Mahatma Gandhi

"In Republics, the great danger is that the majority may not sufficiently respect the rights of the minority."

James Madison

"All, too, will bear in mind this sacred principle, that though the will of the majority is in all cases to prevail, that will to be rightful must be reasonable; that the minority possess their equal rights, which equal law must protect, and to violate would be oppression."

Thomas Jefferson

A   A   A   A   A

The law of the majority Unimportant?

"In matters of concience the law of the majority has no place". For instance, a hs student, greatly feels peer pressure would choose not to smoke eventhough the majority of his peers feel that it is a desirable thing to do. According to the statement this student should make his choice based on what he believes not to be right, regardless of the general consesnus of his peers.

There are some situations in which the laws of majority is important in matters of conscience. For instance, a politician that believes in firearms can not make a law to force his constituents to carry guns, if they are herrible opposed to such weapons in the first place. Therefore the politician, in doing what he feels is right wouldn't be able to ignore the general consensus of the people of his province about firearms because his decision about such a law would affect them as well as him.

Certain circumstances would govern whether the law of majority is important or not in matters of conscience. If a person acts in such a way that he can live with, and it doesn't have adverse effects on other people who may

IF YOU NEED MORE SPACE, CONTINUE ON THE NEXT PAGE.

A   A   A   A   A

feel quite differently, then the law of majority is unimportant. If a person's conscience tells them to act in ways that hurt others, then the conscience of the majority must be taken into account. For instance, a Christian school teacher can't force her class that is majority Jewish to sing christmas songs because she believes it's the proper thing to do during the christmas holidays. That would antagonize the class, which would have been taken into consideration when she wanted to do what's right.

IF YOU NEED MORE SPACE, CONTINUE ON THE BACK OF THIS PAGE.

Analysis of Sample Essay #1

Score
2/6   44–50

Task 1 – not really achieved. Although the statement was used in the first sentence, it was never really defined as a thesis nor otherwise defined. Encountering the typographical error "concience" instead of "conscience" or the mistake in spelling the quote in the beginning, seriously hurts the credibility of the writer. Peer evaluation or pressure is somewhat analogous to the making of laws by the majority, but quite loose as an association. For these reasons, clarity of thought and concrete examples to support a given thesis seem cloudy and unfocussed.

Task 2 – an antithesis is never really developed to the extent needed. While the politician example whom is juxtaposed in relation to a general consensus, could be developed, the idea of "forcing" people to carry weapons, seems an example, a bit absurd and reaching. The credibility of the writer is also questioned, when the use of "horrible" instead of the correct "horribly" (Para. 2, Line 2) is used adding to a general tone of inconsistency in care of grammar, and overall approach to the subject.

Task 3 – Because neither of the above tasks were completed with the necessary organisational and supportive devices and materials, providing a synthesis of arguments presented is impossible. A touchy feely context-based qualification in the surmounting to a "well, it all depends on the circumstance," is an intellectual and academic cop-out. The example of the Christian school teacher with Jewish students not forcing them to sing Christian songs, could be developed in more detail, if such an example is chosen.

Overall – some good ideas, but unfocused, not organised to the extent needed. There seems to be some misunderstanding of the quote. The writer needs to reveal the Gandhi meaning that non-violent resistance to certain political repressions was not only necessary, but morally correct and in opposition to the laws of the majority. Hypothetical examples could be explored also: suppose that there was a law passed that said you could not protest or peaceably assemble to protest, or a law prohibiting you from enjoying "life, liberty, and the pursuit of happiness." In many ways, the subject of the essay concerns "personal liberty" vs. "collective responsibility" or "subjective reactions" to "legislative mandates or laws." This juxtaposition, or fulcrum needs to be explored and balanced to a larger degree.

Technical errors, spelling, and typographical errors deflated the essay – as previously noted. A stronger organisational pattern is needed, which follows a sequential and logical progression.

Evaluation (see WC 4.5): 2/6. This essay completely fails to address adequately one or more of the tasks. There may be recurring mechanical errors (i.e. spelling and grammar). Problems with analysis and organisation are typical (though organisation was fine in this instance).

2	These essays may show some problems with clarity or complexity of thought. The treatment of the writing assignment may show problems with integration or coherence. Major ideas may be underdeveloped. There may be numerous errors in mechanics, usage, or sentence structure.

A   A   A   A   A

My Rights Begin Where Yours End

In our democratic society, we have created many laws or rules gained through legislation. These rules are discussed, developed and enacted by elected officials who represent the (most) majority of their constituents. However, the laws produced in this manner may be in conflict with a particular individual's beliefs or values. Thus the statement suggests that when such a conflict is evident, the individuals beliefs superceed the law, rendering the rules of the majority irrelevant. "In matters of conscience, the law of the majority has no place" spoken by a man of peace regarding a non violent struggle. However, there are those who have used such ideas for darker purposes...

For example, in 1996 many churches frequented by the African-American community were set ablaze by individuals - some of whom were members of racist movements. Both arson and such race-based acts are illegal in America. As in this case, the individuals who acted in defiance of the law of majority claimed they were abiding by their own beliefs and values. Thus they acted with a clear conscience destroying the lives and communities of innocent victims. Such a crime is immoral, unacceptable and - according to the rules of

IF YOU NEED MORE SPACE, CONTINUE ON THE NEXT PAGE.

A A A A A A

the majority — illegal. Clearly, the law of majority must supercede the conscience of the perpetrators of such a crime.

The dividing line becomes clear. Life, liberty and the pursuit of happiness are the foundations of Constitution. The concept is both logical and moral. Our conscience should be our guide as we excercise our our freedom. However, since our neighbors and fellow Americans share the same rights, someone's conscience should never be used as a reason why someone's Constitutionally protected rights are stripped away. In conclusion, one's conscience should be one's guide but when it interferes with the rights of others, the law of majority becomes more important.

Analysis of Sample Essay #2

Score
5/6   65–71

Task 1 – A quick example could help buttress Task 1 in outlining the thesis matter, where subjective liberties are at odds with social, legislative, or governmental mandates. As noted in Essay #1, hypothetical examples could be used in supporting the thesis outline. Identifying the source of the quote as Gandhi, as a man of peace, helps further establish the credibility as a writer.

Task 2 – effective transition into an antithetical notion of when a sinister turn is taken between the dialectic of individual rights-beliefs and governmental mandates. Very good *specific* example and portrayal of the paradoxes of such a balance.

Task 3 – follows a logical progression, sequential with good analysis and reasoning. Good use of quotes in relation to a most relevant document concerning this juxtaposition: The Constitution (naturally, there are many effective international, national or regional examples depending on where you live or where you attend school).

Overall – good logical sequence, completion of tasks to an above average extent, clarity of focus, good development of ideas, clear and simple style of language.

The title did not necessarily - nor correctly - represent the outline of the ideas presented to the adequacy needed. The title is somewhat ambiguous and polysemantic, having several ways to interpret. Another minor observation – rules and laws are conflated to some extent, they could be differentiated more effectively, or simply omit the use of the word "rules".

Examples of some minor technical and typographical errors – "gained" in Paragraph (P) 1, Line (L) 2 is redundant, omit; P1, L9 – "supercede" not "superceed"; P3, L2 – insert "the" before "Constitution"; P3, L3 should be "These concepts are . . ."; P3, L4 doubled "our our"; P3, L9 – "constitutionally" – use lower case.

Evaluation (*see* WC 4.5): 5/6: All tasks are addressed by this essay. The treatment of the subject is substantial but not as thorough as for a 6 point essay. While some depth, structure and good vocabulary and sentence control are exhibited, this is at a lower level than for a 6 point essay.

> **5**   These essays show clarity of thought, with some depth or complexity. The treatment of the rhetorical assignment is generally focussed and coherent. Major ideas are well developed. A strong control of language is evident.

4.9 Frequently Asked Questions

Over the last 5 years, our Gold Standard GAMSAT Essay Correction Service has corrected thousands of student essays en route to improved GAMSAT Section II scores. From our experience, students tend to have similar concerns about essay writing for the GAMSAT.

How many quotes should I choose?

Your first 5 minutes of Section II is "reading time" and thus not counted as part of the overall time of 60 minutes for Section II. This is your opportunity to read all 10 quotes and begin the process of brainstorming. For example, keeping the overall theme in mind, which quote or quotes generate(s) the best ideas?

There are students who have obtained exceptionally high scores exploring only 1 quote for their essay as there have been students who have explored 3 or more quotes. As long as you stick to the theme, the number of quotes that you choose should not be your focus. Compelling ideas which are well-illustrated must be the focus of your essay.

From our experience, an average science student without essay-writing experience tends to optimise their score by choosing 2 quotes in opposition for the argumentative essay (Writing Test A), and one quote - well explored - for the reflective essay (Writing Test B). Your personal experience and skills

may lead you to a different path in order to optimise your score.

Ultimately, it all boils down to your experiences, writing skills and knowledge of the theme of the quotes.

Which quote should I choose?

Writing Test A: Consider the 3 tasks that we described as applied to the 5 quotes. Which generates the most clear, specific ideas? Can you mention dates with confidence? Can you mention names other than those provided alongside the quotes? Other specifics? Answering these questions will lead you naturally down the path to the ideal quote for you to optimise your score.

Writing Test B: Consider personal experiences/reflections to illustrate any of the 5 quotes. If that truly does not work, try the reverse (i.e. an argumentative approach). Consider the social implication for that point of view. Any quote, within the context of the overall theme, that generates the best ideas, should be pursued with vigour.

How do I quote a statement that has been listed without any attribution in a writing task?

First, let's establish the academic protocol for quoting statements. Ideally, you would require the parenthetical after the quote: (Anonymous, Year). Considering that themes are given on-the-spot in the exam, it is unlikely that you will know the year, so you could just write: (Anonymous). This would be effective in an argumentative, formal essay such as in Writing Task A. For example: "Good friends are hard to find, harder to leave, and impossible to forget." (Anonymous)

On the other hand, if you are using an informal style (which is common for Writing Task B), then you could write something similar as follows: As has been said anonymously, "Write a wise saying and your name will live forever."

It all boils down to style. As long as you treat the quote with as much respect as you would any quote, then your GAMSAT score is unlikely to be significantly affected by the style used regarding this issue.

As an aside: If it is a long quotation, it is unlikely to benefit your essay if you were to rewrite the whole statement. You can simply quote from the most powerful part of the statement or comment while providing context for the rest. Alternatively, you can just refer to the statement and then paraphrase it completely while providing an example or examples.

What do I do if I have strong argumentative ideas for Writing Test B?

Go with it! If your creative juices flow in a particular direction, you must go with the flow of ideas. The point of understanding the Gold Standard structure for Writing Tests A and B (WC 4.25 and WC 4.2.6) is that you keep in mind the objective. For example, even if you pursue an argumentative essay for Test B, consider the social implication and, most importantly, reflect on the personal meaning and related experience(s).

Accordingly, you can use a reflective or a personal narrative in response to Writing Test A. As discussed in WC 4.2.3, you may appeal to a reader's pathos in an argument. Besides, ACER does not impose any format for Section II. What they simply require is for you to generate a valuable response for the socio-cultural theme of Test A and the personal-social one in Test B. We've had past students who did well in Section II using the reflective approach for both tasks.

How personal is personal?

Your GAMSAT Writing Test B may include personal experiences that you are willing to share with, obviously, a stranger who is professional at marking essays (i.e. this is not your psychiatrist!!). In other words, this is unlikely to be the ideal venue to share experiences that you have never shared with anyone in your entire life.

On the other hand, "personal" must be sincere and must exemplify the point that you are trying to make. Being sincere and practicing your essay-writing skills optimise the chance that the reader buys into the experience that you are describing in your essay.

Examples of meaningful, personal expressions that, within context, seemed sincere: I wept, I felt, I failed, I was able to overcome my failure, I was hurt, I was the cause of his/her pain, I realised, I adapted, I was forced/compelled to reconsider, etc.

How many essays do top GAMSAT Section II students complete prior to the exam?

Top students complete 20-40 timed essays prior to the actual GAMSAT. Of course, students with natural charisma expressed by the pen or with a non-science background can get away with much less practice and still obtain a high Section II score.

How can I gauge my essay-writing progress?

We have placed our suggested scoring system in this book (WC 4.7). You can have someone that you respect (a friend, family member, high school teacher or university professor), score some of your essays. ACER has a new automated GAMSAT Section II scoring service, which you can access by going to their website. Gold Standard has a personalised essay correction service, which you can access at GAMSAT-prep.com.

Is there anything useful to review for Section II the night before the exam?

Yes! Consider reviewing the answers you create for the Section II exercises in this book; the quotes, helpful words and Latin expressions from this book or from your per

sonal notes; and review the notes you take from your practice exam experiences and/or from your exposure to the various resources we have previously described. In the end, well-explored ideas combined with 2-3 powerful words and/or expressions can produce tremendous results for GAMSAT Section II.

What is the ideal length of a GAMSAT essay?

Unless you can think fast and write as fast by hand at the same time, you really have time for only one and a half up to two pages. The most important thing is to finish a well-organised essay with great ideas that is also easy to understand.

What level of English skills would be required in Section II?

Part of the assessment is being able to put your ideas and emotions in words that are clear, appropriate and accurate. This means that your spelling skills must be decent enough that you can tell the difference between "eel and "ill" or "peach" and "pitch", for example.

You must also be able to construct complete sentences. Keep in mind that spoken English and written English have their own nuances. Colloquial terms and tone are highly discouraged. After all, you are applying for a graduate medicine program. It is only reasonable that you are expected to write formal, academic essays.

Another option is to enroll in a short-term writing class. You can inquire from your university's Student Services office to aid you in this area.

I have never been good at writing essays. My head goes blank every time I attempt to start writing. Do you have any suggestions?

You need to find out what could be causing the problem. Two common root causes are **exam anxiety** and **limited reading exposure**.

Sometimes, when you are too nervous trying to beat the limited time to write your essays, you end up with nothing essential - "your head goes blank". The solution is really very simple. Practice as often as you can. Just like any skills training, you have to keep practicing until you master the techniques.

If the problem is because you are always faced with unfamiliar topics and you have no idea on what to talk about, you need to read as much varied materials as you can - news, blogs, even scientific articles, and so on. But because you are preparing for the GAMSAT, an exam that requires you to write short essays, you might want to choose short articles from which to emulate good writing and concise arguments.

Is a title important?

A title is not required but if something original or engaging comes to mind after hav-ing planned your essay, then it could be of benefit. Please avoid writing a title that says "Comment no. 1" or "Quote no. 2" though. Remember that the main purpose of a title is to catch a reader's interest, so make it interesting, witty and beautifully worded (for example, an expression from your national anthem or a Latin expression).

How much time do I need to prepare for Section II?

Preparation time highly depends on your academic training and English writing skills. First, forming well-reasoned opinions for an on-the-spot topic can entail reading several sources prior to the test. Otherwise, you may be able to express agreement or disagreement on an idea, but you might find yourself inadequate to support your view with strong examples.

Even with candidates whose first language is English, expressing thoughts in a clear, logical manner may not be an easy task. You may feel like you have so many things to say within such a limited time. This entails discipline, and can take time to develop, in filtering only the most salient ideas that you will discuss in your essay.

Developing language skills and a writing style that suits you best can indeed take some time. The key is to determine your strengths and weaknesses months before the exam. Simulate a timed Section II test then do a post-test analysis. Most likely, you will then be able to know how much time and what kind of help you need.

4.10 Common Grammatical Errors

Please do not read the following section unless either it is more than 6 weeks before the real exam or you have done some practice essays and you find that generating ideas and producing a well-structured essay is no longer challenging. At this point, improving details such as grammar and flexibility in the use of language can now become more interesting to explore as you aim to go from a very good score to an excellent score.

Some Basic Concepts

By definition, a sentence has the following properties:

> it contains a *subject*
>
> it contains a *verb*
>
> it expresses a *complete thought*

E.g., the sentence *"China prospers."* has a subject: "China"; a verb: "prospers"; and it conveys a complete thought or idea that makes sense.

Most sentences also have an *object* (receiver of the action); e.g., in the sentence "Mary baked a cake," the object is "a cake."

Run-on Sentences (fused sentences)

Incorrect usage	Correct usage	Explanation
He watched the movie ten times he really loved it.	He watched the movie ten times. He really loved it. He watched the movie ten times; he really loved it. He watched the movie ten times, for he really loved it. Since he really loved the movie, he watched it ten times.	Run-on sentences occur when two main clauses have no punctuation between them. Separate the two main ideas into separate complete sentences and punctuate each properly. Use a conjunction preceded by a comma to combine two ideas. Subordinate one of the main ideas into a clause.

Comma Faults (comma splices)

Incorrect usage	Correct usage	Explanations
He watched the movie ten times, he really loved it.	He watched the movie ten times, for he really loved it. He watched the movie ten times; he really loved it.	Comma faults occur when two main clauses are joined by only a comma. Use comma before a conjunction (*and, but, for, nor, or, so,* or *yet*) to join two complete thoughts (sentences). Use a semicolon to join two sentences. Omit the use of a conjunction, and start the second sentence in lowercase. Form two complete thoughts as separate sentences with the proper end marks. (See preceding example.) Join two thoughts by subordinating one of them. (See preceding example.)

Sentence Fragments

Incorrect usage	Correct usage	Explanation
Luke can read a book. And memorise it right after.	Luke can read a book and memorise it right after.	A sentence must have a subject and a verb.

Faulty Subordination

Incorrect usage	Correct usage	Explanation
I gazed out of the bus window, noticing a person getting mugged.	Gazing out of the bus window, I noticed a person getting mugged.	Place what you want to emphasise in the main clause, not the subordinate clause. Here the mugging should be emphasised and so should be in the main clause.

Errors in Subject-Verb Agreement

Rule: The verb should agree with the subject in terms of number (singular or plural) and person (first, second, or third).

Incorrect usage	Correct usage	Explanation
There is no glasses.	There are no glasses.	In this sentence, the subject is *glasses*, not there. *glasses* is plural; therefore, the verb should be plural (i.e. *are*).
She like diamonds.	She likes diamonds.	The subject *she* is in the second person, and is singular; therefore, the verb should also be in the second person, and be singular (i.e. *likes*).
Neither Emma nor Harry were there.	Neither Emma nor Harry was there.	In sentences where subjects are joined by *or* or *nor*, the verb agrees with the subject closer to it. In this example, "Harry" is the nearer subject. It is singular, so the verb should be also.
Neither Mary nor the others was there.	Neither Mary nor the others were there.	"Others" is the subject that is nearer to the verb. It is plural, so the verb should be also.
All of the team were there.	All of the team was there.	"Team" is singular, so the verb should be also.
All the players was present.	All the players were present.	"Players" is plural, so the verb should be also.
There are a variety of fruits.	There is a variety of fruits.	"Variety" is singular.
	There is a lot of birds here *or* there are a lot of birds here.	Both are correct. The first is correct since "lot" is singular. The second is correct because it is gaining acceptance through popular use.
Here is your shoes and tie.	Here are shoes and tie.	This sentence is in the inverted order, i.e., the subject/s come/s after the verb. When re-stated in the normal order, this sentence will be: *Your shoes and tie are here.* Subjects joined by *and* always take the plural form. Therefore, "shoes and tie" is plural, so the verb should be also.

Incorrect usage	Correct usage	Explanation
Fiona is one of the worst singers who has performed in this bar.	Fiona is one of the worst singers who have performed in this bar.	When relative pronouns *who*, *which*, or *that* are used as subjects of dependent adjective clauses, the verb of the adjective clause must agree in number with the antecedent of the pronoun. In this sentence, the antecedent of *who* is *singers*. "Singers" is plural, so the verb should be also (i.e. "have").
"I forget" or "I forgot".	I've forgotten.	Note that "I often forget" and "I forgot my umbrella yesterday" are correct.
Everybody are happy with the results.	Everybody is happy with the results.	Words like *everybody, everyone, everything, somebody, someone, each, either, nothing* and *anything* are examples of indefinite pronouns in singular form. Always remember that only the following are indefinite pronouns that are plural in form: *both, few, many, others,* and *several.* *All, any, more, most, none, some* may take singular or plural forms depending on the context of the sentence.
The queen, together with invited guests, face the media.	The queen, together with invited guests, faces the media.	The subject in this sentence is "queen". "Invited guests" is a noun of the intervening phrase that merely adds information about the subject. "Queen" is singular, so the verb should be also in its singular form, "faces".
Two-thirds of the project were assigned to me.	Two-thirds of the project was assigned to me.	When the subject is a fraction, the verb agrees with the noun in the of-phrase (i.e. "project").
The number of applicants remain unaccounted.	The number of applicants remains unaccounted.	*The number of* is always singular. *A number of* is always plural.

Errors in Noun-Pronoun Agreement

Rule: Pronouns should agree with their nouns in terms of number (singular or plural), person (first, second, or third), and gender (masculine or feminine).

Incorrect usage	Correct usage	Explanation
Did everyone remember their assignment?	Did everyone remember his assignment?	*Everyone* is singular, so the pronoun should be as well.
It was them who apologized.	It was they who apologized.	The nominative case (I, you, he, she, it, we, you, they, who) is used following some form of the verb *to be*.
If I were him, I would go.	If I were he, I would go.	As above.
It is me.	It is I.	As above.
Whom will succeed?	Who will succeed?	A simple rule-of-thumb is to use "who" when "he" would also make sense; and use "whom" when "him" would also make sense (e.g. "Him will succeed" does not sound right, while "he will succeed" does).
Who did you give it to?	Whom did you give it to?	As above. "You gave it to he" does not sound right, while "you gave it to him" does. Thus, use "whom".
It belongs to he and I.	It belongs to him and me.	The *objective* case of pronoun (i.e. me, you, him, her, it, us, you, them, whom) is used as the object of a preposition, such as "to".
Hugh fired he.	Hugh hired him.	The *objective* case of pronoun (i.e. me, you, him, her, it, us, you, them, whom) is used as the *object* of a verb.
He is as proficient as me.	He is as proficient as I.	Try stretching the sentence out: "He is as proficient as *I am proficient*, not "he is as proficient as *me am proficient*."
He was in the same class as us.	He was in the same class as we.	Try stretching the sentence out: "He was in the same class as *we were in*."
I trust Bob more than he.	I trust Bob more than him.	Try stretching the sentence out: "I trust Bob more than *I trust him*."
Now sing without me coaching you.	Now sing without my coaching you.	Use the *possessive* case of the pronoun (i.e. my, your, his, her, its, our, your, their, whose) in sentences like this.

Special Problems in Pronoun Agreement

Incorrect usage	Correct usage	Explanation
The movie was disappointing because *they* never made the plot seem realistic.	The *movie* was disappointing because *it* never made the plot seem realistic. The movie was disappointing because *the writers* never made the plot seem realistic.	Pronoun must agree with antecedents that are either clearly stated or understood. Otherwise, use a specific noun.
In 17th century England, *you* had to choose between following the Church or the King.	In 17th century England, *Puritans* had to choose between following the Church or the King.	Use *YOU* only when the reference is truly addressed to the reader.
Charles asked *William* about the state of his marriage. William tried to evade the topic, but confused about the situation, *he* tried to carry on a pleasant conversation.	*Charles* asked *William* about the state of his marriage. *William* tried to evade the topic, but confused about the situation, *Charles* tried to carry on a pleasant conversation.	Always use a pronoun close enough to its antecedent to avoid confusion.
I placed my passport in my bag, but I can't find *it*.	I placed my passport in my bag, but I can't find *my bag*.	Use pronouns to refer to an obvious antecedent.

Dangling Modifiers

Rule: Avoid dangling modifiers (i.e. adjectives or adverbs that do not refer to the noun or pronoun they are intended to refer to).

Incorrect usage	Correct usage	Explanation
While dialling the phone, the lights went out.	While *I was* dialling the phone, the lights went out.	The modifying phrase "while dialling the phone" does not refer to a particular noun or pronoun (i.e. it dangles).
After attending the mass, pizza was eaten.	After attending the mass, we ate pizza.	As above.

Misplaced Modifiers

Incorrect usage	Correct usage	Explanation
Nina won almost 1 million euros.	Nina almost won 1 million euros.	The first sentence does not mean what it is intended to mean. The modifier "almost" is misplaced.
I only want you.	I want only you.	Same as above.

"Were" to be used in the Subjunctive Mood

Rule: Use *"were"* in the subjunctive mood, i.e. when expressing a wish, regret, or a condition that does not exist.

Incorrect usage	Correct usage	Explanation
If I was prettier, I would be famous.	If I were prettier, I would be famous.	This sentence is in the subjunctive mood.
Mum treats him as if he is a slave.	Mum treats him as if he were a slave.	As above.

That, Which, and Who

Incorrect usage	Correct usage	Explanation
This is the novel which he loved.	This is the novel that he loved.	When commas are not used, use "that".
This gown, that is designed by Monique, is expensive and elegant.	This gown, which is designed by Monique, is expensive and elegant.	When commas are used, use "which".
She is the person that designed the gown.	She is the person who designed the gown.	For persons, use "who". Do not use "who" for animals.
The President, which is an avid golfer, was on the course.	The President, who is an avid golfer, was on the course.	For persons, use "who", even when commas are used.

Note: Often the above pronouns can be omitted making a sentence more concise. Thus:

This is the novel he loved. ("That" is implied.) This gown, designed by Monique, is expensive and elegant. She designed the gown. The President, an avid golfer, was on the course.

Faulty Parallelism

Incorrect usage	Correct usage	Explanation
She likes to read, swim and shopping a lot.	She likes to read, swim and shop a lot. She likes to read, to swim and to shop a lot.	Similar ideas should be expressed in grammatically similar forms. (E.g., nouns with nouns, adjectives with adjectives, words with words, phrases with phrases)
The professor was asked to submit his report quick and accurately.	The professor was asked to submit his report quickly and accurately.	Similar ideas should be expressed in grammatically similar structures (i.e. same word order, consistent verb tenses).

Mixed Constructions

Incorrect usage	Correct usage	Explanation
Will asked Lizzie to marry him?	Will asked Lizzie to marry him?	Don't mix a statement with a question.
The reason is because I don't have a nanny.	The reason is that I don't have a nanny.	Don't mix two different sentence constructions.

Split Infinitives

Incorrect usage	Correct usage	Explanation
I need to mentally prepare.	I need to prepare mentally.	"To prepare" is an infinitive. Splitting infinitives with other words tends to be awkward.

Commas

Incorrect usage	Correct usage	Explanation
Uncle has money, wealth and power.	Uncle has money, wealth, and power.	Use a comma before the last item in a series to avoid any confusion.
The food was served late cold and smelly.	The food was served late, cold, and smelly.	Use commas to separate adjectives that could be joined with "and." You could say that "the food was served late and cold and smelly."
Jonas is a popular, varsity player.	Jonas is a popular varsity player.	Don't use commas to separate adjectives that could not be joined with "and." It would be ridiculous to say that " Jonas is a popular and varsity player."

Incorrect usage	Correct usage	Explanation
You wait here, and I'll get your coat.	You wait here and I'll get your coat.	Don't use a comma to set off clauses that are short or have the same subject. However, always use a comma before "for", "so," and "yet" to avoid confusion.
The doctor gave detailed precise instructions to the nurse.	The doctor gave detailed, precise instructions to the nurse.	Use commas to separate adjectives of same or equal rank.
India has a rigid, social caste system.	India has a rigid social caste system.	Do not use commas to separate adjectives that must stay in a specific order.

Semicolons

Incorrect usage	Correct usage	Explanation
The car is old, however, it is in good condition.	The car is old; however, it is in good condition. The car is old; it is, however, in good condition.	Use a semicolon with a conjunctive adverb (e.g. nevertheless, however, otherwise, consequently, thus, therefore, meanwhile, moreover, furthermore).

Apostrophes

Correct usage	Explanation
Maggie Holmes' dog is lost. Maggie Holmes 's dog is lost.	Since there is disagreement on which is correct, both are acceptable.
The girl's doll fell in the mud. The girls' doll fell in the mud.	Common errors arise when apostrophes are misplaced in singular and plural nouns. In the first sentence, placing the apostrophe in between the noun and an *s* indicates a singular noun. In the second sentence, an apostrophe placed after a plural noun hints that the "doll" is commonly owned by at least two girls.

Troublesome Verbs

TRANSITIVE (followed by an object)	INTRANSITIVE (not followed by an object)
raise, raising, raised: The farmer is raising chickens.	**rise, rising, rose**: The moon is rising.
lay, laying, laid: I am laying the dress on the bed.	**lie, lying, lain**: I am lying on the bed.

"A" or "The"

Correct usage	Explanation
I dated **the** cheerleader back in college.	The definite article **the** is used when referring to a specific subject or member of a group. The speaker in the sentence could have been acquainted with many cheerleaders; but he was able to date only one particular cheerleader.
I dated **a** cheerleader back in college.	Use the indefinite article **a** to refer to a non-specific subject. The sentence implies that the speaker dated someone who could have been any member of a cheerleading group.

Proper Usage of "The"

• The Thames flow through Oxford and London. • The Gibson Desert is home to indigenous Australians. • Myths say that Santa Claus lives in the North Pole. • The equator is approximately 3,500 miles from the southernmost part of the United Kingdom. • The Chinese are hardworking people.	USE **the** when referring to • the proper names of rivers, oceans and seas; • deserts, forests, gulfs, and peninsulas • geographical areas • points on the globe • some countries like *the* Netherlands, *the* Dominican Republic, *the* Philippines, *the* United States • the people of a nation
Anna shops in Bond Street. Blue Lake attracts many tourists in Australia. St. Patrick's Island is a sanctuary for seabirds. Galtymore ranks 14th among Ireland's highest mountain peak. English is the main language used in the United Kingdom.	DO NOT USE **the** when referring to • street names • names of lakes except with a group of lakes • bays • most countries/territories but NOT cities, states or towns • names of mountains in general • names of continents • names of islands except with island chains • names of languages and nationalities

Verb or Participle

Not all verbs demonstrate an action. There are those that merely express a condition or an existence. These are called linking verbs. Words that describe (adjectives) or identify (another noun) should follow the linking verb.

Examples:

Incorrect Usage	Correct Usage
Nicole Kidman **sounds** sarcastically in the interview.	Nicole Kidman **sounds** sarcastic in the interview. The verb "sounds" expresses the state of emotions (sarcastic) of the subject (Nicole Kidman) at the time of the interview.
	Sir Edward Hallstrom **is** a philanthropist. The verb "is" connects the noun "philanthropist" to the subject "Sir Edward Hallstrom".

Participles are words that look like verbs but function in the sentence as nouns.

Example: **Exploring** Lake Argyle is one of the most wonderful outdoor adventures in Australia.
"Exploring" is a participle that functions as the noun-subject in the sentence and should not be confused with the main verb "is".

Common errors involving confusion between verbs and participles lead to **Sentence Fragments.**

Incorrect Usage	Correct Usage	Explanation
Dancing on her toes. The ballerina **was** superb.	**Dancing** on her toes, the ballerina **was** superb.	The main thought of the sentence is a description of the level of performance of the subject (ballerina) - "superb". The action word "dancing" merely adds information about what the subject (ballerina) does.

4.11 Section II Practice Worksheets

Section II Practice Worksheet I (Formulating the Thesis Statement)

Comment #	Repeated words	Ideas for or against the subject
1		
2		
3		
4		
5		
Topic:		
Theme or Issue:		
My Debatable Claim		

Section II Practice Worksheet II (Writing the Introduction)

This is where you express your interpretation of the comments' theme. You may state it as a direct statement or you may use a creative device.	
This is where you expound your ideas in relation to your initial statement by quoting or paraphrasing one or two of the given comments. Alternatively, you can continue discussing your narrative or metaphor.	
Your last sentence in the paragraph is your thesis statement. Make sure that it is clear, and it is debatable claim.	

Section II Practice Worksheet III (Task A Template)

Note: This template may also be used if you are more comfortable using an argumentative format for Writing Task B.

(Optional) Choose a title that summarises - in one short phrase - the overall idea of your essay.	
This is your introductory paragraph. Remember to include the following: - Aim to open with a catchy statement or anecdote - Express what the overall theme or one of the comments means to you - Include your debatable thesis statement in the last sentence of the paragraph (**Note:** Sometimes, if your introduction is too lengthy, you can discuss your thesis statement in the second paragraph.)	
In this paragraph, your aim is to explain and support your thesis statement. - Give one reason or argument in support of your thesis - Provide a concrete example or examples to support your argument - Explain how the examples relate to the argument	

This is where you present the strongest counterargument to your thesis. - Your counterargument should be related or parallel to the thesis' supporting example - Provide a clear illustration of your counter-argument's example.	
This is the paragraph where you show that your thesis' arguments are superior to the antithesis. Your aim here is to show that you have carefully considered all arguments for and against your idea and you have made up your mind to choose your arguments because it is better than the best opposition to it.	
This is your closing paragraph. - Summarise the main ideas discussed in the preceding paragraphs. - Tie up or reconcile conflicting ideas. - Propose your plan of action for the consideration of the reader - End with a memorable statement.	

Section II Practice Worksheet IV (Task B Template)

Note: This template may also be used if you are more comfortable using a personal piece for Writing Task A.

(Optional) Choose a title that summarises - in one short phrase - the overall idea of your essay.	
This is your introductory paragraph. Remember to explain: - what the comment's mean to you. - why you agree or disagree with the comment's idea. Briefly present your thesis statement towards the end of the paragraph.	
This is where you begin your personal narrative. It must be about an event that is pivotal in your life. It must also be relevant to the theme of the comments and/or your thesis.	

This is where you share your realisations from the personal narrative. Describe: - how you felt - how you thought and - what made you change your mind or point of view **There must be a 'before-and-after' description of your state of mind and state of heart.**	
This is where you state an application of your personal realisation. Cite a social problem that is relevant to your experience. How can your life-lesson serve as an inspiration to those who may be similarly situated? What new perspectives can you offer to the social problem that you cited?	

4.12 Breaking the Rules: Exploring Creativity

Now that you have understood the basic requirements and criteria for each writing task, you can start exploring creative ways of presenting your ideas without necessarily following the 'rules' to a tee. If you have an excellent command of the English language and believe that you have what it takes to come up with outstanding, unique Section II pieces on exam day, then you may consider adopting the following options for 'breaking the rules'. The key is to practice and refine your format, making sure that you demonstrate sophisticated writing and thinking skills.

- Analogy

You can use an object as a point of reference to express your views and feelings on a theme. For example, if you are into photography or filmmaking as a hobby, you could describe different stages of your argument as "scenes" that build up to a conclusion or a personal realisation. See WC 4.2.2 for more examples of analogy, metaphor, and simile.

- Letter

Even in Writing Task A, you can choose to write a "Letter to the Editor" or a "Dear Mr President / Madam Prime Minister" letter to express your strong opinion on an important sociocultural issue. Your letter must still be evidence-based but the letter format and tone will make your piece quite interesting for the markers to read.

For the more personal Writing Task B, you can write a "Dear Mum" or "Dear Dad" letter. A break-up letter or a resignation letter would also be unique when discussing a personal issue (whether it is fictional or not) that most readers would find relatable.

- Short Story

You can write a fictional short story, a fairy tale or a historical narrative. Depending on your academic background and training, writing in this format can take several practice in order to generate an engaging story which is highly relevant to the given theme, the appropriate narrative tone, relatable characters, etc.

- Debate or Conversation

You can also write a hypothetical debate between two of the authors who are quoted in the list of comments.

- Poem

- Diary Entry

- Social Media Post

5.1 Gold Ideas

One of the main ingredients in obtaining an excellent Section II score is constant practice. Write as many essays as you can based on as many themes that you can reasonably explore during your GAMSAT preparation timetable (see the table of themes from past exams in WC 4.1). You will note that many of the real past Section II topics can be prescribed a more broad categorization. For example, affirmative action and meritocracy fall under the general topic of equality; optimism, humour, and life goals are quite germane to the theme of happiness, and so forth.

This means that you can actually prepare and polish possible arguments, stories, and supporting examples which you can conveniently use in case you encounter a related theme in the writing tasks during your exam. Most importantly, train your mind to form opinions on important social, cultural and personal issues, which you can support with sound and concrete evidence.

The following essays are meant to expose you to various perspectives on typical Section II topics, as well as different presentation styles. These essays were submitted to our GS Essay Correction Service by actual students under timed conditions, hence you may observe some grammatical errors - albeit minimal and tolerable - in some of the pieces.These written responses will hopefully advance your development of unique and creative ideas to help you produce punchy Section II essays that offer fresh insights vis-à-vis the themes presented to you on exam day. And finally, consider taking very brief notes ('Gold Notes', at most 2-3 sentences per essay) especially when you encounter content that impresses you in some way. Enjoy!

Main Topic: Equality
Related Themes or Subtopics: Affirmative Action, Meritocracy, Rights of the Majority vs the Minority

Sample Response 1

The idea of equality is sound in principle yet is seldom achieved in practice. In George Orwell's allegorical novella about Stalinism, the author highlights how quickly the idea of equality can be corrupted by those in a position of power. The original ethos of all being created equal with equal rights is swiftly modified to suit a powerful dictator's position. The contradictory sentence of some being more equal than others is attached to the original mantra to suit a minority and not represent the majority. These personal agendas are easier to achieve when power is within reach. As said by Lord Acton, "Power tends to corrupt and absolute power corrupts absolutely." This is why equality is so difficult to achieve when individuals are given more responsibilities and powers to govern.

When absolute power is given, narrow-mindedness generally ensues because it is the view of one or a small group of individuals. An example is Adolf Hitler's Nazi party who rose to power in Germany after being democratically elected to begin with. The views Hitler held on his preferred Aryan race and prejudices towards the Jewish community are antithetical to that of equality but were not highlighted until he could command absolute power after removing limits to legislation and receiving extra powers after the Germany parliamentary building was burnt down and the chancellor's office dissolved. Equality was quickly dispatched and a dictator's will was enforced upon Europe. Thousands were then sent to concentration camps and stripped of their humanity and had no rights whatsoever in comparison with those in power.

For equality to be allowed to exist, checks and balances are required to be put in place to prevent corruption and the temptation of absolute power. Nearly everywhere, past and present, there has been a social and political hierarchy and this is needed because, to some degree, all cannot be equal and all cannot have the same power. If all are equal, then a child should have the same standing in society as a Prime Minister and be capable of making the same decisions. This is not feasible and society would not function so we have modified this being by amending it to "all have equal opportunity" and are "equal in the eyes of the law". The checks and balances aforementioned are to prevent these 'equalities' from being taken away. Society should not fear their elected leaders gaining too much power and dismantling the idea of equality; otherwise, there would be different levels of humanity. Guy Fawkes said to those in power that "people shouldn't be afraid of their governments; governments should be afraid of their people." This can prevent others from being more equal than you or I.

Sample Response 2

An Honourable Rise

My grandfather came from an impoverished family where education was either a matter of privilege or luxury. However, this never dampened his hopes of becoming an engineer some day. As a young boy, he would make models of engines and buildings. As he grew older, he would take extra miles to gain merit-based scholarships in getting into university.

From a curious boy who modelled ingenious train designs on the village streets in Indonesia, my grandfather is now a well-respected lecturer in the field of engineering in one ofAustra lia's most reputable universities. He never gained any favours from an official party or the government. He prided himself of his hard-earned degree and eventually, his upright work ethics which gained him the status he holds now. Whilst equality rights, policies and systems, such as affirmative action and meritocracy, have been discussed significantly over the past decades, my grandfather's inspiring story demonstrates that there is no greater feeling than being fulfilled in a self-built career - without the influence or manipulations of someone in power.

I believe that the only way to have a successful workplace is to ensure that people are employed based on merit. When companies or institutions hire individuals based on physical characteristics that they have no control over, they are washing their pro-fessional standards down the drain. Some may say affirmative action allows individuals who come from a minority due to disability, race or socioeconomic background a chance in the work force. Indeed, affirmative action does. However, we must consider the impacts this would have on our economy and the quality of our services if we did not hire the best person for the job. People would feel like they have a sense of entitlement just because they were born to a specific family or community. More importantly, work places should not succumb to these demands of entitlement.

I believe that the only way to have a successful workplace is to ensure that people are employed based on merit. When companies or institutions hire individuals based on physical characteristics that they have no control over, they are washing their professional standards down the drain. Some may say affirmative action allows individuals who come from a minority due to disability, race or socioeconomic background a chance in the work force. Indeed, affirmative action does. However, we must consider the impacts this would have on our economy and the quality of our services if we did not hire the best person for the job. People would feel like they have a sense of entitlement just because they were born to a specific family or community. More importantly, workplaces should not succumb to these demands of entitlement.

For us to have well-functioning businesses we need to understand that every individual is different and can bring something different to the plate. Take affirmative action for example. It has the 'power' to remove the identity (individual quality) of an individual within both the workplace and within the community in general. When one is placed in a category by affirmative action, he or she is inadvertently being stereotyped and classified by other members of society. John Kasich once claimed that 'affirmative action has a negative effect on our society when it means counting us like so many beans and dividing us into separate piles'. If affirmative action is employed in the world of careers, individuals are going to become merely cogs in the machine, without a sense of identity and worth other than what is being labelled by the officials implementing the affirmative action.

Affirmative action is hard-pressed to succeed practically in the workplace. It is quite idealistic to claim that everyone will receive the same rights if a few government policies are in place. Even if more individuals from minority groups are employed, this does not break the glass ceiling that will be inevitably reached if employers are not supportive of affirmative action. Respect in the workplace is gained through the quality of work that is being displaced not merely because you work there. By handing individuals a free spot to a certain job, this could lead to hostility and resentment by others in the workplace that had to work harder or gain extra qualifications and fight the rat race to secure their position. Affirmative action leads to hostility in the environment and does not break the barriers that the people instilling it believe.

In every workplace the individuals hired must be employed based on their merit and no other personal characteristics such as socioeconomic background or race. If affirmative action does come into place, it has the power to remove the identity of the individuals and what can be truly be offered by workers can be easily lost. Furthermore, it is difficult to truly succeed in the workforce if the affirmative action policies are merely placed as a formality.

My grandfather is considered successful by many of his peers, not because of his role at the university but rather of the fact that he was able to work hard from a young age to achieve his goal. He did not need to accept 'gifts' from anyone nor did he take advantage of any special government policy. He supported himself on his own merit. For this, he is appreciated by his colleagues who feel he is definitely entitled to what he has achieved.

Sample Response 3

In the following extract, a conversation between Thomas Jefferson and a bystander takes place. Jefferson claims, "If the measures which have been pursued are approved by the majority, it is the duty of the minority to acquiesce and conform." The bystander strongly disagrees and aims to refute:

Bystander: "Tell me Mr. Jefferson, you are essentially conveying the idea that public opinion trumps that of the minority?"

T. Jefferson: "Why yes, I believe I am. What use is democracy when the majority vote does not trump that of the minority?"

Bystander: "Although what you're proposing is noted, it is quite preposterous to expect the minority to conform to public opinion. This goes against basic human rights. Take slavery as an example, the approved measure (slavery) was accepted by the majority, but clearly disputed by the minority (African-American slaves). Obviously in this instance, it is appalling to propose that the minority must conform to the rule… is it not?"

T. Jefferson: "Yes, it is a valid observation but think of it logically –"

Bystander: "Oh… I am!"

T. Jefferson: "If the majority school of thinking was right-wing, then the left-wing minority in this instance must conform to said proposals. If they did not there would be utter chaos."

Bystander: "But that is where you're wrong, sir. This is why we have opposing political views, so that we can find a middle-ground hospitable to both the left and the right. That is why the minority must not just conform, but instead stand-up to fight the majority. Just like Abraham Lincoln did when abolishing slavery – fundamentally disproving the idea that the minority must conform. I finally put this to you, without individuals standing-up for the minorities, we would have not progressed and seen change."

Topic: Digital Piracy
Related Themes or Subtopics: Consumer Rights, Copyright Protection

Sample Response 4

Managing Consumers' Rights

Digital Rights Management involves various technologies developed in an attempt to prevent unlawful copying of digital files such as music and videos. Mass illegal copying and distribution for profit, otherwise known as piracy, is an immoral and illegal practice and should be prevented. However, in an attempt to restrict piracy, DRM also affects household consumers. It inherently infringes on their rights to fair use of digital files that they have purchased and is, therefore, an impractical method of piracy prevention.

Piracy of digital files is widely acknowledged as an illegal practice. It essentially involves people making a profit from another individual's work, which is not only unlawful but also unfair. Artists have a right to make a profit from their own creativity and inventions, and copyright laws protect this right. However, mass production and distribution of illegal copies of digital files pose threats to artists and the wider media business and is ultimately breaking the law. It is, therefore, important that efforts are made to prevent such practices. DRM attempts to do this by preventing digital files being copied, effectively restricting any use of the digital files that have not been unauthorised by the provider. Many companies such as iTunes and Sony implement DRM methods to protect their files.

However, DRM not only influences pirates but also consumers. As David Safford recognises, it essentially "takes away existing rights of consumers". Legitimate consumers, who have legally purchased these digital files, possess the right to fair use of the file. DRM somewhat restricts this use, as it makes it difficult to transfer files between two computers, for family members to share files and for the copy of music onto other devices so that it can be listened to outside the home. Fundamentally, DRM infringes on the rights of the consumers to use the files in fair, low-impact, non-threatening ways.

Further, the success of DRM methods in preventing piracy is unclear. It has been suggested that for the most parts, pirates have easily been able to evade any restrictions. In order to combat this, updated DRM methods are constantly needed, and are often only successful for a few months. For example, it was not long before Blue Ray discs were able to be easily copied by pirates. As David Safford notes, DRM "can never be effective".

Ultimately, a better solution needs to be found. DRM methods place huge disadvantages on legitimate consumers in relatively unsuccessful attempts to stop large-scale piracy. Better, more feasible methods must be developed which target music piracy more directly without infringing on household consumers.

Sample Response 5

The question of whether managing and protecting digital rights is beneficial to artists and the development of their works is a controversial one. There is also no consensus on the issue as to how this affects consumers' rights. On the one hand, digital rights protection measures prevent the illegal downloading of music, videos and software and force people to take the legal way in purchasing the products they like. On the other hand, those who have good computer skills can easily override any digital protection and obtain the private copy anyway. Ultimately, however, I believe that managing and protecting digital rights is not only effective, but it also violates people's rights to access information.

First, there are a number of websites such as Pirate Bay, where individuals with very limited knowledge can access illegal copies with little effort. This relates not only to the download of the latest music and films but also to software programs and e-books that further education.

Second, while illegal copies may impact the sales of artists' products, this also increases their popularity by gaining a wider reach of their work. Many who get a copy of an e-book for free might decide to order a real product and pay for it.

Finally, many artists and developers learned that showing their creations online for free brings benefits not only to them but also to people who allow it. Enabling access to their songs, for instance, makes a bigger group of fans that will be interested in attending their concerts or buying their other products. Similarly, a software for editing texts that is free might become so popular that organisations start using it and pay full price, which creates a bigger profit for the developers.

In conclusion, there are more benefits to free digital information than they are to digital rights restrictions. Of course, the principle behind copyright protection is one of academic respect. It is one educated person's means of recognising another person's intellectual property. Certainly, there are negative implications to piracy. It puts one's integrity in question. However, providing free access to online information in a way that benefits both sides, creators and consumers, is the way forward that has already commenced. This is not stealing - unlike what digital piracy does. Sooner or later, some leeway needs to be granted in order to adapt to the changes of our time and the advancing technology.

Sample Response 6

Good afternoon, TED audiences. Let me start us off by sharing with you an experience I had during my university years.

I was a student of a program called [Company A] course. It's a course that helps you get into medical school by providing a smorgasbord of practice questions. On the second day of the two-day course, I asked the teacher whether I could gain access to the printable versions of the online practise exams. I felt that a paper copy would better prepare me for the real exam. However, the reply I received from the teacher was "HAHA… No." I was pretty offended by his response. I thought, "What's wrong with having a paper version of something I already paid for?" However, in hindsight, I understand where this teacher was coming from. You see, many med school preparation organisations went bankrupt because students would copy and distribute the 'supposedly' paid mock exams. Organisations such as such as [Company B] and [Company C] would spend thousands of dollars (or so I heard) PER QUESTION. However, they were not gaining any the income they deserved because of these students. You see, I realise now that test preparation companies have to hire quality writers, editors, and examiners to write the practice tests. How else could they sustain the required overhead expenses to continue producing high-calibre content if they were not getting any legitimate sales from their products?

Therefore, to prevent [Company A] from going bankrupt, the teacher needed to minimise the illegal distribution of their practise exams. Although I, myself, would not stoop to such low levels of selling stolen files, I can't say the same for others. Yet, despite the regulations put in place to prevent illegal distribution of the files, I find myself agreeing with Tom O'Reilly when he pointed out how "copy protection on software" was not accepted by consumers. Whether it be pay-per-use or using encryption codes, thieves will always find a way to steal and distribute "protected" digital files. By "digital files", I am referring to everything that can be found on a computer's operating system – whether it be software or PDFs, etcetera.

Failures in preventing illegal distributions of digital files are evident throughout our history. For example, Windows have long used a pay-for-activation-codes system to minimise the distribution of their Microsoft Office products. Despite them saying how the codes are "unique", internet users have managed to work their way around the system and consequently, distributed them online. How do I know this exists? You see, during my high-school years, I got provided a USB with the Microsoft Office files and a program to override the activation system. Okay, okay. Before you all get up and on me, let me tell you that I have no interest in ripping companies off for their good products. I hope many of you are in the same boat. Another event where the prevention of distributing digital files have failed miserably was when the governments teamed up with media industries to place warnings before movies and videos. Remember those "You wouldn't steal a car. You wouldn't steal a handbag. You wouldn't steal a movie. Downloading pirated films is stealing." captions? Did anyone ever see those warning signs on a video you saw online? If you did, then, naughty! Jokes aside, the evidence is there. Despite the warnings – the activation-code systems and the internet-blocks placed to prevent illegal distribution of digital files – the very sad thing is happening.

Now, some of you may disagree with me in saying that digital files can be protected. Yes, there is a limited few software out there that have managed to prevent their novel system become a victim to internet thieves. Such limited evidence includes the uniqueness in domains has helped prevent many website owners from having their site-link stolen. This means that no two links are the same – like snowflakes! [...] However, it still doesn't mean the content on this site is protected. Stealing the digital information can take the form of a screenshot, copy-and-paste or retyping the content. So, truly, these digital files are not protected. It is no wonder why Bruce Schneier once said: "Digital files cannot be made uncopyable".

Although many organisations have teamed up and put in a tremendous amount of effort to protect the rights to digital files, true protection is hard to achieve. Such cases are more prominent for highly desirable and costly digital files – such as the Windows Office. Only in exceptional cases, where the entire system is built on uniqueness, can you see digital systems being protected. It's unfortunate that the hard work of a team is easily ripped by internet thieves. However, I'll prefer to believe consumers that use stolen-goods are doing it not because of causing a company to go bankrupt. I believe, if you are a user of a ripped digital file, and if you have the financial resources to do so, please support the company that you have ripped the files from. Whether it be buying their cheapest product or buying the ACTUAL product, let us live honest lives and pay for the resources. Ripping each other off isn't the society we should be establishing, should we?

Topic: Environmental Protection
Related Themes or Subtopics: Global Warming, Greed, Responsible Citizenship

Sample Response 7

The Air-conditioned Nightmare

Such is the current global demand for energy that humanity now purportedly faces its greatest challenge: the growth of consumption while slowing and eventually reversing environmental impact. The issue surrounds developed society's inability to manage the exponential growth of consumption that has come with great affluence. In energy per capita, Australians consume 8 times the world average and a staggering 50 times the average of developing nations. Such figures are the premise of Toyota Chairman Fujio Cho's statement that, "Environmentally friendly cars will soon cease to be an option, they will become a necessity.' Cho's advocacy for efficiency is relevant in any age: why would any engineering-savvy civilisation opt for inefficient means of living when there are alternatives? Implicitly, Cho also warns of the impending end of the fossil fuel age and society's need to embrace what most would deem 'green' technology. While 'greener' technologies are the most promising technology for the long-term amelioration of our seemingly mutually exclusive aims of growing consumption and cleaning up the biosphere, it will be argued herein that in the medium-term, green technology is insufficient. Instead the solution to the current crisis entails words few would like to hear: the developed world needs to reduce its consumption.

Firstly, Cho's quote can be endorsed by a brief analysis of the energy requirements of the world, and the inherent inefficiencies in world energy use. When we talk of the world's energy needs, it is safe to reduce the discourse to that of the developed world due to its enormous proportion of world consumption (as detailed above). Developed nations consume most of the world's annual demand of 6×10^{20} joules of energy, and a significant amount is driven by desire rather than necessity. Ignoring the 75% of waste energy lost as heat in modern power plants, we will focus our discussion on the household and the individual. Many people continue to drive heavy vehicles with large capacity engines; build homes with minimum efficiency standards and live lifestyles that are unnecessarily energy intensive. For instance, most Australian and North American homes are built to the minimum standard utilising 2x4 inch framework while studies have shown that the price of a home built using 2x6 inch framework would only cost 5% more yet save 50% of the energy required for perpetual climate management. Cho's statement can be extrapolated from vehicles to – in this instance – houses and many other energy intensive aspects of life. For instance, studies have also shown that individuals will select an average air-conditioner temperature at a level low enough to trigger the desire for heating if the season were winter. On reflection of the current lifestyle of the affluent Westerner, it would appear that there is no perception of a necessity to restrict consumption and or become more efficient as Cho suggests.

Secondly, one becomes more sceptical of Cho's statement when his position and the state of fossil fuel capacity is considered critically. Despite the current schedule of communication, the world is not 'running out' of any of its resources if we consider this to mean the world will have no fossil fuels left in the medium term. Until the late nineteenth century, the primary fuel of the US remained wood (in China, this was the case until 1960) and it was not until the 1960's that the primary fuel of the great machine that is the USA became oil. The 20th century was very much the world's century of coal, not oil. The switch to oil as a primary fuel only came later due to easier access and efficiencies of energy generation. Today, the energy evolution continues and natural gas is becoming more popular due to the price of oil. Tomorrow, better extraction and refinement techniques –such as horizontal drilling - will see shale-gas/oil become a more economical alternative and this pattern will continue into the future: before the world runs out of any resource, it will become so expensive that demand for the resource on a global scale will reach zero. Cho is correct to say that cars and lifestyles in general need to become more efficient for the betterment of the envi-ronment, however his statement feels more like an endorsement of the current 'green' pandemic that many corporations have endorsed on the premise of positioning and selling their products.

The last two decades have witnessed an explosion in environmentally friendly products, institutions, government advisory bodies and even political parties such as the Greens. The purpose of the 'green' groundswell is noble: to prevent further destruction and pollution of the natural environment. Solutions such as solar, wind, geothermal and hydroelectric power are put forward by this movement in an attempt to unify growing consumption with environmental utopia. At the level of the household, these solutions are viable. For instance, much like water tanks, solar-powered households are able to consume electricity as desired as they have invested in technology that is future proofing their level of consumption. However, on a national scale this is not possible. On his Twitter account, scientist Dr. Karl Kruszelnicki recently endorsed plans for a 30-kilometre square solar farm in Africa's Sahara desert. The farm is the result of an energy think-tank and in theory is capable of supplying the world with a surplus of energy. In reality, there are no means of storing or transporting this amount of energy. The largest battery in the world can only store 1.3×10^{11} joules meaning virtually every citizen in the world would need one these batteries. Furthermore, there exist no global networks for energy distribution. The US estimates it would cost US$12 trillion to replace its own failing power grid habitually rated a D- in annual audits by civil engineers. Pragmatically, these considerations also apply to the hero electric product from Cho's Toyota corporation: the Prius. Toyota is not alone. GM also spent billions developing its Volt model and the Tesla was also developed by the US Tesla corporation at great cost. So far, sales of these vehicles have been much lower than forecast. Like much of the green movement's ideas, the products are more idealistic than functional. To date, there exists no network to publicly recharge such vehicles outside of the pioneering California state. More critically, the root resource of powering these vehicles remains fossil fuels. The same 25% efficiency steam-turbo generators that power our houses and pollute the atmosphere will be required to charge these electric cars. While all of these 'green' efforts are dignified and should remain in development, humanity should not be expecting them to become the primary source of energy for a long time – they remain in their infancy.

As the environmental programs of governments and private enterprise remain underdeveloped, the only solution for managing current environmental pressures and the emergence of developing nations is for the developed world to consume less. Efforts are already underway to mitigate consumption. While free-markets shoulder a significant portion of the responsibility for the destruction of the natural world, they are now effecting a redress. This can be seen in the pricing of emissions such as in Australia's move initially toward a carbon tax and now toward an emissions trading scheme. These policies are required as an interim mea sure to minimise the damage of fossil fuels while other tech-nologies are developed. As in many areas of life, restrictions and parameters breed innovation and though many people will choose to ignore the increasing price of energy in the future, forced behaviour modification in the form of reduced consumption will be inevitable. It is an indictment on Western norms that we would prefer to work so hard to develop a host of new technologies rather than make what can only be defined as simple but effective modifications to mitigate our profligacy.

Sample Response 8

Money Cannot Save Us!

Nowadays, it is common knowledge that the earth's environment is worsening due to extensive pollution contributed by the rapid growth of industrialisation. "Only when the last tree has died and the last tree has been poisoned and the last fish been caught will we realise that we cannot eat money." This Indian Cree proverb suggests that financial wealth cannot sustain us once our natural resources are ruined or depleted. Humans need to take responsibility for the earth's pollution because what we do today will have an impact on the future generations of people to come. We must not procrastinate in restoring the environment of our only home here on planet Earth.

The rise of modern technology has given rise to more factories being built so that the products or energy produced can benefit the needs of civilisation. It is interesting to note that many countries have welcomed the establishment of foreign industries to boost their economic growth despite toxic bi-products and fumes resulting in greenhouse gasses that further contribute to global warming. It is obvious that humans hold a major responsibility for emitting pollution into our environment. However, the drive for economic success is so desirable that it facades the underlying health of the country's environmental well-being.

Some may argue that it is important to invest plenty of money and attention to strengthen a country's economic development. Certainly, the rise of industrialisation and infrastructure has brought benefits to the country such as creating new employment, increasing the attractiveness of tourism and increasing the country's competitiveness in foreign trade. However, it is disappointing to note that the consequence of pollution not only affects the environment but also the health of its population. For example, China is one of the fastest developing countries in the world but Beijing is considered one of the most polluted cities where hazardous air may potentially spread to neighbouring provinces and countries. With such detrimental effects, the city may become less attractive for tourism hence causing a negative impact in terms of social and economic values. Moreover, research performed by the World Health Organisation suggest there to be a positive correlation between pollution and birth defects. These health outcomes are disgraceful and immediate measures should be taken to minimize the output of pollution because the health of the environment and population is under threat.

Furthermore, it is clear that the strategy of gaining financial wealth through rapid industrial growth has taken a toll on developing countries like China. It can be examined that the making of money is not the only issue but the methods and processes utilised which compromise the quality of life should be strongly discouraged. The preservation of public health should take priority over selfish desires for industrial investments and profits because life is much more precious. Life provides opportunities for people to have purpose, respect and dignity through relationships and communities. A selfish desire breeds temporal satisfaction whereas selfless motives such as the preservation of human life are rewarding as future generations of people arrive. Thus it can also be agreed that "every human has a fundamental right to an environment of quality that permits a life of dignity and well-being."

It is clear that the earth is suffering from the consequences of pollution and humans are responsible for their actions. It is highly suggestive that actions should be taken immediately to minimise environmental pollution. In order for that to occur, governments need to be convicted of their country's poor environmental status so they can endorse a national culture of environmentally friendly trends and habits. Some possible actions include reducing operational times of industrial factories, endorsing a culture of recycling products and materials, investing in research and development of renewable energy sources and applying strict fines for breaches of these policies. We need to start now and develop a culture of environmentally friendly trends because generating money alone cannot sustain us once our natural resources are depleted.

Sample Response 9

A recent BBC radio documentary investigated the devastating impact that rising sea levels have on many Islands in the South Pacific. The desperation heard in the voices of individuals and the sheer helplessness of these communities to singularly turn the tides, speaks volumes about the impossibility of continuing the current patterns of development in an increasingly volatile environment. Yet there are key moments of progressive thinking attempting to reverse the damage done, or at least preserve what is left. The primary issue, in my eyes, remains, however, the role that industry and private enterprise must play in securing an environmentally sustainable future.

For too long, the debate surrounding climate change and global environmental sustainability has been directed towards governments. Although economic partnerships such as the EU, ASIAN and alike may produce memorandums; global talks may develop signed documents such as the Kyoto Protocol; and countries such as Australia may ratify the Carbon Tax - their sustained impact is meaningless without strict adherence, and largely ineffective without industry support.

Furthermore, many of these measures are blunt instruments, meaning they are economy wide rhetoric with a simple lack of specified targets, plans or adaptable measures. In effect, they are punishments for pollution, rather than encouragement for change. While there have been some notable exceptions such as the Clean Energy Bill which contained some provisions for investing into clean energy proposals and development, the lack of government support and confusion have rendered this position stalled and defunct with the change of leadership.

Business and industry are wholly complex and each is driven by a multitude of factors. Yet undoubtedly, business is driven by opportunity and profits. The quote, "Environmentally friendly cars will soon cease to be an option. . . they will become a necessity" by Fujio Cho demonstrates some elements of this by lamenting that environmentally friendly cars will become a necessity. While this is an almost unconscionable extreme, it nonetheless points the way for industry.

There are boundless opportunities for innovative and entrepreneurial thinkers to capitalise on this market. And a profitable market at that! Science and technology have already played an enormous role in instigating projects such as the Frozen Ark, which is collecting DNA samples of endangered species for scientific research and preservation. Solar panelling technologies are powering many homes in Australia, and there are countless innovations being made to sophisticated industries.

The success of Smart Grid Technologies being thrilled through a joint venture by the agency Energy Australia and the Federal Government point the way for the intersection of industry and government. The benefit here is that it is driven by profit and opportunity seen by the industry. This will ensure that more technologies are driven to the fore. Thus it is industry, not the government, that has the best impact on climate change.

Topic: Liberty
Related Themes or Subtopics: Democracy, Free Speech, Censorship, Government

Sample Response 10

The Muted Demos

Democracy. The word stems from the Greek words for 'people' and 'power'. Democracy is the manifestation of the populace's desire through choice. When Alastair Farrugia made his statement that "freedom is when the people can speak, democracy is when the government listens," he was separating the expression of the people's wishes from their actual practice by the official government. The following examines the void that exists between the expressed voice of the people and political implementation of the people's wishes in Australia. While Australians have access to freedom of speech, one would be ignorant to believe they lived in a democracy where the government listens.

Australia is a lucky country due to many of the land's characteristics, none more so than the freedom to speak about one's desires. Largely due to the melting pot of cultures, Australia is tolerant of many opinions and creeds. Many of these opinions are able to be expressed openly without attracting oppression. The media landscape in Australia is also well protected from those who might wish to depose freedom of reporting as evidenced by protections for journalistic freedom such as the Shield Laws which were recently enacted in each state. While the country is open to dialogue on sensitive issues such as homosexual marriage, there seems to be very little done about these issues in terms of concrete policy. The government is aware of the issues, however, they do not act to address them. For many years, there has been great public sentiment for the support of homosexual unions. However, no political leader has shown any desire to effect the democratic mass of opinion. If Australia were a true democracy, politicians would not only hear what the people are saying but also act on their desires. Instead, Australia's creeky nineteenth-century political structure rewards inactivity. Until an election is impending, Australian political leaders are unwilling to address the larger issues of public discontent such as refugee intake, homosexual unions and carbon taxation. Prime Minister Kevin Rudd had yet to make up his mind on whether same sex couples should be allowed to formally marry. As a result, the country could not move forward on this issue. With Rudd's polling figures on the wane, he announced that he was in full support of same sex marriage. Rudd even went so far as to say that they were totally natural. This is evidence that politicians understand clearlyv what it is that the public desires, they are simply unwilling to implement policy when it does not suit their agenda.

Of course, one cannot underestimate the amount of work that needs to be done in taking public sentiment and refining it down into fitting policy, much like a whittler carves away at a piece of timber. There is only so much time and resource to be shared around in government of a nation. Some would argue that every minority cannot have what they desire all of the time. Therefore, it is up to the public to freely express their desires to the government, and for the government to decide what is possible.

One cannot argue that politicians are the individuals most suited to managing a country's people, policy and resources. However, it should not be politicians who tell people what to do; politicians should be asking Australians 'What do you want?' before putting their considerable skill set to bear on corresponding policy. This is the function of government: to deliver policy reflecting the desire of the polis. However, in modern day Australia, the desires of the populace only become relevant at times such as the short sprint to an election which is currently underway. It is unfathomable to think that the people of a nation are only consulted once every 4 years - at election campaign time - about policies such as the $5.5billion Paid Parental Leave Scheme (PPLS), Carbon Tax, homosexual unions and other large infrastructure projects such as the National Broadband Network. This is a sign of a sick the execution of the democracy; one that is, at best, seasonally received.

The challenge for the elected government is thus to provide better mechanisms for communication between the populace and the government. It can only be assumed that politicians require more clarity when it comes to the wants of the people. One wonders why Australians only get to have their speech heard once every 4 years. Why are there no referendums for major policy initiatives in the interim? The logistics of such mechanisms would be simple. For instance, options for key social issues could be listed online for people to analyse and vote upon. By allowing those who are interested - via a non-mandatory referendum - to vote on key issues during a government's term, the government would go a long way toward Farrugia's definition of democracy: a government that truly listens.

Sample Response 11

#CensorshipIsDead

~~TRUMP~~ will make America great again!

Could you imagine how many Facebook and Twitter users would have been imprisoned if there was a strict censorship law against posting memes and hashtags against Donald Trump during the US elections? #wicked, right?

With the advent of social media and the internet, the question of whether censorship has a useful place in today's society has become a topic of controversy. Many people believe that censorship is a pragmatic way of protecting individuals from immoral, harmful, or insensitive content. However, others would argue that censorship is a method of putting limits on liberty, and thus a hindrance to true freedom of speech and expression. On consideration, I would disagree with the need for censorship in Western society. In an era where we fight for freedom; freedom for the minorities, freedom in art and creativity. In an era where we fight for freedom - freedom for the minorities, freedom in art and creativity, and freedom through technology and social media - the need for censorship has become something of the past.

If we learn anything from history, it's that censorship has always been a fine line between protection and oppressive control. In 399 BC, Socrates, an ancient philosopher, was sentenced to death for his corruption of youth and his acceptance of unorthodox beliefs. He violated the moral and political codes of his time. For authorities, this was a convenient method to stop the spread of "incorrect" ideas within society. Today, however, the western world lives with a sense of candidness, open-mindedness and exposure. With social media outlets such as Facebook, Twitter, and Instagram, sharing has become trendy. Many people use these methods to project creative thinking or challenge the moral constructs of society and what was deemed immoral. One such example was the marriage ceremony performed for gay and lesbian couples at the 2014 Grammys award show. Through the use of technology and music pop-culture, artists and celebrity were able to project a political pro-gay marriage message to its audiences. While some may disagree with this message, the whole notion is that society has reached a point where it allows people to make choices for themselves. For the majority, there is no longer a necessity or desire to have authorities deem what is appropriate and what is damaging.

Conversely, some may argue, censorship is still necessary for the protection of the young and vulnerable. For example, many claim censoring violence in the media is necessary for a reduction in future crime rates. However, I would suggest internal censoring of material. By this I mean, within the home, parents and guardians should act as the buffer between the appropriate and the inappropriate. Whether it be at home, at school, or through the world of internet and social media, children can easily be exposed to unsuitable material daily. However, in a society where liberty is sought in every scenario, the best approach would be to teach children how to deal with these things rather than try and shield them from it. By censoring material, all you do is create a generation with ignorance on how to approach a potentially controversial or harmful situation.

For all these reasons, I believe that censorship is something that, while once accepted, is now just a method of oppression on liberty and free expression. Whether it be through a painting, music, books or any other means, censorship of these materials is placing a limit on the artist's ability to exercise their own creativity. In a world where everything can be found with just a click of the mouse, censorship has no use or benefit to society.

For all these reasons, I believe that censorship is something that, while once accepted, is now just a method of oppression on liberty and free expression. Whether it be through a painting, music, books or any other means, censorship of these materials is placing a limit on the artist's ability to exercise their own creativity. In a world where everything can be found with just a click of the mouse, censorship has no use or benefit to society. I say, #censorshipisdead.

Sample Response 12

Is the rule by the majority absolute? In democratic societies, there is always a majority that wins elections and referenda and there is always a minority composed by those who vote for the losing candidate and the losing proposition in the referendum. In a democracy, the majority's choice will always win. After all, this is the core concept of a democracy: a rule by the majority. However, the majority cannot simply pass laws that take away certain basic civil and political rights of minorities. Majorities in democratic governments may have the inherent power to pass laws, but it should not be any law or policy they like, especially if those laws encroach upon the civil and political rights of minorities.

History has taught us to be vigilant in protecting our freedom and basic human rights. One such lesson in history about a majority voting to deprive a minority of its basic rights is what happened in Nazi Germany to the Jews. In the first place, Adolph Hitler's Nazi Party was voted into power by a majority of the German population. Then, when the Nazi Party was already in power in the legislature, the Nazi majority party began to pass laws that deprived the Jewish minority of its basic civil and political rights. First, the Jews were made to register in order to identify them as Jews – the names of their relatives were all registered. Second, all Jews were made to wear yellow stars. Third, the Jews were prohibited from worshipping in their temples and synagogues. Fourth, it was forbidden for Jews to marry Germans. Fifth, Jews were removed from government offices and private offices where they worked. Sixth, Jewish businesses were closed and they were not allowed to own businesses, lands or any bank deposits – these were all confiscated in favour of the government. Seventh, the Jews were forbidden to travel to any other part of Germany or the world. They were imprisoned in what was called Jewish Ghettoes – cramped living spaces for only hundreds were made to house deported Jews by the thousands. Lastly, without any criminal charges, indictments, trials or convictions, Jews were herded into cattle cars and imprisoned under guard in concentration camps. Some of those Jews were exterminated (like termites or ants or rats) in gas chambers. By several acts passed by the legislature controlled by Hitler's Nazi Party, the majority succeeded in depriving a minority (the Jews) their basic civil and political rights: the right to be secure in their persons and their homes against unreasonable searches and seizures, the right not to be deprived of life, liberty or property without due process of law, the right not to be condemned to imprisonment or death without a trial and without the opportunity to defend themselves in a court of law.

Germany under Hitler had all the appearances of a democracy (they had a parliament and people were able to vote). However, the Parliament under Hitler was not really democratic because the majority did not respect the most basic and civil political rights of a minority (the Jews). The democratic process of "majority rules" was perverted into depriving a minority group of its existence. This is what is not supposed to happen in a democracy: the majority has a right to make laws and to "rule" by imposing its will through elections and through the passage of laws. But one thing a majority cannot do in a democracy is to vote to deprive a minority of its basic civil and political rights.

It is true that democracy is indeed the dictatorship of the majority. In Ancient Rome, democracy was the rule of the mob – whoever controlled the mob controlled Rome. In modern times, however, our democracy is no longer a direct democracy (mob rule) but a representative democracy. We vote for representatives who represent our views and preferences as a constituent. In the legislature or in Parliament, our representatives still vote by the majority. What is prohibited in constitutional democracies is that the majorityor the vote of the majority be used to oppress or deprive the minorities their basic civil and political rights. "Individual rights are not subject to a public vote; a majority has no right to vote away the rights of a minority." (Ayn Rand) This is why most modern constitutions have what is called a Bill of Rights – this is a list of the basic civil and political rights and liberties that individuals are guaranteed. These are guaranteed in the constitution or basic law of the land so that the majorities cannot act to deprive the minorities of these basic civil and political rights. They are rights that are so basic as to be universal – they are considered inherent in our very humanity.

Topic: Power
Related Themes or Subtopics: Violence, War, Revolutions

Sample Response 13

Much of the world seems to be in a never-ending, self-perpetuating struggle for power. Each proponent believes that his or her own solution to the problem is the "right one". However, there never seems to be an absolute solution to any one conflict that faces a nation - or the world for that matter. Many countries may have altruistic agendas, yes; but the truth is, the solution often chosen, or imposed, is the one that is supported by the most power to do so. While peaceful means should be the first course of action in any problem, the use of weaponry and military force should not be totally disregarded when no other means seems to work.

The pursuit of peace by altruistic means is always ideal in any situation; otherwise, it risks setting a precedent that contradicts the foundation in which a nation or a movement was established. Martin Luther King Jr's ideals to achieve civil rights for the African-American via non-violent protests was one such instance. However, with the advent of new technology and an increasingly complex society, it seems the ideals of peace cannot be achieved by just "good intentions". In this day and age, countries would laugh in the face of another that tried to advocate for certain ideals, no matter how peaceful the intentions, unless they were backed up by the ability to do so.

Al Capone, a famous American gangster, once said, "you can get more with a kind word and a gun than you can with just a kind word." This gives pause for thought. Although the means he employed to achieve his goal were not altruistic ones, or in the pursuit of existential ideals, he still achieved them. To extrapolate this ideal into modern society is a sad reality that must be faced.

Similarly, during Nazi occupied Germany in World War II, many attempts were made by the allied nations to reach an agreement of peace so as to avoid the unnecessary loss of more innocent lives. It is evident in this case that the ideal of peace was not going to be met by pacifist ideals and appealing to the humanitarian aspect of a Nazi government that had ingrained in it such draconian agendas.

After diplomatic negotiations fell through, it was only via war, and more specifically the atomic bomb dropping on Hiroshima, that the goal of peace was eventually reached.

It may be believed that the precedent that is set by the ability to destroy someone or something, which does not conform to proposed ideals, is a dangerous one. It may also be true that "a man of courage never wants weapons". However, a courageous man must demonstrate a willingness to use them if the situation warrants it. The aim to achieve peace through gentle, kind, and altruistic means should always be at the forefront of one's mind, but with an ever complex society, in which war and conflict is intrinsic to human existence, the sad reality is that the right ideals must be supported and backed by the power to impose them. If not, it risks a decay of our somewhat peaceful existence.

Sample Response 14

The origin of a revolution is for change, a good change. When corruption and injustice reign in a nation, the people must act. The objective must be for the people to be unshackled from the chains of inequality and strive for liberty and ultimately, the pursuit of happiness.

Revolutions have occurred in many stages of history for the pure reason of disdain and unfairness of the people against the governance of the country. Revolutions aim in restoring equal law and order for all levels of citizens and to give opportunities for anyone in a society to live in liberty and happiness. There have been many revolutions against injustices in the social system, such as the Haiti revolution against slavery, and the French revolution against corruption and poverty. The American Revolution marked the independence of the United States from British rule, and help lay the foundations of a great nation that enjoys freedom and wealth for the last 200 years. The reasons for many revolutions were demands of freedom from oppression and to govern and prosper for the nation rather than being taken away by a coloniser or an oppressive government.

It is imperative for revolutions to be coordinated and led by pragmatic leaders who must control the movement as to ensure the image of the revolution is not hypocritical and not a mirror-image of their own oppressors. Egypt, in 2012, had its first "democratically-elected" government; the once "terrorist-branded" Muslim Brotherhood, led by Dr Mohamed Morsi. Besides the background of the brotherhood party, this was the opportunity to see if the "brotherhood" had the resources and values to lead the nation. Instead of sharing power with the parliament, Morsi began a tirade of "power grabbing", with some of his policies giving him absolute powers in regards to foreign policy, the economy and legal systems. He developed many opponents, such as one of the highest judges in Egypt. He soon came to resemble the previous Mubarak-era "totalitarian government". In June 2013, over 4 million Egyptians protested on the streets, and Morsi was toppled by the Egyptian military led by Field Marshal el Sisi.

If revolutions lose their focus and their initial objectives, then the foundations of the revolution will soon become fragile and will collapse until another revolution comes knocking in its place.

Leadership and keeping to values are imperative for a revolution to stay legitimate in the eyes of the nation. Revolutions catalyse change the political and social environment of a nation. We have seen many revolutions that have been coordinated and executed precisely, and this is due to the elements of liberty and justice acting as the banner for the movement. Revolutions can bring forth prosperity for a nation and lay down the foundation for future generations to enjoy. And let's hope that the revolution only becomes a legacy, not a living reality.

Sample Response 15

Gen. Douglas MacArthur once said, "Whoever said the pen is mightier than the sword obviously never encountered automatic weapons." In our day and age, wars come in forms that do not even involve armies anymore. The fact is, most wars in the past were preceded by negotiation before violence exploded. Those were the rules of engagement in time gone by. Of course, guns are mightier than pens – pens can only maim, but guns can kill. But pens create words and words create ideas and ideas live on longer than guns. Ideas make people decide to strap dynamite onto their chests and walk into a crowded supermarket and detonate them. In other words, our problem nowadays is no longer whether the pen is mightier than guns but which ideas can be so powerful as to inflict harm on innocent civilians.

Ideas make people create improvised explosive devices and leave them by the roadside indiscriminately to hurt passing convoys of soldiers, or passing groups of school children, whichever trips over them first. Ideas cause people to hijack airplanes and crash airplanes into two office buildings. "Pens" and "guns" are symbols for the contradictory concepts of "diplomacy" and "armed violence". Moreover, people, indistinguishable from each other, carry mobile phones that detonate suitcase bombs. Extremists acting as suicide bombers are commonplace now. Religious ideas such as the "jihad" are coupled with the violence of bombs. When American Navy Seals (all sixteen of them) dropped parachutes in a field and in the dead of night, enter a three-story house and kill Osama bin Laden, it was not an act of war as Osama bin Laden was not a head of state. He was head of a terrorist organisation. Wars are no longer the preoccupation of countries and nations and states. Wars are between interests and ideas, ideologies and ways of life.

In our modern and digital age, the traditional argument of which is mightier, the pen or the sword, is no longer relevant. Terrorists do not negotiate anymore. They just detonate bombs in markets and offices of newspapers, cafes, restaurants and even concert halls and football stadiums. Wars were more civilised in that they were restricted to targeting military bases, depots and outposts. They were only to fire upon armed combatants. Civilian populations were still affected, but generally, they were not targeted. Exceptions to this rule were the atrocities of the Japanese Imperial Army and the crimes against humanity during the Nazi Holocaust. But now, terrorism targets huge civilian populations. The fighting in World War I was confined to certain geographical areas in France and in Turkey. The fighting in World War II was confined to "theatres" of conflict in Asia and the Pacific. Now, every football game could be a target. Even a small Christmas party in a suburb in California and the Boston Marathon became the targets of a terrorist attack. The terror attack was motivated by ideas – jihadist ideas. Violence, therefore, is merely the expression of dangerous ideas.

Topic: Happiness
Related Themes or Subtopics: Humour, Money vs Happiness, Work, Life Goals, Optimism

Sample Response 16

What's So Funny?

"In the end, everything is a gag." These profound words, uttered by Charlie Chaplin, one of the earliest comedians of the 20th century, speak a myriad of truth about the double-edged nature of humour. Sadly, in our current culture, even the most sensitive subjects are not safe from ridicule and parody. As a young adult growing in this often cruel society, I am often questioning the extent of what we consider to be humorous. Taken in the same frame of mind as Charlie Chaplin's words, if something can be made fun of, then it will eventually be ridiculed. This extreme line of thought left an uneasy impression on me when I least expected it.

For a greater part of my childhood, I have been an avid fan of the cartoon show, South Park. South Park is well known for its risque and offensive parody type of humour. In one particular episode, the show satirised the sensitive issue of AIDS. Despite laughing at its comical moments, that specific episode left a disturbing afterthought. Would I have found that type of humour entertaining if I was afflicted with the deadly AIDS disease? This led to other questions of why the general population sees this as acceptable humour. Decades ago, during the initial outbreak of AIDS, such humour would have caused outrage nationwide and led to the cancellation of South Park. However, in today's society, it barely caused a ripple. It seems that all issues in our contemporary world are being sucked into a vortex of no-limits all out comedy, and people don't seem to care as much as before.

Similarly, the show 'Chaser's War on Everything' did a parody sketch on real terminally ill children. This epitomises the idea that nothing is safe from ridicule and parody. Children on their death beds, being ridiculed on national television! Comedy has evolved in great magnitudes since the days of Charlie Chaplin. But even then, Chaplin rightly predicted that eventually, all issues can and will be subject to satire.

I have come to realise that even though nothing is safe from ridicule, we must keep an open mind on what is an acceptable form of comedy. Though it may be hilarious to one person, we must empathise with those being ridiculed. It will only be a matter of time before something close to your heart will be taken by the growing 'black hole of comedy'.

Sample Response 17

The Speedos Modelling Contract

Every time he made me laugh, it hurt. Even to form a broken-toothed smile was painful. "What about your speedos contract?" Bart quipped and nearly fell off his bedside chair laughing. I was lying in a hospital bed with a jaw broken on both sides, a broken nose, broken teeth and broken ribs. It was the first major trauma of my life. And we all face adversity in our lives. That's a reality. But as Marjorie Pay Hinckley put it, "The only way to get through life is to laugh your way through it." My friend Hugh helped me see that, and he may have saved my future.

In April 2004, I was attacked by three men. I don't really remember much, but after being hit square in the jaw for the first time, I remember the slow-motion sensation of falling to the ground. Fifteen minutes later, they left the scene, and I was in a pool of blood. I have a vague recollection of being bundled into a taxi and then lying in a hospital bed. Two things struck me. I couldn't close my teeth, and my trousers were wet.

I couldn't talk. I was terrified. Not I-just-watched-an-Alfred-Hitchcock-movie terrified. Actually afraid for my life. Tears streamed down my face and pooled behind my ears on the pillow, even though it hurt to cry. What had happened? Why was I here? Where was I? What was going on? Everyone winced when they saw my face, adding further to the terror. Doctors and nurses whispered to each other and shook their heads. In fact, everyone whispered around me, like I had died. Everyone except Hugh. He swished back the hospital curtain and said "Jesus, mate, you wet your pants! And you look like crap! What about that speedos modelling contract I was organising for you?" It hurt to laugh... but he stopped the tears. He brought normality back to a whirlpool of uncertainty, fear, anger, distress and trauma. I thought, well if he's laughing about it, it can't be too bad.

I lay in the recovery after the surgery that night and reflected on Hugh's very brief role in what had happened. He had been with me on my evening out before the attack, a very close friend. I had been care-free, a student with the world at his feet, doing what twenty somethings do. I had gotten home (almost) after an evening out and three guys set up on me. They turned me - and my world - upside down. They shattered a previously idyllic view of the world in 15 minutes. And as I slid helplessly down the abyss of self-pity, rage, anger and terror, Hugh came and cracked a joke. He started laughing at the fact that I had urinated in my pants. I was still me. And if I was me, then I was open to ridicule as normal, like it or not. Just as we always did. And it struck me then. He had halted that seemingly inexorable descent. He showed me that the world can be miserable sometimes, but you have a choice. You can let it get you down, or you can laugh. Either way, life goes on and you can choose how you allow that life to affect you.

All of our lives are full of challenges, some more than others. The 21st-century lifestyle brings with it pressure and stress. Traffic, bills, childcare costs, health care costs and property costs. It would be facetious to say that laughing cures all ails, but we can learn that a healthy positive attitude is always a good thing. Science is telling us now that smiling even when you are not happy helps release dopamine and serotonin, the happy chemicals. If we're stuck in traffic, we're stuck in traffic. Blowing the horn won't help. Pull out the sense of humour from that survival kit. Smile at the person in the next lane. Switch radio stations to something more upbeat. When life fires lemons at you, laugh, joke and sing while you rattle together a nice, fresh lemonade.

Sample Response 18

My brother died when he was only 6 years old. It was the 5th of August. He fell from a window as he was trying to 'fly'. His death was so sudden and so unexpected. We could not comprehend it and for the first few days, all we could do was shed tears. I shed tears when I was alone and when I caught my sister's eye. I could not keep myself from crying. The loss was so real, it brought on a hollow kind of feeling in my stomach, an emptiness that was gnawing at my insides.

At his funeral, my father was inconsolable. My Dad was a joker. He usually cracked jokes and teased us. For the first time in my life, I saw my father shed tears. My father was sobbing. My brothers, sister and I were all seated together during the service. My father was seated across from us. As we were listening to the eulogy, my father started crying – he was bawling like a child whose favourite toy got broken, a child who had skinned his knee and was crying for his mum. We stopped and stared at my Dad. Tears were still streaming down our faces but my father's sobs got our attention. We started laughing at the sight of my Dad's face: red and contorted with his sobs. He looked like a clown.

It was so out of place, the sound of our laughter at the funeral service. It was so contradictory, the sound of our laughter while my Dad was wracked with sobs. But we couldn't help it – my Dad's face looked so funny as he sobbed. We have never seen him cry before and we found it funny to see our Dad shedding tears like a child – like ourselves. Pretty soon, my Dad looked at us – wondering what we found so funny. We couldn't tell him – we all tried to contort our faces imitating the way he looked when he was crying and we all started laughing.

When we first learned that my brother had died, I wondered to myself if we would come out of that situation intact – if we would fall apart, if we would become bitter or deathly afraid. I wondered if any of us would get depressed or anxious. A death in the family – it alters the family. Grief alters people. When I started laughing at my brother's funeral, I had a fleeting thought that I was becoming unhinged. I was afraid that I was falling apart, but then, I also felt relief. I knew that we would be alright at some point in the future. I was crying now, but the fact that I could still see something funny and laugh at it could only mean that my brother's death had not unhinged me.

It was alright, I realised, to feel the hurt, to grieve and to mourn, to cry and shed tears – the death and loss of someone so dear is reason enough for all that. However, I also realised that the grief will someday lose its sharpness until it becomes a dull ache and then, a memory and a sigh. It will leave a mark on us but we had a choice as to how our grief will mark us. I realised that we could let the grief overwhelm and overshadow us, or else, we could let it motivate us to cherish each other more because life is so short and death is so sure. We could live our lives so afraid of death, or we could live our lives thankful for another day.

Every August 5th, I remember my brother. I remember his death, and the grief has become a dull ache. Every April 11th – my brother's birthday, I mark just how old he would have been. I sigh. The grief is still real but it has lost its power over me. My grief has been transformed by time. It is now mingled with hope. I realise that I too will die someday, and it doesn't seem as scary as it did years before. When I think of dying, I feel sad at the pain my death will inflict on those I love and those who love me and who will miss me. But with this sadness, there is also a hope that death will not be so uncertain – I can look forward to being with my brother.

I realise that I cannot control life or death, I cannot predict when death will come or how it will come. Death can come when we least expect it. Grief is intense and the loss is often unfathomable. However, the grief passes, too. Grief is a process that one must go through. Grief however, does not need to rob me of my joy forever. The ability to laugh in the midst of grief, even at the most trivial things - is a sign of hope that grief will pass and laughter will become more precious, more intense because it provides a counterpoint to the grief. When I can still laugh even in the midst of my grief, it only means that I am coping and doing my best to mend what death has broken inside me.

Topic: Solitude vs Loneliness
Related Themes or Subtopics: Self-identity, Friendship

Sample Response 19

Overcoming the Barrier of Loneliness

"Loneliness is a barrier that prevents one from uniting with the inner self". Carl Rogers' words allude to the idea that the feeling of loneliness prevents us from truly connecting with ourselves. Loneliness is a feeling that essentially arises from being alone. However, loneliness is a negative feeling that is hinged on a low self-esteem and the precon-ception that being alone is coupled with being unwanted and unloved.

I have personally experienced this aversion to loneliness. I remember when I was in high school I hated to be seen alone because I dreaded the idea that people would think that I had no friends or was a 'loner'. As a result, I made great efforts to always be in the company of other people. However, as I grew older, I was thrust into situations such as attending university, where I was forced to be alone. While I initially experienced aversion to being alone, I gradually overcame the feelings of loneliness and instead, began to value the time that I could spend with myself. It allowed me moments of introspection and reflection, leading me to appreciate who I was as a person as I embrace my flaws but also treasured my positive traits. It was in my moments of solitude that I was able to reflect on my wonderful life, be grateful for what I have, and ultimately foster a deep sense of fulfilment.

Self-esteem is the view that people have of themselves. People with positive self-esteem are comfortable and happy with who they are. They are not often affected by the actions or criticisms of other individuals as they possess an internal sense of self-affirmation. However, to be totally comfortable with one's self is a rare trait. Often, people possess some degree of low-self esteem and, therefore, struggle to deflect negative words or disapproval from others as they do not have a sturdy sense of self on which they can rely on in order to avert such comments. Therefore, they often strive to obtain external sources of affirmation.

It is because of this desire for external affirmation that people often struggle to be alone without feeling lonely. Often, people place a large emphasis on being valued and needed by others and belonging to a group. Being alone, therefore, renders feelings of sadness and being unwanted. The views of society do not help with this – there is a social stigma that surrounds being alone as it is associated with being friendless.

As a result, most people who are not comfortable with themselves avoid being alone, or when they are alone, they feel negative as a result. This creates a problem because it is when we are alone that we are truly able to connect with our inner self and understand who we truly are. With this connection comes an appreciation of our internal beauty.

The wisdom in Carl Rogers words is clear – loneliness prevents one from embracing solitude, and in doing so restricts interactions with one's self. It is these moments of isolation that allow us to gain satisfaction with who we truly are and develop a positive sense of self. There is, therefore, a vicious cycle that must be broken – those with low self-esteem must overcome the barrier of loneliness in an attempt to connect with themselves and therefore find a sense of self-worth.

Sample Response 20

Dear Father,

Perhaps, after all these years, my kick of honesty has led to my current situation. I have persisted with your dream for me to take over the family business and continue our legacy of success, for far too long, and years of unease and discomfort, are finally manifesting in this recent revelation of mine. I am lonely, father, but not for the reasons you may first believe. It is true, I have a gracious and loving family, whose ability to live is without boundaries. I have a dedicated and admirable set friends who are as loyal as they are ambitious. I have every facet of life required to avoid isolation. But I have been living a lie pretending to be interested in our business and have developed a ruthlessness and tenaciousness that I do not relate with anymore. I have strayed from my inner nature and turned into someone I don't recognise anymore; I have lost myself, and can no longer continue to deny how isolated I feel.

I should have recognised this phenomenon when I first started working at the firm. I was not initially proficient in the management of people, but it was a skill I developed over years of exposure and practice. I was not innately gifted with the tenacity for negotiation, nor the veracity required to chase contracts and foster prosperity. Most of all, however, I was never partial to the ruthlessness required for business. I was uneasy at the prospect of having to make cutbacks; unwilling to administer punishment when the situation demanded it. I only became that person over time. I engaged on downsizing when times were tough, despite my total reluctance to cause harm to anyone. I have fired more people than I can bear. I know that is what is inherently required in business; however, it has turned me into someone I can barely recognise anymore. I never envisioned that I would sink into the monotony of the rat race, with wealth being my only goal and feeling a continual level of stress and depression at my situation.

I don't admire what I have turned into. I look around and I am in the company of people who I don't relate to. I am not inclined to ferociously climb the ladders of success like everyone else at this company. My friends, as well meaning as they are, do not share my inherent passion for creativity, my love of art and music, my desire to connect with people, or my craving desire to travel the world. I have lost the sense of beauty and adventure that invigorated my youth. I have not the zeal that I once had. I feel alone. Not only because I don't relate to the people around me, but because I don't ever relate to my current identity. I do not desire the life I currently lead but my persistence with it has led me to completely disengage from pursuing my inherent passions.

I feel lost and almost detached from my day to day lifestyle, simply floating through without consciously experiencing emotion or care. I cannot continue to live with this sense of isolation from surroundings. I need to care about myself before I can ever hope to achieve happiness in the future. That is why I have decided to resign from the company.

Mark Twain once remarked that 'the worst loneliness is not to be comfortable with yourself'. I am not inherently the man I have become, and I can no longer continue under the pretense that I identify with the life I am leading. I hope you understand my decision, and accept that I must now find my own path to success, and hopefully satisfaction.

Sincerely,
Your Son

Sample Response 21

The Loneliest Hour of Night

I always hated this time of the night. Everyone in my family had already gone to bed, and I had the house to myself as I finished up my studies and prepared for bed. I didn't really understand how to explain the feeling, other than labelling it as loneliness. Was it really the absence of others around me that contributed to the loneliness? I would have to say no. It was rather the whispers that sprung up inside my head. Without the distractions that the interaction with my family provided, I could no longer ignore the doubt, insecurity, and questions posed by my own mind. I was experiencing what Twain calls, "the worst loneliness - not to be comfortable with yourself".

While my family would typically describe me as a rather carefree individual, emanating endless positivity even in the face of "disaster" this was not the complete story. In a superficial sense, I was such a person. I just found that it was easy to avoid thinking about the negative things in life, by taking the opportunity instead to encourage others or maintain a happy atmosphere. My true nature, however, would creep out in the solitude of the night. "What if I don't get the scores I need? How did I let myself do so badly on the last test... I'm such a failure." These were just some of the thoughts that plagued me. I would constantly replay events in my head, and chastise myself for the way I acted, the mistakes I made in retrospect. Simply put, I was not comfortable being alone, where I had ample time to reflect on my own actions.

In an attempt to avoid coming to terms with my introspective thoughts. I began to read before bed. I would not stop until I literally passed out from fatigue. There was one night where I suddenly woke up, stiff from having fallen asleep in an upright position. This is ridiculous, I thought. Why was I going to such an extent to avoid confronting loneliness? There was simply nothing that could be accomplished from shying away from myself. I promised myself that this would end, I would try a new method. In the following nights, when I was all but alone, I began to process my own thoughts. I organised them on paper, into my fears and mistakes. I linked them to ways in which I could improve, and attempt to prevent their reoccurrence. Gradually, I realised that those whispers of insecurity began to die down. I started to feel more peace when I was alone.

I actually enjoy the time I have for myself now. It is a chance to communicate with one's own thoughts. An opportunity to be comfortable in my own skin, or pursue actions which lead to more comfort. Expand in connection with loneliness. What you have learnt.

I think, in our present day society, many of us are afraid of being alone. Perhaps a legitimate reason behind this is the fact that solitude challenges whether we are comfortable with ourselves. Facing our own fears, doubts, and guilt can result in an unbearable sense of loneliness. Instead of distracting ourselves with interaction with others, or through activities, we should endeavour to reflect on our thoughts. It is only if we become comfortable with ourselves, will we be able to mitigate the loneliness of being alone. Putting this off may result in undesirable consequences, stemming from our urge to escape the loneliness. These could include addictions, leading to insomnia and further health complications.

Topic: Beauty
Related Themes or Subtopics: Self-confidence, Self-identity

Sample Response 22

Beauty Is Invisible To The Eye

I read the Little Prince when I was young and I never fully understood the concept of hidden beauty until I was in high school. Growing up, I would always be bombarded with magazines and television that depict flawless models and place importance on external looks. In today's society, not much importance is given to building one's character and every individual is adamant on looking good on the outside. The perverse notion of outer beauty is gone to such an extent that people are undergoing surgery to obtain the perfectly chiselled jawline of Brad Pitt or the sculpted rear of Jennifer Lopez.

During my high school days, I relished on the attention that I received from boys my age. They thought I was beautiful and I loved being called beautiful. I placed a great deal of importance, energy and money in the way I looked on the outside. I bought expensive makeup products, booked monthly salon appointments for my highly coloured and extensions-ridden hair. However, I paid little importance to who I was becoming on the inside. Being popular was my forte and I excelled at it. All of that changed when I noticed my hair falling out in the shower. I had a patch of my scalp that was visible. When I went to see the dermatologist, I was diagnosed with Alopecia.

Within months, I had lost all my hair and this greatly impacted my emotional well-being and self-esteem. Going to a high school in which the students place importance on one's outer appearance, it was a hard downfall from being the popular student in school to becoming someone who was completely bald. When my boyfriend ended our relationship because of my condition, I realised that outer beauty is just a facade, a mask, for your inner self. I found strength in the knowledge that my outer appearance is not a representation of who I am on the inside. I started joining more clubs and societies in school and met amazing and like-minded individuals who did not rate someone based on their appearance but on their character. Learning the hidden treasures of someone's true character that is concealed by their outward mask was an important life lesson for me.

Not many people in today's society realise that beauty is just a transient mask. What lies underneath is the true representation of a person. A person's beauty can be withered into nothingness due to old age but the character of a person stands true through time. There have been countless cases in which young girls are so obsessed with looking beautiful like the actors or singers on television that they surgically change their appearance. What they do not realise is the extent of the prevalence of Photoshop in the industry. A societal change needs to be undergone to educate the people about the crucial nature of developing one personality rather than beauty. Personality cannot go through liposuction for enhancement, it needs to be cultivated. Singers and actors should set an example as role models for the younger generation by promoting inner beauty instead of focusing solely on the outer. After all, maybe the next unappealing person you meet in the future could be the nicest and most helpful individual that you have ever come across.

Sample Response 23

Confidently Beautiful With A Heart

"Why should you be the next Miss Universe?" asked Steve Harvey during the final round of the question and answer portion of Miss Universe 2015. All three ladies were absolutely stunning. They captured everyone's attention as each one of them walked down the stage to answer the question. "I will use my voice to influence the youth and I will raise awareness to certain causes, like HIV awareness," answered Miss Philippines. This answer exemplified the candidate's inner beauty, which made Miss Philippines significantly different from the rest of the other candidates. Her good personality captured the hearts of the judges. She was crowned Miss Universe 2015.

Our society has different standards of beauty. Despite the variation in those standards, some people feel insecure about their body and wish to change their physical appearances. From curly hair to straight hair. Muffin top to flat tummy. Shorter to taller. For teenagers who are undergoing identity crisis, it is a struggle for them to accept their physical appearance when they do not "fit" in the category of beauty within their peers. I, myself, have experienced insecurities when I was in high school.

I was jealous of the other girls in school because I was only five feet tall. Although I was skinny, I was not tall enough to feel like a super model. I would wear heels when I go out with my friends but at school, heels were not allowed. I did not have a boyfriend. I did not have confidence. I was timid.

As a fully-grown woman, I am still petite, but in a relationship. As I have been interacting with more people, I have developed better social skills. I have realised that my idea of beauty, embedded in my "petite girl profile", was masking my true beauty, which is my personality. My partner told me that one thing he likes about me is the fact that I have a good heart. After reflecting on my past, I have learned that I may be small, but I have a big heart, which is appreciated by the people around me.

Beauty can make people turn their heads around on someone. It is astonishing. However, without interaction, true beauty can be hard to unravel. A person's behaviour and character encompass the entire exquisiteness of a person. All men and women should find the goodness and greatness within themselves, despite flaws in their physical appearances. My big heart makes me attractive. Like Miss Universe 2015, I can also say that I am confidently beautiful, with a heart.

Sample Response 24

When Will We Be Beautiful?

Beauty goes beyond skin deep. This is the way we teach children to perceive the world. Homo sapiens have the highest degree of cognitive ability throughout the animal kingdom. The fact that we are aware makes it our duty to reason and moralise. As such, it has become our inherent nature to differentiate between good actions and bad actions. A philosopher resides within us all. The philosopher within Antoine de Sait Exupery said, "What makes the desert beautiful is that somewhere it hides a well."

While we do our best to impart moral values onto new generations, we can also observe that it is not within the nature of the human race to be prejudiced. Prejudice usually comes from the teachings of others or out of instinct to be wary of our differences. So why then, is it still necessary to teach moral values? It could be possible that without guidance, people would naturally attain the outlook we would aim for anyway. I was taught moral values as a child. Although my family had a religion, we weren't always very good at practising it. However, moral values and religious values are one and the same, and so they superseded religious rituals.

When I was nine, I moved to a new school and was almost immediately befriended by a girl in my class who suffered from cerebral palsy. She didn't have many friends because it seemed that the other students quickly grew tired of her. Everyone had trouble understanding her when she spoke because of her partial paralysis, and she wasn't as physically able as the rest of us. I immediately thought everyone was terribly shallow for not having patience with her until I found that I was also strained from my companionship with her. It felt like a real struggle being slowed down all the time. I was her only friend and I was finding it difficult. I knew that beauty went beyond skin deep but that didn't seem to make it any easier. Upon reflection now, many years later, I realise that people are not immoral. They simply struggle between whether to put themselves first or to put others with greater needs first.

It is necessary to teach moral values but it is infinitely more necessary to us to realise them. Everyone is an individual within a community. Most people have opinions. Some express those opinions.

Everyone is trying to achieve the right outcome, but do we truly realise our morals? Until it becomes our goal to find the well in the desert, the inner beauty we all have, we will always be putting ourselves before others.

Topic: Home
Related Themes or Subtopics: Family, Memories

Sample Response 25

Of Bikes and Cakes

Today, my boyfriend broke up with me. I wanted so much to run home and tell my mum and dad how much I was in pain, but I couldn't. They are miles away from where I am now. So I took out my bike and pedalled my blues away around the block.

I remember how my now ex-boyfriend actually found it ridiculous that I'd still hang my childhood bike in the apartment. Now I understand how the presence of that bike around makes me feel like I never really left home. It constantly reminds me of the first time that my dad taught me how to ride the bike; how he was patient and reassuring; and how he promised he would never let me down. Today, that sense of security - of making me feel that despite the heartbreak, life will eventually get better - came handy. To my dad's eyes, I will always be the best girl and he will always have my back.

When I returned to the apartment, I decided, "I should bake a cake!" And while mixing the flour and sugar and eggs, all my childhood memories with mum came rushing in...

In grade school, I used to wear thick glasses and braces, and kids at school would tease me with all sorts of hurtful names like nerdy, ugly daisy, just to name a few. I felt like an outcast. But every time I got home, mum, upon hearing my footsteps at the door, would exclaim, "My beautiful princess is home! Now let's bake this princess a cake." All the pain I felt during those days would instantly disappear. At home, I was royalty - with the tastiest cake in the world on the platter! - regardless of my appearance.

So I had my slice of cake today. I can't say it stopped me from crying over my boyfriend's rejection. But then again, it made me felt right at home in the warmth of my mother's arms. I knew the 'princess' in me will never be beaten emotionally - at least, not for long.

It is this acceptance that William Jerome speaks of when he mentioned that "any old place [he] can hang [his] hat is home sweet home". Just like the house I currently live in is not my childhood home, it is the memories I bring in it that makes me feel like I never really left home.

Home is where I can retreat at the end of the day: a secure haven, filled with love and free from judgement. It is my own space, a space I choose to share with those I love, and those who love me in return. It is the love and simplicity of my childhood memories that make a home: a haven of memories, my mother tenderly teaching me to bake a cake, or Dad teaching me to ride a bike; promising he would never let go.

Sample Response 26

Throughout life and its many experiences, many of us move houses, cities, states or countries; but coming back to any previous home always fills us with some little bit of warmth. The truth, time and time again, is that home is found because of the people and the memories; not the materials or the locations. With the right company, we can find a home on Mars or the moon if we wanted to.

The idea that "it takes hands to build a house, but only hearts can build a home" reminds me of the book Samurai's Garden. In this novel, the main character Stephan is forced to leave his home in New York and go to Japan for the summer. At first, he is extremely upset and unwilling to open up his mind to the experience that is ahead of him. Throughout the novel, he meets several people and forms several deep, meaningful friendships. By the end of the novel, through a beautiful telling of the story of Stephan's life in which readers personally connect to the characters, the author makes the point to the reader that home is truly where such relationships are made and experiences are felt. This is done through exploring Stephan's hesitation and internal conflict of returning back to New York, the place he considered home, as he will be leaving his newfound family behind.

Home need not be through real-life relationships but can be felt through connections to television shows or movies as well. Another example of how homes are created by people and experience is the television show Gilmore Girls. The show is set in a small town and follows the lives of a mother and her daughter. Throughout the show, viewers are also exposed to all of the characters within the town, each with their own quirks and characteristics. Add in the music and the fast-paced sarcastic dialogue and every viewer becomes hooked. No matter how long it has been since I have seen an episode, I start to feel the nostalgia of returning home and meeting the characters, when I watch one.

Thus it is evident that home is not determined by location, space, or other physical attributes. Home is where one makes friends, lives life experiences, grows into a better person, makes memories, and so much more. It has everything to do with one's heart and the hearts of those around them, and this is what makes the feeling of home one of the most special feelings of all time.

Sample Response 27

Home is essential in our lives; it is where we can be our own selves and free to do the things we want to do. Having a home gives us a feeling of comfort and security. However, like many material possessions, a physical home is something that we may not be able to keep forever. Such was my experience when we migrated to Australia and left our home overseas.

I struggled to overcome the feeling of "homesickness" and it took me quite a while to feel at home in a new country. My first few weeks in Australia were hard for me. From a two-storey, five-bedroom house overseas, we moved to a three-bedroom apartment in Sydney. I used to have my own room. This time, I had to share my bedroom with my younger sister. I used to ask mum why we had to sacrifice our big house for a small apartment in Sydney. She kept on reminding me that physical things in life can fade or be taken away from me, hence, I should focus on the intangible ones and be not attached to our old home overseas.

I started reflecting on our old home. Why was it so valuable to me? How could I develop the same feeling to our new home? Then I realised that it was not the aesthetics and the space or measurements of the house. I liked our old house and valued it because that was where I grew up and all my childhood memories were there. Having said that, I shook my head and recognised that memories stay in the heart and soul, not in a physical house. It is something that I could bring with me all the time.

I began helping out mum in "building" our new home. Aside from buying appliances and furniture, I also added the care, love, and family spirit in our new home. I realised that what I needed was just right next to me: my family to complete the corners of our home; and the healthy family bonding and long-lasting memories we share together, which light up our home. Since then, I felt complete, I felt at home and there was no longer a feeling of homesickness.

As a multicultural country, Australia has a huge number of migrants from around the world, and many are yet to arrive here. They might face the same struggle as I had when I first moved here. In order to overcome this, they may do the same thing as I did; that is, to build the home in their hearts and souls. Through this, I was able to have an irrevocable condition of having a home to myself. I can go from one place to another, bringing my own home with me, as I have made a home for myself inside my heart and soul and found the things needed to furnish it.

Main Topic: Wealth
Related Themes or Subtopics: Money vs Happiness, The Meaning of Richness

Sample Response 28

Paypal the Pain Away

Western society, largely influenced by the media and advertising, has established a rigid set of criteria for success; wealth, beauty, popularity and power. This definition of success is intrinsically linked to possession and dominance. Consumerism advocates that possession is achieved by wealth. Despite evidence and experience continually challenging the idiom that "there is nothing that money can't buy," society is infatuated with the notion that money can relieve all pain, illnesses and debts.

Society is captivated by the romantic idea of wealth. This ideal concept is perpetuated by advertising which suggests that beauty is valued at eight monthly payments of $89.99 plus shipping and handling; that isolation is cured by rapid weight loss; that illness is remedied by low-fat yoghurt; and that your lifestyle is dictated by the car you drive. This fanciful notion is challenged in literature.

F. Scott Fitzgerald's classic American novel The Great Gatsby has been said to capture the American Dream. That is, by earning money, one can achieve their desires and create something of themselves. Gatsby fashions himself a life of parties, champagne and beautiful women to win a woman's heart. Fitzgerald suggests that Gatsby's life was theatrical and insincere; his house was an extravagant replica of a castle in Europe, his parties were filled with colourful strangers and his wealth was achieved through bootlegging. Gatsby's death at the conclusion of the novel affirms the idea that money and extravagance cannot win a lady's heart, that hosting parties for the masses does not relieve one of isolation and that happiness is intangible.

Additionally, George Bernard Shaw's play Pygmalion affirms that wealth and status are fickle. The title of the play was derived from the Greek myth, in which an artist creates a sculpture of a perfect woman and falls in love with her. Professor Higgins gave the flower girl Eliza Doolittle the markings of wealth - clothes, dress mannerisms, to pass her off as a duchess. This play affirmed that superficial transformations do not contribute to happiness or respect but are promoted to appease society.

As is evident in literature, the notion that money cannot buy happiness is continually challenged. However, we continue to buy the latest Apple product to ensure our credibility among colleagues, spend money on products to alter our appearances and ensure our success in finding love, to ultimately conform to the idea of success. American Express rewards us for spending. Maybelline assures us that "We're Worth It". Well, retail therapy is a myth, a fantasy.

Sample Response 29

The Game Called Life

From an early age, my father and I didn't have the best relationship. I never got piggyback rides from him or he never tried to braid my hair. We didn't do what 'normal' father and daughters did and I was in no shape or form of what people coined the term as 'daddy's little girl' and somehow I got used to it. It's not that he didn't love me, he loved me a lot, but he loved money more.

Money to many people may seem like the most important reason to be alive, which is exactly what my father believed in. And I accepted that to be the truth as well. He worked day and night, dropping me off at daycare, going to work in a crisp new suit and coming back with it being ruffled from stress. He had every new gadget that came out within hours, copious numbers of cars and not to mention the clothes. His stress lines around his eyes and forehead didn't matter because he had everything of the latest model. That was what he deemed as happiness.

Looking back at it now, 15 years later, it is the sad truth. In our modern lifestyles, we're so caught up in worrying about ourselves, how big our houses are, what brand of clothes we are wearing that it almost seems like we buy things we don't actually want ourselves but that other people want to see. Each and every one of us is climbing the same ladder of what we regard as life, but have we stopped to appreciate what life has given us? Is money the only reason life is worth living for?

"After a certain point, money is meaningless. It ceases to be the goal. The game is what counts." (Aristotle Onassis) My father realised this the instant his life was on the verge of ending. He never expected the heart attack, but it opened his eyes. That's what happens when you've been hit hard, you gain consciousness of what really is valuable. Amidst the sea of emotional pains that I went through my childhood, it gives me happiness that my father is a changed man. He no longer invests days in working all the time but rather has picked up new hobbies that he enjoys and finds fulfilling. He spends quality time with his family now and eventually, stress lines have turned into laugh lines.

Of course, money is important, we all know that it's a necessity in life. However, it is not everything. The game of life is more important. That is what I learnt from my father.

Sample Response 30

There are many ongoing debates surrounding the issue of money, and whether or not money can buy happiness. On the one hand, some argue that money cannot buy happiness; on the other, proponents argue that money is, in fact, essential for a happier, or less miserable life. Aristotle Onassis once said. "After a certain point, money is meaningless. It ceases to be the goal. The game is what counts." From the experiences thus far in my life, I believe this to be true.

My mother retired several years ago after working in her dream job as a flight attendant for 20 years. It wasn't long after that she was diagnosed with clinical depression. To say that she struggled gravely to adjust to her new life at home would be an understatement. She had imagined what her life would be like as a stay at home mum and wife: fun; cooking fancy family meals for the family of four; taking her children shopping on the weekends, and endless dinner table conversations. Although she had all of those things, she found that most of her days were spent idly - "not doing anything at all". "I feel like I've lost my purpose in life," my mother would tell, and I would respond by telling her that she was being overly dramatic again. I couldn't have been more wrong.

My mother was phenomenal at her job, she climbed to the top of the metaphorical food chain in the airline industry and she made more money than she had ever imagined possible. But at home, all that money did nothing to make her happy. As opposed to her sedentary life in suburbia, her old job was challenging; it gave her a sense of purpose, it made her life meaningful. She definitely wasn't in it for the money. This, I believe, is what Onassis refers to in saying "(Money) ceases to be the goal. The game is what counts." For my mother, the 'game' and what counted were the challenges. It was the feeling of accomplishment after a hard day's work, and it was the notion that she was doing something meaningful. Once she lost that, she lost herself, and the dark cloud of depression reared its ugly head. No amount of money could change that. Money was essentially meaningless at this point.

Of course, money is indeed important, to a certain point. It is the means by which we survive, especially in modern society. Money affords us the necessities for basic survival; food, water, shelter, and the list goes on - except, of course, if we were living outside of civilisation; which most of us engaging in this debate, do not. This arbitrary "certain point" is, of course, unique to each individual. I would simply define it as the point at which one decides they have enough money, and their lives are no longer dedicated merely to the pursuit of more money, but also other, intangible things. For some, it may be the point at which survival is no longer a struggle; the point at which one can live comfortably within their means. Regardless, this, I believe, is when "(money) ceases to be the goal" and "the game is what counts".

Fundamentally this "game" or "what counts" comes down to individual values. For my mother, it was the sense of purpose and meaning that her job gave her that counted. This was "the goal" that she strived for.

Caring for my mother through her depression drove me to research more about the condition and those it affects. The results were eye-opening. Depression and other mental health issues are often stigmatised. However, there is a growing body of evidence that the incidence of depression is skyrocketing, and among those highly affected are the rich. This may be an indicator then, that indeed, money cannot buy happiness, although, to a certain point, it is essential for survival.

If you wish to assess more essays chosen by our staff at the GS GAMSAT Essay Correction Service, you can review them for free at gamsat-prep.com/forum.

If you give a sincere effort and really develop content for WC 4.5.1, 4.5.2, 4.6.1, 4.6.2 and 4.11, then in the days and hours leading up to the GAMSAT, reviewing that content will be one of your most valuable tools to optimize your Section II GAMSAT score. Good luck!

Gold Standard
GAMSAT* Exam

THE GOLD STANDARD GAMSAT
Pull-out, Full-length GAMSAT Practice Test

Introduction

Prior to sitting this practice test, section 2.3 from Part II - Understanding the GAMSAT - should be reviewed.

The following full-length practice Gold Standard (GS) GAMSAT is designed to challenge you and to teach you at a whole new level. You will need to take the tools you have learned and build new structures and create new paths to solving problems. The problems will range from very simple to very challenging, but they will all be very helpful for your GAMSAT preparation. Do not be afraid of making mistakes - it is part of the learning process. The student who makes the most mistakes has the greatest learning potential!

Timing is critical. Many students do not complete various sections of the exam. If you decide to do a few problems from time to time then you have never practiced for the GAMSAT. A full day exam is a rigorous event. It requires practice that simulates exam conditions. An important aspect of the latter is timing. Practice according to the prescribed exam schedule.

Upon finishing the exam, the next challenge is the equally important thorough review. Mistakes, and even correct answers for which some doubt existed, should be examined without time restrictions for maximum learning benefit.

Preparing the Tests

To sit the GAMSAT, you will need a watch or stopwatch, # 2 pencils, an eraser, and a pen with blue or black ink for Section II. During the actual administration, you will not be permitted a calculator for Section III. Calculations or notations must be made in the test booklet (scrap paper is not permitted).

For your practice GAMSAT test, you will find 3 test booklets and two answer documents. To create your test booklets tear your sheets out gently and systematically. Place the front of the book flat on a table and open to the pages just after the full-length exam where you will find Answer Document 1 and Answer Document 2. Tear along the perforation.

The page numbers reflect the exam section to which the page belongs. For example, GS3-8 is the 8th page of Section III (3) of the GS GAMSAT. Begin pulling out pages while paying close attention to the page numbers. Once the complete exam is removed, you will require a stapler. Each of the 3 test sections has a cover page. Staple along the left margin of the cover page 5 times: the topmost and bottommost parts of the margin, once in between the two, and finally, staple once between the top and the middle staple, and again between the middle and the bottom staple. You should now have three test booklets.

Now you can use Answer Document 1 for multiple choice questions. Answer Document 2 will be used for Section II. Answer Document 2 should be stapled together forming a booklet similar to the other exam booklets.

Exam Schedule

You can expect to arrive at the designated exam center by 8 am, local time. Usually logistics are settled and students are sitting the exam by 9 am. About 7 hours later, the exam would have ended. Please see Section 1.2 in Part II of this textbook for your exam day schedule.

Answer Key Information

The answer key to Section III is cross-referenced. In other words, if you make a mistake, the answer key will direct you either to a specific area in a passage or to a specific section in the science review of the Gold Standard GAMSAT textbooks. Alternatively, a key word, concept or equation might be written. If a problem strictly relies on reasoning skills, "deduce" may be written in the answer key without a cross-reference, or, with a cross-reference but only for background information. The hope is that you will find this new answer key informative and helpful as a quick reference. In addition, of course, the original owner of this textbook has 1 year of free online access to the explanations plus access to a Forum with a specific thread for each individual question.

Table 2: Identification of abbreviations and symbols for GS GAMSAT Answer Keys.

Ap	Appendix		PoE	Process of Elimination
B	Background Information		PT	Periodic Table
C	Concept		Q	Question
cf.	Compare		R	Reaction
D.A.	Dimensional Analysis (*see* Part II, 2.3, #16)		T	Table
E	Equation		X.	Answer Choice X
EN	Electronegativity		X. = ba	emphasizes Choice X as being the *best* answer
endo	Endothermic		X.:T/F	Choice X is true but does not answer Q
ESR	Electron Shell Repulsion		X. ↔ …	Choice X is wrong because...
exo	Exothermic		Δ	Change, difference in
F	Figure		↑	Increase, higher
G	Graph		↓	Decrease, lower
info	Information		→	Proceeds to... , next step...
KS	Key Step		∴	Therefore
KW	Key Word		*	Important!
L	Line(s) where info can be found		10.5–7	Section 10.5 to 10.7
P	Paragraph where info can be found		10.5/7	Section 10.5 and 10.7

TEST GS-1

Section I:
Reasoning in Humanities and Social Sciences

Questions 1-75
Time : 100 Minutes

INSTRUCTIONS: Of the 75 questions in this test, many are organised into groups preceded by stimulus material. After evaluating the stimulus material, select the best answer to each question in the group. Some questions are independent of any descriptive passage or each other. Similarly, select the best answer to these questions. If you are unsure of an answer, eliminate the alternatives that you know to be incorrect and select an answer from the remaining alternatives. To indicate your selection, use a pencil to blacken the corresponding oval on Answer Document 1, GS-1. If you wish to make notes, it must be done ONLY in the test booklet. No scrap paper is permitted. No marks are deducted for wrong answers.

The Gold Standard GAMSAT* has been designed exclusively to test knowledge and thinking skills. The exam may contain hypothetical statements and/or express controversial ideas. Statements contained herein do not necessarily reflect the policy, position, or view of RuveneCo Inc.

You have 10 minutes reading time allocated for the content of this test booklet during which it is forbidden to mark your exam paper in any way. After your reading time is complete, you may begin the exam.

OPEN BOOKLET ONLY WHEN TIMER IS READY.

**Worked solutions are available to the original owner
at gamsat-prep.com.**

The following two passages discuss different indigenous values.

Questions 1 – 2 refer to Passage I.

PASSAGE I

"Mitakuye Oyasin" is a Native American prayer and expression. Even though it only consists of two words in the Lakota Sioux language, the expression is considered the most powerful prayer when uttered. The phrase translates roughly as "all my relations" and "we are all-connected", within the same utterance.

The Lakota Sioux also honoured, respected, and can be said to have worshipped the Buffalo. Their ceremonies had rites and rituals and every part of the animal, after it was killed, was used for food, clothing, tools, and weapons.

In many ways, the Lakota Sioux exhibited wisdom in their views of the environment. Their prayer implies that all life deserves honour and respect, because all life is valued, and intertwined with each other. Their rituals also showed that from the smallest ant to the greatest and strongest creatures of the Earth, all are connected and useful in a biological system.

1. For the Lakota Sioux, "honour and respect" connotes:
   A   worship.
   B   interconnection.
   C   value.
   D   parity.

2. ". . . all life deserves honour and respect, because all life is valued, and intertwined with each other" is closest to which Native American proverb?
   A   Respect the gift and the giver.
   B   When we show our respect for other living things, they respond with respect for us.
   C   With all things and in all things, we are relatives.
   D   Treat the earth well: it was not given to you by your parents; it was loaned to you by your children. We do not inherit the Earth from our Ancestors; we borrow it from our Children.

Questions 3 – 6 relate to either Passage II or both passages.

PASSAGE II

For the Indigenous Australians, kinship to the land is a core spiritual value. While geographical boundaries such as lakes, rivers, and mountains distinguish each Aboriginal clan, these "traditional lands" bind the identity of its people to their territory. There are areas in a territory that certain clan members have a special connection with, like for example, the place where one's mother first conceived. This gives them a deeper affinity, respect and care for that locale and the lives surrounding it.

Understandably, an Aboriginal clan does not only possess the right to use their land and benefit from its returns; they also take on the duty to cultivate and preserve their own environment, including its animals. As one Kakadu elders, Bill Neidjie puts it, "Our story is in the land. . . it is written in those sacred places. . . My Children will look after those places, that's the law."

3. The phrase "Our story is in the land" connotes that:
   A   Aboriginal tribes are eternally bound to their land by tradition and history.
   B   among the Aborigines in Australia, the land and identity are inseparable.
   C   traditional lands embody the values and belief systems of the Aborigines.
   D   Aboriginal folklore is rich in stories about the origins of their land.

4. According to the Indigenous Australians, "respect and care" for the environment is an expression of:
   A   tribal worship.
   B   ancestral affinity.
   C   fiduciary duty.
   D   ethnic custom.

5. The Lakota Sioux and the Aborigines of Australia are only two of the native tribes which were labelled by 17th century European colonisers as "savages". However, the indigenous values presented in the two passages parallel much of today's principles about ecology. Which of the following statements would alter the old European perception regarding the culture of these native people?
   A   Indigenous people have always had a great sense of indebtedness and respect for the environment.
   B   The culture of the natives has always been guided by natural insights as compared to the highbrow rationalism of the Europeans.
   C   Native tribes have always had an advanced culture save for their unrefined wardrobe fashion.
   D   Indigenous people have long had a sophisticated code of conduct, which includes the preservation of and the harmonious co-existence with nature.

6. In both passages, the following is a common idea on the environment:
   A   both native cultures illustrate the interrelationships of all life.
   B   both cultures honour and respect ecosystems.
   C   indigenous tribes have a long history of worshipping nature.
   D   the two passages highlight indigenous spiritual orientation.

UNIT 2

Questions 7 - 16

*The following is an excerpt from **The Grapes of Wrath** by John Steinbeck.*

The owners of the land came onto the land, or more often a spokesman for the owners came. They came in closed cars, and they felt the dry earth with their fingers, and sometimes they drove big earth augers into the ground for soil tests. The tenants, from their sun-beaten dooryards, watched uneasily when the closed cars drove along the fields. And at last the owner men drove into the dooryards and sat in their cars to talk out of the windows. The tenant men stood beside the cars for awhile, and then squatted on their hams and 5 found sticks with which to mark the dust.

In the open doors the women stood looking out, and behind them the children – corn headed children, with wide eyes, one bare foot on top of the other bare foot, and the toes working. The women and the children watched their men talking to the owner men.

They were silent.   10

Some of the owner men were kind because they hated what they had to do, and some of them were angry because they hated to be cruel, and some of them were cold because they had long ago found that one could not be an owner unless one were cold. And all of them were caught in something larger than themselves. Some of them hated the mathematics that drove them, and some were afraid, and some worshipped the mathematics because it provided a refuge from thought and from feeling. If a bank or 15 a finance company owned the land, the owner man said, The Bank – or the Company – needs – wants – insists – must have – as though the Bank or the Company were a monster, with thought and feeling, which had ensnared them. These last would take no responsibility for the banks or the companies because they were men and slaves, while the banks were machines and masters all at the same time. Some of the owner men were a little proud to be slaves to such cold and powerful masters.   20

The owner men sat in the cars and explained. "You know the land is poor. You've scrabbled at it long enough, God knows."

The squatting tenant men nodded and wondered and drew figures in the dust, and yes, they knew, God knows. If the dust only wouldn't fly. If the top would only stay on the soil, it might not be so bad.

The owner men went on leading to their point: "You know the land's getting poorer. You know what cotton does to the land; robs it, sucks all the blood out of it."   25

The squatters nodded – they knew, God knew. If they could only rotate the crops they might pump blood back into the land.

Well, it's too late. And the owner men explained the workings and the thinkings of the monster that was stronger than they were. "A man can hold land if he can just eat and pay taxes; he can do that."   30

"Yes, he can do that until his crops fail one day and he has to borrow money from the bank."

"But – you see, a bank or a company can't do that, because those creatures don't breathe air, don't eat side-meat. They breathe profits; they eat the interest on money. If they don't get it, they die the way you die without air, without side-meat. It is a sad thing, but it is so. It is just so."

7. The tenants are portrayed in the excerpt as:
   A   hard workers.
   B   poor and impoverished.
   C   well rewarded.
   D   lazy and incompetent.

8. "Monster" (line 17) in the passage refers to which of the following?
   A   The Dust
   B   The dying off of crops
   C   The banking system
   D   The owners of the land

9. The tone of the narrative in this passage suggests:
   A   perseverance.
   B   hopelessness.
   C   rage.
   D   anger.

10. The passage seems to describe a historical setting that took place during which American event listed below?
   A   The Great Depression
   B   World War 2
   C   The Dust Bowl
   D   The Great Immigration to the U.S.

11. "Scrabbled" (line 21) would mean:
   A   squandered.
   B   scrubbed away at.
   C   squatted on.
   D   tilled.

12. There are many references to "squatting" in the narrative. What would be the best definition listed below?
   A   Waiting for good soil
   B   Wasting time idly, not working
   C   Staying on the land, to own it
   D   Ready to get orders from the bosses

13. To some extent, the workers are portrayed as slaves in the excerpt. How are the bosses portrayed?
    A   Mean, cruel, and without conscience
    B   As slaves to the banks
    C   Supportive of the worker's rights
    D   As hard working farmers

14. Based on the excerpt, owners:
    A   are genuinely concerned about the squatters.
    B   are in cahoots with the banks.
    C   want the squatters to leave.
    D   have no interest in the squatters.

15. In this excerpt, the predominant image is:
    A   machinery.
    B   cotton.
    C   soil.
    D   dust.

16. In the colloquial phrase "cat side-meat" (lines 32-33), what does "cat" refer to?
    A   Stealing
    B   Eating
    C   Hording
    D   Portioning

Questions 17 – 18

17. Even though we may not be familiar with quintic equations (which are polynomials as groups of 5, hence "quin"), the humour of this cartoon is due to which of the following?
     A   Math and geeks
     B   The diversity of meanings in language
     C   The unintended irony
     D   The logical fallacies presented

18. We can infer from the party or social get together context of the cartoon that:
     A   there is always somebody radical at an event.
     B   radicals are very significant in relation to quintic equations.
     C   the get together is for brainiacs and math whizzes.
     D   the author is not playing with language.

Questions 19 – 21

The following is a short parable by the German philosopher Schopenhauer.

In a field of ripening corn I came to a place which had been trampled down by some ruthless foot; and as I glanced amongst the countless stalks, every one of them alike, standing there so erect and bearing the full weight of the ear, I saw a multitude of different flowers, red and blue and violet. How pretty they looked as they grew there so naturally with their little foliage! But, thought I, they are quite useless; they bear no fruit; they are mere weeds, suffered to remain only because there is no getting rid of them. And yet, but for these flowers, there would be nothing to charm the eye in that wilderness of stalks. They are emblematic of poetry and art, which, in civic life – so severe, but still useful and not without its fruit – play the same part as flowers in the corn.

19. The speaker in this parable regards the flowers as:
    A   symbolic of the colours and abundance of life.
    B   representative of the beautiful but useless in life.
    C   unnecessary splendour that makes life bearable.
    D   ideal symbols of poetic and artistic creations.

20. The parable suggests that the speaker regards poetry and art as:
    A   superfluous.
    B   purely ornamental.
    C   uplifting.
    D   purposive.

21. This parable could best be described as:
    A   comparing and contrasting useful corn and beautiful flowers.
    B   illustrating the functional aesthetics of poetry and art and nature.
    C   pointing out how diverse nature is.
    D   showing how poetry and flowers are like weeds.

Questions 22 – 33

Extended Unit on Romanticism (in broken paragraphs)

PARAGRAPH I

The Romantic era, period, or movement, can be viewed as an artistic, political, and philosophical response to classical ideals and political dogma, the burgeoning paradigm of scientific rationalism, and the emergence of the industrial revolution. Within the historical context of the French and American Revolution, the individual was gaining new liberties over tyranny. The romantic hero emerged as a cultural icon becoming manifested in literary, philosophical, and historical stereotypes.

22. In Paragraph I, why would scientific rationalism, be considered a burgeoning paradigm?
    A   Because as a model of inquiry, it would be the dominant example to follow.
    B   Because the experimental method was beginning.
    C   Because technological innovations were at the forefront of culture.
    D   Because it was in direct opposition to poetic modes of thought.

PARAGRAPH II

Emphasizing subjective experience over objective agreement, as in Browning's phrase "the mind is a thousand times more beautiful than nature could ever be", the romantic hero became a common figure in lyrical poetry and theatre. This passionate, talented hero, rejects societal ideals and norms, yet is instilled with some tragic flaw, which leads to his demise. Imbued with the attainment of perfection, the romantic hero could easily utter Browning's remarks, "A man's reach must exceed his grasp, or what is a heaven for?"

23. In reference to one of Lord Byron's major works, he is often quoted as saying: "Man's greatest tragedy is that he can conceive of a perfection which he cannot attain." Lord Byron's statement and Browning's "A man's reach must exceed his grasp, or what is a heaven for":
    A   differ in their perceptions of a perfect society.
    B   differ in their outlook towards man's pursuit of achieving perfection.
    C   are similar in their positive views about obtaining a perfect world.
    D   are similar in their assumptions about the nature of worldly pursuits.

PARAGRAPH III

Such is the basic nature of Moliere and Lord Byron's "Don Juan", whose unattainable appetites and libertine excesses bring about his own downfall. During this era, William Blake, visionary poet, remarked "the road of excess leads to the palace of wisdom" as if predefining a Byronic type of hero. Byron's own exploits paralleled his literary creations, as well, as a kind of "unattainable excess". Keats would describe this affliction or obsession as "egotistical sublime", and we find it in different personae in this era. Goethe's Faust suffers from the same malady but also ultimately redeems himself.

24. Paragraph III implies that, for Keats, a typical Byronic hero:
    A   is a failed perfectionist.
    B   is an obsessive, soul-searching hero.
    C   has no defined identity.
    D   is an excessive pleasure-seeker.

PARAGRAPH IV

In history, we find this same overachieving ego-figure in Napoleon, releasing the serfs from oppression, insisting on equality, founding the Napoleonic code of law, extending his megalomaniacal military reaches across the globe, until he is turned away from Russia, and defeated at Waterloo. Finally Napoleon was exiled, like The Count of Monte Cristo, and brought down by his own lust for power.

25. When describing Napoleon's military reaches, the term "megalomaniacal" is used. This term roughly equates to:
    A   slovenliness.
    B   prestige.
    C   military-like.
    D   ego.

PARAGRAPH V

The maestro violinist, Niccolò Paganini, whose persecution by the Church, can be seen as a romantic hero. Undeterred in his efforts to compose and perform, many legends and myths surround him. Supposedly slowly poisoned by mercury used to treat his tertiary syphilis, he was believed to be a fiddling devil, being able to play virtuoso on one string, caricatured as the mad genius who sold his soul, much like Faust. Being that the romantic mind was fascinated with things distorted or beyond nature, in a word – grotesque, as evidenced in Mary Shelley's Frankenstein, the demonic character of Paganini was a perfect example of how romantic ideas could enter into popular folklore.

26. In Paragraph V, the association between a romantic mind and the characters of Frankenstein and Paganini suggests that:
    A   being experimental was a Romantic tendency.
    B   the Romantic Movement was preoccupied with the unconventional and bizarre.
    C   the duality of human nature polarized between the sinister and the extraordinary, between good and evil, was a typical characteristic of a Romantic hero.
    D   Romanticism was distorted.

PARAGRAPH VI

While the beginnings of the scientific method were being refined, many poets and philosophers stood in bleak contrast to the rational logico-deductive models, and also drifted away from the classical Apollonian muses. In fact, the concept of imagination was offered by the romantics as diametrically opposed. "We murder to dissect" was Wordsworth's herald and "contemplation of nature" was given the highest priority against reductionist forms of thought. By finding voice in Dionysian modes of expression, without the Hellenic order and restraint of tempered meter or rhyme, these romantics located truth in the individual. In philosophy, subjective idealism was finding its groundings in Leibniz and Berkeley, and later more radically, with Nietzsche. In Germany, the romantic virtuoso was Beethoven and later Wagner, whose operas portrayed the pinnacle of German Romanticism, with its excessive exuberance, reigniting Nordic myths into national epics.

27. Wordsworth's quote in Paragraph IV, "We murder to dissect" is a poetic response to:
    A   extreme egoism.
    B   the fatal flaw.
    C   fallacies of myth.
    D   the scientific method.

28. In Paragraph VI, an opposition between the classical Greek gods – Apollo and Dionysus – symbolizes which of the following?
    A   Truth and Illusion
    B   Order and Freedom
    C   Music and Poetry
    D   Ego and Pride

PARAGRAPH VII

Blake, Wordsworth, Keats, Shelley, et al. helped define poets "as unacknowledged legislators of the world, (Shelley)," who should break free of "the mind-forged manacles (Blake)" of contemporary thought through contemplation with and of nature. Keats' "Truth is Beauty, Beauty is Truth" is symptomatic of the romantic impulse to find an alternative to the reductive process of science, which many poets found "dissective" in its scope and process.

Perhaps the epitome and end of Romantic philosophers can be found in Nietzsche, who in virtual isolation from humanity, writes of a greater humanity, located in the 'Superman', beyond good and evil. Peering into the abyss and limits of philosophy, as such, brought about his own downfall in the form of madness.

29. According to Paragraph VII, which of the following is NOT true about the Romantic era?
    A   The Romantic era was concerned with individual experience.
    B   The Romantic era sought freedom from different constraints.
    C   The Romantic era was concerned with contemplation with Nature.
    D   The Romantic era was logical and scientific.

30. The description of Nietzsche "who in virtual isolation from humanity, writes of a greater humanity" is an example of what?
    A   Madness
    B   Contradiction
    C   Irony
    D   Metaphor

Questions 31 – 33 pertain to all paragraphs.

31. Which of the following statements does NOT describe the Romantic spirit implied in the preceding paragraphs?
    A   Do what you will, this world's a fiction and is made up of contradiction.
    B   Come forth into the light of things, let nature be your teacher.
    C   I have love in me the likes of which you can scarcely imagine. A rage, the likes of which you would not believe. If I cannot satisfy one, I will indulge in the other.
    D   I love you the more in that I believe you had liked me for my own sake and for nothing else.

32. A certain type of support in relation to the author's interpretation was extensively used in the paragraphs. Which of the following would be the best answer in defining this type of support?
    A   Historical examples
    B   Literary quotations
    C   Various juxtapositions
    D   Contrasting analogies

33. Based on the paragraphs, the term "subjective" in the Romantic context is:
    A   outside, verifiable.
    B   dependent upon.
    C   subject to.
    D   personal, individual.

Questions 34 -37

The following is Graham's "Hierarchy of Disagreement".

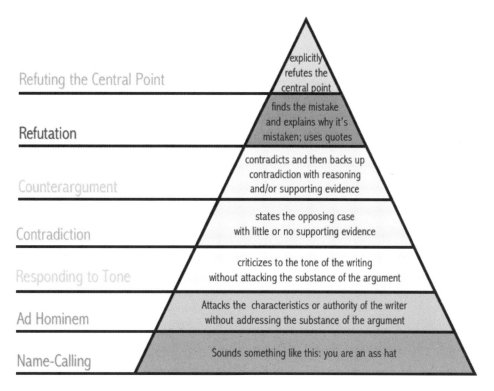

34. Based on the diagram, what makes "Responding to Tone" a weak form of disagreement?
    A   Tone is hard to judge.
    B   It overlooks the correctness of the writer's point.
    C   The response is still fundamentally a personal attack on the writer.
    D   It allows the critic to disagree without valid evidence.

35. This diagram shows that:
    A   it is necessary to differentiate between name-calling and Ad Hominem attacks.
    B   refuting the main point of an argument does not need supporting evidence.
    C   the tone of the argument is more important than the substance of the argument.
    D   the hierarchy moves from an emotional response to logical refutation.

36. Graham's "Hierarchy of Disagreement" seems to emphasize that:
    A   argumentation is inherently impassioned.
    B   anger makes argumentation personal.
    C   disagreeing essentially means arguing.
    D   it is possible to disagree without necessarily being angry.

37. The disagreement hierarchy is presented in the form of a pyramid in order to show that:
    A   disagreements occur in stages.
    B   forms of disagreement are arranged in an ascending manner.
    C   the more rational the disagreement, the less it is employed.
    D   rationality should govern disagreements.

Questions 38 – 42

Afternoon in School - The Last Lesson

When will the bell ring, and end this weariness?
How long have they tugged the leash, and strained apart
My pack of unruly hounds: I cannot start
Them again on a quarry of knowledge they hate to hunt,
I can haul them and urge them no more.   5
No more can I endure to bear the brunt
Of the books that lie out on the desks: a full three score
Of several insults of blotted pages and scrawl
Of slovenly work that they have offered me.
I am sick, and tired more than any thrall   10
Upon the woodstacks working weariedly.

And shall I take
The last dear fuel and heap it on my soul
Till I rouse my will like a fire to consume
Their dross of indifference, and burn the scroll   15
Of their insults in punishment? - I will not!
I will not waste myself to embers for them,
Not all for them shall the fires of my life be hot,
For myself a heap of ashes of weariness, till sleep
Shall have raked the embers clear: I will keep   20
Some of my strength for myself, for if I should sell
It all for them, I should hate them -
- I will sit and wait for the bell.

D. H. Lawrence

38. The learning atmosphere depicted in the poem is:
A   exhausting because of the healthy exchange of ideas.
B   challenging.
C   unruly and hateful.
D   indifferent, therefore pointless.

39. What is meant by "slovenly work" (line 9)?
A   Done obediently like a dog
B   Repetitive and unnecessary
C   Terse and unfocused
D   Done in a hasty and sloppy fashion

40. The literary style of Lawrence's poem, with its series of rhetorical questions, theatrically most resembles a(n):
A   dialogue.   B   soliloquy.
C   imbrications.   D   aside.

41. Line 23 suggests that the attitude of the speaker is one of:
A   impatience.
B   detachment.
C   resignation.
D   frustration.

42. The ringing of the bell in this poem connotes:
   A a relief from boredom.
   B freedom from the burdens of teaching.
   C a signal of opportunity for the speaker to channel his noble efforts to a more rewarding endeavour.
   D hope for a better classroom situation the next day.

UNIT 8

Questions 43 – 47

From late 1950s to early 1960s, the issue of African-American Civil Rights was crucial in shaping the eventual structure of politics and image of democracy in America. The following are excerpts from speeches of two of the most influential advocate-leaders of the time.

Questions 43 – 44 pertain to Passage I.

PASSAGE I

The political philosophy of black nationalism means that the black man should control the politics and the politicians in his own community; no more. The black man in the black community has to be re-educated into the science of politics so he will know what politics is supposed to bring him in return. Don't be throwing out any ballots. A ballot is like a bullet. You don't throw your ballots until you see a target, and if that target is not within your reach, keep your ballot in your pocket.

The political philosophy of black nationalism is being taught in the Christian church. It's being taught in the NAACP. It's being taught in CORE meetings. It's being taught in SNCC Student Nonviolent Coordinating Committee meetings. It's being taught in Muslim meetings. It's being taught where nothing but atheists and agnostics come together. It's being taught everywhere.

Black people are fed up with the dillydallying, pussyfooting, compromising approach that we've been using toward getting our freedom. We want freedom now, but we're not going to get it saying "We Shall Overcome." We've got to fight until we overcome.

The economic philosophy of black nationalism is pure and simple. It only means that we should control the economy of our community. Why should white people be running all the stores in our community? Why should white people be running the banks of our community? Why should the economy of our community be in the hands of the white man? Why? If a black man can't move his store into a white community, you tell me why a white man should move his store into a black community. The philosophy of black nationalism involves a re-education program in the black community in regards to economics. Our people have to be made to see that any time you take your dollar out of your community and spend it in a community where you don't live, the community where you live will get poorer and poorer, and the community where you spend your money will get richer and richer.

"The Ballot or the Bullet" by Malcolm X
(Founder, Muslim Mosque Inc.)
April 3 1964

43. Based on the passage, Malcolm X associates the ballot with:
   A wise decision-making.
   B freedom to act out one's choice.
   C a means for achieving advancement.
   D civil rights.

44. Malcolm X proposes that the way for African-Americans to attain freedom is through:
  A   a drastic change in the national political system.
  B   the indoctrination of Black Nationalism.
  C   exigent measures.
  D   voting wisely.

PASSAGE II

Every American citizen must have an equal right to vote.

There is no reason which can excuse the denial of that right. There is no duty which weighs more heavily on us than the duty we have to ensure that right.

Yet the harsh fact is that in many places in this country men and women are kept from voting simply because they are Negroes. Every device of which human ingenuity is capable has been used to deny this right. The Negro citizen may go to register only to be told that the day is wrong, or the hour is late, or the official in charge is absent. And if he persists, and if he manages to present himself to the registrar, he may be disqualified because he did not spell out his middle name or because he abbreviated a word on the application. And if he manages to fill out an application, he is given a test. The registrar is the sole judge of whether he passes this test.

He may be asked to recite the entire Constitution, or explain the most complex provisions of State law. And even a college degree cannot be used to prove that he can read and write.

For the fact is that the only way to pass these barriers is to show a white skin. Experience has clearly shown that the existing process of law cannot overcome systematic and ingenious discrimination. No law that we now have on the books – and I have helped to put three of them there – can ensure the right to vote when local officials are determined to deny it. In such a case our duty must be clear to all of us. The Constitution says that no person shall be kept from voting because of his race or his colour. We have all sworn an oath before God to support and to defend that Constitution. We must now act in obedience to that oath.

from "We Shall Overcome" by Lyndon Baines Johnson
(Thirteenth President of the United States)
March 16 1965

Questions 45 – 47 apply to either Passage II or both passages.

45. Former U.S. President Johnson views equality in voting rights as a(n):
  A   social responsibility.
  B   constitutional right.
  C   political duty.
  D   affirmation of freedom.

46. In reference to the failure of granting equal rights to the African-Americans, both speakers assign the culpability to:
  A   the biased government system.
  B   segregation.
  C   cunning politicians.
  D   arbitrary legal provisions.

47. The two passages seem to suggest that:
  A   Malcolm X favours racial segregation while President Johnson favours integration.
  B   unlike Malcolm X, President Johnson maintains his confidence in the U.S. Constitution.
  C   both speakers claim that the government is responsible for racial inequities in America.
  D   Malcolm X views the act of voting as a choice while President Johnson views it as a must.

Questions 48 – 54

Consider the following passage and comments in answering the questions.

Some aspects of postmodern art concern self-consciousness of the art act itself, the laying bare of the devices used to construct the illusion or representation, and blurring the divisions between the audience and the art. For example, John Cage, a pianist and to some extent experimentalist in art, recorded only audience noise for one of his compositions: the shuffling about in seats, coughs, whispers, etc… all to some extent, what would be considered noise. His most famous work is the 4'33", which he composed in 1952. This piece is performed in three movements without the musician hitting a single note for four minutes and thirty three seconds. The composition is supposed to consist of the sounds of the surroundings that the listener hears while it is performed.

The following remarks are quoted from Cage himself:

Comment I

Wherever we are, what we hear is mostly noise. When we ignore it, it disturbs us. When we listen to it, we find it fascinating.

Comment II

People who are not artists often feel that artists are inspired. But if you work at your art you don't have time to be inspired.

Comment III

Ideas are one thing and what happens is another.

Comment IV

The grand thing about the human mind is that it can turn its own tables and see meaninglessness as ultimate meaning.

Comment V

Art's purpose is to sober and quiet the mind so that it is in accord with what happens.

Comment VI

The first question I ask myself when something doesn't seem to be beautiful is why do I think it's not beautiful. And very shortly you discover that there is no reason.

Comment VII

The highest purpose is to have no purpose at all. This puts one in accord with nature, in her manner of operation.

48. In Comment I, which of the following could be reasonably inferred about John Cage's view of music?
    A   Music takes different forms.
    B   Music is an affirmation of life.
    C   Silence is music in itself.
    D   The appreciation of music depends on how you listen to it.

49. Comments V and VII support the notion that the purpose of music is to:
  A have no purpose at all.
  B bring about internal order out of chaos.
  C reveal the natural motion of life.
  D liberate the listeners from artificial conventions.

50. How many of the comments would contradict the concept that art should be an expression of the artist's inner state rather than his or her subject?
  A 4
  B 2
  C 3
  D 1

51. Which of Comments I to VII is closely similar to the idea of "art for art's sake"?
  A Comment II
  B Comment IV
  C Comment V
  D Comment VII

Questions 52 – 54 relate to the pictures or the comments, whichever is applicable.

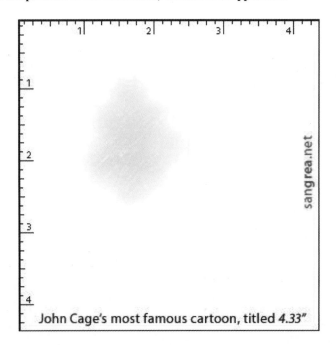

John Cage's most famous cartoon, titled 4.33"

Picture 1

52. Which among Comments I to VII does Picture 1 relate with?
  A Comment III
  B Comment IV
  C Comment VI
  D Comment VII

53. In relation to the comments, what makes Picture 1 humorous?
  A Its self-referentiality
  B There is nothing there, except the two axes.
  C It mocks the pretensions of such notions.
  D All of the above

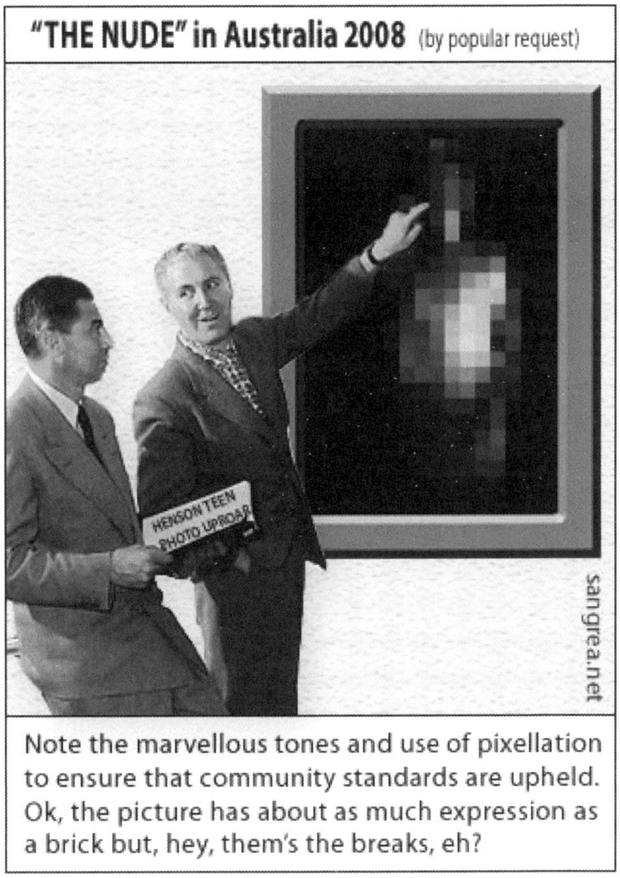
"THE NUDE" in Australia 2008 (by popular request)
HENSON TEEN PHOTO UPROAR
sangrea.net
Note the marvellous tones and use of pixellation to ensure that community standards are upheld. Ok, the picture has about as much expression as a brick but, hey, them's the breaks, eh?

Picture 2

54. The humour in this picture is derived from the overbearing standards of:

A censorship.
B representation.
C traditional art.
D colour contrast to black and white.

Questions 55 – 57

The following compilation of crime percentages were based on some Thailand research in relation to other countries of the Western world.

Table 1. Crimes Statistics: Thailand and selected Western Countries

Assaults (per thousand people)	Burglaries (per thousand people)
US 7.6	Australia 21.7
UK 7.5	UK 13.8
Canada 7.1	Canada 8.9
Australia 7.0	US 7.1
France 1.8	France 6.1
Germany 1.4	Japan 2.3
Thailand 0.3	Thailand 0.2
Japan 0.3	Germany N/A

Rapes (per hundred thousand people)	Gun Murders (per hundred thousand people)
Australia 79	Thailand 31
Canada 73	US 2.8
US 30	Canada 0.5
UK 14	Germany 0.5
France 14	Autraslia 0.1
Germany 9	UK 0.1
Thailand 6	Japan N/A
Japan 2	France N/A

55. The number of violent crimes (listed as Assaults, Rapes, and Murders) were committed in Australia and Thailand in this selected temporal frame. Which country had the LEAST amount of violent crimes listed?
   A   Japan
   B   Thailand
   C   France
   D   Germany

56. Which country would define the closest approximation to a mean or average of the crime of rape listed?
   A   Germany
   B   US
   C   UK
   D   France

57. The main purpose of the chart provided could be inferred to:
    A   assess Thailand's crime rates in relation to other countries.
    B   promote gun control measures or legislation in Thailand.
    C   provide statistics for analysis in Thailand's violent and non-violent crimes.
    D   compare and contrast the different crimes worldwide in relation to Thailand.

UNIT 11

Question 58

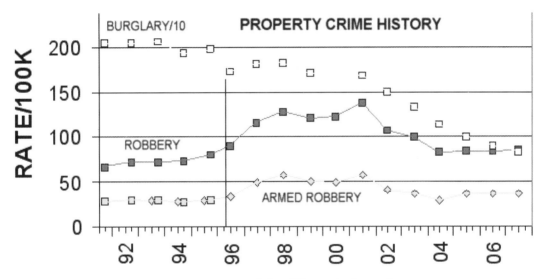

Figure 1. Property Crime History in Australia

58. Which of the following would make the best generalization concerning Australian crime rates based on Figure 1?
    A   The decline of burglary, over the years, corresponds to a rise in robbery.
    B   The rates for robbery and armed robbery rose faster after 1996, and stayed higher for a few years.
    C   All three types of crime do not decline after 1993.
    D   It appears that a short term increase in armed robbery occurred after 2002.

Questions 59 – 65

The Englishman and Music

Englishmen have never cared for music as they care for football or film stars. They like singing, most of them, either making a noise themselves or listening to others. There is a long tradition both of religion and conviviality by which men and women who would not claim to be musical will gladly take part in a hymn or join in a chorus. There has been a tradition centuries old by which choral singing in parts has been a fairly widespread pastime. In Elizabethan times, it was something more: for about forty years it appears to have been a fashionable craze among cultivated people, and, though it is easy to overestimate the excellence of their performance, the singers of those days conferred an incalculable benefit upon the art of music and a rich heritage upon English musical life by their assiduous practice, thereby stimulating to activity a whole school of first-rate composers. Assuredly England has never been a "land without music", as the reproachful German phrase went a couple of generations ago. But music, musical affairs, musical politics, new compositions, the status of individual artists, have never in this country been "front page news": the bulk of the population does not really care how music gets along provided that on occasion it can obtain what it wants for ceremonial occasions, for occasional polite entertainment, for lubricating the wheels on which its theatrical or restaurant entertainment runs. . . Our festivals, our opera seasons, and the performance of our virtuosi, even our musical competitions, leave our national phlegm unmoved. The tantrums of a prima donna have a certain human interest for our popular newspapers, but by and large the great public does not care. Are we then a musical people?

. . . Are we a blue-eyed people? Some of us are blue-eyed and some of us are musical. The musical enthusiasts are a small minority, but the potentially musical are a much larger number. Perhaps five percent are definitely insusceptible to music. . . The rest are capable of having their interest, and perhaps ultimately their love, aroused for the art. There are many things in this beautiful world that compete for our attention, for our limited time, for our not unlimited mental energy, and for our pocket-money, and many will sacrifice music to fly-fishing or watching birds. . . many a gifted person with artistic abilities that run in several directions at once will devote himself to water-colours instead of the piano. But the coming of the wireless broadcasting has at least made numbers of people, running into the hundreds of thousands, aware of music as a factor in their experience of life.

The kind of satisfaction that comes from music. . . is one of the things that give value to life. Possibly it is the most perfect example of those higher disinterested values that give significance to life, in that it is unmixed with social, political and ethical purposes and so provides us with an instance of what is valuable in and for itself alone without further object. Not everyone will want this particular kind of satisfaction from music; some take a more hedonistic view of it and value it as just one more ingredient in the good life. Still others are content with the opiate of light music. But whichever of the many sorts of psychological satisfaction that can be getting from music may be found by any individual, it is so far a part of his life's experience, and more and more people are coming to be aware of it as such and to value it as an enrichment of their lives.

Adapted from Frank Howes, Fontana Guide to Orchestral Music, 8 1958 by Collins Clear Type Press

59. According to the passage, the attitude of the English during the Elizabethan era was most influential in resulting to:
    A   an interest in musical affairs which had never been there previously.
    B   increased participation in hymn and choir singing in churches.
    C   a revival in choral singing in parts.
    D   great musical compositions by a new era of composers.

60. The author rhetorically asks "Are we a blue-eyed people?" in order to:
    A   exemplify that nearly half of the population is, at least, partially musical.
    B   convey the irrelevance of questioning whether the English are musical or not.
    C   affirm that, as a whole, the English are a musical people.
    D   emphasize the contrasting attitudes towards music between the English, Germans and Russians.

61. The passage suggests that the English might be less interested than the Germans in news concerning:
   A   football and the newest developments in that sport.
   B   issues in musical entertainment that might affect business.
   C   outdoor hobbies.
   D   developments in the music and theatre industry.

62. According to the author, someone who is "insusceptible to music" is someone who:
   A   is uninterested in musical affairs, musical politics, and the state of individual artists.
   B   would rather not waste their time fly-fishing or bird-watching.
   C   is incapable of having their interest for music aroused.
   D   would rather devote their time to water-colours.

63. The passage indicates that the renewed musical awareness in England can in part be attributed to:
   A   the assiduous practicing of singers over the years.
   B   the introduction of wireless broadcasting into society.
   C   the emergence of a whole new school for talented composers.
   D   a decline of interest in football that has occurred over the years.

64. Based on the passage, one could conclude that the author believes that music's greatest value lies in the fact that:
   A   it has a great ability to bring joy.
   B   it is a form of expression which is detached from politics, social and cultural issues.
   C   it is a component of the good life.
   D   it has the power to enrich the life of every individual who becomes aware of it.

65. Which of the following would be the best reason why the English are NOT musically inclined as other Germanic countries?
   A   They are more interested in hobbies and sports.
   B   They have no great composers, in relation to Bach or Beethoven.
   C   Look at modern culture, such as the British invasion of Rock and Roll.
   D   Their musical proclivities are in the nascent stages of development.

Questions 66 – 69

The following are two short passages from Shakespeare (Macbeth and King Lear).

Macbeth, after his queen's death, makes the following famous speech in Act 5, Scene 5, lines 17-28.

MACBETH: Wherefore was that cry?

SEYTON: The queen, my lord, is dead.

MACBETH: She should have died hereafter;
There would have been a time for such a word.
To-morrow, and to-morrow, and to-morrow,
Creeps in this petty pace from day to day
To the last syllable of recorded time,
And all our yesterdays have lighted fools
The way to dusty death. Out, out, brief candle!
Life's but a walking shadow, a poor player
That struts and frets his hour upon the stage
And then is heard no more: it is a tale
Told by an idiot, full of sound and fury,
Signifying nothing

Act III, Scene IV, during the terrible storm. While his fool takes shelter in a hovel, Lear, after learning of his daughter's treachery, throws himself into the wilderness, losing his sanity or so it seems. Here he remains standing for a moment in the rain and meditates on the poor citizens of his kingdom:

Poor naked wretches, whereso'er you are,
That bide the pelting of this pitiless storm,
How shall your houseless heads and unfed sides,
Your loop'd and window'd raggedness, defend you
From seasons such as these? O, I have ta'en
Too little care of this! Take physic, pomp;
Expose thyself to feel what wretches feel,
That thou mayst shake the superflux to them,
And show the heavens more just.

66. In the Macbeth passage, the tonality of Shakespeare suggests:
   A   remorse.
   B   despair.
   C   grief.
   D   anxiety.

67. In the King Lear passage, the tonality of Shakespeare suggests:
   A   shattered innocence.
   B   profound enlightenment.
   C   remorseful compassion.
   D   indignant defiance.

68. In the passage from King Lear "Take Physic, pomp" is a strange and anachronistic utterance. Based on the context of the passage, this would mean in modern day language:
    A to understand the poor's suffering.
    B to feel the elements of the storm arrogantly.
    C to strive to make things just.
    D pompous men take a taste of this medicine.

69. Which of the following generalizations could be inferred concerning both passages?
    A Life is unjust.
    B Life is meaningless.
    C Life is constantly changing.
    D Life is storm-like.

UNIT 14

Questions 70 – 73

The following are pictures from World War 1 and World War 2.

Picture 1–from China ("You will be defeated!" - translation)

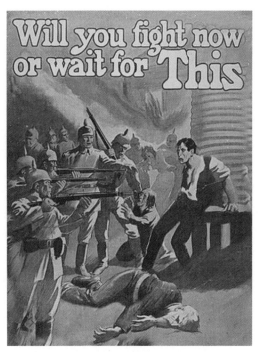

Picture 2–from Australia (WW1)

Picture 3–from the U.S.

Picture 4–from the U.S.

Picture 5–from the UK

It can be argued that all of the 5 pictures represent propaganda to at least some extent.

70. Which of the pictures appeals mostly to a "sense of patriotism and homeland"?
    A   1
    B   5
    C   3
    D   2

71. Which of the following ratios depict the representations' use of emotional appeals respectively (1-5)?
    A   Quantity, quality, labour, taxes, derision
    B   Rage, sentiment, workers, money, laughter
    C   Intimidation, fear, demonization, economic insecurity, humour
    D   Polarization, patriotism, caricatures, foolhardiness

72. Which picture is the most emotionally charged?
    A   3
    B   4
    C   1
    D   5

73. Which picture "polarizes"? (either/or thinking)
    A   2
    B   5
    C   1
    D   3

Questions 74–75

How to Learn the Lost "Art of Memory"

Many scholars have claimed that "the art of memory" or lost art was due to the rise of the written word. The ancient Greeks and Romans supposedly had enormous memories, based on a few architectural tricks. Essentially, they would accomplish these by using mental rooms or diagrams, which were known as "loci". Even the internet has shown an increase of interest in such a lost art, with slogans, such as "memorize" by rooms of your house, or toolbox, or even building a mental palace which is compartmentalized to the extent that it can hold whatever you wish to remember! The pictures below were from Giordano Bruno, who tried to reinvent the art, in the late dark ages.

Even though orators such as Cicero and Quintilian have offered advice on how to do such an outrageous act of mental imagery, categorization, compartmentalization, and memory, below are some contemporaneous suggestions on how to start and accomplish this feat of mnemonics.

How to Build Your Memory Palace

At the World Memory Championships, top competitors memorize the order of 20 shuffled decks of cards in an hour and more than 500 random digits in 15 minutes, among other events. A Secret is to build a memory palace, an image in your mind.

- Decide on a blueprint for your palace. Real or imagined. You can use your home, if you wish, but it has to have route, and places of storage, for your items you need to memorize.

- Define a route. Take a walk through. If you need to remember items in sequence, it is important to do this, as imagery in your mind, walking through your home or palace.

- Identify specific storage locations in your palace or along your route. You can store things you need to remember, in specific rooms, closets, drawers, chests, and so forth. For example, if you wish to remember things you need to get at the store, store those items in the respective places, with a visual image–shampoo, toothpaste–bathroom, etc. Be Creative.

- Memorize your memory palace. Draw out your map, graphic or blueprint, with the rooms and items which you need to memorize–this will help you greatly by matching the visual image on paper, with the image in your mind.

- Place things to be remembered in your palace. Based on your route, place items you need to remember in select places.

- Use symbols. You may want to associate a symbol which is placed in a room, with something you need to remember–such as a musical note or staff, by the entertainment centre, indicating that new music you wish to purchase.

- Be creative. Associate rooms, objects, items, with each other in different ways. Experiment!

- Stock your palace with other mnemonics. You may have a special place where you keep old letters and pictures from your past, which trigger memories. Put such devices as the musical treble clef of "Every Good Boy Does Fine" (EGBDF) in this place.

- Explore your palace. Once you have stocked your palace with evocative images, you need to go through it and look at them. Visualize the walk through the rooms, the symbols and devices; if you cannot do this, write them out again on a pad.

- Use your palace. Try it out, see if it works. If not, rebuild sections, where there is a logical progression and association to assist your memory.

- Build new palaces. You can dump the current contents out, and start fresh on other things you need to remember such as parts of a speech, math formulas, birthdays, anything of importance which requires memory.

- Practice, Explore, Visualize, Associate.

74. According to the passage, such a memory device is based mainly on:
    A visual and internal imagery.
    B rigorous analysis and induction.
    C hypnagogic dream states.
    D associative synthesis.

75. Based on the passage, we do not have as much of a memory as the ancient Greeks and Romans due to:
    A the blossoming of the scientific method.
    B the rise of religion.
    C the loss of instructional texts.
    D the rise of literacy and the written word.

TEST GS-1

Section II: Written Communication

2 Writing Tasks (A and B)
Time: 60 Minutes (total)

INSTRUCTIONS: This test is designed to evaluate your writing skills. There are two writing assignments. You will have 5 minutes to read the instructions and the quotations in the two writing tasks. During your reading time, you are not permitted to mark or write in your exam booklet nor the answer document in any way. Thereafter, you will have 60 minutes to complete writing your responses for both tasks. Your response to Writing Task A must be written only on answer sheets marked "A," and your response to Writing Task B should be written only on answer sheets marked "B." If you finish writing before time is up, you may review your work.

Use your time in an efficient manner. Prior to writing your response, read the assignment carefully. The empty space on the page with the writing assignment may be used to make notes in planning your response. Scratch paper is not permitted. Corrections or additions can be made neatly between the lines but there should be no writing in the margins of the answer booklet. You are not expected to use each page of your answer document but do not skip lines. Use a black or blue pen to write your response. Illegible essays cannot be scored.

OPEN BOOKLET ONLY WHEN TIMER IS READY.

WRITING TASK A

Read the following statements and write a response to any one or more of the ideas presented.

Your essay will be evaluated on the value of your thoughts on the theme, logical organization of content and effective articulation of your key points.

* * * * * * * * *

Comment 1

    Whoever said the pen is mightier than the sword obviously never encountered automatic weapons.

Gen. Douglas MacArthur

* * * * *

Comment 2

    Political power grows out of the barrel of a gun.

Chairman Mao Zedong

* * * * *

Comment 3

    A man of courage never wants weapons.

* * * * *

Comment 4

    Before a standing army can rule, the people must be disarmed, as they are in almost every country in Europe.

Noah Webster

* * * * *

Comment 5

    You can get more with a kind word and a gun than you can with just a kind word.

Al Capone

WRITING TASK B

Read the following statements and write a response to any one or more of the ideas presented.

Your essay will be evaluated on the value of your thoughts on the theme, logical organization of content and effective articulation of your key points.

* * * * * * * * * *

Comment 1

Each friend represents a world in us, a world possibly not born until they arrive, and it is only by this meeting that a new world is born.

Anais Nin

* * * * *

Comment 2

A friend is one who walks in when the rest of the world walks out.

* * * * *

Comment 3

The best mirror is an old friend.

* * * * *

Comment 4

One friend in a lifetime is much; two are many; three are hardly possible. Friendship needs a certain parallelism of life, a community of thought, a rivalry of aim.

Henry Adams

* * * * *

Comment 5

Friendship is unnecessary, like philosophy, like art... It has no survival value; rather is one of those things that give value to survival.

C.S. Lewis

TEST GS-1

Section III:
Reasoning in Biological and Physical Sciences

Questions 1-110
Time : 170 Minutes

INSTRUCTIONS: Of the 110 questions in this test, many are organised into groups preceded by a passage. After evaluating the passage, select the best answer to each question in the group. Some questions are independent of any descriptive passage or each other. Similarly, select the best answer to these questions. If you are unsure of an answer, eliminate the alternatives that you know to be incorrect and select an answer from the remaining alternatives. To indicate your selection, use a pencil to blacken the corresponding oval on Answer Document 1, GS-1. Rough work is to be done ONLY in the test booklet. No scrap paper is permitted. No calculator is permitted. No marks are deducted for wrong answers.

The Gold Standard GAMSAT* has been designed exclusively to test knowledge and thinking skills. The exam may contain hypothetical statements and/or express controversial ideas. Statements contained herein do not necessarily reflect the policy, position, or view of RuveneCo Inc.

You have 10 minutes reading time allocated for the content of this test booklet during which it is forbidden to mark your exam paper in any way. After your reading time is complete, you may begin the exam.

> **OPEN BOOKLET ONLY WHEN TIMER IS READY.**

**Worked solutions are available to the original owner
at gamsat-prep.com.**

Questions 1–6

The last step in translation involves the cleavage of the ester bond that joins the complete peptide chain to the tRNA corresponding to its C-terminal amino acid. This process of termination, in addition to the *termination* codon, requires release factors (RFs). The freeing of the ribosome from mRNA during this step requires the participation of a protein called ribosome releasing factor (RRF).

Cells usually do not contain tRNAs that can recognize the three termination codons. In *E. coli*, when these codons arrive on the ribosome they are recognized by one of three release factors. RF-1 recognizes UAA and UAG, while RF-2 recognizes UAA and UGA. The third release factor, RF-3, does not itself recognize termination codons but stimulates the activity of the other two factors.

The consequence of release factor recognition of a *termination* codon is to alter the peptidyl transferase center on the large ribosomal subunit so that it can accept water as the attacking nucleophile rather than requiring the normal substrate, aminoacyl-tRNA.

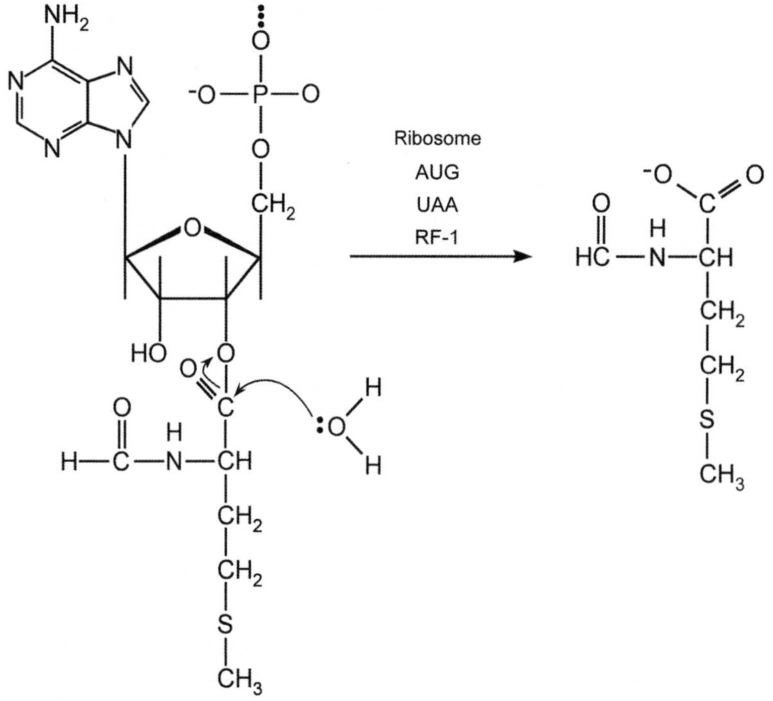

Figure 1

1. Where would the RFs be expected to be found in the cell?
   A Within the nuclear membrane
   B Floating in the cytosol
   C In the matrix of the mitochondria
   D Within the lumen of the smooth endoplasmic reticulum

2. The alteration to the peptidyl transferase center during the termination reaction serves to convert peptidyl transferase into a(n):
   A exonuclease.
   B lyase.
   C esterase.
   D ligase.

3. Sparsomycin is an antibiotic that inhibits peptidyl transferase activity. The effect of adding this compound to an in vitro reaction in which *E. coli* ribosomes are combined with methionine aminoacyl-tRNA complex, RF-1 and the nucleotide triplets, AUG and UAA, would be to:
   A inhibit hydrolysis of the amino acid, allowing polypeptide chain extension.
   B inhibit peptide bond formation causing the amino acid to be released.
   C induce hydrolysis of the aminoacyl-tRNA complex.
   D inhibit both hydrolysis of the aminoacyl-tRNA complex and peptide bond formation.

Figure 2 shows the kinetics of inhibition of rabbit red blood cell peptidyltransferase by Sparsomycin. The time plots shown were done using Sparsomycin concentrations of (*) 0.1×10^{-6} M, (▲) 0.2×10^{-6} M, and (●) 0.4×10^{-6} M. The percentage (x') of the remaining active peptidyltransferase is shown, as well as the percentage at equilibrium (x'_{eq}) for each curve which is indicated by the dashed --- lines.

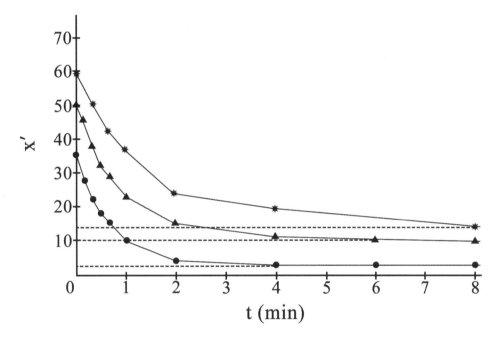

Figure 2
Adapted from D. Synetos, Molecular Pharmacology June 1, 1998 vol. 53 no. 6 1089-1096.

4. Which of the following is NOT true concerning the curves in Figure 2?
   A The equilibrium point of the curve using 0.4×10^{-6} M Sparsomycin is obtained at a point where more than 95% of the peptidyltransferase is not active.
   B The fact that the 3 plots are curved, does not in itself indicate if the reaction is first order or second order.
   C The curve where 0.2×10^{-6} M Sparsomycin is used is most consistent with a first-order reaction because the active concentration of peptidyltransferase decreases by approximately 50% at just under 1 minute, and then by another 50% (approximately) at just under 1 minute later.
   D If the curves were linear, they would be most consistent with zero-order and first-order reactions.

5. Which of the following graphs is consistent with the data in Figure 2?

The following estimates may be of assistance: log 6 = 0.8, log 4 = 0.6.

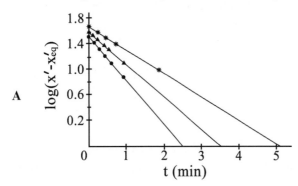

A

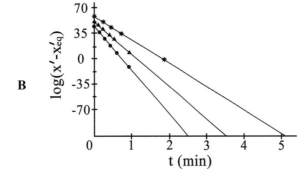

B

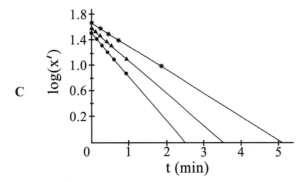

C

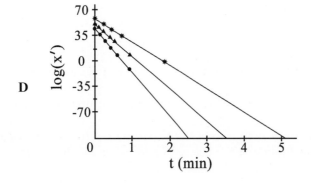

D

6. According to Figure 2, if 0.2×10^{-6} M of Sparsomycin is applied to 70 picograms of peptidyltransferase from rabbit red blood cells, estimate the rate of inhibition at t = 2 minutes.

   A   30 picograms/minute
   B   25 picograms/minute
   C   15 picograms/minute
   D   3.5 picograms/minute

Questions 7-11

Reduction potentials (also referred to as *redox potentials*) reveal the tendency of a chemical species to acquire electrons and thus be reduced. Each species has its own intrinsic redox potential; the more positive the potential, the greater the species' affinity for electrons and tendency to be reduced.

A reduction potential is measured in volts (V). Because the true or absolute potentials are difficult to accurately measure, reduction potentials are defined relative to the standard hydrogen electrode (SHE) which is arbitrarily given a potential of 0.00 volts. Standard reduction potential is measured under standard conditions: 25 °C, a 1M concentration for each ion participating in the reaction, a partial pressure of 1 atm for each gas that is part of the reaction, and metals in their pure state.

Table 1: Standard State Reduction Potentials. Ions are in aqueous form.

Half-reactions	Standard reduction potential (E°)
$F_2 (g) + 2e^- \rightleftharpoons 2F^-$	2.87 V
$Cl_2 (g) + 2e^- \rightleftharpoons 2Cl^-$	1.36 V
$Br_2 (aq) + 2e^- \rightleftharpoons 2Br^-$	1.09 V
$Ag^+ + e^- \rightleftharpoons Ag (s)$	0.80 V
$Fe^{3+} + e^- \rightleftharpoons Fe^{2+}$	0.77 V
$Cu^{2+} + 2e^- \rightleftharpoons Cu (s)$	0.34 V
$2H^+ + 2e^- \rightleftharpoons H_2(g)$	0.00 V
$Pb^{2+} + 2e^- \rightleftharpoons Pb (s)$	−0.13 V
$Ni^{2+} + 2e^- \rightleftharpoons Ni (s)$	−0.41 V
$Zn^{2+} + 2e^- \rightleftharpoons Zn (s)$	−0.76 V
$Na^+ + e^- \rightleftharpoons Na (s)$	−2.71 V

7. What should happen when a piece of copper is placed in 1M HCl?
    A   The copper is completely dissolved by the acid.
    B   The copper is dissolved by the acid with the release of hydrogen gas.
    C   The copper bursts into greenish flames.
    D   Nothing happens.

8. What should happen when a piece of lead is placed in 1M HCl?
    A   The lead is completely dissolved by the acid.
    B   The lead begins to dissolve with the release of hydrogen gas.
    C   The lead bursts into flames.
    D   Nothing happens.

9. If standard state oxidation potentials are used instead of standard state reduction potentials and the half reactions are listed in descending order according to their standard state oxidation potentials, which one of the following would be true?

    A   The lead reaction would be above the silver reaction.
    B   The fluorine reaction would be above the chlorine reaction.
    C   The iron reaction would be above the nickel reaction.
    D   The hydrogen reaction would be below the copper reaction.

10. According to Table 1, which of the following species is the strongest reducing agent?

    A Fe^{3+}
    B Fe^{2+}
    C Zn^{2+}
    D Zn (s)

11. Only considering the standard half-cell reactions of the species listed in Table 1, how many different voltaic cells with a voltage greater than 2V can be made?

    A   Fewer than 7
    B   7
    C   15
    D   More than 15

Questions 12–16

The four forces that act on a plane are lift, weight, drag or air resistance, and thrust, the last of which is produced by the plane's engine.

Impact pressure produces 30% of the lift. It results from the fact that wings are given a *dihedral* angle where the distance from the tip of the wing to the ground is greater than that from the root of the wing to the ground.

The other 70% of lift can be accounted for by the Bernoulli effect. A cross-section of an airplane's wing reveals greater surface area above the wing compared to a flatter, lower surface. Thus air, moving in streamline flow, must move more rapidly over the top of the wing.

Bernoulli's equation, $P + 1/2\rho v^2 + \rho gh = $ constant, is often modified when discussing an airplane's wing. The "ρgh" component is usually left out since the difference in distance from the top of the wing to the ground compared to the bottom of the wing to the ground is usually negligible.

Note that:
- Streamline flow is governed by the continuity equation where $A_1 v_1 = A_2 v_2$
- For Bernoulli's and/or the continuity equation: P is pressure, ρ is density, v is velocity, g is gravity, h is the height and A is the cross-sectional area.

12. Newton's Third Law states that for every action there must be an equal and opposite reaction. This is applicable to lift and the dihedral angle because:
    A the fast moving air above the wing increases the pressure.
    B drag must be as low as possible to improve forward motion.
    C there is a large pressure difference between the wings.
    D the wing deflects the air downward and the air in turn deflects the wing upward.

13. Compared to the wing's upper surface, the air moving along the undersurface has:
    A greater velocity, greater pressure.
    B greater velocity, lower pressure.
    C lower velocity, greater pressure.
    D lower velocity, lower pressure.

14. An airplane is encircling an airport with DECREASING speed. When the airplane reaches point P, what is the general direction of its acceleration?

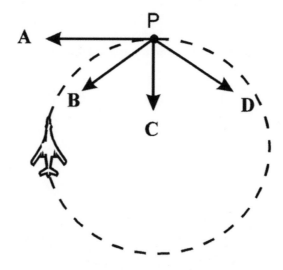

15. The following represents an incompressible fluid in laminar flow through pipes. Where is the pressure highest?

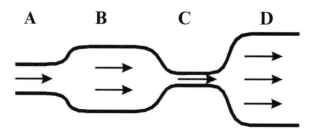

16. Flow is defined as volume per unit time. Concerning the preceding diagram, what can be determined regarding the flow?
    A   It is highest at C.
    B   It is highest at D.
    C   It cannot be determined.
    D   It is constant throughout.

UNIT 4

Question 17

17. What would be the expected change in terms of the solubility of a gas when a solution containing the gas is heated and when a solution containing the gas has the pressure over the solution decreased, respectively?

   A   Increase, increase
   B   Increase, decrease
   C   Decrease, increase
   D   Decrease, decrease

UNIT 5

Question 18

18. The structure of β-D-glucose is shown below in two different projection systems. The circled hydroxyl group in Fig. 1 would be located at which position in the modified Fischer projection depicted in Fig. 2?

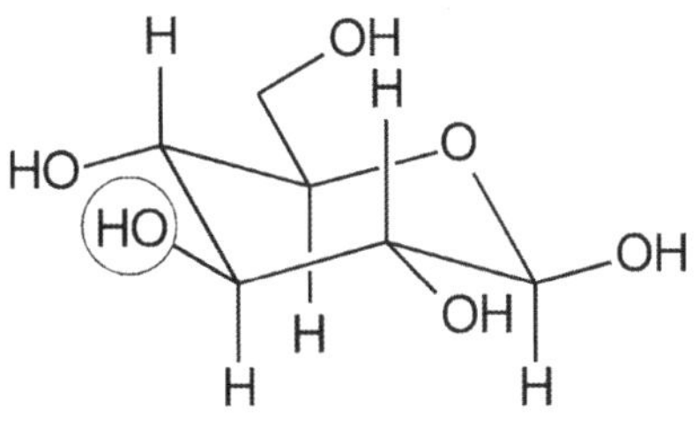

Figure 1 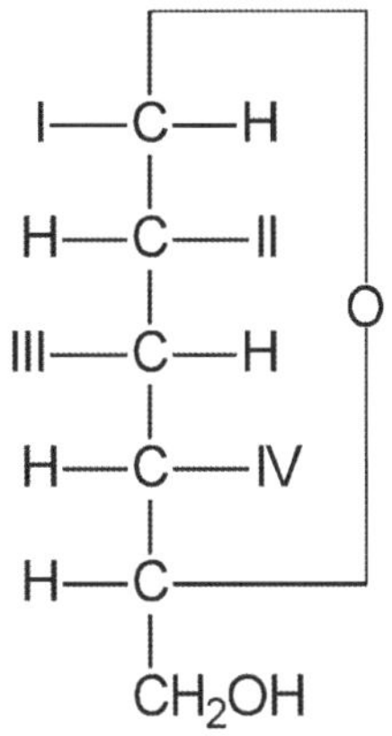   Figure 2

   A   I
   B   II
   C   III
   D   IV

Questions 19–24

The essential stages in the manufacture of H_2SO_4 and H_2SO_3 involve the burning of sulfur or roasting of sulfide ores in air to produce SO_2. This is then mixed with air, purified and passed over a vanadium catalyst (either VO_3^- or V_2O_5) at 450 degrees Celsius. Thus the following reaction occurs.

$$2SO_2(g) + O_2(g) \rightleftharpoons 2SO_3\ (g) \qquad \Delta H = -197 \text{ kJ mol}^{-1}$$

Reaction I

If the SO_2 is very carefully dissolved in water, sulfurous acid (H_2SO_3) is obtained. The first proton of this acid ionizes as if from a strong acid while the second ionizes as if from a weak acid.

$$H_2SO_3 + H_2O \rightarrow H_3O^+ + HSO_3^-$$

Reaction II

$$HSO_3^- + H_2O \rightleftharpoons H_3O^+ + SO_3^{2-} \qquad K_a = 5.0 \times 10^{-6}$$

Reaction III

The concentration of H_2SO_3 in cleaning fluid was determined by titration with 0.10 M NaOH (strong base) as shown in Fig.1. Two equivalence points were determined using 30 ml and 60 ml of NaOH respectively:

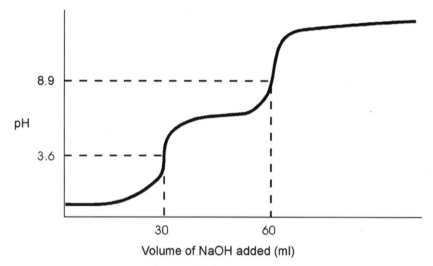

Figure 1

Note: You may find some of the following information helpful. Relative atomic masses: H = 1.0, N = 14.0, O = 16.0, S = 32, Cl = 35.5

19. What is the oxidation number of sulfur in sulfurous acid?
    A +3
    B +4
    C +5
    D +6

20. What is the percent by mass of oxygen in sulfurous acid?
    A 31.9%
    B 19.7%
    C 39.0%
    D 58.5%

21. Which of the following acid-base indicators is most suitable for the determination of the first end point of the titration shown in Figure 1?
    A Cresol red (color change between pH = 0.2 and pH = 1.8)
    B p-Xylenol blue (color change between pH = 1.2 and pH = 2.8)
    C Bromophenol blue (color change between pH = 3.0 and pH = 4.6)
    D Bromocresol green (color change between pH = 3.8 and pH = 5.4)

22. The equilibrium constant K_a is also called the acid dissociation constant and K_b is the base dissociation constant. The value of K_a given in Reaction III is relatively low which would mean that, relatively, its:
    A pK_a is low and the pK_b of its conjugate base is high.
    B pK_a is high and the pK_b of its conjugate base is low.
    C pK_a is low and the pK_b of its conjugate base is low.
    D pK_a is high and the pK_b of its conjugate base is high.

23. If no catalyst was used in Reaction I, which of the following would experience a change in its partial pressure when the same system reaches equilibrium?
    A There will be no change in the partial pressure of any of the reactants
    B SO_3 (g)
    C SO_2 (g)
    D O_2 (g)

24. If the temperature was decreased in Reaction I, which of the following would experience an increase in its partial pressure when the same system reaches equilibrium?
    A There will be no change in the partial pressure of any of the reactants
    B SO_3 (g)
    C SO_2 (g)
    D O_2 (g) and SO_2 (g)

UNIT 7

Question 25

25. The patella (i.e. kneecap) is a thick, mostly circular bone which articulates with the femur (thigh bone) and covers and protects the front (anterior) part of the knee joint. Approximate the rate of growth of the anterior surface area of the human patella from birth to age 20 years old.
    A 1.1×10^{-4} cm^2 per hour
    B 1.1×10^{-4} nm^2 per hour
    C 1.1×10^{-2} cm^2 per second
    D 1.1×10^{-2} nm^2 per second

Questions 26–31

Much of the study of evolution of *interspecific* interactions had focused on the results rather than the process of coevolution. In only a few cases has the genetic bases of interspecific interactions been explored. One of the most intriguing results has been the description of "gene-for-gene" systems governing the interaction between certain parasites and their hosts. In several crop plants, dominant alleles at a number of loci have been described that confer resistance to a pathogenic fungus; for each such gene, the fungus appears to have a recessive allele for "virulence" that enables the fungus to attack the otherwise resistant host. Cases of character displacement among competing species are among the best evidence that interspecific interactions can result in genetic change.

Assuming that parasites and their hosts coevolve in an "arms race," we might deduce that the parasite is "ahead" if local populations are more capable of attacking the host population with which they are associated than other populations. Whereas the host may be "ahead" if local populations are more resistant to the local parasite than to other populations of the parasite.

Several studies have been done to evaluate coevolutionary interactions between parasites and hosts, or predators and prey. In one, the fluctuations in populations of houseflies and of a wasp that parasitized them were recorded. The results of the experiment are shown in Fig. 1.

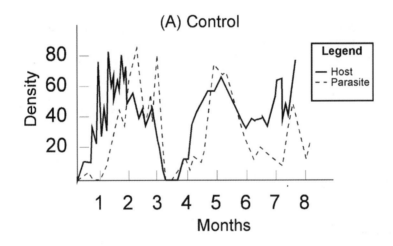

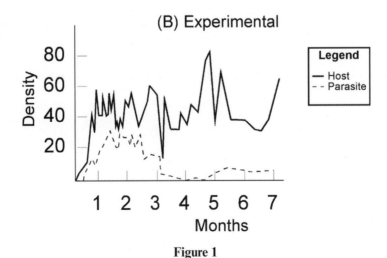

Figure 1

26. A pathogenic fungus is more capable of growth and reproduction on its native population of its sole host, the wild hog peanut, than on plants from other populations of the same species. It is reasonable to conclude that:
   A   the fungus, in this instance, was capable of more rapid adaptation to its host than vice versa.
   B   the fungus, in this instance, was capable of more rapid adaptation to all populations of the host species than vice versa.
   C   the host, in this instance, was capable of more rapid adaptation to the fungus than vice versa.
   D   all populations of the host species were capable of more rapid adaptation to the fungus than vice versa.

27. Allopatric refers to areas isolated geographically from one another whereas sympatric populations occupy the same or overlapping geographical areas. The passage suggests that one result of interspecific interactions might be:
   A   genetic drift within sympatric populations.
   B   genetic drift within allopatric populations.
   C   genetic mutations within sympatric populations.
   D   genetic mutations within allopatric populations.

28. According to Fig. 1, the experiment showed that over time:
   A   coevolution caused a decrease in both the host and parasite populations.
   B   coevolution caused both a decrease in fluctuation of the host and parasite populations, and a lowered density of the parasite population.
   C   coevolution caused a marked increase in the fluctuation of only the host population, and lowered the density of the parasite population.
   D   coevolution caused a decrease in the population density of the parasite population but caused a marked increase in the density of the host population.

29. The control in the experiment likely consisted of:
   A   members from different populations of the host and parasite species used in the experimental group, that had a short history of exposure to one another.
   B   members of the host and parasite species used in the experimental group, that had a long history of exposure to one another.
   C   members of the host and parasite species used in the experimental group that had no history of exposure to one another.
   D   members from different populations of the host and parasite species used in the experimental group, that had a long history of exposure to one another.

30. Which of the following is the least likely explanation of the results obtained for the control group in Fig. 1?
   A   A low parasite population results in a lowered host population by the sheer virulence of the parasite.
   B   A low host population can increase a parasite population by forcing the parasite to seek an alternate source for food.
   C   A high parasite population destroys the host population resulting in a lowered host population.
   D   A high host population creates a breeding ground for parasites thus increasing the parasite population.

31. Penicillin is an antibiotic which destroys bacteria by interfering with cell wall production. Could the development of bacterial resistance to Penicillin be considered similar to coevolution?
   A   Yes, a spontaneous mutation is likely to confer resistance to Penicillin.
   B   No, an organism can only evolve in response to another organism.
   C   Yes, as antibiotics continue to change there will be a selective pressure for bacterial genes which confer resistance.
   D   No, bacteria have plasma membranes and can survive without cell walls.

Questions 32–37

The Diels–Alder reaction is a cycloaddition reaction that can occur between a conjugated diene (= 2 double bonds separated by a single bond) and a substituted alkene (= the dienophile) to form a substituted cyclohexene system.

Diene + dienophile = cyclohexene

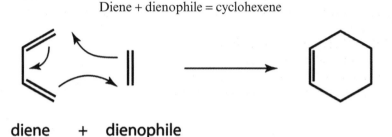

diene   +   dienophile

All Diels-Alder reactions have four common features: (1) the reaction is initiated by heat; (2) the reaction forms new six-membered rings; (3) three π bonds break and two new C-C σ bonds and one new C-C π bond are formed; (4) all bonds break and form in a single step.

The Diels-Alder diene must have the two double bonds on the same side of the single bond in one of the structures, which is called the *s-cis* conformation (= *cis* with respect to the single bond). If double bonds are on the opposite sides of the single bond in the Lewis structure, this is called the *s-trans* conformation (= *trans* with respect to the single bond).

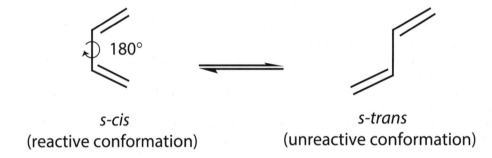

s-cis
(reactive conformation)

s-trans
(unreactive conformation)

32.   Consider Table 1.

Table 1:   Neutral carbon's bond hybrids

When bonded to...	Hybridization	Shape	Bond angle
2 atoms	sp	linear	180°
3 atoms	sp^2	trigonal (triangular)	120°
4 atoms	sp^3	tetrahedral	109.5°

All of the following are true regarding the neutral, non-cyclic molecule, *allene* (C_3H_4) EXCEPT one. Which one is the EXCEPTION?
A   The C-H bond angles are 120°.
B   The hybridization of the carbon atoms are sp and sp^2.
C   The bond angle formed by the three carbons is 180°
D   Allene is a conjugated diene.

33. Which of the following would be the least reactive diene in a Diels-Alder reaction?

A

B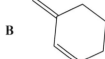

C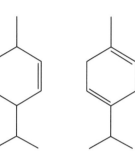

D

34. The number of conjugated dienes among the 5 structures below is:

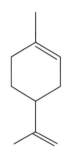 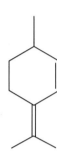 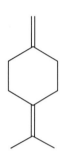

A 1 only.   **B** 2 only.   **C** 3 only.   **D** more than 3.

35. Choose the diene and dienophile that could be used to produce the Diels-Alder product.

? $\longrightarrow$

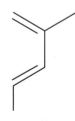
CO_2Me

CO_2Me

CO_2Me

i   ii   iii   iv   v

A i and iv   **C** iii and iv
B ii and iv   **D** iii and v

36. Each of the following represents a pair of resonance structures EXCEPT:

I   [structure]   and   [structure]

II   [structure]   and   [structure]

III   [structure] $-CH_2$ and   [structure] $=CH_2$

IV   [structure] $-CH_2$ and   [structure] $-CH_3$

A   I
B   II
C   III
D   IV

37. How many possible structural isomers are there for C_4H_8?
A   2
B   4
C   5
D   More than 5

Questions 38–43

The phenomenon of refraction has long intrigued scientists and was actually used to corroborate one of the major mysteries of early science: the determination of the speed of light.

The refractive index of a transparent material is related to a number of the physical properties of light. In terms of velocity, the refractive index represents the ratio of the velocity of light in a vacuum to its velocity in the material. From this ratio, it can be seen that light is retarded when it passes through most types of matter. It is worth noting that prisms break up white light into the seven "colors of the rainbow" because each color has a slightly different velocity in the medium.

Snell's law allows one to follow the behavior of light in terms of its path when moving from a material of one refractive index to another with the same, or different refractive index. It is given by: $n_1 \sin\theta_1 = n_2 \sin\theta_2$, where "1" refers to the first medium through which the ray passes, "2" refers to the second medium, and the angles refer to the angle of incidence in the first medium (θ_1) and the angle of refraction in the second (θ_2).

A ship went out on a search for a sunken treasure chest. In order to locate the chest, they shone a beam of light down into the water using a high intensity white light source as shown in Fig.1. The refractive index for sea water is 1.33 while that for air is 1.00.

Table 1: Common values for sine and tangent

θ	$\sin\theta$	$\tan\theta$
30°	1/2	$1/\sqrt{3}$
45°	$1/\sqrt{2}$	1
60°	$\sqrt{3}/2$	$\sqrt{3}$
90°	1	-

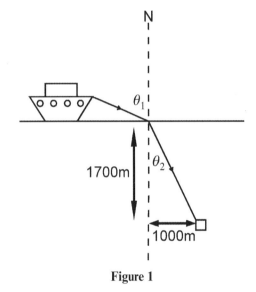

Figure 1

38. From the information in the passage, how would you expect the speed of light in air to compare with the speed of light in a vacuum (which is given by "c")?
    A   It would be approximately equal to c.
    B   It would be greater than c.
    C   It would be less than c.
    D   This cannot be determined from the information given.

39. Using the information in the passage, what must be the approximate value of θ_2 such that the beam of light hits the chest as shown in Figure 1?
    A   15°
    B   30°
    C   45°
    D   60°

40. How does the refractive index in water for violet light compare with that of red light given that violet light travels more slowly in water than red light?

A $n_{violet} = n_{red}$

B $n_{violet} < n_{red}$

C $n_{violet} > n_{red}$

D   This depends on the relative speeds of the different colors in a vacuum.

41. Total internal reflection first occurs when a beam of light travels from one medium to another medium which has a smaller refractive index at such an angle of incidence that the angle of refraction is 90°. This angle of incidence is called the critical angle. What is the value of the sine of this angle when the ray moves from water towards air?

A 2π

B   0.75

C   0.50

D   0

42. What would happen to the critical angle, in the previous question, if the beam of light was travelling from water to a substance with a greater refractive index than air, but a lower refractive index than water?

A   It would increase.

B   It would decrease.

C   It would remain the same.

D   Total internal reflection would not be possible.

43. Which of the following would you expect to remain constant when light travels from one medium to another and the media differ in their refractive indices?

A   Velocity

B   Frequency

C   Wavelength

D   Intensity

Questions 44–49

Aside from diabetes, thyroid disease is the most common glandular disorder. Millions of people are treated for thyroid conditions, often an underactive or overactive gland. Overwhelmingly, women between the ages of 20 and 60 are much more likely than men to succumb to these conditions. The etiology lies in the failure of the immune system to recognize the thyroid gland as part of the body and thus antibodies are sent to attack the gland.

The plasma proteins that bind thyroid hormones are albumin, a prealbumin called thyroxine-binding prealbumin (TBPA), and a globulin with an electrophoretic mobility, thyroxine-binding globulin (TBG). The free thyroid hormones in plasma are in equilibrium with the protein-bound thyroid hormones in the tissues. Free thyroid hormones are added to the circulating pool by the thyroid. It is the free thyroid hormones in plasma that are physiologically active (increasing the metabolic rate) and imbalances in these hormones result in thyroid disease. In thyroid storm, a form of hyperthyroidism, the normal body temperature of 37.5 °C may rise to over 40 °C.

In addition, in humans there are four small parathyroid glands that produce the hormone, parathormone, which is a peptide composed of 84 amino acids. Parathormone and the thyroid hormone calcitonin work antagonistically to regulate the plasma calcium and phosphate levels. Overactive parathyroid glands, *hyperparathyroidism*, can lead to an increase in the level of calcium in plasma and tissues.

Table 1: Different plasma proteins and their binding capacity and affinity for thyroxine.

Protein	Plasma Level (mg/dl)	Thyroxine Binding Capacity (µg/dl)	Affinity for thyroxine	Amount of thyroxine bound in normal plasma (µg/dl)
Thyroxine binding globulin (TBG)	1.0	20	High	7
Thyroxine binding prealbumin (TBPA)	30.0	250	Moderate	1
Albumin	...	1000	Low	None
Total protein-bound thyroxine in plasma	...	...	...	8

44. Is it reasonable to conclude that thyroid disease is sex-linked?
    A No, because thyroid disease appears to be caused by a defect of the immune system and not a defective DNA sequence.
    B No, because if the disease was sex-linked, there would be a high incidence in the male, rather than the female, population.
    C Yes, because the high incidence of the disease in women suggests that a gene found on the X chromosome codes for the disease.
    D Yes, because the same factor increases the risk of women getting the disease, regardless of familial background.

45. According to Table 1, it would be expected that:
    A TBG has the highest binding capacity for thyroxine while TBPA has the highest affinity.
    B TBG has the highest binding capacity for thyroxine while albumin has the lowest affinity.
    C albumin has the highest binding capacity for thyroxine while TBPA has the highest affinity.
    D albumin has the highest binding capacity for thyroxine while TBG has the highest affinity.

Question 46 refers to Fig. 1.

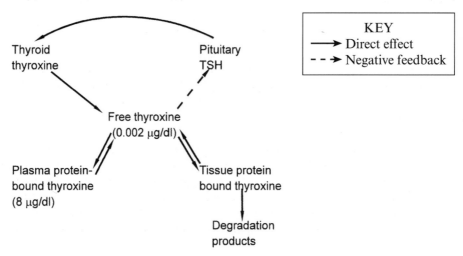

Figure 1

46. According to the equilibrium shown in Fig. 1, an elevation in the concentration of free thyroid hormone in the plasma is followed by:
    A   an increase in tissue protein-bound thyroxine.
    B   an increase in tissue protein-bound thyroxine and plasma protein-bound thyroxine.
    C   an increase in the amount of TSH secreted from the pituitary gland.
    D   an increase in both the amount of TSH secreted from the pituitary gland and the release of thyroxine from the thyroid gland.

47. Symptoms that can be inferred to be consistent with hypothyroidism and hyperthyroidism, respectively, include:
    A   a fine tremor and diminished concentration.
    B   brittle nails and kidney stones.
    C   rapid heart beat and increased irritability.
    D   lethargy and nervous agitation.

48. Which of the following is an example of positive feedback?
    A   A body temperature of 39 °C causes a further increase
    B   Elevated TSH results in elevated thyroxine
    C   Calcitonin and parathormone regulate calcium levels
    D   Increased TBG leads to an increase in TSH

49. Parathormone influences calcium homeostasis by reducing tubular reabsorption of PO_4^{3-} in the kidneys. Which of the following, if true, would clarify the adaptive significance of this process?
    A PO_4^{3-} and Ca^{2+} feedback positively on each other.
    B   Elevated levels of extracellular PO_4^{3-} result in calcification of bones and tissues.
    C   Increased PO_4^{3-} levels cause an increase in parathormone secretion.
    D   Decreased extracellular PO_4^{3-} levels cause a decrease in calcitonin production.

Questions 50–54

The enthalpy of solution (ΔH_{soln}) of a salt depends on two other quantities: the energy released when free gaseous ions of the salt combine to give the solid salt (lattice energy: ΔH_{latt}) and the energy released when free gaseous ions of the salt dissolve in water via solute-solvent interactions to yield the solvated ions (enthalpy of hydration: ΔH_{solv}) where:

$$\Delta H_{soln} = \Delta H_{solv} - \Delta H_{latt} \qquad \text{Equation I}$$

From the formal definition of the quantities, it can be seen that both ΔH_{latt} and ΔH_{solv} are exothermic. Although these values seem to be in competition, the factors that affect ΔH_{latt} and ΔH_{solv} do so in the same way. Firstly, the smaller the ion, the closer the association of the ion with either other ions in the crystal lattice, or, with water molecules and thus the more negative ΔH_{latt} and ΔH_{solv} become. Also, the greater the charge on the ion, the greater the increase in electrostatic forces of attraction between itself and other ions or water molecules, and the more negative ΔH_{latt} and ΔH_{solv} become.

Although ΔH_{latt} and ΔH_{solv} undergo similar changes, the change in ΔH_{solv} up or down a group is much more profound than that of ΔH_{latt}. A good example of this is seen in the solubility changes of the Group II carbonates.

However, there is one exception to these general rules. If the cation of the salt is approximately the same size as the anion, the arrangement of ions in the crystal lattice is more uniform and hence the lattice is more stable and ΔH_{latt} is more negative.

Table 1: Note the order going down the periodic table is Mg, Ca, Sr, Ba.

Group II Carbonate	Solubility (mol L^{-1} H_2O)
$MgCO_3$	1.30×10^{-3}
$CaCO_3$	0.13×10^{-3}
$SrCO_3$	0.07×10^{-3}
$BaCO_3$	0.09×10^{-3}

50. It is often useful to determine the solubility product (K_{sp}) of compounds that are sparingly soluble like those in Table 1. In this context, K_{sp} can be defined as the mathematical product of ion concentrations raised to the power of their stoichiometric coefficients. The solubility product for $MgCO_3$ is:
    A 1.3×10^{-4}
    B 2.6×10^{-4}
    C 1.7×10^{-6}
    D 6.7×10^{-8}

51. $Ca(OH)_2$ has approximately the same K_{sp} as $CaSO_4$. Which of them has the greater solubility in terms of mol L^{-1}?
    A   They both have the same solubility.
    B $Ca(OH)_2$
    C $CaSO_4$
    D   It depends on the temperature at the time.

52. Given the information in the passage, the $CO_3{}^{2-}$ anion is approximately the same size as:
    A Mg^{2+}.   C Sr^{2+}.
    B Ca^{2+}.   D Ba^{2+}.

53. The ΔH_{solv} for a doubly charged anion X^{2-} was found to be more negative than that for the carbonate anion. Given the information in the passage, which of the following is the most likely explanation?
   A X^{2-} is the same size as the carbonate anion.
   B X^{2-} is larger than the carbonate anion.
   C X^{2-} is smaller than the carbonate anion.
   D   It depends on the H_{latt} for the salt containing the anion.

54. A solution of $SrCO_3$ in water boils at a higher temperature than pure water. Why is this?
   A $SrCO_3$ increases the density of water.
   B $SrCO_3$ decreases the vapour pressure of the water.
   C $SrCO_3$ has a low solubility in water.
   D $SrCO_3$ decreases the surface tension of the water.

UNIT 13

Question 55

55. The following system includes a frictionless pulley and a cord of negligible mass. Since the system is at rest, what can be said about the force of friction between the platform and the large weight?

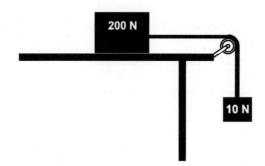

   A   It is 200 N.
   B   It is 10 N.
   C   It is 190 N.
   D   In this case, the force of friction is not necessarily present.

Questions 56–61

In the simple model of a gas as described by the kinetic molecular theory, a gas is pictured as an assembly of particles travelling at high velocities in straight lines in all directions. The particles are constantly colliding, but they are supposed to be perfectly elastic so that no momentum is lost on impact. They are also supposed to be point masses, that is, they have mass but occupy no space. In addition, no attractive or repulsive forces are exerted between particles.

From this theory, and the work of other great scientists like Boyle and Charles, the ideal gas law was devised: $PV = nRT$ where P = pressure of the gas, V = volume of the gas, n = number of moles of gas particles present, T = Kelvin temperature of the gas and R = universal gas constant.

However, no "real" gas conforms to this "ideal" gas theory, that is, no real gas obeys all of these laws at all temperatures and pressures. These deviations were investigated by the French physicist Amagat, who used pressures up to 320 atmospheres and a range of temperatures to investigate these deviations. The following diagram shows how the PV/nRT value varies with pressure for certain gases at 50 °C.

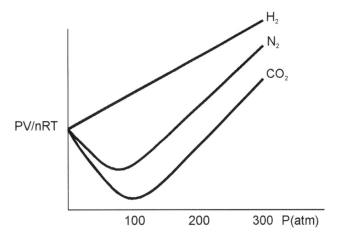

The deviations of real gases from ideality confers a number of properties on the gas which could not be explained by the kinetic molecular theory.

56. What would the PV/nRT versus P graph look like for an ideal gas?

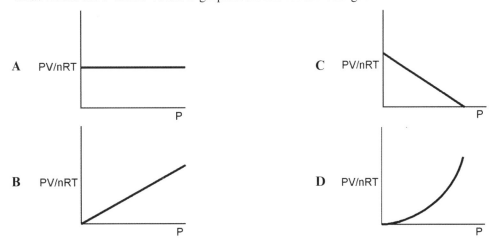

57. From the information in the passage, if 1 dm³ of H_2 gas initially at 50 atmospheres had its pressure increased to 100 atmospheres at a constant temperature, which of the following would be true?
A Volume = 500 cm³
B Volume > 500 cm³
C Volume < 500 cm³
D The change in volume will depend on the rate of increase of the external pressure.

58. Which of the following does not contribute to the explanation of the deviation of "real" gases from ideality?
A Gas particles occupy space.
B Gas particles have an attraction for each other.
C Gas particles possess mass.
D Gas particles do not undergo elastic collisions.

59. A sample of N_2, known to contain traces of water, occupied a volume of 200 dm³ at 25 °C and 1 atm. When passed over solid Na_2SO_4 (drying agent), the increase in mass of the salt was 35.0 grams. What was the partial pressure of the N_2 in the sample? (Assume ideality and molar volume at 25 °C = 24 dm³)
A 0.1 atm
B 0.2 atm
C 0.4 atm
D 0.8 atm

60. For a given quantity of an ideal gas, there are state changes in which one of the characteristics of the gas or process remains constant. The processes are defined as follows:
- Isothermal: the temperature remains constant
- Isobaric: the pressure remains constant
- Isochoric: the volume remains constant
- Adiabatic: the heat is not transferred into or out of the system

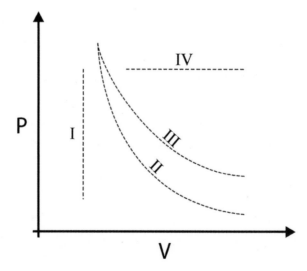

Figure 1: Pressure (P) vs Volume (V) graphs

Which of the following labels in Figure 1 is most consistent with the shape of a graph for the isothermal, isobaric, isochoric and adiabatic processes, respectively?
A III, IV, I, II
B III, IV, II, I
C I, II, IV, III
D II, IV, III, I

61. Consider the following graph illustrating the evolution of carbon dioxide gas under ideal conditions.

$$CaCO_{3(s)} + 2HCl_{(aq)} \rightarrow CaCl_{2(aq)} + CO_{2(g)} + H_2O_{(l)}$$

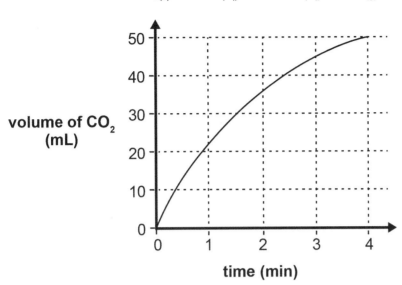

The average rate of reaction is greatest in which of the following time intervals?
A   0-30 seconds
B   30-60 seconds
C   0-1 minute
D   0-4 minutes

UNIT 15

Question 62

62. Von Willebrand's disease is an autosomal dominant bleeding disorder. A man who does not have the disease has two children with a woman who is heterozygous for the condition. If the first child expresses the bleeding disorder, what is the probability that the second child will have the disease?
A   0.25
B   0.50
C   0.75
D   1.00

Questions 63–66

Ozone (O_3) reacts vigorously with alkenes. The reaction (= *ozonolysis*) breaks carbon-carbon double bonds to generate carbon-oxygen double bonds (= *oxidative cleavage*) which can produce ketones, aldehydes or a combination thereof. The overall reaction is illustrated below.

For the reaction above to occur, a reducing agent such as zinc metal or dimethyl sulfide must be used. Alternatively, an oxidative workup would oxidize any aldehydes to carboxylic acids (i.e. complete oxidation).

Note that:
- R, R′, R″ and R‴ can each be any of hydrogen, an alkyl or an aryl group.
- if the starting material is an alkyne, the result of ozonolysis with oxidative workup is oxidative cleavage and complete oxidation.

63. If the starting compound is a disubstituted alkene, which of the following must be true?
    A   Formaldehyde must be one of the 2 products
    B   At least one aldehyde must be one of the 2 products
    C   Two aldehydes must be the 2 products
    D   Both A and B are correct.

64. Ozonolysis of 5-chlorohexane-1-ene under reductive workup would be expected to produce 2 products. Which of the following would be one of those 2 products?
    A   Methanal
    B   Methanoic acid chloride
    C   Acetic acid
    D   Acetic acid chloride

65. Ozonolysis of cyclopentene under reductive workup would be expected to produce which of the following products?
    A   *cis*-Cyclopentane-1,2-diol
    B   *trans*-Cyclopentane-1,2-diol
    C   Pentane-2,4-dione
    D   Pentanedial

66. Ozonolysis of cyclodecyne under oxidative workup would be expected to produce which of the following products?
    A   *trans*-1,2-dihydroxycyclodecanene
    B   Decanedioic acid
    C   Decanone
    D   Decanedial

Questions 67-69

Because of the symmetry of the benzene ring, if a monosubstituted benzene is evaluated, there could only be one such molecule. The one substituent, or ligand, replaces hydrogen at a carbon which would then be referred to as carbon-1.

However, when the benzene ring already has a substituent then substituted isomers are possible. Consider the following structure of methylbenzene.

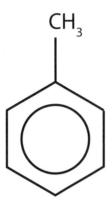

Any single hydrogen - whether from the ring or from the substituent - on methylbenzene can be replaced (monosubstituted) but that does not always result in a different isomer. For example, there are 3 hydrogens on the methyl substituent, but replacing any one of them with another atom (e.g. fluorine) would produce three identical molecules because the connectivity would not have changed. Whereas, substituting non-equivalent hydrogens like a methyl hydrogen vs. one of the ring hydrogens would produce 2 different isomers. Occasionally, the number of disubstituted or trisubstituted isomers must be determined.

For each of the following three questions, assess the substitution of any hydrogen in methylbenzene by fluorine and then determine if the products created are different from one another.

67. How many different monosubstituted isomers of methylbenzene are possible?
   A   2
   B   4
   C   5
   D   7

68. How many different disubstituted isomers of methylbenzene are possible?
   A   4
   B   6
   C   8
   D   10

69. As compared to disubstituted isomers of methylbenzene, how many trisubstituted isomers of methylbenzene are possible?
   A   Fewer
   B   Same
   C   An increase of 50%
   D   An increase greater than 50%

UNIT 18

Questions 70–71

70. The following equation is used to relate force and fluid viscosity η:

$$F = -2\pi r l \frac{v}{R} \eta$$

where F is force, r is radius, l is length, v is speed, R is distance and η is the viscosity. What are the dimensions of viscosity in the fundamental quantities of mass (M), length (L) and time (T)?

A $\quad M \cdot L^3 \cdot T^{-3}$
B $\quad M \cdot L^{-1} \cdot T^{-1}$
C $\quad M \cdot L^2 \cdot T^{-1}$
D $\quad M \cdot L^{-2} \cdot T^{-2}$

71. In the fundamental quantities described in the previous question, which of the following is equivalent to L^3?

A $\quad$ (joules)/(pascals)
B $\quad$ (joules)(pascals)
C $\quad$ (volume)(joules)(pascals)
D $\quad$ (volume)(joules)/(pascals)

UNIT 19

Questions 72-74

Viral hepatitis type B (serum hepatitis) is an infection of humans that primarily damages the liver. The causative agent is a virus called HBV, which is transmitted in much the same way as the HIV virus.

If HBV could be cultivated in the laboratory in unlimited amounts, it could be injected into humans as a vaccine to stimulate immunity against hepatitis type B. Unfortunately, it is not yet possible to grow HBV in laboratory culture. However, the blood of chronically infected people contains numerous particles of a harmless protein component of the virus. This protein, called HBsAg, can be extracted from the blood, purified, and treated chemically to destroy any live virus that might also be present. When HBsAg particles are injected into humans, they stimulate immunity against the complete infectious virus.

Of late, a new source of HBsAg particles have become available. Thanks to genetic engineering, a technique for cloning the gene for HBsAg into cells of the common bread yeast *Saccharomyces cerevisiae* has been developed. The yeast expresses the gene and makes HBsAg particles that can be extracted after the cells are broken. Since yeast cells are easy to propagate, it is now possible to obtain unlimited amounts of HBsAg particles.

72. Before being injected into humans, the HBV virus would first have to:
A $\quad$ be cloned in yeast cells to ensure that enough of the virus had been injected to elicit an immune response.
B $\quad$ have its protein coat removed.
C $\quad$ be purified.
D $\quad$ be inactivated.

73. The following graph shows the immune response for an initial injection of HBsAg and a subsequent injection of the HBV virus. Which of the following best explains the differences in the two responses?

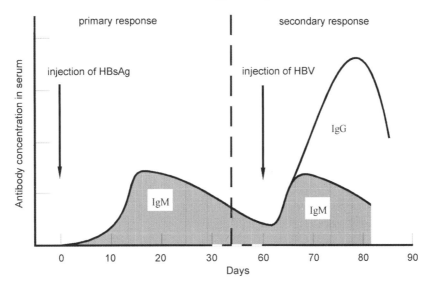

A   During the initial response, the immune response was carried out primarily by macrophages and B-lymphocytes.
B   During the secondary response, T-cells possessing membrane receptors, recognized and attacked the viral antigens.
C   Memory cells produced by T- and B-cells during the first exposure made the second response faster and more intense.
D   Memory cells produced by macrophages during the first infection recognized the viral antigens more quickly during the second infection, causing antibody production to be increased.

74. According to the preceding diagram, all of the following are correct EXCEPT:
A   if the slope of the curve was taken at any time t, the units could be in mg/day.
B   the time difference between the peak IgM and IgG secondary responses is less than the delay in the IgM primary response.
C   the peak IgM primary response has a delay similar in duration to the peak IgG secondary response.
D   the difference between peak IgG and peak IgM concentrations is greater than the peak IgM concentration.

UNIT 20

Question 75

75. A mass of 100 kg is placed on a uniform bar at a point 0.5 m to the left of a fulcrum. Where must a 75 kg mass be placed relative to the fulcrum in order to establish a state of equilibrium given that the bar was in equilibrium before any weights were applied?
A   0.66 m to the right of the fulcrum
B   0.66 m to the left of the fulcrum
C   0.38 m to the right of the fulcrum
D   0.38 m to the left of the fulcrum

Questions 76–80

Sweat is a watery fluid containing between 0.1 and 0.4% sodium chloride, sodium lactate and urea. It is less concentrated than blood plasma and is secreted by the activity of sweat glands under the control of pseudomotor neurons. These neurons are part of the sympathetic nervous system and they relay impulses from the hypothalamus.

When sweat evaporates from the skin surface, energy as latent heat of evaporation is lost from the body and this reduces body temperature. Experiments have now confirmed that sweating only occurs as a result of a rise in core body temperature. Blood from the carotid vessels flows to the hypothalamus and these experiments have indicated its role in thermoregulation. Inserting a thermistor against the eardrum gives an acceptable estimate of hypothalamic temperature.

76. The transport of electrolytes in sweat from blood plasma to the sweat glands is best accounted for by which of the following processes?
   A   Osmosis
   B   Diffusion
   C   Active transport
   D   All of the above

77. Drinking iced water results in a lowering of core body temperature. Thus, a trial exposing the skin to heat while drinking iced water would result in which of the following according to the passage?
   A   If the person had been sweating prior to exposure to the trial then there would be an increase in sweating.
   B   If the person had been sweating prior to exposure to the trial then there would be a decrease in sweating.
   C   Irrespective of whether the person had been sweating prior to the trial, there would be an increase in sweating followed by a decrease in sweating.
   D   Irrespective of whether the person had been sweating prior to the trial, there would be no change in sweat production.

Questions 78-80 refer to Figure 1

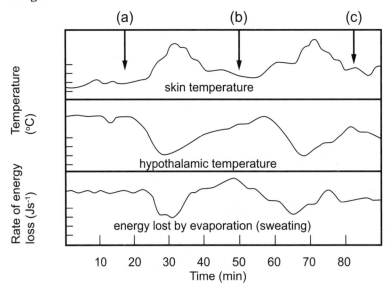

Figure 1: The relation between skin temperature, hypothalamic temperature and rate of evaporation for a human in a warm chamber (45 °C). Iced water is swallowed at points labeled (a), (b) and (c).

78. During the first 20 minutes the temperature and evaporation rate remain relatively constant because during this time:
   A evaporation was at a minimum.
   B the energy loss was not constant.
   C the subject was allowed to equilibrate with his surroundings.
   D 45 °C was considerably higher than the mean body temperature.

79. The relationship between hypothalamic temperature and rate of sweating could be best described as:
   A direct, suggesting that the rate of sweating is controlled by hypothalamic activity.
   B direct, suggesting that hypothalamic activity is controlled by the rate of sweating.
   C inverse, suggesting that changes in the rate of sweating occur in the opposite direction to changes in hypothalamic temperature.
   D independent, suggesting that the rate of sweating and hypothalamic activity change independently of each other.

80. Shortly after ingestion of the iced water, skin temperature rises. This can best be explained by which of the following?
   A As the evaporation rate falls, latent heat is no longer being lost from the skin, causing a rise in skin temperature.
   B The unusually high temperature of the chamber over the 30 minute period caused the rise in temperature.
   C The skin temperature rose to counteract the disturbance in body temperature caused by ingestion of the iced water.
   D Change in skin temperature always occurs in the opposite direction to change in hypothalamic temperature.

Question 81

The body mass index (BMI) provides a measure of the relative mass based on the weight and height of an individual.

- Metric units: BMI = Weight[kg] / (Height[m] × Height[m])
- Imperial units: BMI = 703 × Weight[lb] / (Height[in] × Height[in])

Consider Figure 1.

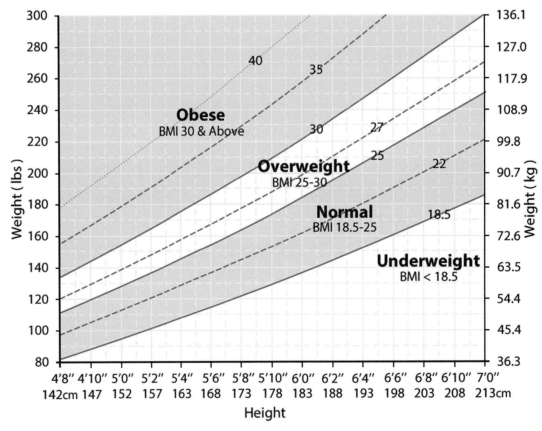

Figure 1: Body Mass Index (BMI) Chart for Adults. Intermittent shading from upper left to bottom right represents Obese, Overweight, Normal, and Underweight, respectively. Note that Height is given in feet (′) and inches (″) as well as centimeters (cm). For example, a 'Normal' BMI of 22 can be seen for a person who 6′0″ or 183 cm, and 160 lbs or 72.6 kg. Adapted from Vertex 42 LLC.

81. Which of the following statements is most accurate?
  A A height of 1.75 m with a weight of 96 kg is categorised as 'overweight'.
  B With an increase in height, the effect of height on the ratio that constitutes BMI is exponential, whereas the change in weight has a linear effect.
  C An increase in weight by 5 kg due to muscle is likely to have a greater impact on the BMI than an increase of 5 kg due to fat.
  D Doubling the weight in kilograms for a person who is 'underweight' is more likely to make that person 'obese' as compared to doubling their weight in lbs.

Questions 82–87

Active transport is the energy-consuming transport of molecules against a concentration gradient. Energy is required because the substance must be moved in the opposite direction of its natural tendency to diffuse. Movement is usually unidirectional, unlike diffusion which is reversible.

When movement of ions is considered, two factors will influence the direction in which they diffuse: one is concentration, the other is electrical charge. An ion will usually diffuse from a region of its high concentration to a region of its low concentration. It will also generally be attracted towards a region of opposite charge, and move away from a region of similar charge. Thus ions are said to move down *electrochemical gradients*, which are the combined effects of both electrical and concentration gradients. Strictly speaking, active transport of ions is their movement against an electrochemical gradient powered by an energy source.

Research has shown that the cell surface membranes of most cells possess sodium pumps. Usually, though not always, the sodium pump is coupled with a potassium pump. The combined pump is called the sodium-potassium pump. This pump is an excellent example of active transport.

Table 1: Concentration of Na^+, K^+, and Cl^- inside and outside mammalian motor neurons. The sign of the potential (mV) is inside relative to the outside of the cell.

Ion	Concentration (mmol/L H_2O)		Equilibrium potential (mV)
	Inside cell	Outside cell	
Na^+	15.0	150.0	+60
K^+	150.0	5.5	−90
Cl^-	9.0	125.0	−75

Resting membrane potential (Vm) = −70 mV

The value of the equilibrium potential for any ion depends upon the concentration gradient for that ion across the membrane. The equilibrium potential for any ion can be calculated using the Nernst equation. The following is an approximation of the equation for the equilibrium potential for potassium (E_k in mV) at room temperature:

$$E_k = 60 \log_{10} \frac{[K^+]_O}{[K^+]_i}$$

$[K^+]_o$ = extracellular K^+ concentration in mM
$[K^+]_i$ = intracellular K^+ concentration in mM

82. All of the following explain the ionic concentrations in Table 1 EXCEPT:
    A Na^+ and Cl^- ions passively diffuse more quickly into the extracellular fluid than K^+ ions.
    B Na^+ ions are actively pumped out of the intracellular fluid.
    C   the negative charge of the cell contents repels Cl^- ions from the cell.
    D   the cell membrane is more freely permeable to K^+ ions than to Na^+ and Cl^- ions.

83. If the concentration of potassium outside a mammalian motor neuron were changed to 0.55 mol/L, what would be the predicted change in the equilibrium potential?
   A   12 mV
   B   120 mV
   C   60 mV
   D   600 mV

84. A graph of E_k vs $\log_{10}[K^+]_o$ would be:
   A   a straight line.
   B   a logarithmic curve.
   C   an exponential curve.
   D   a sigmoidal curve.

85. In the process of osmosis, the net flow of water molecules into or out of the cell depends primarily on the differences in the:
   A   concentration of protein on either side of the cell membrane.
   B   concentration of water molecules inside and outside the cell.
   C   rate of molecular transport on either side of the cell membrane.
   D   rate of movement of ions inside the cell.

86. Active transport assumes particular importance in all but which of the following structures?
   A   Cells of the large intestine
   B   Alveoli
   C   Nerve and muscle cells
   D   Loop of Henle

87. At inhibitory synapses, a hyperpolarization of the membrane known as an inhibitory postsynaptic potential is produced rendering V_m more negative. This occurs as a result of:
   A   an increase in the postsynaptic membrane's permeability to Na^+ and K^+ ions.
   B   an increase in the permeability of the presynaptic membrane to Ca^{2+} ions.
   C   the entry of Cl^- ions into the synaptic knob.
   D   an increase in the permeability of the postsynaptic membrane to Cl^- ions.

Questions 88

Infrared (IR) spectroscopy is an instrumental technique used to identify substances by keying in on functional groups. By measuring the absorption of infrared radiation over a range of frequencies and then comparing such data to tables for known substances, it is possible to reveal the underlying identity of the chemical.

Table 1: IR Absorptions

Functional Group	Characteristic Absorption(s) (cm^{-1})	Notes
Alkyl C-H Stretch	2950–2850	Alkane C-H bonds are fairly ubiquitous and therefore usually less useful in determining structure.
Alkenyl C-H Stretch Alkenyl C=C Stretch	3100–3010 1680–1620	Absorption peaks above 3000 cm^{-1} are frequently diagnostic of unsaturation
Alcohol/Phenol O-H Stretch	3550–3200	Specifity of the absorption is in part dependent on surrounding functional groups.
Carboxylic Acid O-H Stretch	3000–2500	
Amine N-H Stretch	3500–3300	Primary amines produce two N-H stretch absorptions, secondary amides only one, and tetriary none.
Aldehyde C=O Stretch Ketone C=O Stretch Ester C=O Stretch Carboxylic Acid C=O Stretch Amide C=O Stretch	1740–1690 1750–1680 1750–1735 1780–1710 1690–1630	The carbonyl stretching absorption is one of the strongest IR absorptions, and is very useful in structure determination as one can determine both the number of carbonyl groups (assuming peaks do not overlap) but also an estimation of which types.
Amide N-H Stretch	3700–3500	As with amines, an amide produces zero to two N-H absorptions depending on its type.

All figures are for the typical case only – signal positions and intensities may vary depending on the particular bond environment.

88. Consider the following reaction.

The infrared spectrum of the product can be distinguished from that of the starting material by the:
A   disappearance of IR absorption at 3360 cm^{-1}.
B   disappearance of IR absorption at 2820 cm^{-1}.
C   appearance of IR absorption at 3360 cm^{-1}.
D   appearance of IR absorption at 1740 cm^{-1}.

Questions 89–96

It is well known that there are two major forms of carbon, that is, carbon has two main allotropes: graphite and diamond. These differ greatly from each other with respect to their physical properties as shown in Table 1. The physical properties of silicon are also shown in Table 1 for comparison as carbon and silicon belong to the same group in the periodic table.

Table 1

Physical properties	Graphite	Diamond	Silicon
Density (g cm^{-3})	2.26	3.51	2.33
Enthalpy of combustion to yield oxide (ΔHc) kJ mol^{-1}	−393.3	−395.1	−910
Melting point (°C)	2820	3730	1410
Boiling point (°C)		4830	2680
Conductivity (electrical)	Fairly good	Non-conductor	Good
Conductivity (thermal)	Fairly good	Non-conductivity	Good

Graphite possesses what is commonly known as a layer structure: carbon atoms form three covalent bonds with each other to yield layers of carbon assemblies parallel with each other. These layers are held together via weak Van der Waals' forces which permit some movement of the layers relative to one another.

Both diamond and silicon (see Figure 1) form a diamond crystal lattice. The crystal lattice can be thought of as an array of 'small boxes', or cells, infinitely repeating in all three spatial directions: x, y and z. Continuing with the box analogy, consider that an atom in, for example, a top corner is shared by 3 other boxes at the same level plus another 4 boxes above. Fractions of atoms can be added to be equivalent to a full atom or atoms. There are 4 atoms completely within the lattice while all other atoms are shared between boxes to one degree or another. The length of one side of a crystal lattice for silicon is 0.543 nm.

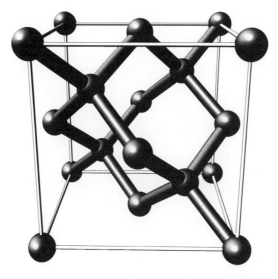

Figure 1: Diamond crystal lattice: Like a small box, or cell, that constitutes a repeating structure. Atoms are represented as spheres. Each of the 6 faces of the 'box' has 1 centrally-located atom which is equally shared with 1 adjacent box.

A phase diagram is a graph that shows the relation between the solid, liquid and gaseous states. Any point in the graph is where 2 phases exist at equilibrium except the triple point where all 3 exist at equilibrium. Solid CO_2 is called "dry ice" because it can go directly from solid to vapour (sublimation) at room pressure (i.e. 101.3 kPa). The triple point of CO_2 occurs at 217 K and 515 kPa. A reduction in CO_2 pressure directly correlates with changes in its sublimation, melting and boiling points.

89. Which of the following is a correct representation of the phase diagram for carbon dioxide?

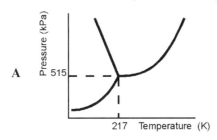
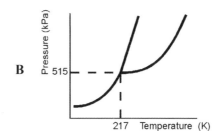
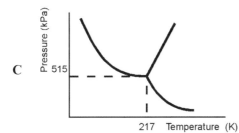
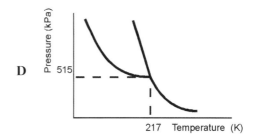

90. The properties of the layer-like structure of solid graphite stated in the passage would lend it to which of the following industrial uses?
A   Insulator
B   Structural
C   Corrosive
D   Lubricant

91. Using the information in the table, calculate the enthalpy change for the following process:

$$C_{graphite} \rightarrow C_{diamond}$$

A $+1.8 \, kJ \, mol^{-1}$
B $-1.8 \, kJ \, mol^{-1}$
C $+1.0 \, kJ \, mol^{-1}$
D $-1.0 \, kJ \, mol^{-1}$

92. It is possible to convert graphite into diamond via various chemical processes. Based on the information in the passage, which of the following would facilitate increased amounts of diamond assuming that the system is in equilibrium?
A   Higher pressures
B   Lower temperatures
C   A catalyst
D   None of the above

Questions 93 and 94 refer to the following additional information:

At a given temperature T in kelvin, the relationship between the three thermodynamic quantities including the change in Gibbs free energy (ΔG), the change in enthalpy (ΔH) and the change in entropy (ΔS), can be expressed as follows:

$$\Delta G = \Delta H - T\Delta S$$

93. The sublimation of carbon dioxide occurs quickly at room temperature. What might be predicted for the three thermodynamic quantities for the reverse reaction?
    A   Only ΔS would be positive.
    B   Only ΔS would be negative.
    C   Only ΔH would be negative.
    D   Only ΔG would be positive.

94. Which of the following statements is consistent with the triple point of carbon dioxide?
    A   The absolute temperature dominates the effect on Gibbs free energy.
    B   The reaction is spontaneous, Gibbs free energy is negative.
    C   The enthalpy change is equal to the effect of the entropy change.
    D   The entropy change is negative because there is more disorder overall.

95. To calculate the number of atoms per unit cell (crystal lattice), the degree to which atoms at the surface or corners are shared, as well as the number of whole atoms within the cell, must be taken into account. Considering the information in the passage and Figure 1, how many silicon atoms are there per unit cell (one crystal lattice)?
    A   4
    B   8
    C   16
    D   18

96. Given the information provided, which of the following is most consistent with an estimate of the number of silicon atoms per cm^{-3}?
    A 5×10^{22}
    B 5×10^{24}
    C 5×10^{26}
    D 5×10^{28}

Questions 97–99

Hückel's Rule was developed to determine if a planar ring molecule, whether neutral or in ionic form, would have aromatic properties.

If a compound does not meet all the following criteria, it is likely not aromatic.
1.   The molecule is cyclic.
2.   The molecule is planar.
3.   The molecule is fully conjugated (i.e. p orbitals at every atom in the ring).
4.   The molecule has $4n + 2$ π electrons, where $n = 0, 1, 2, 3$, and so on.

If rules 1., 2. and/or 3. are broken, then the molecule is non-aromatic. If rule 4. is also broken then the molecule is antiaromatic.

Of course, benzene is aromatic (6 electrons, from 3 double bonds), but cyclobutadiene is antiaromatic, since the number of π delocalized electrons is 4.

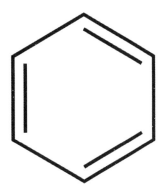

Note: All cyclic molecules among the following questions can be assumed to be planar except cyclodecapentaene which has many conformations including a boat-like conformation.

97.   Which of the following would you expect to be aromatic?

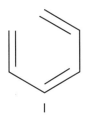   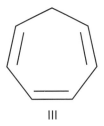   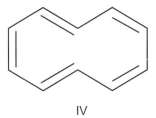

I   II   III   IV

A   None
B   I only
C   II and III only
D   I, II, III and IV

98. Which of the following is aromatic?

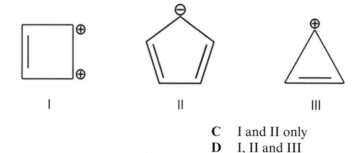

I   II   III

A	I only	**C**	I and II only
B	II only	**D**	I, II and III

99. Consider planar conformations of the following molecules. In that instance, which of the following would be considered anti-aromatic?

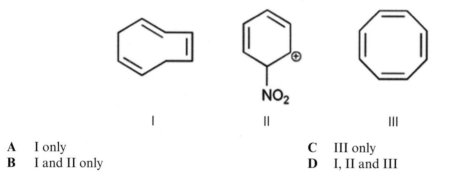

I   II   III

A	I only	**C**	III only
B	I and II only	**D**	I, II and III

UNIT 27

Question 100

Apoptosis is the process of programmed cell death that can occur in multicellular organisms. The proteins involved in apoptosis are associated with pathways for cell cycle arrest and DNA repair. These processes are mostly regulated through the interplay of various proteins involved in feedback loops including some of the ones shown in Figure 1.

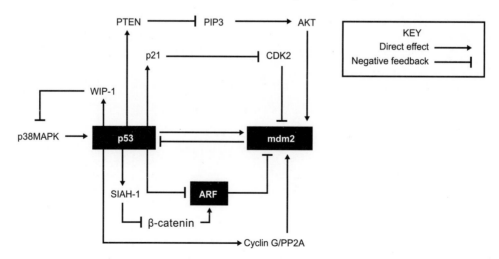

Figure 1: Feedback loops forming a regulatory network affecting apoptosis, cell cycle arrest and DNA repair. (Bioformatics Institute)

100. According to Figure 1, CDK2 activity would most reasonably increase due to all of the following EXCEPT:
A   degradation of p21.
B   high cyclin G concentrations.
C   a mutation in the gene that produces PTEN.
D   high p53 concentrations.

UNIT 28

Question 101

101. The data in Table 1 were collected for Reaction I:

$$2X + Y \rightarrow Z$$ Reaction I

Table 1

Exp.	[X] in M	[Y] in M	Initial rate of reaction
1	0.050	0.100	8.5×10^{-6}
2	0.050	0.200	3.4×10^{-5}
3	0.200	0.100	3.4×10^{-5}

What is the rate law for the reaction?
A   Rate = $k[X]^2[Y]$
B   Rate = $k[X]^2[Y]^2$
C   Rate = $k[X][Y]^2$
D   Rate = $k[X][Y]$

Questions 102–104

The following represents a summary of nucleophilic acyl substitution followed by nucleophilic addition:

- Carboxylic esters, R'CO₂R", react with 2 equivalents of organolithium or Grignard reagents to give tertiary alcohols.
- The tertiary alcohol that results contains 2 identical alkyl groups (R in the mechanism shown).
- The reaction proceeds via a ketone intermediate [Step (1)] which then reacts with the second equivalent of the organometallic reagent or Grignard reagent [Step (2)] .
- Et = ethyl

102. Which of the following represents the product of the reaction between propyl ethanoate and 1 equivalent of 2-butyl lithium (*sec*-butyllithium)?
   A   2-hexanone
   B   3-methyl-2-pentanone
   C   4-methyl-3-hexanone
   D   3-heptanone

103. Given the mechanism provided, in order to produce a secondary alcohol, which of the following must be true?
   A   R' must be a hydrogen
   B   One R must be a hydrogen
   C   R' and R" must be hydrogens
   D   Either one R or R' must be hydrogen

104. Using 2 equivalents of the first and 1 equivalent of the second, respectively, which of the following pairs of compounds can be used to form the following tertiary alcohol?

   A   Propyl lithium and methyl butanoate
   B   Butyl magnesium bromide and propyl butanoate
   C   Butyl lithium and pentyl pentanoate
   D   Propyl magnesium bromide and hexyl pentanoate

UNIT 30

Questions 105-108

The viscosity of a fluid, that is, a gas, a pure liquid or a solution is an index of its resistance to flow. The viscosity of a fluid in a cylindrical tube of radius R and length L is given by:

$$n = \pi \Delta P R^4 t / (8VL)$$
            Equation I

where n = viscosity of fluid, ΔP = change in pressure, t = time, V = volume of fluid and V/t = rate of flow of fluid. This equation can be applied to the study of blood flow in our bodies. The heart pumps blood through the various vessels in our bodies to supply all of its tissues. At rest, the rate of blood flow is about 80 cm^3 s^{-1} and this is maintained in all blood vessels. However, the radii of the blood vessels decreases the further away blood moves from the heart. Therefore, in order to maintain the rate of blood flow, a pressure drop occurs as one moves from one blood vessel to another of smaller radius.

A great number of physiological conditions can be explained using Equation I, for example, hypertension.

105. What would be the pressure drop per cm of the blood in the first blood vessel leaving the heart if the blood vessel is of unit radius and the body is at rest?

$$n_{blood} = 0.04 \text{ dyn s cm}^{-3}$$

   A $25.6/\pi$ dyn cm^{-3}
   B $16000/\pi$ dyn cm^{-3}
   C $\pi/25.6$ dyn cm^{-3}
   D $\pi/16000$ dyn cm^{-3}

106. Which of the following has the greatest effect on the viscosity of a fluid per unit change in its value?
    A   Volume of the fluid
    B   Length of the tube
    C   Pressure of the fluid
    D   Radius of the tube

107. The equation for the rate of flow of a fluid (from Equation I) has often been compared to Ohm's law. Given that P can be likened to the voltage and flow rate can be likened to the current, which of the following can be likened to resistance?
    A πR^4
    B $\pi R^4/(8Ln)$
    C $8Ln/(\pi R^4)$
    D $8Ln$

108. Hypertension involves the decrease in the radius of certain blood vessels. If the radius of a blood vessel is halved, by what factor must the pressure increase to maintain the normal rate of blood flow, all other factors being constant?
    A   2
    B   4
    C   8
    D   16

UNIT 31

Questions 109–110

The red bread mold *Neurospora crassa* grows well on a cultural plate with "minimal" medium which is a fluid containing only a few simple sugars, inorganic salts, and vitamin. *Neurospora* that grows normally in nature (wild type) has enzymes that convert these simple substances into the amino acids necessary for growth. Mutating any one of the genes that makes an enzyme can produce a *Neurospora* strain that cannot grow on minimal medium. The mutant would only grow if the enzyme product were to be added as a supplement. On the other hand, if a "complete" medium is provided, containing all required amino acids, then *Neurospora* would grow, with or without mutation.

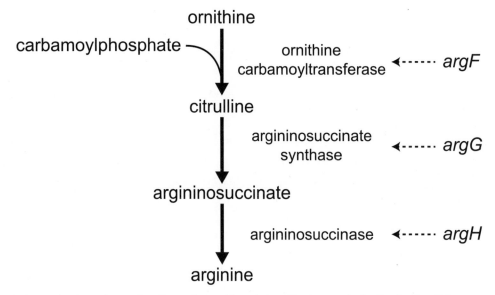

Figure 1: A synthesis pathway for the amino acid arginine. Each gene in italics in the diagram produces one enzyme necessary for the synthesis of this essential amino acid required for growth.

mutant strain	nothing	ornithine	citrulline	argininosuccinate	arginine
P	-	-	-	+	+
Q	-	-	-	+	+

Table 1: Growth response of mutant strains in "minimal" media with supplements as indicated. Growth is indicated by (+), and no growth is indicated by (−).

109. According to the information provided, a conclusion that can be made with certainty is that neither mutant strain P nor Q has the defective enzyme:
    A carbamoyltransferase.
    B argininosuccinate synthase.
    C argininosuccinase.
    D None of the above enzymes are defective in either mutant strain P nor Q.

110. Experiments using the two mutant strains P and Q, reveal that strain P accumulates citrulline, but strain Q does not. Which of the following statements is most consistent with the data provided?
    A Strain Q has only one mutation.
    B Strain P has a mutation in *argF* only.
    C Strain P has mutations in *argF*, *argG* and *argH*.
    D Strain P has a mutation in *argG* only.

END OF REASONING IN BIOLOGICAL AND PHYSICAL SCIENCES. IF TIME REMAINS, YOU MAY GO BACK AND CHECK YOUR WORK IN THIS TEST BOOKLET.

GAMSAT SCORE!

After you have completed test GS-1, you should spend the equivalent of a full day reviewing errors and guesses. Time must be taken to create "Gold Notes" which are high-density notes from your exam experience (preferably a maximum of 2 pages per exam section). By having a manageable number of pages, you can review all your exam experiences (ACER and GS tests) several times every week leading up to the real GAMSAT. This way you can always build on the progress you are making.

Worked solutions are available online for the original owner of this textbook by going to gamsat-prep.com, registering as an owner, clicking on Tests in the top Menu and scrolling down. Every question in the GS-1 exam also has a forum thread at gamsat-prep.com/forum so that if you do not understand the worked solution, we are happy to clarify any teaching points with you. There is no charge for this service.

We also have a free GS GAMSAT Score Calculator so that you can input your raw scores from this GS-1 exam to convert to scaled scores and a percentile rank.

The Gold Standard GAMSAT has put together a suite of home study materials, online courses, essay correction services and classroom lectures across Australia, Ireland and the UK. We recognize that everyone learns differently. Thus we created a multimedia, integrated approach so you can choose the tools that help you study best. Good luck!

Gold Standard GAMSAT Practice Exams Summary

- GS-Free (1/3 length) available for free in all gamsat-prep.com accounts
- Full-length GS-1 which you have just completed; full solutions online
- Full-length GS-2, GS-3, and GS-4: available separately online only
- Full-length GS-5: available online or as an on-campus mock exam (paper)

All practice exams are revised every year to best reflect the current exam.

Answer Keys & Answer Documents

Answer Document

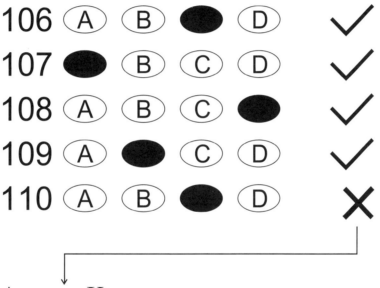

Answer Key

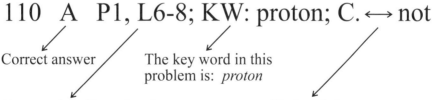

110   A   P1, L6-8; KW: proton; C. ⟷ not

Correct answer

The key word in this problem is: *proton*

Paragraph 1, lines 6 to 8, is where the answer can be found

Choice C. is wrong because of the word "*not*"

Test GS-1

ANSWER KEY   SECTION I

1.	D	20.	C	39.	D	58.	B
2.	A	21.	B	40.	B	59.	D
3.	B	22.	A	41.	C	60.	C
4.	B	23.	B	42.	C	61.	D
5.	D	24.	B	43.	C	62.	C
6.	B	25.	D	44.	C	63.	B
7.	B	26.	C	45.	A	64.	D
8.	C	27.	D	46.	C	65.	B
9.	B	28.	B	47.	D	66.	B
10.	C	29.	D	48.	B	67.	C
11.	B	30.	C	49.	C	68.	C
12.	C	31.	D	50.	C	69.	D
13.	B	32.	B	51.	A	70.	D
14.	C	33.	D	52.	A	71.	C
15.	D	34.	A	53.	D	72.	A
16.	B	35.	D	54.	A	73.	A
17.	B	36.	D	55.	A	74.	A
18.	B	37.	C	56.	B	75.	D
19.	C	38.	D	57.	B		

Common Abbreviations Used for the GS-1 Section 3 Answer Key
Note that 'sections' refers to The Gold Standard GAMSAT books

PHY = physics section;   *GM = GAMSAT Math sections;*   *G = graph;*
CHM = chemistry section;   *T = table;*   *L = line(s);*
BIO = biology section;   *E = equation;*   *P = paragraph;*
ORG = organic chemistry section;   *F = figure;*   *KW = key word.*

*See **GS Part V**, **Table 2**, for a complete list of symbols and abbreviations.*

Cross-reference   *Cross-reference*

1.	B	P2, S3; BIO 1.1, 5.2–P4	56.	A	PV/nRT = 1 = const. (ideal); CHM 4.1.6
2.	B	P2, S5; BIO 5.1.1–5.1.2	57.	B	#1: F1; CHM 4.1.4/8
3.	B	P2, S6; deduce; BIO 5.1	58.	C	CHM 4.1.2, 4.1.8
4.	D	F1 (2); BIO 5.1	59.	D	CHM 1.3, 4.1.1/7
5.	D	F2, deduce; BIO 5.1.2	60.	A	GM 3.5; PHY 1.4.1; CHM 4.1
6.	A	F2	61.	A	GM 3.5; CHM 9.1
7.	D	CHM 10.1, 10.2	62.	B	BIO 15.3
8.	B	CHM 10.1, 10.2	63.	B	ORG 4.2, 7.2.1
9.	A	CHM 10.1, 10.2	64.	A	ORG 4.2, 7.2.1
10.	D	CHM 10.1, 10.2	65.	D	ORG 4.2, 7.2.1
11.	C	CHM 10.1, 10.2	66.	B	ORG 4.2, 4.3, 7.2.1
12.	D	PHY 2.3	67.	B	ORG 2.1, 2.2, 2.3, 5.1
13.	C	P3, L5; PHY 6.1.3	68.	D	ORG 2.1, 2.2, 2.3, 5.1
14.	B	PHY 3.3; A + C = B	69.	D	ORG 2.1, 2.2, 2.3, 5.1
15.	D	PHY 6.1.3; Continuity then Bernoulli	70.	D	P2, S 1, S 4, deduce; BIO 2.1
16.	D	PHY 6.1.3	71.	A	GM 2.1.3, 2.2; PHY 5.1, 6.1
17.	D	CHM 5.3, 8.10, 9.10; BIO 12.4.2	72.	A	P2, S3; BIO 2.1
18.	C	ORG 3.1, 12.3.2	73.	C	G; BIO 8.2
19.	B	CHM 1.6	74.	A	G
20.	D	CHM 1.4	75.	A	PHY 4.1, 4.1.1
21.	C	CHM 6.9	76.	D	P2; PHY 4.3/4
22.	B	CHM 6.1/2/3/7/8	77.	B	E; PHY 4.3/4, 4.4.1
23.	A	CHM 9.7, 9.8	78.	C	E; PHY 3.2; F = f < fmax; KW: tries
24.	B	CHM 9.9	79.	C	PHY 3.2, 3.2.1
25.	A	Deduce; GM 2.1.3, 2.2	80.	A	PHY 5.4, 1.1.2
26.	A	P2; BIO 2.1, 2.3, 16.2	81.	B	GM 3.5-3.9
27.	B	P2; BIO 16.3; cf BIO 15.5	82.	A	deduce; T1; P2, S2-3; BIO 1.1.2, 5.1.1 - 5.1.3
28.	B	F1 (B), cf (A); BIO 16.2 - 16.3	83.	B	T; E; CHM 6.5.1
29.	C	App C	84.	A	E; App A.4.3
30.	A	F1, deduce, App C; BIO 16.3	85.	B	BIO 1.1.1
31.	C	deduce; P1-2; BIO 16.2; A. ↔ BIO 15.5	86.	B	BIO 1.1.2, 12.3
32.	D	CHM 3.5; ORG 1.2, 1.3, 4.1, 4.2	87.	D	T1; BIO 5.1.1 - 5.1.3
33.	B	ORG 4.1, 4.2, 4.2.4	88.	C	ORG 7.2.1, 8.2, 14.1
34.	A	ORG 4.1, 4.2	89.	B	P3; B: CHM 4.3.3
35.	B	ORG 4.1, 4.2	90.	D	P2, S2, deduce
36.	D	ORG 1.4, 4.1	91.	A	CHM 8.3, 1.4, ORG 3.2.1
37.	C	Explanation: ORG 2.1, 2.2, 2.3	92.	A	CHM 9.9
38.	A	P2; P4; PHY 11.4	93.	D	E; CHM 8.10
39.	B	PHY 1.1.1, 1.1.2	94.	C	E; P3, S2; CHM 8.10
40.	C	PHY 11.4	95.	C	P5; ORG 4.2.2, 6.2.4; B: CHM 6.10
41.	B	P4, L5; PHY 11.4	96.	C	GM 1.5, 2.2
42.	A	PHY 11.4	97.	A	ORG 5.1, 5.1.1
43.	B	P2; PHY 11.4	98.	D	ORG 5.1, 5.1.1
44.	B	P1, S3; BIO 15.3	99.	C	ORG 5.1, 5.1.1
45.	D	T1	100.	B	ORG 1.6, 7.1, 8.1, 9.4
46.	B	F1; CHM 9.9, BIO 6.3.3, 6.3.6	101.	A	ORG 1.6, 7.1, 8.1, 9.4
47.	D	BIO 6.3.3	102.	D	ORG 1.6, 7.1, 8.1, 9.4
48.	A	P2, S4/5; F1; BIO 6.3.6/7	103.	A	E1
49.	B	deduce; BIO 5.4.4, 6.3.3	104.	D	E1; PHY 6.1.4
50.	C	CHM 5.3.2	105.	C	E1; PHY 10.1
51.	B	CHM 5.3.2; B →more moles	106.	D	E1; PHY 6.1.4
52.	C	P4, T; CHM 5.3.2	107.	D	BIO 3.1, 4.4-4.10, 6.3.6, 6.3.7
53.	C	P2, L4-7	108.	C	BIO 3.1, 4.1-4.3
54.	B	CHM 5.1.1/2	109.	D	BIO 3.1, 4.1-4.3
55.	B	PHY 3.2, 3.2.1, 3.4	110.	B	KWs: *no enantiomer*; ORG 2.2, 2.3.3

The Gold Standard GAMSAT

Answer Document 1

Test GS-1

CANDIDATE'S NAME _____ STUDENT ID _____

Mark one and only one answer to each question. Be sure to use a soft lead pencil and completely fill in the space for your intended answer. If you erase, do so completely. Make no stray marks.

Section I

1 (A) (B) (C) (D)   39 (A) (B) (C) (D)
2 (A) (B) (C) (D)   40 (A) (B) (C) (D)
3 (A) (B) (C) (D)   41 (A) (B) (C) (D)
4 (A) (B) (C) (D)   42 (A) (B) (C) (D)
5 (A) (B) (C) (D)   43 (A) (B) (C) (D)
6 (A) (B) (C) (D)   44 (A) (B) (C) (D)
7 (A) (B) (C) (D)   45 (A) (B) (C) (D)
8 (A) (B) (C) (D)   46 (A) (B) (C) (D)
9 (A) (B) (C) (D)   47 (A) (B) (C) (D)
10 (A) (B) (C) (D)   48 (A) (B) (C) (D)
11 (A) (B) (C) (D)   49 (A) (B) (C) (D)
12 (A) (B) (C) (D)   50 (A) (B) (C) (D)
13 (A) (B) (C) (D)   51 (A) (B) (C) (D)
14 (A) (B) (C) (D)   52 (A) (B) (C) (D)
15 (A) (B) (C) (D)   53 (A) (B) (C) (D)
16 (A) (B) (C) (D)   54 (A) (B) (C) (D)
17 (A) (B) (C) (D)   55 (A) (B) (C) (D)
18 (A) (B) (C) (D)   56 (A) (B) (C) (D)
19 (A) (B) (C) (D)   57 (A) (B) (C) (D)
20 (A) (B) (C) (D)   58 (A) (B) (C) (D)
21 (A) (B) (C) (D)   59 (A) (B) (C) (D)
22 (A) (B) (C) (D)   60 (A) (B) (C) (D)
23 (A) (B) (C) (D)   61 (A) (B) (C) (D)
24 (A) (B) (C) (D)   62 (A) (B) (C) (D)
25 (A) (B) (C) (D)   63 (A) (B) (C) (D)
26 (A) (B) (C) (D)   64 (A) (B) (C) (D)
27 (A) (B) (C) (D)   65 (A) (B) (C) (D)
28 (A) (B) (C) (D)   66 (A) (B) (C) (D)
29 (A) (B) (C) (D)   67 (A) (B) (C) (D)
30 (A) (B) (C) (D)   68 (A) (B) (C) (D)
31 (A) (B) (C) (D)   69 (A) (B) (C) (D)
32 (A) (B) (C) (D)   70 (A) (B) (C) (D)
33 (A) (B) (C) (D)   71 (A) (B) (C) (D)
34 (A) (B) (C) (D)   72 (A) (B) (C) (D)
35 (A) (B) (C) (D)   73 (A) (B) (C) (D)
36 (A) (B) (C) (D)   74 (A) (B) (C) (D)
37 (A) (B) (C) (D)   75 (A) (B) (C) (D)
38 (A) (B) (C) (D)

Section III

1 (A) (B) (C) (D)   38 (A) (B) (C) (D)   75 (A) (B) (C) (D)
2 (A) (B) (C) (D)   39 (A) (B) (C) (D)   76 (A) (B) (C) (D)
3 (A) (B) (C) (D)   40 (A) (B) (C) (D)   77 (A) (B) (C) (D)
4 (A) (B) (C) (D)   41 (A) (B) (C) (D)   78 (A) (B) (C) (D)
5 (A) (B) (C) (D)   42 (A) (B) (C) (D)   79 (A) (B) (C) (D)
6 (A) (B) (C) (D)   43 (A) (B) (C) (D)   80 (A) (B) (C) (D)
7 (A) (B) (C) (D)   44 (A) (B) (C) (D)   81 (A) (B) (C) (D)
8 (A) (B) (C) (D)   45 (A) (B) (C) (D)   82 (A) (B) (C) (D)
9 (A) (B) (C) (D)   46 (A) (B) (C) (D)   83 (A) (B) (C) (D)
10 (A) (B) (C) (D)   47 (A) (B) (C) (D)   84 (A) (B) (C) (D)
11 (A) (B) (C) (D)   48 (A) (B) (C) (D)   85 (A) (B) (C) (D)
12 (A) (B) (C) (D)   49 (A) (B) (C) (D)   86 (A) (B) (C) (D)
13 (A) (B) (C) (D)   50 (A) (B) (C) (D)   87 (A) (B) (C) (D)
14 (A) (B) (C) (D)   51 (A) (B) (C) (D)   88 (A) (B) (C) (D)
15 (A) (B) (C) (D)   52 (A) (B) (C) (D)   89 (A) (B) (C) (D)
16 (A) (B) (C) (D)   53 (A) (B) (C) (D)   90 (A) (B) (C) (D)
17 (A) (B) (C) (D)   54 (A) (B) (C) (D)   91 (A) (B) (C) (D)
18 (A) (B) (C) (D)   55 (A) (B) (C) (D)   92 (A) (B) (C) (D)
19 (A) (B) (C) (D)   56 (A) (B) (C) (D)   93 (A) (B) (C) (D)
20 (A) (B) (C) (D)   57 (A) (B) (C) (D)   94 (A) (B) (C) (D)
21 (A) (B) (C) (D)   58 (A) (B) (C) (D)   95 (A) (B) (C) (D)
22 (A) (B) (C) (D)   59 (A) (B) (C) (D)   96 (A) (B) (C) (D)
23 (A) (B) (C) (D)   60 (A) (B) (C) (D)   97 (A) (B) (C) (D)
24 (A) (B) (C) (D)   61 (A) (B) (C) (D)   98 (A) (B) (C) (D)
25 (A) (B) (C) (D)   62 (A) (B) (C) (D)   99 (A) (B) (C) (D)
26 (A) (B) (C) (D)   63 (A) (B) (C) (D)   100 (A) (B) (C) (D)
27 (A) (B) (C) (D)   64 (A) (B) (C) (D)   101 (A) (B) (C) (D)
28 (A) (B) (C) (D)   65 (A) (B) (C) (D)   102 (A) (B) (C) (D)
29 (A) (B) (C) (D)   66 (A) (B) (C) (D)   103 (A) (B) (C) (D)
30 (A) (B) (C) (D)   67 (A) (B) (C) (D)   104 (A) (B) (C) (D)
31 (A) (B) (C) (D)   68 (A) (B) (C) (D)   105 (A) (B) (C) (D)
32 (A) (B) (C) (D)   69 (A) (B) (C) (D)   106 (A) (B) (C) (D)
33 (A) (B) (C) (D)   70 (A) (B) (C) (D)   107 (A) (B) (C) (D)
34 (A) (B) (C) (D)   71 (A) (B) (C) (D)   108 (A) (B) (C) (D)
35 (A) (B) (C) (D)   72 (A) (B) (C) (D)   109 (A) (B) (C) (D)
36 (A) (B) (C) (D)   73 (A) (B) (C) (D)   110 (A) (B) (C) (D)
37 (A) (B) (C) (D)   74 (A) (B) (C) (D)

The Gold Standard GAMSAT

Answer Document 2

Test GS-1   Section II

CANDIDATE'S NAME _____   STUDENT ID _____

> When your timer is ready, you may turn the page and begin.

IF YOU NEED MORE SPACE, CONTINUE ON THE NEXT PAGE.

A　　**A**　　**A**　　**A**　　**A**

IF YOU NEED MORE SPACE, CONTINUE ON THE BACK OF THIS PAGE.

STOP HERE FOR WRITING TASK A.

B   **B**   **B**   **B**   **B**

IF YOU NEED MORE SPACE, CONTINUE ON THE BACK OF THIS PAGE.

B   **B**   **B**   **B**   **B**

IF YOU NEED MORE SPACE, CONTINUE ON THE NEXT PAGE.

STOP HERE FOR WRITING TASK B.